Literary Darwinism
Evolution, Human Nature,
and Literature

Joseph Carroll

Routledge
Taylor & Francis Group
New York London

Routledge
Taylor and Francis Group
270 Madison Avenue
New York, NY 10016

Routledge
Taylor and Francis Group
2 Park Square
Milton Park, Abingdon
Oxon OX14 4RN

Library of Congress Cataloging-in-Publication Data

Carroll, Joseph, 1949–
    Literary Darwinism : evolution, human nature, and literature / by Joseph Carroll.
        p. cm.
Includes bibliographical references (p.) and index.
    ISBN 0-415-97013-X (alk. paper) — ISBN 0-415-97014-8 (pbk. : alk. paper)
    1. English fiction—19th century—History and criticism. 2. Evolution (Biology) in literature. 3. English fiction—20th century—History and criticism. 4. Literature—History and criticism—Theory, etc. 5. Darwin, Charles, 1809–1882—Influence. 6. Literature and science—Great Britain. 7. Social darwinism in literature. 8. Human beings in literature. 9. Adaptation (Biology) 10. Nature in literature. I. Title.
    PR878.E95C37 2004
    823'.80936—dc22

                                                                            2003017569

Contents

Introduction

An Emerging Research Program

In the past decade or so, a small but rapidly growing band of literary scholars, theorists, and critics has been working to integrate literary study with Darwinian social science. These scholars can be identified as the members of a distinct school in the sense that they share a certain broad set of basic ideas. They all take "the adapted mind" as an organizing principle, and their work is thus continuous with that of the "adaptationist program" in the social sciences. Adaptationist thinking is grounded in Darwinian conceptions of human nature. Adaptationists believe that all organisms have evolved through an adaptive process of natural selection and that complex functional structure in organic development gives *prima facie* evidence of adaptive constraint. They argue that the human mind and the human motivational and behavioral systems display complex functional structure, and they make it their concern to identify the constituent elements of an evolved human nature: a universal, species-typical array of behavioral and cognitive characteristics. They presuppose that all such characteristics are genetically constrained and that these constraints are mediated through anatomical features and physiological processes, including the neurological and hormonal systems that directly regulate perception, thought, and feeling.

Adaptationist social scientists identify "the adapted mind" as the foundation of human culture. Adaptationist literary scholars concur, and they seek to bring literature itself within the field of cognitive and behavioral features susceptible to an adaptationist understanding. They identify human nature as a biologically constrained set of cognitive and motivational characteristics, and they contend that human nature is both the source and subject of literature. They are convinced that through adaptationist thinking they can more adequately understand what literature is, what its functions are, and how it works—what it represents, what causes people to produce it and consume it, and why it takes the forms it does.

In this introduction, I shall try to give a sense of where Darwinian literary study now stands and suggest where it might be headed. After sketching out the history of Darwinian social science, I shall distinguish the adaptationist research program from other forms of "evolutionary" thinking in literary study. I shall identify the main contributors to adaptationist literary study and list some of their accomplishments. I shall also take up two large theoretical issues that remain to be resolved: the exact structure of "human nature," and the adaptive function of imaginative constructs. In the final section, I shall describe the essays that are included in this volume.

The *Origin of Species* was published in 1859 and within a decade it had almost completely changed the general view of evolution in the minds of the educated public. While writing the *Origin*, Darwin had been fearful of endangering his general theory of evolution by alarming people in their most tender ideological anxieties. Consequently, he had mentioned human beings only in passing. Close to the end of the *Origin*, surveying the prospects for the theory he has propounded, he declared, "In the distant future, I see open fields for far more important researches. Psychology will be based on a new foundation, that of the necessary acquirement of each mental power and capacity by gradation. Light will be thrown on the origin of man and his history" (2003, p. 397). The future was not so distant as Darwin fancied, at least not in the short run. Darwin was himself much surprised by the magnitude of his success in establishing the basic principle of "descent with modification," and the success gave him the heart to fulfill his own prediction—to throw light on man and his history, and to place psychology on a new foundation. In *The Descent of Man, and Selection in Relation to Sex* (1871), he located human beings in their ancestral lineage as primates. On the basis of evidence from comparative anatomy and embryology, he concluded that "man is descended from a hairy quadruped, furnished with a tail and pointed ears, probably arboreal in its habits" (vol. 2. p. 389). (*The Expression of the Emotions in Man and Animals*, first published in 1872, is a psychological and anatomical sequel to *The Descent of Man*).

Like many (but not all) of their primate cousins, the specifically human descendants of this hairy quadruped were highly social in nature, and much of *The Descent of Man* is given over to analyzing the origin, function, and character of human social behavior. Darwin provides a classic account of human moral psychology. He identifies two central elements in moral feeling: an evolved social sympathy that humans share with other social animals, and a capacity for assessing the significance of particular actions within longer rhythms of life. This latter capacity is one of those peculiarly human cognitive aptitudes. The rudimentary elements for such aptitudes can be found, Darwin argues, in other animals. There is no human characteristic that is not continuous with characteristics of other primate species, but in human beings those characteristics develop and combine in ways that produce capacities unique within the animal kingdom. One such capacity is the moral sense. Another is language, and it is on language, Darwin speculates, that all higher cognitive human development depends. Darwin succeeds in analyzing human psychology and culture in ways that lead back through unbroken causal sequences to the elementary biological drives toward survival and reproduction. He is thus the first sociobiologist and the first evolutionary psychologist, and it is for this reason that one will often see the epithet "Darwinian" used more or less synonymously with epithets like "sociobiological" or "adaptationist."

The revolution Darwin began in psychology and the other social sciences has not yet been completed. Through the first decade of the twentieth century, educated people interested in society and literature understood that their own ideas had to be integrated with Darwin's new conception of man's place in nature. Among his distinguished successors in this period, we can identify T. H. Huxley, Leslie Stephen, Francis Galton, William James, John Dewey, and Thorstein Veblen. Literary figures heavily influenced by Darwinian naturalism include George Eliot, H. G. Wells, Joseph Conrad, Thomas Hardy, and an array of naturalists such as Émile Zola, Frank Norris, Arnold Bennett, and Jack London. (Literary Darwinism extends down to the present through a lineage that includes Aldous Huxley, William Golding, Kurt Vonnegut, and Ian McEwan.)

In the second decade of the twentieth century, an anti-Darwinian counterrevolution conquered the social sciences and from there spread out to become the dominant public ideology of the century. Social theorists such as Émile Durkheim, Franz Boas, Alfred Kroeber, and Robert Lowie propounded the doctrine that culture is an autonomous agency that produces all significant mental and emotional content in human experience. From this culturalist perspective, innate, evolved characteristics exercise no constraining influence on human motives or thoughts. Evolution produced the human brain, but that brain invented culture, and culture has succeeded in cutting itself loose from all direct biological influence. This concept of cultural autonomy became the cornerstone of standard social science, and until the 1970s Darwinism essentially disappeared from professional social theory. Important work in Darwinian epistemology was accomplished in the mid-century period by both Konrad Lorenz and Karl Popper, but the first major professional challenge to cultural autonomy as the ideology of the social sciences appeared in 1975, with the publication of Edward O. Wilson's *Sociobiology: The New Synthesis*. Wilson offered a comprehensive analysis of the social behavior of animals within the explanatory framework of natural selection. His final chapter, extending this analysis to the human animal, provoked a series of violent rebuttals, but it also helped inaugurate a line of research that has since grown at ever-accelerating rates. (On the history of Darwinian social science, see Alcock, 2001; Brown, 1991, pp. 1–38; Buss, 1999, part 1; Degler, 1991; Fox, 1989, chapters 3 and 4; Freeman, 1992, 1999, pp. 17–27; Segerstråle, 2000; Tooby and Cosmides, 1992, p. 28; E. O. Wilson, 1994, chapter 17.)

Over the past three decades, Darwinism has had a major impact on psychology, philosophy, political science, linguistics, and aesthetics. Dozens of books and thousands of articles have been published in these areas; many distinguished Darwinian researchers now hold key positions at major research institutions; and there is a steady stream of serious but accessible publications aimed at both professional scientists and the educated lay public. Every year, the nonfiction bestseller lists include some work of Darwinian psychology or Darwinian ethical theory. It could not yet be said that Darwinism dominates the social sciences, but it can reasonably be predicted that within two decades this transition will have advanced far enough so that the modifying term "Darwinian" will be quietly dropped from the substantive term "social science." The epithet will be redundant because all educated people will take it for granted that no reputable psychologist or anthropologist can ignore the findings of biologically oriented study, and even sociologists and political scientists will have to accommodate themselves to the reality of what is empirically known about the biological basis of human behavior. (Representative contributions to sociobiology and evolutionary psychology include Alexander, 1979, 1987; Arnhart, 1998; Betzig, 1986, 1997; Bickerton, 1990; Bowlby, 1982; Brown, 1991, 2000; Buss, 1990, 1994, 1995, 1999, 2000; Chagnon, 1979; Chagnon and Irons, 1979; Chiappe and MacDonald, 2003; Cosmides and Tooby, 1992, 1994; Crawford and Krebs, 1998; Cronk, Chagnon, and Irons, 2000; Daly and Wilson, 1983, 1988; Darwin, 1981, 1998; Dawkins, 1987, 1989; Eibl-Eibesfeldt, 1989; Ekman, 2003; Eysenck, 1967, 1980; Geary, 1998; Hamilton, 1996, 2001; Hrdy, 1999; Irons, 1998; Low, 1998, 2000; MacDonald, 1990, 1995a, 1995b, 1997; McGuire and Troisi, 1998; Maxwell, 1991; Mithen, 1996, 2001; Pinker, 1994, 1997b, 2002; Ridley, 1997, 1999; Rushton, 1995; Segal, 1999; Segal and MacDonald, 1998; Symons, 1979, 1992; Tiger and Fox, 1971; Tooby and Cosmides, 1992, 2001; Trivers, 1972, 1985; Williams, 1966; D. S. Wilson, 1999, 2002, in press; E. O. Wilson, 1975, 1978, 1998; J. Q. Wilson, 1993.)

It seems likely that within two decades the sheer force of progressive empirical knowledge will almost inevitably bring about a fundamental transformation in the social sciences. In all likelihood, the humanities will eventually follow in the train of this movement, but they will probably be slow and late in catching up. The conceptual shift that takes place when moving from the Darwinian social sciences to the humanities can be likened to the technological shift that takes place when traveling from the United States or Europe to a country in the Third World. While traveling in space, one also moves backward in time. In the humanities, scholars happily confident of their own avant-garde creativity continue to repeat the formulas of Freud, Marx, Saussure, and Lévi-Strauss—formulas that have now been obsolete, in their own fields, for decades. It is as if one were to visit a country in which the hosts happily believed themselves on the cutting edge of technological innovation and, in support of this belief, proudly displayed a rotary-dial phone, a manual typewriter, and a mimeograph machine.

There are many literary scholars, and especially younger scholars, who are eager to make productive use of the best available information about the human mind and human behavior. The conceptual time lag in the humanities presents grave institutional problems for these scholars. Among their colleagues in the mainstream literary establishment (exemplified by the Modern Language Association), they are almost certain to meet very often either with blank incomprehension or with outright hostility. This problem is particularly acute for young scholars at the beginning of their careers, trying to put together dissertation committees or flinging themselves on a job market that is already sufficiently inhospitable even for those who are willing to conform to established views

Despite these real and serious institutional obstacles, a substantial body of work has now been published in Darwinian literary studies, and it seems likely that this movement will not only continue but also that it will expand at an increasing rate. The more that is published, the more momentum the whole movement has—the more there is to work with, and the more plausible and possible the whole enterprise seems. One element certain to be important, but hard to calculate, is the simple exhaustion of rhetorical variations in the movements that have now been current for some two or three decades—a period of time sufficient for a fresh doctoral graduate to have passed through maturity and to have entered into the declining phase of his or her career. Deconstruction as a method pure and sufficient unto itself lasted scarcely a decade before giving way to the politically saturated discourse theory of Foucault, and radical political ideology has perhaps already exhausted the range of important social groups that can plausibly be represented as oppressed minorities. After the vast groundswell of feminism and the minor tides of postcolonialism and queer theory, no truly new political impulse has animated literary study now for more than a decade, and no essentially intellectual impulse has been felt for something like three decades. The only major new subject area that has appeared in the past decade or so has been ecological literary study, or "ecocriticism," and in respect to its theoretical orientation this school has teetered uncertainly between postmodernism and a quasi-Darwinian naturalism. (See Fromm, 1996, 1998, 2001; Glotfelty and Fromm, 1996; Love, 1999a, 1999b, 2003; and in this vol., see part 1, chapter 8; part 2, chapter 4.)

How soon will the stale and etiolated rhetoric of postmodernism crumble from within? How quickly will judicious practitioners make use of the robust theory and provocative information flooding in from adaptationist social science? In *Evolution and Literary Theory* (1995), I glumly foretold dim decades of obstruction and stasis in literary studies. Now, just a few years later, I am more hopeful for faster movement. In the middle of the 1980s, how many people foresaw the imminent collapse of the Soviet Union? I have no basis for confident predictions about the pace of change. What I can say, repeating my earlier conclusion, is that for those of us who cannot tolerate the prospect of stagnating in the backwaters of self-trivializing ideologies, there is no need to wait for the established intellectual bureaucracy to shift its own massive bulk and break through its own obstructions. "Whatever happens within the critical institution as a whole, the pursuit of positive knowledge is available to anyone who desires it. Within this pursuit, the opportunities for real and substantial development in our scientific understanding of culture and of literature are now greater than they have ever been before" (p. 469). In the few years that have elapsed since that statement was written, the developments in positive knowledge have continued to accumulate, and the programmatic claim that literary scholars can make use of this knowledge has been rapidly confirming itself as a practical reality. Even just a few years ago, the term "adaptationist literary study" could claim to be little more than a speculative and predictive abstraction. Through the work they have already done, a substantial cadre of scholars has now given definition and detail to that abstraction.

Non-Adaptationist Forms of Evolutionary Criticism

Adaptationist literary study can be distinguished from other forms of "evolutionary" literary study by reference to a simple causal sequence. Adaptationists would affirm the following two causal propositions: (1) the mind has evolved through an adaptive process of natural selection; and (2) the adapted mind produces literature. Adherence to this causal sequence can be contrasted with at least three other distinct ways of integrating evolution with literary study: (1) cosmic evolutionism; (2) evolution taken as an analogical model; and (3) evolution taken as a normative value. All three of these alternatives to the adaptationist program seem to me fundamentally misconceived. Here I shall only briefly characterize them and explain why I think they are misconceived.

The theory of cosmic evolution is the belief that the universe itself is evolving, driven by some inner principle of complexification. In most versions, this principle is teleological and spiritualistic; that is, the universe is conceived as evolving *toward* some higher, ultimate state of spiritual and/or social perfection. In the field of metaphysics and cultural theory, this general view of things can be credited to Herder, Hegel, and the German Romantics and proponents of *Naturphilosophie*, but it is a diffusive, pervasive aspect of cultural and literary theory throughout the nineteenth century. In social theory, it animates Marx as much as Hegel, and it shapes the thinking of progressive liberals like Arnold and Mill and even of utilitarians like Comte and Spencer. In biology proper, it is a distinguishing feature in the theory of Lamarck, and it is continued in the biological thought of Spencer (1862) and of Teilhard de Chardin. Among contemporary literary theorists, its adherents include Walter Koch (1993), Frederick Turner (1992), Alex Argyros (1991), and Richard Cureton (1997a, 1997b). When they adopt its most robust forms, proponents of this theory are metaphysical formalists. That is, they identify some autonomous, self-generating and self-regulating formal process, and they depict this formal process as the central causal force that is responsible for "evolution" or "development" on every level of phenomenal process: cosmology (astronomy), geology, biology, psychology, culture, language, and literature. As a set of comprehensive cosmic formulas, such theory can be combined with virtually any other conceptual apparatus or set of jargon terms. In recent times, it has been combined with, among other things, structuralist anthropology and linguistics, deconstructive epistemology (if that is not itself an impermissibly oxymoronic designation), chaos theory, and ecological theory.

In my own view, such thinking sounds the last echo of medieval theological speculation. It operates chiefly in the range of fanciful metaphysics. Insofar as it makes use of empirical information, it subordinates that information to abstract formulas that are generated *a priori*. Empirical information is used only to ornament and illustrate preconceived ideas, and these ideas are not subject to falsification through new empirical findings. In its style and manner, work done in this vein tends to exemplify a variety of quirks and defects. Some of it (Koch, Cureton) is truly medieval in its pseudo-technical proliferation of formal patterns—a style reminiscent of the symbolic elaborations of alchemical and astrological theory. Some of the writing in this school is verbally opaque, either through an affinity with scholastic theology (Koch) or deconstructive metaphysics (Argyros). In the work of Frederick Turner, cosmic evolution articulates itself in an effusively lyrical manner that seeks affiliation with the poetry of the English Romantics and the American Transcendentalists. (Koch, Turner, and Argyros are reviewed in this vol., part 1, chapter 5.)

The second misconceived way in which to adapt evolutionary theory to literary purposes is to take evolution as an analogical model—to use a metaphor as a conceptual framework. This is a shortcut to causal thinking, and it is another version of formalism. The analogical theorist takes it for granted that the causal processes in one field will provide a neat and reliable pattern for processes in other fields. In evolutionary theory proper, organisms vary in random ways. Variations differ in the degree to which they enable the organism to survive and reproduce. Variations are heritable, and the heritability of more adaptive variations leads in time to speciation, or, in Darwin's terms, "descent with modification by means of natural selection." How can this causal sequence be adapted to the problems of culture and literature? Thomas Kuhn envisioned scientific disciplines as branching into separate, incommensurable "species" (1991, pp. 7–8). Psychologist Donald Campbell (1988) sought to generalize all intellectual creativity as a form of random variation and adaptive selection; and there is now afoot a project at the University of Michigan to provide statistical data supporting the notion that science fiction "evolves" through an adaptive evolutionary process. Describing the underlying logic of the University of Michigan Genre Evolution Project, Rabkin and Simon explain, "Cultural creations evolve in the same way as do biological organisms, that is, as complex adaptive systems that succeed or fail according to their fitness to their environment" (2001, p. 45). This theoretical assertion does not appear to be the result of empirical inquiry or reasoned causal analysis. It is an imaginative inspiration supported only by emphatic affirmation. The likelihood that complex causal processes in any one phenomenal area will exactly parallel those in some other area is vanishingly slight. It is for this reason that, as biological historian Michael Ghiselin observes, "the history of thought is strewn with the corpses of strictly analogical argument" (1969, p. 146).

The currently most popular use of evolution as an analogical causal model is the idea of "memes" first conceived by sociobiologist Richard Dawkins (1982, 1989). Memes are supposedly units of cultural symbolism that survive and replicate in a fashion parallel to that of "genes." Examples of successful memes include Christianity, Mickey Mouse, and the idea of "memes" itself. The supposed parallel between genes and units of cultural symbolism is radically imperfect. Genes are "self-replicating," but units of cultural symbolism are repeated only if they activate responses in a human mind; they are stimuli, not organic mechanisms organized for self-replication. The causal mechanisms involved in transmitting cultural patterns involve complex interactions of psychological dispositions and environmental circumstances. Theorists who use the "meme" metaphor as a shorthand designation for these complex processes almost invariably get caught up in confusing causal associations that are appropriate to the source of the metaphor (genes as self-replicating units), but not to the subject the metaphor is taken to illustrate (semiotic stimuli the repetition of which depends on complex causal processes external to the stimuli).

The use of evolution as an analogical causal model has a clear kinship with the third literary misuse of evolutionary theory: taking evolution as the basis for normative value judgments. This application is perhaps most familiar in the form associated with the social Darwinists and the Nietzscheans. In this scheme of things, all natural relations are conceived as violent and hostile, and that conception of nature is used to authorize violent domination as a social, political, or literary norm. In a contrasting scheme, utopian conceptions of the natural order as a harmonious ecosystem are used to authorize norms of pacific concord. In contemporary literary theory, violent domination is not often touted as a viable norm, but the idea of evolution as random and chaotic has sometimes been taken to support deconstructive principles of indeterminacy. In all such conceptions, whether aggressive or pacific, evolution is reduced to one aspect, an aspect that correlates with human values, and that reduction is then used to justify the human norm that guided the reduction in the first place. This process is a little like selectively using the Bible to justify whatever social, political, or aesthetic values one wishes to propound. The appeal of such usage is that the source can be taken to justify virtually anything, even values radically opposed to one another. That universal utility is of course also a fatal theoretical weakness. Evolutionary processes involving speciation operate at time scales and on levels of biological organization far broader than those of human social interaction, but the adaptive process has produced humans with species-typical moral and aesthetic dispositions. The adaptationist understanding of ethics and aesthetics operates at the level of those dispositions, not at the level of the large-scale causal processes that produced them.

We can mention one more school that cites some of the same sources as the adaptationists but remains distinct from them. The "cognitive rhetoricians" affiliate themselves with a branch of cognitive psychology that confines itself largely within the range of linguistic philosophy—thus avoiding the questions of basic human motivational structures that interest evolutionary psychologists. The main theoretical source of the cognitive rhetoricians is the work of language philosophers Mark Johnson and George Lakoff, who have developed a system for analyzing abstract concepts as metaphors drawn from basic percepts of physical space and bodily orientation. The most prominent practitioner in this field is Mark Turner, and it is represented also by Mary Thomas Crane, Tony Jackson, Alan Richardson, Ellen Spolsky, Francis Steen, and Lisa Zunshine. The distinction between these two schools is by no means absolute, and some scholars occupy a borderline position between them (see Boyd, 1999; Easterlin, 2002). The cognitive rhetoricians tend to seek common ground with the discourse theory of poststructuralism, and they are uncomfortable with adaptationist claims that human nature consists in a highly structured set of motivational and cognitive dispositions that have evolved through an adaptive process. Such claims are, they feel, "reductive." The adaptationists would not disown the epithet. They would concur with E. O. Wilson's assertion that "the heart of the scientific method is the reduction of perceived phenomena to fundamental, testable principles" (1978, p. 48). (For a sympathetic survey of cognitive rhetoric, see Hart, 2001; and in this vol., less sympathetically, see the commentary on M. Turner in part 1, chapter 5, and part 2, chapter 1.)

Contributions to Adaptationist Literary Study

Adaptationist thinking in literary theory can be traced back as far as the work of Darwin's contemporary Hippolyte Taine, and it enters into the literary theory and criticism of a few major writers in the later nineteenth and early twentieth centuries, notably into that of Émile Zola, Leslie Stephen, and (with heavy qualifications) Carl Jung. Except for the indirect influence of Darwin through Jung's archetypalism—as in the work of Northrop Frye—adaptationist thinking had little influence on the development of mainstream critical theory through most of the twentieth century. The New Critics who dominated the academic establishment from the 1930s through the 1970s propounded ostensibly formalist doctrines that were, for the most part, grounded in romantic and Christian conceptions of the autonomous power and quasi-spiritual significance of the literary imagination. The main contextualist or "extrinsic" alternatives to the formalist or "intrinsic" criticism of the New Critics were those of old-fashioned Freudian and Marxist theory. The poststructuralist regime ushered in by deconstruction inverted the New Critical orientation toward harmony and resolution but perpetuated and extended New Critical doctrines on the hermetic autonomy of the textual universe. (See Abrams, 1995, 1997; Carroll 1995; and in this vol., see part 1, chapter 2.) With a few exceptions, most of the biologists, anthropologists, and psychologists who have made seminal contributions to Darwinian social science have had little expertise in the humanities and have not had much to say about art or literature as a product of the adapted mind. The first stirrings of adaptationist thinking among literary scholars began in the late 1980s and early 1990s.

My own interests were turned in this direction in the early 1990s. I was profoundly dissatisfied with the irrationalism and textualism of the prevailing literary doctrines, and in adaptationist research I found a solid basis for developing alternative views about such matters as personal identity, sexuality, gender, the family, social motives, and the relation between the mind and the world. Unbeknownst to me at the time, similar dissatisfactions, hopes, and ambitions were animating several of my contemporaries. While I was conducting the research that eventuated in *Evolution and Literary Theory*, Robert Storey was working on *Mimesis and the Human Animal: On the Biogenetic Foundations of Literary Representation* (1996; reviewed in this vol., part 1, chapter 5). A preview article from Storey's book appeared in a collection of essays, *After Poststructuralism: Interdisciplinarity and Literary Theory*, coedited by Nancy Easterlin and Barbara Riebling (1993). This collection also contained one of Easterlin's own articles, "Play, Mutation, and Reality Acceptance: Toward a Theory of Literary Experience," and in the subsequent decade Easterlin (1999a, 1999b, 2000, 2001a, 2001b) has remained an active contributor to adaptationist literary studies. In the late 1980s, Brett Cooke had already begun producing a series of articles taking an adaptationist perspective on Russian literature, science fiction, opera, ballet, and cinema, and he has coedited two collections of essays, *Sociobiology and the Arts* (Bedaux and Cooke, 1999) and *Biopoetics: Evolutionary Explorations in the Arts* (Cooke and Turner, 1999). (Both volumes were based on small conferences and contain essays of varied quality.) Cooke's theoretical and interpretive efforts (1995, 1999a, 1999b, 1999c, 1999d) have now culminated in the first scholarly and critical book focusing on a single literary work, *Human Nature in Utopia: Zamyatin's We* (2002). One way to get a sense of the diverse sorts of work being done in this field is to dip into the three special journal issues that have been devoted to adaptationist literary study: *Human Nature: An Interdisciplinary Biosocial Perspective* 6, no. 2 (1995); *Interdisciplinary Literary Studies* 2, no. 2 (2001, edited by Brett Cooke); and *Philosophy and Literature* 24, no. 2 (2001). In addition to essays by the scholars already mentioned (Carroll, Cooke, Easterlin, and Storey), these collections contain essays by Brian Boyd (2001), Robin Fox (1995), Jon Gottschall (2001), Ian Jobling (2001a), Margaret Nesse (1995), and Michelle Sugiyama (2001b). Jobling (2001a, 2002) and Sugiyama (1996, 2001a, 2001c) have published other articles in the field, and Boyd, Gottschall, and Sugiyama have articles in press. Articles in Darwinian literary study have also been published by Barash and Barash (2002), Evans (1998), Fromm (2003a, 2003b), Nordlund (2002), Thiessen and Umezawa (1998), and Whissel (1996). Gottschall and D. S. Wilson have in press a coedited volume, *Literature and the Human Animal*, that will contain articles by both literary scholars and social scientists—including articles by Carroll, Gottschall, Nettle, and D. S. Wilson. (For more detailed commentary on specific contributions to adaptationist criticism, see Carroll, 2003a, in press.)

In the middle of the 1990s, several of the scholars who took an adaptationist approach felt it necessary to clear the ground by conducting polemical campaigns against the prevailing postmodern views. Easterlin's collection *After Poststructuralism* contained a diverse array of scholars hostile to poststructuralism and anxious to bring literary study within the general purview of a realist and rationalist orientation. In *Evolution and Literary Theory*, I integrated adaptationist theory with concepts from traditional literary theory and used the resulting theoretical system to repudiate poststructuralist precepts—specifically the ideas that language constructs the world and that the world is fundamentally incoherent and unknowable. The book was about evenly divided between positive theoretical construction and polemical assault. Similar aims and proportions characterized Storey's *Mimesis and the Human Animal*. In the wider field of an adaptationist aesthetics concerned with all the arts, Ellen Dissanayake conducted a similar campaign in *Homo Aestheticus: Where Art Comes from and Why* (1995b). In "Jane, Meet Charles: Literature, Evolution, and Human Nature" (1998), Brian Boyd offered an introductory exposition of evolutionary psychology, summarized the opposition between adaptationism and poststructuralist doctrines, and illustrated the interpretive potential of adaptationism by giving a sharply focused sociobiological reading of Austen's *Mansfield Park*.

I would say that we are now finally getting past the need for such polemics. It is not that the mainstream literary establishment has seen the error of its ways and has humbly set about amending them. Far from it. But the case against poststructuralism has been made very thoroughly from a number of angles. Those who care to rehearse these issues have ample sources at their disposal. More recent work has concentrated on the constructive side of the adaptationist project—assessing theoretical problems within the adaptationist framework and engaging in specific tasks of scholarship and interpretive criticism. This capacity to turn away from polemic and to engage in genuinely new and constructive work marks a fundamental difference between adaptationist literary study and the often merely negative, reactive responses against poststructuralism that characterize the critiques of many older, traditional scholars.

Hovering on the Verge of a Paradigm

Evolutionary psychology has already produced an immense body of useful research, and adaptationist literary study has now produced a much smaller but still substantial and valuable body of work. It nonetheless remains the case that we do not yet have a full and adequate conception of human nature. What we have are the elements that are necessary for constructing that conception. I shall list here a few questions that need to be answered before we can put these elements together in a way that makes good on our claims for possessing a science of human nature.

At what level do the analytic reductions of biology and psychology become distinct motives, with their attendant emotions? How firmly do we draw the line between the "ultimate" regulative principles of inclusive fitness or reproductive success and the "proximal" mechanisms that operate on the level of immediate triggers to behavior? Is reproduction itself a motive, or do people only want sex? (Sociobiologists emphasize reproductive success; evolutionary psychologists look at people as "adaptation executors.") Do people desire children? Or is parenting a behavioral repertoire activated only by the presence of children? (The answer to this question seems obvious to me; many people, though not all, actively want children, but many evolutionary psychologists would balk at that common observation.) Can human behavior be organized into whole "behavioral systems" like "mating" and "parenting," or are all motives only localized mechanisms ("cognitive modules" or "domain-specific mechanisms") triggered by specific stimuli? If behavior is in fact organized into coherent and integrated behavioral systems, what are these systems? How many are there? Is "technology" a separate system? Is "social life" a system or a complex set of systems? How much flexibility is built into any system? That is, how wide a range of possible response to contingent circumstance is possible within a given system? (Too wide, and it is no longer a system; it is drifting toward the infinite flexibility of cultural constructionist views of human behavior. Too narrow, and the systems are not specifically human at all; they are merely the forms of programmed behavior we associate with the less complex neural anatomy of "lower" organisms.)

Is cognition itself a behavioral system? Does cognition consist only of a discrete array of specialized cognitive modules, as Tooby and Cosmides would have it, or does it consist also of a certain range of "general intelligence" that mediates among modules, synthesizing them and bringing them into productive and creative interaction, as Steven Mithen argues? If, as I believe, cognition is itself a distinct behavioral system, on a par with those for "technology," "mating," "parenting," and "social life," that means that the mind itself has motives, that mental needs and processes are distinct and irreducible, with their own particular satisfactions and frustrations. Like all other motives, mental motives interact with the motives of other behavioral systems. People need to understand the world around them, and they thus construct religions, philosophies, sciences, and the arts. But they also need resources, sex, and status, so they use their cognitive activities, like all their other capacities, as means for obtaining the "good things" in life (as Trollope calls them). The interaction of distinct motives should not blind us to the distinctness of the motives.

Within the last few years, since about 1999, evolutionary psychology has progressed to the textbook phase—that is, the phase of institutional success in which a burgeoning academic industry stimulates a proliferation of textbooks designed for use in introductory survey classes. These books range in quality from David Buss's thorough and circumspect survey *Evolution: The New Science of the Mind* to works that could be fairly described as the dual offspring of amateur enthusiasm and commercial ambition. In one respect, the onset of the textbook phase is a good sign. It means that there is a large audience and that the field has won sufficient general respect to warrant official recognition in academic programs. In other respects, the textbook phenomenon is a cause for some concern, and even dismay. Until it has answered questions like those I have listed above, evolutionary psychology can make no valid claim to have achieved intellectual maturity. Textbooks tend to affirm incomplete and uncertain propositions as settled doctrines to be comfortably memorized and replayed on exam questions. One thinks of the old joke about America having passed from barbarism to decadence with no intervening period of civilization.

Despite the threat of premature ossification in textbooks, I am hopeful that serious scientists and scholars will continue to pursue the important questions about human nature that have been the subject of adaptationist study. Perpetual suspension is not the goal. The goal is valid synthesis. One way to measure the validity of any proposed synthesis will be to judge the degree to which that synthesis comprehends the adaptive functions of the human imagination. Literary scholars can do evolutionary psychologists an important service by keeping this criterion of success steadily in view.

The Adaptive Function of Literature and Other Arts

The adaptive function of literature and the other arts is still very much a live question among adaptationists. In "Narrative Theory and Function: Why Evolution Matters" (2001b), Sugiyama argues that narrative is a universal human disposition, that it develops reliably and spontaneously in all known cultures, no matter how isolated they might be, and that it takes the same basic form in all cultures—a form involving characters, goal-oriented action, and resolution. Sugiyama's arguments for *why* narrative should be considered adaptive seem cogent to me. Her arguments for *how* narrative functions adaptively seem right as far as they go, but in my view they do not go as far as they should. She argues that narrative is primarily a means of conveying adaptively important information, and in this respect her arguments are congruent with those put forth by Steven Pinker in his encyclopedic expositions of evolutionary psychology, *How the Mind Works* (1997) and *The Blank Slate: The Modern Denial of Human Nature* (2002). Pinker argues that plot situations in narrative serve as models for behavior, that they are like game plans and that in this respect they are roughly parallel with the model chess games laid out in chess training books. Many authors have no doubt conceived of their work in this way. The epistolary novels of Samuel Richardson had their origin in the book of model letters he published as a guide to writers who were uncertain about the conventions of epistolary propriety. And Anthony Trollope regarded his novels as useful guides to young women involved in the interesting life choices surrounding courtship and marriage. But the didactic side of things clearly does not exhaust the interest and significance in the works of either of these authors, or of any author. I for one have made no use of Richardson's model letters, and as a married, middle-aged male, I am unlikely ever to find myself faced with the interesting life choices Trollope depicts, but I still find both these authors absorbing and stimulating.

In addition to the idea of information transmission or game-plan modeling, there are at least two other theories that have been proposed on the adaptive function of artistic constructs, including literature. (When we speak of literature in a context like this, we must always be understood to include the oral antecedents of written language—"literature" as it is practiced by peoples who are preliterate but who nonetheless have rich traditions of oral narrative.) One theory is that proposed by Geoffrey Miller in *The Mating Mind: How Sexual Choice Shaped the Evolution of Human Nature* (2000), and the other is that proposed by E. O. Wilson in *Consilience: The Unity of Knowledge* (1998).

On the grounds that other primates get along fine without brains of human magnitude, Miller suggests that the higher cognitive capacities of the mind have no particular adaptive utility, at least so far as "survival" is concerned. As an alternative to the idea that the mind has survival value, Miller proposes that the mind evolved through sexual selection as a form of sexual display. The artifacts of the mind—conversation, art, music, literature, and so on—would be forms of display at one remove. Miller's argument against the survival value of the human brain is patently weak. An identical argument could be made about any adaptation not universally shared by all organisms. Many organisms get along fine without eyes, ears, legs, or wings, but few people would conclude from that observation that eyes, ears, legs, and wings contribute in no discernible way to the survival of any organism. Miller's argument against the survival value of the human brain reduces instantly and irresistibly to absurdity.

Miller makes his case for art as sexual display with a good deal of learning and wit, but his central thesis is almost comically far-fetched. In his single-minded pursuit of this one bright idea, he loses sight of a larger principle that undergirds all adaptationist thinking: the idea that complex functional structure gives evidence of adaptive design. Miller argues that all mental activity is a form of sexual ornamentation, and he suggests that "every sexual ornament in every sexually reproducing species could be viewed as a different style of waste" (p. 128). The complex functional structure of the mind thus becomes simply an efficient means of consuming adaptively expensive calories—a sort of neurological incinerator. It is as if a group of workmen were to set up a workshop dedicated to fabricating fine musical instruments, and right next door also to set up a large furnace. All the instruments—oboes, cellos, pianos—are lovingly crafted with immense care and skill, and as soon as each is produced, it is carried over to the furnace and tossed in. Admiring but congenitally tone-deaf females observe this display, marvel at the ostentatious expenditure of superfluous effort, and go soft and warm with sexual excitation. The workmen clearly possess resources so abundant that they can devote the larger part of their productive life to an elaborately senseless process designed to generate highly structured forms of pointless activity.

The functional hypothesis put forth by Sugiyama and Pinker is sensible but incomplete, and the hypothesis put forth by Miller is provocative but ultimately frivolous. The two arguments nonetheless display a common weakness. Neither of them identifies any adaptive function that is specific to art or literature proper. In both hypotheses, literature is a means to an end, in the one case a means for conveying practical information, and in the other a means for generating sexually attractive forms of wasted effort. In the degree to which artistic and literary productions are themselves highly organized in ways that seem designed to fulfill a primary and irreducible psychological need, these functional hypotheses fail to account for the subject at hand. People everywhere have a spontaneous and irrepressible disposition for producing and consuming narratives. Neither the theory of information exchange nor the theory of sexual display offers a convincing explanation for why they have any such need.

In his chapter on the arts in *Consilience*, E. O. Wilson offers a convincing adaptive hypothesis for the universal human disposition to create and consume imaginative artifacts. He argues that the large human brain has adaptive (survival) value, but that in solving some adaptive problems the brain produces a new adaptive problem—it causes confusion and uncertainty. The human brain allows for an unparalleled flexibility of response to variable environmental conditions, but to achieve this flexibility it must cut human cognition loose from any rigidly programmed set of instinctual behaviors. In a dangerous and challenging world that demands decisive action oriented to adaptively functional goals, confusion and uncertainty are potentially fatal disabilities. It is in order to cope with this challenge, Wilson argues, that human beings have created religion and the arts:

> There was not enough time for human heredity to cope with the vastness of new contingent possibilities revealed by high intelligence. . . . The arts filled the gap. Early humans invented them in an attempt to express and control through magic the abundance of the environment, the power of solidarity, and other forces in their lives that mattered most to survival and reproduction. The arts were the means by which these forces could be ritualized and expressed in a new, simulated reality. They drew consistency from their faithfulness to human nature, to the emotion-guided epigenetic rules—the algorithms—of mental development. (p. 225).

Within this general hypothesis, we can formulate more specific hypotheses about the way in which literature and the other arts organize experience in subjectively meaningful ways. We can argue that the arts are indispensable for personal development, for the coherent internal organization of ideas and feelings, and for the organization of shared experience that makes collective cultural life possible. As cognitive paleoanthropologist Steven Mithen observes, imaginative artifacts are not "simply products or representations of our inner thoughts. They play an essential role in formulating, manipulating and sharing those thoughts" (2001, p. 50). In art, music, and literature, people make the forms of experience available to their own conscious minds and to those of others.

When we speak of the literary or artistic "imagination," we mean to signify the complex, integrated set of cognitive, perceptual, and emotional faculties through which we articulate and communicate the felt quality of life. Imaginative constructs are both organized in conceptually intelligible patterns and also weighted with qualitative, subjective affects. The arts make a psychologically indispensable link between conceptual models of experience and the biologically constrained and emotionally mediated dispositions that in common usage we call "human nature." Evolutionary psychologists follow that common usage, and for understandable reasons they are preoccupied with affirming the continuity between human nature and the nature we share with other primates and, in decreasing degrees, with all other animals and all living things. This preoccupation has a sound theoretical basis, and it has proved immensely fruitful for the purpose of analyzing the biological basis of human behavior; but acknowledging the continuity of animal and human nature does not require us to overlook the fact that the arts are themselves one of the most salient and functionally important parts of our specifically *human* nature.

Art provides an emotionally and subjectively intelligible model of reality, and it is within such models that human beings organize their complex behaviors in flexible response to contingent circumstances. The imaginative models that we construct about our experience in the world do not merely convey practical information. They direct our behavior by entering into our motivational system at its very roots—our feelings, our ideas, and our values. We use imaginative models to make sense of the world, not just to "understand" it abstractly but to feel and perceive our own place in it—to see it from the inside out. Making sense of the world in this way, through narrative and through the other arts, is both a primary psychological need and a necessary precondition for organizing our behavior in ways that satisfy all our other adaptive needs. (For arguments to this effect, see Dissanayake, 1995a, 1995b, 2000, 2001, in press; Storey 1996; and in this vol., see part 1, chapters 6 and 7; part 2, chapters 1 and 6.)

The Essays in this Volume

All but three of the essays collected here have appeared previously. Some were published as articles and some as reviews, but the line between the two genres is broad and fuzzy. All of the articles include commentary on current contributions to adaptationist study, and all of the reviews include overt theoretical formulations.

The essays are grouped in three general categories: (1) discussions about the relations among different schools or theoretical perspectives; (2) essays in Darwinian literary theory and practical criticism; and (3) scholarship on Darwin. In each section, the essays are arranged roughly in the order of their composition. The distinction between the first two categories, like that between articles and reviews, is fuzzy. All the essays that are mainly reviews have been placed in the first section, but two of the essays in the first section also contain practical criticism on Victorian novels ("Pinker, Dickens, and the Functions of Criticism," and "Ecocriticism, Cognitive Ethology, and the Environments of Victorian Fiction"). I have placed them in the first section because my primary purpose in these two essays is to assess other theorists or schools of theory. In an essay in the second section, "Organism, Environment, and Literature," I also discuss ecocriticism, but my main purpose there is to trace the development of my own thinking about literary theory over a period of two decades. Similarly, in "The Deep Structure of Literary Representations," I take issue with the cognitive rhetoricians, but I use them only as a foil, and my main purpose is to integrate evolutionary psychology with literary analysis. So that essay too has been placed in the second section.

The essays in the first section, "Mapping the Disciplinary Landscape," delineate historical trends and large party groupings among literary critics and theorists. "The Use of Arnold in a Darwinian World" reflects on the adjustments we have to make when we pass from Arnold's enlightened but prescientific humanism to the Darwinian worldview. "Biology and Poststructuralism" was abstracted from *Evolution and Literary Theory* (1995) and incorporates three main components of that book: the attack on poststructuralism, the formulation of general biological principles that could serve as a new foundation for literary study, and the exposition of a theory of literary figuration. "'Theory,' Anti-Theory, and Empirical Criticism" provides an overview of three main areas in the current disciplinary landscape: (a) the postmodern establishment, (b) the traditional humanist reaction against that establishment, and (c) the newly emerging adaptationist perspective. The review of John Ellis's *Literature Lost* offers a close look at a prime example of the traditional humanist reaction. In the middle of the 1990s, adaptationist study was still a fairly rudimentary enterprise. The lay of the land at that time can be discerned in "Literary Study and Evolutionary Theory: A Review of Books by Alexander Argyros, Walter Koch, Karl Kroeber, Robert Storey, Frederick Turner, and Mark Turner." All six books discussed there claim some affiliation with evolutionary theory, but only one, Robert Storey's *Mimesis and the Human Animal*, could be characterized as adaptationist. The others are instances either of "cosmic evolutionism" or of "cognitive rhetoric." The essays on Steven Pinker and

E. O. Wilson focus on their efforts to provide Darwinian explanations for the functions of literature. Several essays in the second section also discuss the adaptive functions of literature.

In the second section, the first and last essays (chapters 1 and 6) contain comprehensive, synthetic accounts of Darwinian literary theory. The first was written in 1998, the second in 2003. The four middle essays constitute two paired sets. "Universals in Literary Study" can be regarded as a theoretical prelude for the study of human universals in the five novels discussed in "Human Universals and Literary Meaning: A Sociobiological Critique of *Pride and Prejudice, Villette, O Pioneers!, Anna of the Five Towns*, and *Tess of the d'Urbervilles*. "Organism, Environment, and Literature" can be regarded as a theoretical prelude for the appeal to ecological integrity as a criterion of literary value in the subsequent discussion of three novels about Paleolithic life. The last essay in this section sets out a model for human nature, identifies the main elements of literary meaning, and offers a commentary on *Pride and Prejudice* to illustrate the way these ideas enter into practical criticism.

The third section, "Darwin and Darwinism," contains a short review of three biographies of Darwin and a longer commentary on Stephen Jay Gould. Only one of the three biographies (Bowlby's) is itself thoroughly Darwinian in character, and comparing the three Darwin biographies provides an occasion for reflecting on the problems of point of view and interpretive framework in biographical and historical study. The critique of Gould takes up the story of modern evolutionary theory from where I left off in my introduction to an edition of Darwin's *On the Origin of Species* (2003). There, I had carried the story up to the consolidation of Darwin's theory in the "Modern Synthesis"— the integration of genetics with the theory of natural selection—in the 1930s and 1940s. The Modern Synthesis remains the standard framework for the modern, scientific understanding of evolution. In essays published over the past three decades, Gould established himself as the chief opponent of the Modern Synthesis and sought to disconnect Darwinism from the idea of adaptation. Taking account of Gould's work gives me an opportunity to assess the enduring cogency of adaptationist theory. Gould's methods of sophistical argumentation bear a close resemblance to the methods employed by the postmodernists who were the chief targets of polemical animus in *Evolution and Literary Theory*. The critique of Gould thus brings the study of Darwinism into close connection with the commentaries on contemporary critical theory.

The three essays that are here published for the first time are "Adaptationist Criteria of Literary Value: Assessing Kurtén's *Dance of the Tiger*, Auel's *The Clan of the Cave Bear*, and Golding's *The Inheritors*," "Human Nature and Literary Meaning: A Theoretical Model Illustrated with a Critique of *Pride and Prejudice*," and "Modern Darwinism and the Pseudo-Revolutions of Stephen Jay Gould." All the other essays have been published over the past decade. Most of the previously published essays have been retouched but not substantially altered. Some of the titles have been modified for the sake of clarity and specificity. (The original titles and places of publication are identified in the acknowledgements.) In the previously published version of "Ecocriticism, Cognitive Ethology, and the Environments of Victorian Fiction," two paragraphs, one on Austen and one on Hardy, were deleted for reasons of length. Those two paragraphs have here been restored. In the article giving a sociobiological reading of five novels (part 2, chapter 3), the section on Bennett's *Anna of the Five Towns* has been substantially reworked. "Universals in Literary Study" was originally published in a German translation and is here presented in the original English.

Many of the references have been abbreviated, expanded, or brought up to date. All original endnotes or footnotes have been incorporated into the text either as part of the text itself or as parenthetical citations. The style of reference is that of the social sciences, with publications identified parenthetically by author and year of publication. Multiple publications by the same author are listed chronologically in the references, and multiple publications by the same author within a single year are distinguished by lowercase letters following the year. For example: See Cooke, 1995, 1999a, 1999b, 1999c; Easterlin, 2001a, 2001b.

Many friends and colleagues have contributed through discussion or direct criticism to the essays collected here. Particular mention should be made of John Alcock, Larry Arnhart, Brian Boyd, Donald Brown, Napoleon Chagnon, Richard Cook, Brett Cooke, Ellen Dissanayake, Denis Dutton, Nancy Easterlin, David Evans, Harold Fromm, Glen Love, Jonathan Gottschall, Ian Jobling, Kevin MacDonald, Clinton MacHann, Robert Storey, Michelle Sugiyama, and David Sloan Wilson. Harold Fromm first suggested the idea of a collection and has offered shrewd advice and generous help all along the way.

Acknowledgments

The essays in this collection that were previously published originally appeared in the following journals and books and are republished here with the permission of the copyright holders.

The introduction was adapted from "Adaptationist Literary Study: An Emerging Research Program," *Style* 36 (2003): 596–617.

"The Use of Arnold in a Darwinian World," *Nineteenth-Century Prose* 21 (1994): 26–38.

"Biology and Poststructuralism," *Symploke* 4 (1996): 203–219.

"'Theory,' Anti-Theory, and Empirical Criticism." In *Biopoetics: Evolutionary Explorations in the Arts*, eds. Brett Cooke and Frederick Turner. Lexington, KY: ICUS, 1999: 139–154.

"Out of Eden and the Left: A Review of John Ellis's *Literature Lost: Social Agendas and the Corruption of the Humanities*," originally titled "In a Corrupt Shadow," *TLS*, no. 4967 (June 12, 1998): 27.

"Literary Study and Evolutionary Theory: A Review of Books by Alexander Argyros, Walter Koch, Karl Kroeber, Robert Storey, Frederick Turner, and Mark Turner," originally titled "Literary Study and Evolutionary Theory: An Essay Review," *Human Nature* 8 (1998): 273–292.

"Pinker, Dickens, and the Functions of Literature," originally titled "Steven Pinker's Cheesecake for the Mind," *Philosophy and Literature* 22 (1998): 478–485.

"Wilson's Consilience and Literary Study," *Philosophy and Literature* 23 (1999): 393–413.

"Ecocriticism, Cognitive Ethology, and the Environments of Victorian Fiction," originally titled "The Ecology of Victorian Fiction," *Philosophy and Literature* 25 (2001): 295–313.

"The Deep Structure of Literary Representations," *Evolution and Human Behavior* 20 (1999): 159–173.

"Universals in Literary Study," originally titled "Universalien in der Literaturwissenschaft." In *Universalien und Konstruktivismus*, ed. Peter M. Hejl. Frankfurt: Suhrkamp, 2001: 235–256.

"Human Universals and Literary Meaning: A Sociobiological Critique of *Pride and Prejudice*, *Villette*, *O Pioneers!*, *Anna of the Five Towns*, and *Tess of the d'Urbervilles*," *Interdisciplinary Literary Studies* 2 (2001): 9–27.

"Organism, Environment, and Literature," originally titled "Organism, Environment, and Literary Representation," *Interdisciplinary Studies in Literature and Environment* 9 (2002): 27–45.

"The Origin of Charles Darwin: A Review of Three Darwin Biographies," originally titled "The Human Angle: Three Biographies of Darwin Compared," *TLS*, no. 4951 (February 20, 1998): 8–9.

Part 1
Mapping the Disciplinary Landscape

1

The Use of Arnold in a
Darwinian World

Matthew Arnold believes that culture is progressing steadily toward a culminating realization of a universal set of aesthetic and ethical values. He thus maintains that "the world is in a course of development, of *becoming*, towards a perfection infinitely greater than we now can even conceive," and he describes the purpose of culture as an endeavor "to draw towards a knowledge of the universal order which seems to be intended and aimed at in the world" (1965, pp. 83, 93). Arnold himself regards such concepts as correspondent with what "science" can allow, but in both its teleological and transcendental aspects, Arnold's cultural theory is pre-Darwinian. In Darwin's conception, evolution, including human evolution, develops toward no specific goal, and the values of any given culture are relative to a specific adaptive situation. When Arnold sets out the grounds of a modern cultural order, he is prepared to legitimize this order by declaring that it corresponds to "reason and the will of God" (p. 165). A critic operating within a Darwinian conception of cultural order would declare only that this order represents the collective adaptation of a set of social animals operating within specific historical circumstances. The cultural values of these social animals would be contingent on their circumstances. Any particular set of values would represent a temporary adjustment between the innate properties of the organisms and the conditions of their environment, and both the innate properties and the environmental conditions would be caught up in a constant process of change in reciprocally causal relation to one another.

If we accept that the Darwinian conception is basically true, or closer to the truth than any other conception we now have, what value can Arnold's cultural theory have for us at the present time? To pose this question a little more starkly, does the Darwinian conception of culture render Arnold's cultural theory obsolete? Is Arnold's theory of culture now merely an artifact in a museum of ideas that though beautiful have lost all cogency and all current relevance to the structure of our own thought? My answer to this question is in three parts. The first part is that the largest structural components of Arnold's theory are in fact obsolete. In this respect, Arnold's theory shares the fate of all Victorian teleological theories of culture, including that of Marx. The second part of my answer is that much of the substance of Arnold's cultural theory remains as valid today as it was in the second half of the nineteenth century. And the third part is that the two largest substantive values, the regulative norms of Arnold's cultural theory, are themselves obsolete. One of these norms is oriented to the individual and the other to society. For the individual, Arnold projects as ultimate goal and highest regulative principle the "harmonious expansion of *all* the powers which make the beauty and worth of human nature." For society as a whole, he projects a harmonious, universal brotherhood. In this aspect, the idea of "perfection" entails "a *general* expansion of the human family" (1965, pp. 94, 95). What I shall suggest is that these goals are doubly defective. They are defective in the first place because they conflict internally with Arnold's own aesthetic preference for heroism, tragedy, and elegy. And they are defective in the second place because they fundamentally conflict with the order of nature, including human nature, as it appears within the evolutionary scheme of things. The depth of this ethical problematic can be suggested by observing that among the many Victorians who share in the contradictions of Arnold's cultural idealism we can include Darwin himself. Moreover, it should be clear that this final problem, the problem of Arnold's largest substantive values, is not a matter of antiquarian interest. It engages the deepest level of our own ethical consciousness.

Many of Arnold's substantive values are still usable. Here I shall just list some of the larger features of Arnold's general cultural theory: the alternations of Hebraism and Hellenism in the main phases of cultural history; the celebration of Sophocles and of Periclean Athens; the formulation of a classicist aesthetic and its gradual integration with the aesthetic of Romanticism; the contrast of medieval and pagan religious sentiment; the correlation of the phases of cultural history with faculties such as the heart and imagination, the reason and understanding, and then, the conception of "the imaginative reason" as a synthetic faculty; the facultative definitions of prose and poetry, literature and science; the notorious assessments of Chaucer as a minor classic, the Augustans as classics of our prose, and the Romantics as provincial and ignorant; but the compensatory celebrations of the Romantics, and especially of Wordsworth, for their natural magic and their grasp of "life"; the analysis of the three social classes according to criteria of character and aesthetics; and the definition of the state as the best self in its collective and corporate character. Besides mentioning these familiar features of the Arnoldian world, in order to fill out this sketch of substantive Arnoldian values, I shall only recall some of his distinctive phrases and formulas: "the grand style," "the modern spirit," "the best that has been known and thought," "to see the object as in itself it really is," "sweetness and light," "sweet reasonableness," "high seriousness," and "a criticism of life." (See Carroll, 1982.)

The continuing importance of such terms can be suggested by noting that they are commonplace idioms even among those who could not identify the source of these idioms. Arnold is often opposed, sometimes mocked, and by those critics whose historical perspective stops short with our own generation he is usually taken as merely the personification of a now antiquated and thoroughly discredited "humanism." At the highest level of contemporary criticism, however, he remains the critic who is most to be reckoned with. His formulations serve either as a rallying point or as a standard in opposition to which one must establish one's own position. (On Arnold's position within modern criticism, see Carroll, 1982, 1994, 1995, 1998; DeLaura, 1973; Frye, 1971; "The Function of Matthew Arnold at the Present Time," 1983, pp. 415–516; Machann, 1993a, 1993b.)

Many of Arnold's specific cultural values can be stripped of their absolutistic and transcendental character, and they can be assimilated to a relativistic Darwinian model of cultural values. The only essential difference in this adaptation is that, unlike Arnold, we can no longer ground such values in an eternal order sanctioned by "right reason" or "reason and the will of God." Instead, we must recognize that the specifically Arnoldian values emerge out of the cultural history of Western civilization. We must acknowledge that Arnold's formulations of cultural standards are actually descriptions of normative values within Western culture. In order to justify an effort to maintain and even to promulgate such values, we need only declare that we embrace them of our own free choice. In providing a rationale for this choice, we need go no further than declaring a personal preference, but we can, if we wish, explain our preferences, and these explanations can include a comparison of our values with those of other cultures. On the basis of such comparisons, we can maintain, in opposition to the radical multiculturalism prevalent now, that Western civilization represents quite specific achievements in such areas as civil order, science, philosophy, art, architecture, literature, and the activity of critical intelligence; we can maintain that these achievements can be compared with the achievements of other cultures in the same areas, and that in some important respects, within identifiable scales of value, these Western achievements do in fact represent the highest level yet attained by any culture.

Unlike Arnold, I am not claiming that there is any transcendental order that sanctions the scales of value in one culture over those in another culture. I am claiming only that any one culture can identify its own scales of value, can compare them with those of another culture, and, if the scales have points of similarity, can assess relative merit within that specific scale of value. Technology provides a clear instance. A radical cultural relativism would argue that the technology of any given culture is appropriate to that culture and that it cannot be compared with or measured against that of any other culture. But such professions of ideological faith can have no binding force on those who choose to make comparisons. Within our own culture—and indeed within that of any culture—one of the principal criteria by which technology can be measured is that of instrumental efficacy. It is true that within a given culture a stone axe or a wooden plow has its own specific place, but it nonetheless remains true that, measured on the scale of instrumental efficacy, a stone axe is a less efficient weapon than a machine gun, and a wooden plow is a less efficient agricultural tool than a tractor. Developing nations know this. That is why most of them make strenuous efforts to obtain Western technology.

Comparisons similar to those I have made for technology can be made for each of the areas I have identified. For instance, one can compare the kinds of civil order that can be constructed under a government of village elders and under a modern government that involves parliamentary politics, a complex judicial system, and an executive branch delegating major functions to a cabinet. Western science and village folklore can be compared in respect to both the total set of substantive concepts and the regulative principles of research and validation. We can, for instance, compare witchcraft and modern medicine, and we can compare alchemy and modern chemistry. In architecture, cathedrals or skyscrapers can be compared with mud huts or log cabins in respect to the complexity of design, the articulated understanding of the relation of materials to structure, the number and difficulty of problems solved, the sophistication or refinement of specific techniques of construction, and the integration of these techniques with other components of the total cultural order such as commerce or religion. Art and literature do not, of course, develop in any strict correlation with the developments of technology or civic order, but even in art and literature we can compare formal elements such as techniques of perspective or anatomical modeling, complexity and flexibility of syntactic elements, lexical amplitude, sophistication of poetical or narrative structures, refinement of the tonal repertory, and the range and representational potential of available generic forms. In assessing literary works, we can identify whatever scales of value we choose. We could, for instance, choose a scale of value that includes the adequate articulation of highly differentiated individual identities within a complex social order, the sophisticated use of a large lexicon reflecting a highly developed and multifaceted conceptual order, and a continuously developing tradition of literary forms capable of articulating elaborate symbolic and discursive relations among the components within this conceptual order. Such standards can be modulated by any number of components such as originality, stylistic expertise, expressive quality, moral earnestness, rational lucidity, or lyric vividness. Any such scale of value can be used as a basis for comparing Western literature with the literature of other cultures.

In current critical discourse, one frequently meets with a confusion between the issue of comparison and the issue of subjective judgment. Those who would deny the possibility of making comparative cultural value judgments are likely to invoke declarations by anthropologists such as Clifford

Geertz who argue that cultures are simply incommensurable. As I have tried to suggest, the claim for incommensurability is on the face of it merely untrue. Comparison within distinctly identifiable scales of value can in fact be made. But to make comparisons is not to invoke a unitary, transcendent scale of value. Fact and value remain distinct. We can, for example, compare a modern city with a Neolithic village without in any way committing ourselves to a scale of value that favors the modern city. To recognize that modern cities and Neolithic villages are different but comparable in no way prohibits a critic from declaring that in his or her view the total quality of human experience in a Neolithic village was preferable to that in a modern city, that prehistoric peoples lived in a more harmonious relation with their environments, were less dangerous to one another and less damaging to the environment, were more in touch with elementary passions, and so on. Rousseauistic primitivism cannot be repudiated by any appeal to a scale of value; it is itself a scale of value. In similar fashion, democratic egalitarianism cannot be repudiated by an appeal to Nietzschean aristocratic cruelty, nor vice versa. Both are scales of value. Our own particular set of values might well involve tolerance and sympathy for the values of other cultures, but tolerance and sympathy themselves inhere in no transcendent authority that forbids cultures to display exclusionary hostility toward other cultures.

Arnold would have us propagate the "best" that has been thought and said, but within the Darwinian worldview the "best" can only be what seems best to us, not what seems best to God or to "culture" as a displaced version of a providential cultural teleology. A convinced Darwinian might well wish to affirm a preference for, say, a humane and tolerant civil order in contrast to a highly militarized and xenophobic order like that of Nazi Germany, but he would find it both senseless and unnecessary to declare that this preference has the sanction of a transcendent order of value. He would be unwilling to assert that God is on his side, but he might well still be willing to fight, and if necessary to die, to sustain that form of civilization that he himself regards as best.

Finally, let us consider Arnold's belief that culture aims at a harmonious integration both of faculties within the mind and of people within the social order. These complementary forms of integration are the *telos* or goal that governs Arnold's conception of history. If, in accordance with a Darwinian view of development, we reject such teleological concepts, we cannot simply eliminate the teleological aspect of the ideal while leaving the substantive goal intact. At about the time I was writing my book on Arnold several years ago, the solution I am here rejecting was the solution I adopted. I could then imagine no governing norm other than that Arnold himself identified. Even then, though, I realized that this solution brought with it a serious enigma. Arnold's own aesthetic values, it is well known, are heavily oriented to pain and conflict. From the beginning to the end of his career, Arnold placed tragedy, elegy, and heroic epic higher on his own scale of aesthetic value than festive comedy. His love of pastoral lyricism, as in the work of Wordsworth or Senancour, consistently situates itself within a framework of elegy for a lost simplicity. Consequently, if we reject Arnold's ideal of a harmonious expansion and a universal brotherhood, we do not thereby repudiate Arnold's aesthetic temper. The positive elements in Arnold's aesthetic—joy, lyricism, and heroism, not to mention ironic wit—have meaning only within a natural order in which conflict, struggle, and loss are active forces. In other words, the teleological cultural ideal is itself essentially incompatible with the aesthetic ethos that Arnold derives from his normative synthesis of the Western cultural tradition.

Is it possible to valorize literature that deals with social and personal tragedy and still to imagine the possibility of greater harmony? Clearly, as a mere matter of degree, relatively harmonious social units can often be expanded to include larger segments of the total human population, but it nonetheless remains the case, simply as a matter of definition, that if the Arnoldian utopia were ever to be actually achieved—if we were to create a total and permanent world peace that adequately provided for the harmonious development of all people—personal and social tragedy would cease to exist. Whatever else a literature reflecting a utopian world order might look like, we can be quite certain that it would not look like the literature produced by Arnold's masters in the grand style: Sophocles, Homer, Dante, Shakespeare, and Milton. Yet more importantly, from the perspective we now have, within the order of nature as Darwin and his successors have described it, any such utopian literature seems hopelessly vapid and bland.

The goals of harmonious personal development within a universal brotherhood conflicts in deep and unavoidable ways with the whole competitive, antagonistic dynamic that is Darwin's main subject in both *The Origin of Species* and *The Descent of Man*. Darwin himself sometimes embraces the utopian ideal, but his utopian sentiments are essentially incompatible with the implications of his evolutionary theory. Moreover, he expresses other sentiments, irreconcilable with his utopian sentiments, that are far more compatible with his evolutionary theory. In *The Descent of Man*, Darwin identifies three main social qualities: "sympathy, fidelity, and courage" (vol. 1, p. 162). He argues that these social qualities are produced by the process of natural selection, a process that is supplemented by "sexual selection" as part of the human reproductive economy. In a fashion that has been corroborated by modern sociobiology, Darwin argues that sexual selection involves the competition for reproductive advantage among members of the same species and often members of the same social group. The results of sexual selection, in the production of individual and social qualities, has a strong causal effect on the outcome of competition among different social groups. Darwin argues convincingly that a tribe possessing the three main social qualities in a high degree "would spread and be victorious over other tribes; but in the course of time it would, judging from all past history, be in its turn overcome by some other and still more highly endowed tribe. Thus the social and moral qualities would tend slowly to advance and be diffused throughout the world" (vol. 1, pp. 162–163). This explanation remains wholly within the scope of natural history. It provides a fully satisfactory account of the existence and progress of the social virtues, and it convincingly situates human history within the larger processes of natural selection.

There is no scientific reason to posit transcendent causes or faculties outside of or different from the process of competition among human groups described by Darwin, but Darwin himself is unable to tolerate the moral implications of the vision he has himself created: a human world inescapably enmeshed in a process of conquest, assimilation, and extermination. Recoiling from the idea of a human world as violent, cruel, and wasteful as the world of nature, Darwin affirms that the "disinterested love for all living creatures, the most noble attribute of man," can serve as the dominant regulative power in human social relations (1871, vol. 1, p. 105). He describes a three-stage progression in the unit of social organization: from tribe, to nation-state, to universal brotherhood:

> As man advances in civilisation, and small tribes are united into larger communities, the simplest reason would tell each individual that he ought to extend his social instincts and sympathies to all the members of the same nation, though personally unknown to him. This point being once reached, there is only an artificial barrier to prevent his sympathies extending to the men of all nations and races (vol. 1, pp. 100–101).

The "artificial barrier" Darwin would have humans leap is the barrier that separates social organization among competing human groups from a social organization that contains all human beings within a single group. Is it theoretically inconceivable that human beings could extend their sense of group identity to the human species as a whole? From within the worldview established by modern evolutionary theory, any such extension would have to accommodate itself to the largest principle that regulates all of life—the principle of inclusive fitness.

The principle of inclusive fitness, as it is currently understood by evolutionary psychologists does not require us to suppose that all individuals at all times are seeking to maximize their reproductive advantage. Instead, it requires us to suppose that all individuals at all times are operating under the constraints of an evolved psychology that is itself the product of a process of adaptation that has been regulated, throughout the history of life, by the principle of inclusive fitness. The difference is not small. Human beings have evolved a complex set of psychological dispositions, including cognitive and social dispositions, precisely because these dispositions have helped to ensure their reproductive success over millions of years. Reproductive success is thus an ultimate causal force, but the evolved psychological dispositions are themselves proximate causes that are often only indirectly related to the immediate purposes of reproduction. To achieve a world order dominated by universal sympathy would thus not require that the reproductive interests of every individual be harmonized with those of every other individual. It would require, instead, that the evolved psychological dispositions of every individual be harmonized with the evolved psychological dispositions of all other individuals. (On proximate and ultimate cause, see Barkow, 1989, p. 296; Betzig, 1991, p. 140; Symons, 1979, p. 261; Tooby and Cosmides, 1992, p. 54.)

Given the regulative principle of inclusive fitness, organisms animated exclusively by a selfless, self-sacrificing sympathy to other organisms could not have evolved and in fact have not evolved. As Richard Dawkins observes, "Much as we might wish to believe otherwise, universal love and the welfare of the species as a whole are concepts that simply do not make evolutionary sense" (1989, p. 2). Sympathy is only one human motive among others, and all of human history provides us with abundant evidence that under the stimulus of desire, fear, or even simple conformism, this one motive can be easily overridden. Consequently—barring an elementary genetic restructuring of our evolved human psychology—in order to achieve a state in which individual and collective interests were fully synchronized, the evolved psychological dispositions of all individuals would have to be wholly under the administrative direction of a political authority possessing perfect control of all variable factors. This authority would have to be able to regulate the phenotypic interaction of the coordinated mass of individual human beings with all environmental stimuli, and it would have to be sufficiently flexible to anticipate and assimilate all further evolutionary developments emerging from the continuing interaction of random variation and selective retention. While the agents of political authority would thus have to possess perfect control of all variable factors, they would themselves have to be sufficiently constrained by internalized moral sanctions so that they could be trusted not to abuse the powers placed in their hands. (If they were constrained only by external social forces, they would not possess the perfect control necessary to regulate the whole system.)

It should be evident that the biological conditions that would have to be satisfied in order to achieve a utopian world order are of such extreme difficulty as to be, for all practical purposes, unreachable. It is hardly surprising, then, that these conditions are exceedingly remote from the conditions that actually prevail in the world in which we now live. These actual conditions include a good deal of xenophobia and virulent racial, ethnic, national, religious, and ideological hostility, and all this hostility, arising out of various forms of group identity, should alert us to a psychological difficulty inherent in the very idea of a universal brotherhood. Richard Alexander identifies the difficulty. Commenting on efforts to find a solution for nuclear war, Alexander observes that "systems of morality" arise from "within-group altruism" (1987, p. 233). The argument for "'universal brotherhood'" presupposes "that we can achieve peace and prevent war" by expanding this within-group altruism "so as to include the whole world." But any such expansion would obviate the conditions under which the systems of morality arose in the first place. Expectations of universal brotherhood "ignore or seek to override the paradox that extreme within-group altruism seems to correlate with and be historically related to between-group strife" (p. 233). That is, "Brotherly love of the most sincere and intense varieties often, if not universally, correlates with the presence of an enemy" (p. 234). In similar fashion, James Q. Wilson acknowledges that "deeply held loyalties do appear to conflict with generously broad sentiments" (1993, p. 48). Such observations can easily be confirmed by anyone familiar with the literature of war. To give just one example, in an episode in *All Quiet on the Western Front*, the narrator is caught out alone at night in No Man's Land and then hears the voices of his comrades:

> They are more to me than life, these voices, they are more than motherliness and more than fear; they are the strongest, most comforting thing there is anywhere: they are the voices of my comrades.
> I am no longer a shuddering speck of existence, alone in the darkness;—I belong to them and they to me; we all share the same fear and the same life, we are nearer than lovers, in a simpler, a harder way; I could bury my face in them, in these voices, these words that have saved me and will stand by me. (p. 186)

In less extreme form, the civilian population during a war also typically experiences a heightened sense of communal identity that elevates private morale in such a way as to reduce the incidence of social pathology.

In opposition to the utopian moral idealism of Darwin and Arnold, I shall propose two hypotheses, both of which are essentially compatible with Darwin's own theory of social evolution: first, that sympathy is strongly constrained by group-identification; and second, that group-identification is itself strongly constrained by the unit of socioeconomic organization to which any given individual belongs. As a qualification to this second hypothesis, I would acknowledge that socioeconomic organization can be modulated by various forms of cultural identification, but I would also argue that cultural order is itself crucially constrained by socioeconomic organization.

If, as Darwin and many modern evolutionary theorists believe, culture is only a means through which we organize the elementary, biological motives of human nature, "disinterested" values can subsist only as markers of degree within hierarchical orders of interest. One can be disinterested with respect to one's own immediate, individual interests, but only if one has subsumed that individual interest within a larger category of interest such as one's class, political party, ideological group, race, religion, or a concept such as civilization or culture. For instance, Arnold's own inclusive term of interest is "culture," a term that is roughly equivalent to "Western civilization regarded as culminating in Victorian gentlemen with a predominantly classical education and refined literary tastes." (I say this with no intention of disparagement. The characteristics exemplified by Arnold's conception of culture seem to me to constitute one of the finest moments of classical distinction within our cultural history.) Arnold's "culture" coincides with his effective unit of socioeconomic organization, and this convergence is itself no doubt a large factor in the manner of magnanimous confidence that distinguishes his work. Darwin's largest inclusive term is "life" itself. The inclusive breadth of Darwin's sympathy is a major source of his imaginative, literary power, but this imaginative extension of sympathy conflicts sharply with his personal identification with his own socioeconomic and cultural group, a group that is, from an anthropological perspective, very similar to Arnold's, with the difference merely of a scientific rather than a literary emphasis on the primary constitutive elements of civilization. (One might recall in this respect that Arnold and Huxley were personal friends and belonged to the same gentleman's club.)

The expansiveness of Darwin's own ideal of sympathy derives both from his own kindly personality and from the hypertrophic development of his professional naturalist's faculty of sympathetic curiosity into the ways of living things. As a hypertrophic development, this faculty is dependent on leisure— "the leisure to grow wise," as Arnold, echoing Samuel Johnson, formulates it (see Carroll, 1982, p. 176–177). As Darwin himself notes, "The presence of a body of well-instructed men, who have not to labour for their daily bread, is important to a degree which cannot be over-estimated; as all high intellectual work is carried on by them, and on such work material progress of all kinds mainly depends" (1981, vol. 1, p. 169). No doubt partly through association with its enabling condition of leisure, high intellectual work tends to present itself as an activity that is independent of any specific form of socioeconomic organization. This sense of autonomy is delusory. Darwin's cultivation of sympathetic scientific curiosity is itself dependent on the existence of a high civilization, on European and more specifically English civilization. Consequently, in order to sustain his own sense of a universal, disinterested sympathy, Darwin must *also* sustain the priority of his own advanced, Western, scientific civilization. It is for this reason that, throughout his work, he looks forward with equanimity or even with satisfaction to the imminent extermination of all primitive peoples.

In accordance with his kindly nature, Darwin would prefer conversion and assimilation to extermination, and in the *Voyage of the Beagle*, he expresses delighted satisfaction with the progress the Tahitians have made under the tutelage of Christian missionaries, but in *The Descent of Man*, he notes with regret that "it has everywhere been observed that savages are much opposed to any change of habits" (1981, vol. 1, p. 240). Thus, in a letter of 1881 in which he defends the notion that natural selection has contributed to "the progress of civilisation," Darwin remarks, "Remember what risk the nations of Europe ran, not so many centuries ago of being overwhelmed by the Turks, and how ridiculous such an idea now is! The more civilized so-called Caucasian races have beaten the Turkish hollow in the struggle for existence. Looking to the world at no very distant date, what an endless number of the lower races will have been eliminated by the higher civilized races throughout the world" (1959, vol. 1, p. 286 [letter to W. Graham, 3 July 1881]. Similar observations are scattered throughout *The Descent of Man.* For instance, Darwin acknowledges that the inheritance of wealth prohibits children from getting an equal start in "the race for success," but he declares that despite this drawback inheritance is "far from an unmixed evil; for without the accumulation of capital the arts could not progress; and it is chiefly through their power that the civilised races have extended, and are now everywhere extending, their range, so as to take the place of the lower races" (1981, vol.1, p. 169). (On Darwin and the savages, see Duncan, 1991.) In other words, Darwin's sympathy for all living things must itself be constrained by the conditions that enable it to subsist, and these conditions are dependent on the socioeconomic and cultural order to which he himself belongs—that of a modern European and more specifically English civilization that is committed to maintaining a leisure class by means of inherited wealth. (In similar fashion, Arnold recognizes that his own class—the educated elite—is a fourth estate wholly dependent for its existence on the patronage of the dominant socioeconomic classes. See Arnold, 1962a, p. 88, 1965, p. 23.)

When we are secure and prosperous, it is possible to exercise the most benign sympathy for a vaguely universal humanity. When we are threatened—when we are pressed to preserve our territory or maintain our access to the resources on which we depend—we predictably "revert" to the antagonistic mode for which utopian moral visions can provide no adequate account. At this point in history, most of us in the industrialized world are fairly comfortable, but the world population is growing exponentially, and our resources are rapidly diminishing. Threaten our oil, and we instantly dispatch a vast military machine that efficiently obliterates tens of thousands of Iraqi soldiers. Are episodes like this an anomaly? If so, such anomalies have always occurred, and I think it very safe to predict that they will continue to occur. (See E. O. Wilson, 1978, chapter 5.)

Even if it is true that we are not able to escape from the struggle for survival, would it not still be better to adopt the utopian norm propounded by Arnold and Darwin, and to hope that by professing this norm we shall moderate our conflicts and direct our energies toward achieving a universal civilization? Our modern cultural history should give us some pause. The ubiquitous Victorian affirmations of a progressive universal sympathy did nothing to inhibit the frenzy of mass slaughter in the First World War. And of course the First World War led into the Second World War. Since wars absorb an extraordinary amount of energy and require the most intensely organized forms of social effort, I do not think that the wars in this century, or in any previous century for that matter, were mere accidents—just slip-ups on the way to achieving an order of peace and brotherhood that though wholly new in human experience is also somehow normative. Rather than propounding ineffectual utopian ideals based on false psychology, we would do better, I think, to set our sights on sustaining civilization as best we can within the conditions we actually face.

In sum, what is Arnold worth to us at the present time? His values are not absolute and transcendent. They are necessarily conditioned by his own cultural, historical circumstances—circumstances that are not identical to ours—and conditioned also by his own particular temperament, a temperament that is very fine but that has distinct limitations. Parts of Arnold's thinking are obsolete; other parts are enmeshed in the same difficulties and conflicts in which we also are enmeshed. But better than most of the figures in our cultural heritage, and better than most of our contemporaries, he provides us with a model of someone who has assimilated the Western cultural heritage and made it a living medium. His cultural theory is the articulation of this medium. The model he provides is worth only what we choose to make it worth. That is rather less than Arnold himself wanted; but it is considerably more than many of his critics are now willing to grant.

2
Biology and Poststructuralism

The Darwinian Matrix

Darwinian evolutionary theory has established itself as the matrix for all the life sciences. This theory situates human beings firmly within the natural, biological order, and evolutionary principles are now extending themselves rapidly into the human sciences: into epistemology, sociology, psychology, ethics, neurology, and linguistics. The rapidly developing and increasingly integrated group of evolutionary disciplines has resulted in an ever-expanding network of mutually illuminating and mutually confirming hypotheses about human nature and human society. If literature is in any way concerned with the language, psychology, cognition, and social organization of human beings, all of this information should have a direct bearing on our understanding of literature. It should inform our understanding of human experience as the subject of literature, and it should enable us to situate literary figurations in relation to the personal and social conditions in which they are produced. Up to this point, contemporary literary theory has not only failed to assimilate evolutionary theory, it has adopted a doctrinal stance that places it in irreconcilable conflict with the basic principles of evolutionary biology.

I shall describe the current critical paradigm, identify the basic principles in an evolutionary view of knowledge and of culture, outline a theory of literary figuration that corresponds to these larger evolutionary principles, explain how this theory of figuration conflicts with our current critical paradigm, and assess the motives and interests that have established our current critical paradigm as an orthodox creed within the professional institution of criticism.

Textualism and Indeterminacy

The principles that dominate critical theory at the present time can be gathered together under the heading of "poststructuralism," a term here intended to indicate an essential continuity between the Derridean linguistic 1970s and the Foucauldian political 1980s. The central doctrines of poststructuralism are textualism and indeterminacy. Textualism is the idea that language or culture constitute or construct the world according to their own internal principles, and indeterminacy identifies all meaning as ultimately self-contradictory. Textualism treats of human beings and the world in which they live as the effects of a linguistic or cultural system, and indeterminacy reduces knowledge to the spontaneous generation of internal contradictions within this system. J. Hillis Miller offers a representative formulation of the textualist thesis. "We make things what they are by naming them in one way or another, that is, by the incorporation of empirical data into a conventional system of signs" (1986, p. 109; Miller attributes this textualist doctrine, wrongly, to George Eliot.) Fredric Jameson offers a representative formulation of indeterminacy. "'Poststructuralism,' or, as I prefer, 'theoretical discourse,' is at one with the demonstration of the necessary incoherence and impossibility of all thinking" (1991, p. 218).

Together, textualism and indeterminacy eliminate the two criteria of truth: the correspondence of propositions to their objects and the internal coherence of propositions. By affirming that texts do not refer to objects but rather constitute them, textualism eliminates correspondence, and by affirming that all meaning is ultimately contradictory indeterminacy eliminates coherence. By eliminating truth, poststructuralism yields epistemological and ontological primacy to rhetoric or "discourse," and it simultaneously delegitimizes all traditional norms. Since poststructuralism treats all norms as arbitrary, it has a convenient application within the field of radical political ideology. In its political aspect, poststructuralism typically treats of normative intellectual, moral, and social structures within the Western cultural tradition as fraudulent and oppressive—as purely conventional constructs that are designed to perpetuate the exploitative interests of social elites, particularly the interests of white male heterosexuals of the ruling classes. (See Levin, 1993; Searle, 1993.)

The professional advantages of poststructuralist doctrine should be obvious. It enables literature professors to adopt a prefabricated critical stance that depends in no way on the empirical validity of their findings. By connecting the claim to a superior form of insight, transcending reason, with a claim to superior moral authority, poststructuralism invests its adherents with the kind of authority appropriate to a priesthood. The initiates of this doctrinal order must take a vow of intellectual poverty. They necessarily renounce positive, objective knowledge. But in compensation, they automatically occupy a critical perspective that is always already superior to the objective findings of science and that is always already morally superior to the social order in which they themselves participate.

The poststructuralist elimination of truth can, of course, take effect only if one believes that the central poststructuralist doctrines are, in fact, true. In this sense, poststructuralism undermines the ground on which it stands, but the larger poststructuralist position, deriving from the philosophy of Derrida, is that all propositions always undermine the ground on which they stand. Applying this principle specifically to the "law" of genre, Derrida provides a concise formulation of the principle in its broadest import. "What if there were, lodged within the heart of the law itself, a law of impurity or a principle of contamination? And suppose the condition for the possibility of the law were the *a priori* of a counter-law, an axiom of impossibility that would confound its sense, order, and reason?" (1981, p. 53). The "law" of genre here constitutes only a more particular instance of the law in general, that is, the general concept of sense, order, and reason. A central mission of Foucault's work is to apply this principle to the field of intellectual history or, as he calls it, "archaeology." "Archaeological analysis," he explains, "erects the primacy of a contradiction that has its model in the simultaneous affirmation and negation of a single proposition" (1972, p. 155). Synthesizing the principle of contradiction with textualism, Foucault offers an evocative formulation of the poststructuralist conception of discourse as a cosmic principle of linguisticized negativity. "All manifest discourse is secretly based on an 'already said,' " a "writing that is merely the hollow of its own mark. . . . [T]he manifest discourse, therefore, is really no more than the repressive presence of what it does not say; and this 'not-said' is a hollow that undermines from within all that is said" (p. 25). The "hollow"—along with its various synonyms such as the "abyss" and the "void"—serves for poststructuralists as a cosmic framework. Within this framework, the self-canceling nature of poststructuralist repudiations of truth appear as merely exemplary instances of the general claim that incoherence and contradiction are the heart of an ultimate, linguistic reality—"the reality of discourse in general," as Foucault describes it (p. 227). My own position, in contrast, is that the doctrines of textualism and indeterminacy are not true and that truth is itself the primary criterion in assessing the validity of all doctrines.

A fundamental premise of poststructuralist critical theory is that in all specific literary works meaning is preemptively determined by linguistic and cultural codes. Whether taken as purely semiotic textual systems or as ideological structures, from the poststructuralist perspective these codes appear to be constrained neither by individual identities nor by any natural order. To the contrary, the sense of individual identity and the concept of a natural order themselves appear as merely reflexive functions within autonomous sign systems. Under the aegis of deconstructive philosophy, these systems signify their own disconnection from any "ground" outside of themselves. Poststructuralists assimilate descriptive terms from Freudian psychoanalysis and Marxist political economy, but within the poststructuralist synthesis the material determinism of Freud and Marx dissolves into semiosis. Psychosexual and socioeconomic forces cease to be actual forces consisting of concrete circumstances and living agents and become instead components within signifying systems. Under the rubric of "postmodernism," Ihab Hassan describes this vision as one in which languages "reconstitute the universe . . . into signs of their own making, turning nature into culture, and culture into an immanent semiotic system" (1986, p. 508). As Jameson puts it, "Postmodernism is what you have when the modernization process is complete and nature is gone for good." The postmodern world is one in which "'culture' has become a veritable 'second nature.'" This new semiotic cosmology is "an immense and historically original acculturation of the Real, a quantum leap in what Benjamin still called the 'aestheticization' of reality" (1991, pp. ix, x).

In contrast to poststructuralist epistemology, evolutionary epistemology presupposes that, in the formulation of Konrad Lorenz, "All human knowledge derives from a process of interaction between man as a physical entity, an active, perceiving subject, and the realities of an equally physical external world, the object of man's perception" (1979, p. 1). From this specifically biological perspective, meaning is determined, in the first place, not by linguistic and cultural codes that obey only their own internal principles but rather by physiological structures such as "the sense organs and central nervous system" (p. 6). Such structures "enable living organisms to acquire relevant information about the world and to use this information for their survival" (p. 6). Lorenz sets this view of human knowledge in sharp contrast to the view of "transcendental idealists" who assume that "our modes of thought and perception" do not "correspond in the least with things as they really are" (p. 7). Lorenz's views are similar to those of the philosopher Karl Popper, who holds that "Life is problem-solving and discovery" (1979, p. 148). As adaptive organisms, we are concerned to know the truth. The purpose of science is to enable us to discover "a fuller, a more complete, a more interesting, logically stronger and more relevant truth"—relevant, that is, "to our problems." Knowledge is always partial, hypothetical, conjectural, and provisional, but it can correspond more or less adequately to a world that exists independently of human beings.

Biology and Figuration

To designate the total set of affective, conceptual, and aesthetic relations within a given literary construct, I shall use the term "figurative structure." Any element that can be abstracted from a figurative structure is *ipso facto* a figurative element. Thus, representations of people or objects, metrical patterns, rhyme schemes, overt propositional statements, figures of speech, syntactic rhythms, tonal inflections, stylistic traits, single words, and even single sounds are all elements of figuration. Figurative structure, like any other kind of structure, can be analyzed at any level of particularity. A primary concern of literary theory, then, must be to identify the level of analysis at which elements form meaningful units that join with other such units so as to fashion the larger structures of figuration. As evolutionary psychologists John Tooby and Leda Cosmides affirm, "Sciences prosper when researchers discover the level of analysis appropriate for describing and investigating their particular subject: when researchers discover the level where invariance emerges, the level of underlying order. What is confusion, noise, or random variation at one level resolves itself into systematic patterns upon the discovery of the level of analysis suited to the phenomena under study" (1992, p. 63).

In representations of human experience, the most important figurative elements are characters, settings, and plots (a connected sequence of events). For convenience, I shall refer to these elements collectively as the "dramatic" elements of figurative structures. These three elements are the central figurative units in drama, and in both narratives and lyric or meditative poetry the narrator's or speaker's own persona can also be identified as a "character." To be sure, the author's own relation to his story, as this relation is revealed in the narrator's or speaker's persona, is of the first importance in determining the total meaning of the represented action, but it is important precisely because the author, like the represented characters, is a distinct person—a locus for the organization of human experience. On this issue, the traditional wisdom has already identified the units of analysis appropriate to literary study. Until quite recently, character, setting, and plot have formed part of the common vocabulary of literary study, and narrative point of view has been one of the most commonly considered topics of formal analysis. Even the most determined deconstructive effort to repudiate the "subject" cannot avoid surreptitiously or paradoxically reintroducing the concept of character into its analyses of dramatic representations. (See Abrams, 1986, 1997; Booth, 1996; Cain, 1984, pp. 31–50; Leaska, 1996).

The traditional categories—character, setting, and plot—can be explained and validated by invoking the largest principles of an evolutionary critical paradigm. If the purpose of literature is to represent human experience, and if the fundamental elements of biological existence are organisms, environments, and actions, the figurative elements that correlate with these biological elements would naturally assume a predominant position within most figurative structures. Evolutionary theory can thus provide a sound rationale for adopting the basic categories, and it can also provide a means for extending our theoretical understanding of how these categories work within the total system of figurative relations. This theoretical understanding can in turn provide a means for assessing traditional explanations or applications of the categories and measuring their presuppositions against those of an evolutionary paradigm.

I shall argue that representations of characters, settings, or actions constitute a single, continuous scale with realism at one end of the scale and symbolism at the other. Figurations at the realist end of the scale represent people, objects, and actions as they appear to common observation and as they appear to the represented characters themselves. As Samuel Johnson describes it, discussing the new fiction in the first half of the eighteenth century, realist works "exhibit life in its true state, diversified only by accidents that daily happen in the world, and influenced by passions and qualities which are really to be found in conversing with mankind" (1968, p. 18). The definition clearly applies to drama as well as narrative, and it could be applied as well to the objects represented in descriptive poetry. Figurations at the symbolic end of the scale use the dramatic elements to represent or embody the elemental forces and the fundamental structural relations within the author's own world-picture or cognitive order. Typically symbolic forms of representation include fairy tales, myths, and allegories. For instance, the Greek gods represent forces of nature, elemental human propensities and faculties, and human skills and social activities. The personified forces of nature include the sea and sky, sun and moon, lightning and thunder; elemental human propensities include love, jealousy, wisdom, chastity, libidinousness, and artistic talent; and skills and social activities include medical practice, metalworking, war, commerce, and theft. Allegorical figures in *Pilgrim's Progress* depict the basic philosophical and moral elements of a Christian worldview, situate these elements within a sociopolitical landscape, and demonstrate the way all these elements interact in a dramatic sequence leading to damnation or salvation. Characters, settings, and events in *The Faerie Queene* represent a commingling of ancient myths, Christian ethical and philosophical principles, Elizabethan social, economic, and political relations, and like *Pilgrim's Progress*, it locates these relations within the cosmography of a Christian worldview.

The difference between realistic and symbolic forms of representation can be correlated with and, I think, derived from the psycho-physiological polarity of extraversion and introversion. This polar concept was elaborated in the character psychology of Jung, and it has more recently been the subject of intensive empirical research by Hans Eysenck and many other psychologists. (See Bouchard, 1994, 1997; Buss, 1990, 1995; Costa and Widiger, 1994; Digman, 1990; Eysenck, 1967; Eysenck and Eysenck, 1985; MacDonald, 1995b, 1998b; Pervin, 1990, 2003; Pervin and John, 1999; Segal and MacDonald, 1998; Stelmack, 1990; Wiggins, 1996; J. Q. Wilson, 1993.) Put concisely, extraverts are more strongly oriented to absorbing stimuli from the world outside themselves; introverts are more strongly oriented to articulating their own psychic structures. In his essay on Shelley, Robert Browning provides a formulation of this distinction that correlates closely with Johnson's description of realist fiction. Browning declares that there are two kinds of poets, the objective and the subjective. The "objective poet" seeks "to reproduce things external . . . with an immediate reference, in every case, to the common eye and apprehension of his fellow men." In contrast "the subjective poet" is concerned "not with the combination of humanity in action, but with the primal elements of humanity . . . and he digs where he stands, preferring to seek them in his own soul" (1981, pp. 137, 139). Ambrose Bierce offers an incisive formulation of this polarity in respect to the generic distinction between the novel and the romance. "To the romance the novel is what photography is to painting. Its distinguishing principle, probability, corresponds to the literal actuality of the photograph" (1946, p. 314). Leslie Stephen makes a similar distinction in respect to philosophical orientation, and he associates this distinction with the two elementary principles of truth in all representations: coherence and correspondence. "In some minds the desire for unity of system is the more strongly developed;

in others the desire for conformity to facts" (1949, vol. 1, p. 6). The subjective orientation is dominated by the desire for coherence or systemic integrity in a theoretical or figurative structure, and the objective orientation is dominated by the desire for a correspondence between that structure and reality. The objective orientation tends to concentrate on depicting the personal experience of other human beings, and the subjective to concentrate on constructing figurations that exemplify the relations among the elemental components of the author's own cognitive order. Browning's own dramatic monologues provide a good example of objective or realist representation. Characters such as the speakers in "Porphyria's Lover," "The Bishop Orders His Tomb at Saint Praxed's Church," or "Bishop Blougram's Apology" are not primarily projections of components of Browning's own psyche; they are not primarily structural elements within his own cognitive map; they are representations of actual or possible human beings. In this respect, Browning's poems correspond to the criteria for "formal realism" enunciated by Ian Watt: the representation of "particular individuals having particular experiences at particular times and at particular places" (1957, p. 31). The primary purpose of Browning's monologues is not to depict the subjective quality of Browning's own experience; it is to depict the subjective quality of the experience of people who are often radically different from Browning himself. In this respect, Browning is more genuinely "Shakespearian" than most lyric poets.

Northrop Frye's effort to distinguish between the novel and the romance can help to clarify the nature of the differences between realistic and symbolic forms of representation. Frye reifies the distinctions, and he situates them within a metaphysical context radically opposed to that of Darwinian naturalism, but on a certain level of description, his characterization can usefully be compared with the concept of a representational continuum. Frye argues that "the novel tends to be extroverted and personal; its chief interest is in human character as it manifests itself in society. The romance tends to be introverted and personal; it also deals with characters, but in a more subjective way. . . . The romancer does not attempt to create 'real people' so much as stylized figures which expand into psychological archetypes" (1957, pp. 308, 304). In contrast to Frye, I would argue that symbolic figures represent not only "psychological archetypes" but also socioeconomic, ideological, religious, and philosophical elements, that is, the relations among all the conceptual components of a given worldview.

As the quotations from Johnson and Browning suggest, the distinction between realistic and symbolic representation can be associated very closely with a distinction between common understanding and speculative abstraction. It is commonly understood that people occupy a three-dimensional space extending through time, that they undergo the basic biological events of birth and death, and that between these two events they are motivated by certain needs, appetites, or propensities such as hunger, thirst, sexual desire, ambition, fear, curiosity, and affection, that they are vulnerable to injury and sickness, that they are capable of joy and grief, and that they vary a good deal in personality type, in moral character, and in personal development. The common understanding exemplified in realist literature is not "factual" in a way that is qualitatively distinct from observations that would be considered "theoretical"; it is merely theory at a level of such mundane density of cross-referential verification that the theory requires little conscious construction. In other words, "fact" is itself not qualitatively different from theory; it is merely theory at the level closest to our immediate animal needs. Popper argues that "because all our dispositions are in some sense adjustments to invariant or slowly changing environmental conditions, they can be described *as theory-impregnated. . . . [T]here is no sense organ in which anticipatory theories are not genetically incorporated*" (1979, pp. 71–72). The polar terms in propositions of this sort can be turned around: If fact is merely theory at a high level of conviction, theory is merely fact at a level of speculative abstraction remote from the theory already established as fact. Popper argues that "*all science, and all philosophy, are enlightened common sense*" (p. 34). I would myself be less sanguine about the enlightened character of "*all philosophy.*" The extension of common sense in philosophy, as in religion, myth, ideology, and "hermetic" sciences like astrology or alchemy, can produce fanciful worldviews that bear little relation to the actual order of nature. As Leslie Stephen declares, it is perfectly possible for "an erroneous postulate" to survive, so long as it is "not so mischievous as to be fatal to the agent" (1949, vol. 1, p. 4). When regulated by empirically confirmed concepts subject to revision by the criteria of rational judgment, the extension of common sense can also produce valid knowledge. Science is merely that form of speculative abstraction that extends common sense in a series of propositions each of which confirms itself according to the canons of logic and evidence operative also at the lowest level of common sense.

Human Nature, Culture, and Individual Identity

In poststructuralist theories of literature, it is a commonplace that, as Wallace Martin declares, "conventional practices do not separate us from reality but create it" (1986, p. 75). In Stanley Fish's more elaborate formulation, "The givens of any field of activity—including the facts it commands, the procedures it trusts in, and the values it expresses and extends—are socially and politically constructed, are fashioned by man rather than delivered by God or Nature" (1989, p. 485). Fish's formulation depends on tacitly suppressing the idea of a reciprocal interaction between nature and culture and presenting these terms as mutually exclusive antitheses. Taken loosely, the commonplace proposition that culture constructs reality is merely a truism: the idea that cultural conventions vary and that these variations influence individual responses to the world. Taken more strictly, the commonplace is a radical absurdity: the idea that "reality" itself exercises no constraining influence on our conception of the world. Even if we reduce "reality" to the world of human thought and behavior, excluding the physical world in which humans live, this commonplace proposition requires us to suppose that human nature is infinitely malleable and that there are no genetic constraints on behavior, thought, and feeling. In accordance with this supposition, the deep structural similarities across all cultures and between people and other animals would have to be regarded as purely coincidental. (See Brown, 1991; and in this vol., see part 1, chapter 2.)

Human ethology—the evolutionary study of human beings—provides us with a perspective that assimilates the half-truth in the constructivist commonplace but avoids its absurd implications. Sociobiologists and evolutionary psychologists take as their central working hypothesis the idea that innate dispositions, the result of an evolutionary process of adaptation, influence every aspect of human identity: cognition, the psycho-physiological structure of personality, sexual identity, family functions, the organization of individuals in social structures, and the relation of human beings to the nonhuman world of physical nature. Some innate dispositions, such as those regulating vital bodily functions like breathing, are "closed" or hard-wired. Other dispositions, including many of those regulating emotional responses and social behavior, are "open" in the sense that they remain latent until elicited by appropriate environmental stimuli. Dispositions that are not closed are susceptible to varying degrees of modification through cultural conditioning, but cultural forms are themselves the product of a complex interaction among various innate dispositions and between innate dispositions and variable environmental conditions.

Allowing, then, both for genetic disposition and for cultural variation, we can formulate the relation between human nature and culture in the following pair of propositions: (1) innate human dispositions exercise a powerful shaping force on all forms of cultural order; (2) all such forces operate in a tight web of systemic interdependency such that the modification of any one element in the system has a distinct effect on all the other elements within the system. Even elemental forces such as the instinct for mother/infant bonding or for procreation can be suppressed within a given cultural complex, as is evidenced by the institutions of the wet nurse and celibate religious societies, but these suppressions carry with them a heavy psychic cost. Most readers would be able to assess personally and subjectively some of the psychic cost involved in celibacy, and John Bowlby's researches give evidence as to the cost involved in disrupting the mother/infant bond (1973, 1980, 1982). Our society as a whole is still in the process of conducting experiments in such matters as dissolving the nuclear family and eliminating sex-role distinctions for military combat. The most radically constructivist view of all such changes is that traditional social roles and functions are purely arbitrary and can be altered at will by decrees of social policy. These experiments will be interesting to watch. They will enable us to test the constructivist hypothesis and will provide a good deal of empirical data that can be correlated with evolutionary models of human psychology and social organization.

If innate characteristics form a basis both of individual identity and of cultural order, all three areas necessarily overlap, but they do not merge into identity. Genotypes vary, and while the environmental factors that influence individual identity include larger cultural forces, they also include quite particular circumstances of personal history that vary a great deal within any given cultural order. Individual identity is not identical either with cultural order or with all species-typical characteristics, but both cultural order and human nature can be represented only within the cognitive map of an individual mind. That is, all symbolic representations of human nature and cultural order are necessarily interpretations from the perspective of a distinct individual identity.

Poststructuralist theories of language and culture cannot provide an adequate account of either the realistic and symbolic aspects of figuration or the interactions of innate dispositions, cultural order, and individual identity. By eliminating both the individual identity and innate dispositions as principles of organization, poststructuralism locates all literary relations exclusively on the level of culture. If the world antecedent to culture is itself merely an effect of culture or language, there could be no representation of reality. Symbolic order would have to be all-inclusive, but symbolic structures would not articulate dispositions lodged in individual minds. Individual minds would provide no constraining point of force within a given cultural order. Figuration could thus articulate only its own internal relations. The poet could not hold the mirror up to nature, as Hamlet says he should, for nature would itself merely reflect the properties of mirrors. One such property would be the vivid illusion that people are living organisms within a real, physical universe that exists independently of language.

The strongest general claim that could be made for cultural constructivism would be that culture represents emergent cultural phenomena, that is, phenomena that appear only at the level of organization represented by culture. So far as it goes, this claim is self-evidently true. The specifically constructivist claim, however, is that cultural phenomena possess actual or virtual autonomy and assume independent causal priority over human behavior, thought, and feeling. By having all literary works refer only to other literary phenomena, or by having all literary figurations wholly *constitute* their experiences rather than describing them, referring to them, organizing them, expressing them, articulating them, or reconstructing them, poststructuralists render themselves incapable of giving any adequate causal explanation of literary forms. In poststructuralist literary criticism, the skewed causal logic entailed in attributing autonomous causal power to society, culture, or language associates itself intimately with a fundamental falsification of the ontological character of literature. Within the poststructuralist paradigm, the rich world of experience within reality has been emptied out, and in its place we have been given a thin and hectic play of self-reflexive linguistic functions. This is a dreary, impoverished vision of life and literature, but worse, it is a gratuitous and obviously false vision. It depletes the world, and in order to accomplish its depletion it gives a false account of our experience within the world.

The Institutional Situation

My argument, again, is that the evolutionary explanation of human experience is relatively true. It is not absolutely true, since no knowledge is absolute, but it is a more complete and adequate theory of the development and nature of life, including human life, than any other theory currently available to us. It thus necessarily provides the basis for any adequate account of culture and of literature. If a theory of culture and literature is true, it can be assimilated to the Darwinian paradigm; and if it cannot be reconciled with the Darwinian paradigm, it is not true. The poststructuralist explanation of things cannot be reconciled with the Darwinian paradigm. It cannot be modified and assimilated to the Darwinian paradigm. It is an alternative, competing paradigm. It operates on principles that are wholly different and fundamentally incompatible with those of evolutionary theory. It should, consequently, be rejected. Let me face squarely the historical and institutional implications of this rejection. If I am basically right in my contentions, a very large proportion of the work in critical theory that has been done in the last twenty years will prove to be not merely obsolete but essentially void. It cannot be regarded as an earlier phase of a developing discipline, with all the honor due to antecedents and ancestors. It is essentially a wrong turn, a dead end, a misconceived enterprise, a repository of delusions and wasted efforts.

I am myself under no illusions as to the eagerness with which people will embrace a theoretical proposal that necessarily implies that their own theoretical efforts have been wasted. And even without the self-perpetuating dynamic that is built into any system of vested institutional interests, the kind of paradigm shift I am proposing runs counter to ideological prejudices that are deeply rooted in political commitments, in disciplinary interests, and in metaphysical yearnings. I shall briefly consider each of these three sources of prejudice.

For many people, the idea of biological constraints on human nature seems unacceptable because it supposedly limits the range of possible political reform. The norm that typically governs poststructuralist political thinking is that of anarchistic utopianism. Poststructuralism affiliates itself with every form of radical opposition to prevailing or traditional norms. It affiliates itself with Marxist hostility to bourgeois power structures and to the hegemony of Western culture generally, and it emphatically identifies itself with radical feminism and with militant homosexuality. While I am myself opposed to discrimination and in favor of a large civil tolerance for private behavior, I also have a good deal of respect for normative structures, and I would contend that when one adopts a reflexive, automatic hostility to all normative structures, and combines this reflexive hostility with a hostility to all "logocentric" or rational modes of thought, the result is merely a perverse negativity. The basic poststructuralist position, inverting that of Alexander Pope, is that whatever is, is wrong. I would not agree with Pope that whatever is, is right, but I would agree even less with people who are fundamentally opposed to the very principle of normative order.

The radical political motives that animate poststructuralism intertwine themselves with motives of professional ambition. Biologistic thinking threatens the foundational principles through which both the social sciences and the humanities have sought to establish their disciplinary autonomy. The disciplinary motive in literary criticism can be detected in the otherwise incomprehensible eagerness with which academic critics have embraced Derrida's counterintuitive assertions that "writing" constitutes an autonomous matrix of reality. If writing, not ripeness, is all, then literary critics have privileged access to ultimate meaning. It is hardly surprising that rhetoricians, aggrieved at the continually increasing authority and efficacy of science, would insist that the laws of discourse take precedence over the laws of science. Moreover, if literature refers to the world of experience, and is in this sense primary, then criticism, which refers only to literature, would be "secondary." If, however, literature refers only to a world of words, it is in no way prior to criticism. Thus, thirty years ago, the phrase "secondary literature," meaning critical commentary on literary texts, was standard usage. One now almost never hears the phrase. Poststructuralism, it should be clear, invests rhetoricians with an authority at least equal to that both of scientists and of literary authors.

Finally, these political and disciplinary motives form a natural bond with a quasi-religious desire to preserve an area of human subjectivity or spirituality that is somehow, mystically, distinct from the objective world that can be known by science. The realm of rhetoric is the realm of mystical indeterminacy, and the desire to preserve some such realm from science has dominated critical theory from the time of Kant's *Critique of Judgment*. It is a central motive behind Romantic literary theory, phenomenology, Russian formalism, and the more doctrinaire version of New Criticism represented by John Crowe Ransom. The various traditions of transcendental aesthetic theory provide a large context for the poststructuralist hostility to positive scientific understanding.

The three motives I have described—utopian idealism, professionalist ambition, and sublimated religious sentiment—obviously conflict with one another in serious ways, but they all three join forces to obstruct a better motive: the concern for truth. In support of this appeal to truth as a criterion of critical judgment, let me recall the conclusion to Darwin's *Descent of Man*. After acknowledging the distress his theories are likely to produce in many of his readers, Darwin offers consolatory reflections on the nobility displayed in the behavior of certain animals, and he also invokes the hope for still further progress among human beings. Having made these conciliatory points, he returns to his dominant, scientific concern, and he distinguishes unequivocally between his scientific motive and any emotional or ideological motive. "But we are not here concerned with hopes or fears, only with the truth as far as our reason allows us to discover it. I have given the evidence to the best of my ability; and we must acknowledge, as it seems to me, that man with all his noble qualities, with sympathy which feels for the most debased, with benevolence which extends not only to other men but to the humblest living creature, with his god-like intellect which has penetrated into the movements and constitution of the solar system—with all these exalted powers—Man still bears in his bodily frame the indelible stamp of his lowly origin" (1981, vol. 2, p. 405). (For strained efforts to depict Darwin himself as a proto-deconstructive exemplar of irrationalism and indeterminacy, see Barrish, 1991; Beer, 1983; Pitts, 1990; Ulin, 1992.)

The significance of Darwin's concluding observation is only now, more than a century later, beginning to be felt in its full force. I predict that within twenty years the Darwinian paradigm will have established itself as the dominant paradigm in the social sciences. It will have done so in spite of all prejudice and all entrenched interests, and it will have done so because of the irresistible force of its explanatory power. I imagine the Darwinian paradigm will take longer to establish itself in the humanities and in literary theory, partly because literary theory is heavily dependent on developments in other disciplines, partly because it is far less constrained by empirical findings than the social sciences are, and partly because literary theory is the last refuge of mystical indeterminacy; it is the prime medium for the supposedly transcendent autonomy of the human spirit. But even in literary theory, the need for understanding must ultimately take precedence over beliefs that depend on obscurantism and intellectual obstruction. In any case, whatever happens within the critical institution as a whole, the pursuit of positive knowledge is available to anyone who desires it. Within this pursuit, the opportunities for real and substantial development in our scientific understanding of culture and of literature are now greater than they have ever been before.

3
"Theory," Anti-Theory, and Empirical Criticism

People who could be described as evolutionary literary critics presuppose the validity of a scientific understanding of the world, and they believe that the biological study of human beings is the necessary basis for a scientifically valid understanding of literature. These assumptions separate them from most of their colleagues in literature departments, but the assumptions do not go very far toward identifying an actual program of research. In what follows, I shall characterize the two main parties that currently control the field of literary studies—the dominant postmodern party and the traditionalist opposition—contrast them both with critical study that orients itself to a biological understanding of human nature, and then pose a question: what should evolutionary literary critics do? This one large question contains several smaller questions. Where should we start? What guidelines should we follow? What should be the range of our activity? What kind of knowledge can we expect to produce? Is it possible to integrate literary study with empirical social science? What challenges and difficulties do we face in trying to reach this goal?

About thirty years ago, a specific complex of ideological and literary ideas began to emerge on the continent, and in the past twenty years this complex has achieved dominance in Anglo-American academic literary study. There are three central components of the complex: deconstructive linguistic philosophy, Marxist social theory, and Freudian psychology. In their combined scope, these three theories offer a comprehensive account of certain crucial areas of reality: deconstructive philosophy informs us that the ultimate nature of reality is linguistic or rhetorical in character, and it stipulates that this rhetorical order is both self-enclosed and self-subversive, forbidding us access to any realm outside a chain of constantly displaced signifiers. Marxism provides a comprehensive model of social and economic life, including the historical development of social orders, and Freudianism takes in the whole field of individual psychology, sexual relations, and family dynamics. In isolation, each of these three theories has a certain totalizing and self-insulating quality. Moreover, the most cosmically inclusive of the theories, deconstruction, affirms the autonomy of all rhetorical constructs, and it thus covers the whole complex with a defensive force field that renders it impervious to empirical criticism. As Foucault explains in "What Is an Author?" Freudianism and

Marxism must be conceived not as empirical disciplines that are susceptible to disproof but rather as "discursive practices" that transcend all critical categories (1977, p. 132). In this respect, the elements of the poststructuralist synthesis are similar in ontological status to the categories of pure reason analyzed by Kant in the *Critique of Pure Reason*. They are the conditions of possibility of critical thought, the categories without which thinking could not take place.

The comprehensiveness of scope and the self-insulating and self-affirming character of contemporary literary theory can help us to understand one of the striking peculiarities in the attitude of contemporary literary academics. In its positive aspect, as seen from the inside, one might characterize this attitude as one of poise and self-assurance, a stance reflecting a mature and sophisticated intellectual development. From the outside, as seen by practitioners in other disciplines, one might characterize it as arrogance, a certain narrow and overweening vanity, a provincial complacency that is protected by the general laxity of intellectual standards in the humanities.

The attitude I have in mind is apparent in the way critics have become habituated to using the word "theory" itself. More often than not, one hears the word theory used with no limiting adjective. It is not "literary" theory or "postmodern" theory or "current" theory. It is just "theory" *tout court*. Now, since literature is only one of many fields of knowledge, and since efforts to construct theories of literature and of criticism extend back to Plato and Aristotle, this usage has specific implications. It implies that no theory worthy of the name existed before this current theory; and that the current theory is therefore in some way quintessentially and uniquely theoretical. It is not just one among other possible, competing theories; rather, it partakes of some hitherto inaccessible essence of theory, an almost numinous theoreticity or theoriness of theory, something like the thingness or *Dinglichkeit* a phenomenologist seeks to intuit within any actual Thing. The use of the word theory without limiting adjective implies, further, that other fields of knowledge—fields such as history, particle physics, and psychology—fall outside or below the range of "theory." Whatever virtues such disciplines might possess as systematized fields of inquiry, with their own special procedures and vocabularies, and however successful they might be in explaining or manipulating the world, they still lack some special quality of rhetorical or linguistic self-reflexiveness, some savvy, insider sensitivity to the theoricity of theory.

Such claims often resonate tacitly in the very intonation with which the word "theory" is pronounced, but the claims for a particular supremacy in the world of intellect have not of course remained merely latent or tacit. One of the fastest-growing fields in literary studies over the past ten or fifteen years has been the cultural study of science, and it is precisely the motive of this field to extend the province of postmodern theory over the whole realm of scientific knowledge. The confident expansionism of the field has taken a few rude shocks of late, first by the quite unexpected counterblast given by Gross and Levitt in their book *Higher Superstition: The Academic Left and Its Quarrels with Science* (1994), and then by what will surely rank, in historical annals, as one of the great literary hoaxes of all time, Alan Sokal's parody of postmodern science study, "Transgressing the Boundaries: Toward a Transformative Hermeneutics of Quantum Gravity" (1996). (Subsequent publications along this line include Gross, Levitt, and Lewis, 1997; Koertge, 1998; Parsons, 2003; Sokal and Bricmont, 1998). At gatherings such as the annual conference for the Society for Literature and Science, one now hears a new note of caution, defensiveness, and even of propitiation, but these notes are as yet only the reflexive gestures of pained surprise and flustered embarrassment. No substantive changes in theoretical orientation have yet taken place.

There can hardly be any doubt about the dominance of the postmodern paradigm in current literary studies, but there is a party of opposition. This party consists largely of older members of the profession who are still committed to more traditional forms of study, and it now has something of an institutional home, an organization entitled the Association of Literary Scholars and Critics, an offshoot of the intellectually conservative academic organization, the National Association of Scholars. I am myself a member of this organization, but as a member, a reader of the newsletter, and an eavesdropper on the e-mail discussion list, I think it safe to say that the members of the organization would have a very difficult time formulating a consensus view of the positive principles that bind them into a party. They are firm in their dislike of the prevailing paradigm; indeed, they are quite certain of its flagrant iniquity, but they are also haunted by a vague apprehension that their opposition is largely negative and reactive.

Some members of the organization are still affiliated with the New Criticism—the school of close reading that dominated academic literary study from the 1940s through the 1970s—and would thus affirm the virtually autonomous centrality and primacy of individual literary texts. They thus dislike the deconstructive notion of dissolving texts into the amorphous mass of textuality, and they dislike as well the New Historicist extension of textuality to social context. Other members of the organization make more allowance for traditional contextual study—the study of biographical and social influences on texts. Those with a biographical bent dislike the postmodern excision of the author as an originative force, and those with a social bent are made uneasy by the notion that texts only passively reflect larger historical epistemes and do not thus achieve the dignity of critical, reflective power. A good many members are personally committed to a religious view of the world, and they tend to regard literature as a medium for the play of spirit and as a secular vindication for their own sense of a transcendent power embodied in the human imagination. Scholars with this religious bent are deeply alienated by the spirit of nihilistic persiflage that animates much postmodern rhetoric. (On the history of modern academic literary study, see Abrams, 1997; Carroll, 1995; Graff, 1987).

Are there any common ideological or methodological elements here? I think there are. The common ideological element is a residual Arnoldian humanism, that is, a conviction that the canonical texts of Western culture embody a normative set of values and imaginative experiences. Postmodern critics either take literature itself as a subversive agent or regard it as implicated in the hegemonic power structures of the larger culture, and they believe that the function of criticism is to demystify such structures. All the parties within the traditionalist reaction, despite their large differences, are united in their revulsion against the subversive or anti-normative spirit of the postmodern paradigm. Whatever else they might think about literature and how one ought to study it, they feel strongly that one ought to approach it with a respect bordering on reverence. The business of criticism is not to demystify or subvert but to appreciate and affirm. Criticism should illuminate and explain, to be sure, but it should also serve as the archival medium through which a precious heritage is kept alive and transmitted to future generations.

The common methodological element in the traditionalist reaction can be identified, in one of its central guises, as "pragmatic" or "practical" criticism. Pragmatic criticism rejects the subordination of literary texts to "theory." Since "theory" now generally means postmodern theory, in rejecting "theory-controlled" readings, pragmatic critics naturally tend to focus on the kind of theory that currently prevails, but the rejection of "theory-controlled" reading is broader and more fundamental than a rejection of any specific theory or complex of theories. Even among postmodern critics, there are many scholars who wear their theory lightly, accepting it as an unavoidable lingua franca of current academic discourse, but protecting themselves from any coercive influence it might exercise by not taking it altogether seriously. It is taken, instead, as a set of fragmentary and ad hoc heuristic terms, part of the eclectic body of critical terms available for local descriptive and analytic purposes. In the most practical, down-to-earth sort of critical work, the mundane business of discussing literary works in classrooms with students, most critics probably fall back on some not too dissimilar set of traditional and common-language terms, blurring the boundaries of coherent doctrine for the sake of speaking more or less sensibly with student readers. What distinguishes pragmatic critics, as a distinct theoretical group, to put it sympathetically but fairly, is that they feel the need to make their theory coincide with the practice I have just described.

In what, then, does the theory of pragmatic criticism consist? In answering this question, I shall be characterizing views that I myself held just a few years ago. Pragmatic criticism consists in the belief that literary texts have a rich complexity of qualitative meaning that transcends or exceeds any specific theoretical reduction. A pragmatic critic has an intuitive conviction that the psychology in Dickens's depictions of character is more subtle and true than any Freudian premise. He or she believes that George Eliot's depictions of social life display a unique and supreme kind of insight, an understanding by the side of which Marxist analysis is merely a clumsy, hopelessly crude framework for analysis. And he or she feels that the poetic insights of Yeats or Wallace Stevens exhibit an intimate familiarity with the living power of language in comparison to which deconstructive analysis can provide at best a feeble and distorted illumination. Pragmatic critics reject theory-controlled reading because they believe that the theory implicit in canonical literary texts is a much more complete and adequate "criticism of life," to use Matthew Arnold's humanistic phrase (1974, p. 68), than the ideas available in any of standard versions of the social sciences that have been available for humanistic study. In this respect, then, the common methodological element of pragmatic criticism is integrally connected with its common ideological element. Pragmatic critics believe that canonical literary texts have a central normative value in good part because they believe that these texts embody the best intelligence of their civilization. The great books are, in another of Arnold's phrases, repositories of "the best that is known and thought in the world" (1962b, p. 282).

These are, again, views I once formulated as my own, and I shall now briefly try to analyze the conditions and characteristics of literary study that led me to these conclusions. These conditions and characteristics are partly historical and partly inherent in the nature of literature and of criticism. I shall begin with literature itself, and with its historical situation. Until very recently, up to the past century or so, there was no social science. The kind of ethical and social philosophy that dealt with the problems of human behavior and human value operated within the range of common knowledge and more or less inspired speculation. This is the same intellectual range in which literature operates. The ideas about psychology, social life, and nature that are contained in literature, as specifically formulated theses, are roughly concordant with those available in the larger culture in which any given text is written. Philosophy or essayistic commentary is more systematic, but it is thus also more liable to false reductions, to the angularities of single ideas. Literature tends to work with the total lexicon of common language, and thus to be more flexible and subtle in its depiction of personal and social life.

In depicting personal and social life, literature has an advantage in its very nature and purpose. The function of philosophy and of science is to reduce phenomena to valid elementary principles. It is abstract and cerebral. Literature can also engage in philosophical generalization, but it has other purposes as well. It seeks to evoke subjective states of mind, register and stimulate emotional response, and give aesthetic shape to experience. It is thus much closer to the phenomenal surface of life, to life as it is commonly observed and experienced.

The same historical considerations that pertain to literature pertain to criticism. A curious adolescent who is seeking a broad familiarity with human behavior and human circumstances might well feel that literature offers a more valuable guide than any systematic philosophy and most history. Moreover, given the very large overlap between imaginative literature and essayistic belles lettres, students of literature almost inevitably expand the range of their studies to include philosophy and social and psychological commentary. They regard these subjects, understandably enough, as forms of "literature." The result is that critics tend to get absorbed into their subject. They have no standpoint outside of it. They have no Archimedean point of critical leverage. To analyze and explain literature, they can only use the general humanistic knowledge that is generated and limited by literature.

The tendency for critics to become absorbed into their subjects is exacerbated by the peculiarly dual nature of critical study. Critics are both connoisseurs and scholars. As connoisseurs, they share in the subjective aspects of what they study. Unlike physicists, geologists, or biologists, they do not merely try to see the object as in itself it really is; they also deploy a sensitive receptivity to the personal qualities of literary works—to their aesthetic and emotional and moral qualities. As scholars, however, critics are responsible to the same general standards of objective validity that apply to all knowledge: they seek to produce explanations that integrate empirical observations with valid elementary principles. This is a difficult balancing act. The great critics have performed it well within the limits allowed by the inspired amateurism to which they have been historically limited.

In the modern world, as more and more territory is colonized by systematic and progressive empirical science, the productions of inspired amateurism have taken on an ever more problematic cast. Many of us in the humanities have long lived with a half-suppressed sense of uneasiness at the hodge-podge, hit-and-miss character of our inquiries. We have ourselves suspected that we could be judged from the kind of perspective taken by E. O. Wilson, who believes that all knowledge should be assessed by universal standards of empirical validity and that it should be integral with contiguous disciplines. Applying this standard to the finest literary journal articles of the time, he observes that they consist "largely of historical anecdotes, diachronic collating of outdated, verbalized theories of human behavior, and judgments of current events according to personal ideology—all enlivened by the pleasant but frustrating techniques of effervescence" (1978, p. 203). We should note that this chilling assessment falls, chronologically, in the period of transition between old-fashioned humanism and the postmodern synthesis, and that it is broad enough, as a methodological description, so that it can be applied to both.

There are at least three possible responses to the kind of criticism formulated by Wilson. One, the traditionalists' response, is to reject out of hand the standard he uses. The humanities, we are told, are fundamentally and irreconcilably different in nature from the hard sciences, or even the social sciences. There is nothing wrong with the way we have been going about humanistic study, and there is no legitimate alternative to it. We just have to get rid of the postmodern deviations and go back to the old ways. The postmodern response is not to declare the humanities a separate and distinct area but rather to declare that the sciences themselves fall within the province of rhetorical inquiry. The postmodern strategy is to encircle and deconstruct the standard by which Wilson would assess humanistic study. The third response, my own and that of a few other scattered proponents of a sociobiologically oriented criticism, is to accept the criticism as a historically accurate diagnosis of a crucial intellectual failure. Those who adopt this position believe that we are in a historically novel situation and that we now have before us the potential to create an empirically valid study of literature, a kind of study that would be integral with the social sciences that are themselves grounded in biology.

If we adopt this third position, we might well feel like Milton's Adam and Eve leaving the garden of Eden. "The world was all before them"—a daunting wilderness to be explored and settled (1968, p. 1060). What direction do we take? Where do we begin? I shall suggest three basic guidelines. First, we need to identify the elementary concepts that hold good from biology across the social sciences to the humanities. Second, we have to hold these concepts not loosely but empirically, understanding that they are only our best approximations and will almost certainly need to be qualified, and at times even discarded, as our empirical understanding progresses. On this issue, the attitude of empirical science should merge with the prudential skepticism of a traditional humanism that weighs all reductions against a flexible, intuitive, common-level understanding. Third, we must firmly grasp the principle that all subjects of study have their own specific forms of organization, and that the study of literature will thus have to have its own categories and structures embedded within the larger general principles of biology and social science. (Even the social sciences must find mid-level principles that resist premature reduction to elemental biological principles of fitness maximization.)

Let me give one example of what I have in mind when I recommend formulating ideas that are integral across the disciplines but that have their own specific applications and structures within a literary context. One idea that is basic to biological thinking is the idea of organisms and environments. Phenotypes, the observed characteristics of organisms, are the product of interactions between innate characteristics and environmental influences. For the social sciences to advance as sciences, it is necessary that they adopt this principle and thus abandon any exclusive fixation on social or environmental causation. Despite the massive ideological resistance to the idea of innate characteristics, this kind of advance is virtually inevitable. There is now a constantly increasing flood of hard data on genetic and developmental characteristics. Psychologists and other social scientists who ignore this information are condemning themselves to irrelevance. In the literary field, very briefly, the idea of organism and environment has at least two fundamental applications. The first application is to the situations depicted in literary works. These situations involve, as primary components, the interactions of organisms with their environments, including their social environments. To stipulate this much is to affirm that the traditional categories of characters and settings are in fact fundamental categories of analysis. And to affirm even so simple a proposition as this provides us with one basic common point of reference. To possess such points is an indispensable condition for making cumulative contributions to an empirical body of knowledge. The second application is to authors and readers as producers and consumers of literary works. Both authors and readers are organisms in environments. If we are to understand how literary meaning is produced and received, we have to acquire adequate information about the human personality and the way that personality interacts in varying environmental conditions. One primary task for evolutionary criticism is to assimilate that kind of information from biology and the social sciences, including linguistics and cognitive psychology, and use these ideas in the elucidation of literary texts, both as an end in itself—to understand the texts—and as a means of testing and refining the ideas.

If literary studies are ever to satisfy the criteria for empirical validity, they will have to include a range of activities that can be located on a scale of empirical constraint, and these activities will have to be interdependent. At the lower end of the scale, with the least empirical constraint, we can locate most of what we now think of as literary criticism. At the upper end, with the greatest constraint, we can locate the kinds of experimental study—in psychology and linguistics—that are already being conducted but that that have not often been expanded to include literature. As a behavioral science, experimental literary study would affiliate itself closely with observational disciplines like ethology or cultural anthropology. Such disciplinary connections would make it possible to pose and answer empirical questions about how art functions in social groups, what kinds of social needs it satisfies, and how it interacts with other social factors. The results of such study would supply us with the facts for the statistical generalizations that are indispensable for causal explanations of cultural and literary history.

To engage in empirical study, we must be able to propose alternative hypotheses, conduct experiments, confirm or fail to confirm predictions, and thus falsify propositions. So far, even the most conscientious evolutionary criticism has failed to establish any method for testing its theoretical or interpretive hypotheses. The most we have done is to assimilate and integrate the findings of social science, applying them in a speculative way to specific texts or to literature in general. As an illustrative instance, consider a recently published book, Robert Storey's *Mimesis and the Human Animal: On the Biogenetic Foundations of Literary Representation* (1996). Storey goes further than almost everyone else in assimilating empirical study from fields like cognitive psychology, ethology, and personality theory. He integrates these findings with specifically literary forms of meaning in narrative theory, genre theory, and audience psychology, and he applies his theoretical constructs to practical criticism. His work thus exemplifies the kind of program I have been proposing here. The one main thing Storey's book does not do is to propose any means by which the correlations he identifies could be tested and either validated or falsified. In this respect, his work reflects the one central methodological limitation to which interpretive literary study has been subject.

So far, our only constraints are those we impose on ourselves by virtue of our own sense of what seems reasonable. To impose even these constraints, within the framework of evolutionary understanding, is an immense step forward from interpretive caprice within the framework of obsolete social and psychological doctrines like those of Marx and Freud, but it is not enough to shield us from the legitimate reservations of those who take seriously the criteria of validity in the empirical sciences. How would we even begin to overcome this limitation? We need to restrict the possible range of plausible disagreement, and in order to do this we need to start accumulating experimental findings about the production and reception of meaning in literary texts.

Wilson, Near, and Miller (1998) have provided one striking example of experimental literary study. They gave personality tests to experimental subjects, determined their position on a scale of Machiavellianism, and had them write short stories that were then analyzed for content that was correlated with their scores. Apart from the considerable interest of the specific findings, this experiment is important simply because it shows that this one crucial thing can be done. That is, experiments relating to the production of literary meaning can be conducted. Moreover, at this point, when so little is firmly established, almost any specific finding is going to offer us important implications. The results of the experiment in literary Machiavellianism, for example, give evidence in support of the contention that individual psychological differences influence the action of a story. Here is a specific instance in which a finding can provide support for a basic working hypothesis in interpretive criticism.

Generalizing from this example, we can say that virtually any psychological test that can be given to people, and any description of general traits for a given group of people, can be correlated with the study of the production and reception of meaning. For example, magnetic resonance imaging and positron emission tomography now give us access to images of the brain in action. Scientists are already studying the way blood flow changes under specific stimuli. It is not, I think, extravagant to suggest that such stimuli could eventually include the reading of literary texts. We can identify a whole array of mental and emotional characteristics in experimental subjects. We can track mental responses to given stimuli. Could we not then also identify specific literary forms, hypothesize connections between these forms and measurable forms of mental and emotional reaction, and test these hypotheses in experimental subjects? Could we, for instance, take the opening chapter of Jane Austen's novel *Pride and Prejudice*, have an experimental subject read it while under a scanning machine, and find out something about the way comedy actually alters the brain? By correlating the responses of individual people with other data on the same people—psychological and social profiles, for example—and by comparing such correlations across individuals and groups of individuals, we could begin to formulate precise empirical propositions about the conditions under which audience response varies. At the moment, this scenario sounds like science fiction. The technical limitations of scanning do not yet allow for such large-scale study, and progress will probably come through an accumulation of more minute findings, but I see no reason, in principle, that we cannot begin to produce empirical results in interpretive criticism.

Most of the people who concern themselves with evolutionary criticism are engaged in the practice of interpreting literary texts. Such interpretations have characteristically consisted of analyses of plot and character designed to demonstrate that the stories being told illustrate the kind of behavior evolutionary psychology teaches us to expect. One main form of study that has been envisioned for evolutionary criticism is to accumulate large aggregates of such analyses. Examples would include content analyses of plots for the purpose of identifying the frequency of certain sociobiological themes such as mate choice, parent-child conflict, kin selection, or group affiliation behavior. One could imagine plot summaries of, say, 5,000 novels and plays, broken down into categories common to evolutionary psychology and anthropology, with variations graphed historically, and correlated with cultural and socioeconomic variables or variables in the author and audience—variables such as age, sex, and social status. All of this seems to me eminently worth doing. It would give us a substantial set of provisionally stable points of factual reference. I would certainly not urge that we stop doing this, but I shall suggest two reservations or cautions about it.

The first reservation is that we need to be aware of one large and problematic assumption built into the procedure: the assumption that literary authors represent human behavior in ways that correspond to our current understanding of evolutionary psychology. To a remarkable extent, I think authors do in fact do this. Beneath and apart from their structure of conscious beliefs, authors, like people in general, are instinctively attuned to evolutionary psychology. It is the psychology by which they actually operate. If people behave in ways that illustrate evolutionary psychology, and if authors offer reasonably realistic portrayals of human behavior, then no matter what the authors' own belief systems might be, the stories they tell would tend to illustrate evolutionary psychology. But at times they do not, and the deviations are at least as interesting as the normative instances. In examining the represented content of stories, we need to take account of how personal and cultural factors influence the representation of human behavior. To give a few examples, sentimental idealism, cynicism, utopian fantasy, sexual deviance, and other forms of psychological idiosyncrasy can be shown to affect the kinds of actions that are represented in specific stories. (For examples of literary criticism that take account of nontypical behaviors, See Cooke, 2002; and in this vol., see part 2, chapter 3.)

My second reservation expands on the first: represented actions are not the only factors to be considered in literary texts. The presence of the author as registered in tone, point of view, and style, is a crucial feature of meaning in all literature. Simple folktales passed on in oral tradition are the closest thing to an exception to this rule, but even these tales reflect a collective cultural point of view. For literary authors in a culture with more highly developed forms of individuality, the interaction between the collective ethos and that of the author—very often an antagonistic, ironic interaction—becomes a central point of interest. I would suggest, then, that evolutionary criticism should not limit itself exclusively to the analysis of represented content of plot and character. We need to pose more fundamental questions about how meaning is produced in literary texts, and we need to take account of the individual psychology of authors and the way that psychology interacts with their particular set of cultural circumstances. To say this is not to step outside the range of repeatable elementary phenomena that is the domain of science. It is rather to locate an evolutionary study of literature within the same range of historical sciences that includes biology and geology—sciences in which there are large general laws such as natural selection, but in which there are also unique historical phenomena such as speciation events.

In closing, I want to take a step back from the immediate problem of methodology and give a broader, behavioral context to the question, "What should evolutionary literary critics do?" Regarding my own case as fairly typical, I would argue that if our training has been primarily literary and humanistic, we need to engage in a long-range program of basic reeducation. We need to learn more in technical detail about the common knowledge of contemporary physics, astronomy, genetics, and molecular biology, among other disciplines. Why? Partly because the truth of the modern scientific worldview is in the detailed sense of an intricate and elaborately interconnected set of mechanisms. Our own sense of the world needs to be adjusted to this modern scientific worldview. If it did nothing else, this sort of knowledge would give us a chastened sense of what counts as plausible propositions and worthwhile evidence. Yet further, basic scientific literacy is a precondition for engaging in any collaborative work with experimental scientists and even for making intelligent use of the findings from empirical science.

Our historical position presents special challenges. We are seeking to construct a theory of literature that would be integral with a total body of scientific and social-scientific knowledge, but this larger integrated context is itself only now beginning to take shape. While working as speculative theorists and as empiricists in our own practical criticism, we also have to work as polemicists and revolutionists, not only within our own almost wholly hostile discipline but within the much larger field of "the human sciences." At the widest level, then, we have to be reformers, agitating for a fundamental revision in the way we organize higher education. Even while worrying about how to provide minimal employment for our current generation of graduate students, we have to work toward restructuring the humanities curriculum so that future generations of students will be scientifically literate. They would then be much less likely to waste their professional lives in futile rhetorical gambits like those parodied by Alan Sokal, and they would be much more likely to make good on the promise of an empirical, evolutionary study of literature.

4

Out of Eden and to the Left

A Review of John Ellis's Literature Lost: Social Agendas
and the Corruption of the Humanities

John Ellis joins a now large group of commentators who are deeply concerned
about the prominence of the radical left in the humanities departments of
American universities. Alan Bloom, Roger Kimball, Dinesh d'Souza, Richard
Bernstein, William A. Henry III, Christina Hoff Sommers, and Lynne Cheney
have written books on similar themes from a similar ideological standpoint.
Within this broader range of conservative resistance to the academic left, Ellis
defines his own distinct niche. He is a capable literary scholar with a specialized interest in German literature, and in previous books he has established re-
spectable credentials in literary theory. Unlike several previous commentators,
he is not merely blowing the whistle on the radicals and trying to arouse indignation in the general public. He is speaking primarily to other literature professors and to university administrators. He shrewdly analyzes the theoretical
structures and rhetorical techniques of his opponents, and in his own critical
perspective he seeks to exemplify the values of literary humanism, of Enlightenment rationality, and of "a liberal democratic way of life."

The strongest aspects of Ellis's work are his affirmations of the normative
value of Western cultural achievements and his concordant attack on radical
critiques of race, gender, and class. His prose is clear, simple, and direct, and he
displays an integrity of intellectual character that contrasts appealingly with
the sophistry and hypocrisy that so often characterize contemporary critical
theory. The weakest aspect of his work is his failure to formulate an adequate
alternative framework for understanding literary and cultural phenomena.

As an alternative to the radical cultural criticism he deplores, Ellis can offer
nothing more inviting than a return to the way literary study was conducted in
the quarter century after the Second World War. In 1974 he published *The Theory of Literary Criticism: A Logical Analysis*, and in *Literature Lost* he frequently
references this earlier work as an authoritative treatment of important theoretical issues. The earlier work, as he himself acknowledged, was heavily dependent
on Wellek's and Warren's *Theory of Literature*, which was first published in 1942.

Wellek and Warren offered a comprehensive survey of traditional literary
scholarship from a formalist perspective, and Ellis has absorbed their central

formalist credo. "The object of literary criticism," he asserts in the earlier book, "is an interpretive hypothesis as to the most general principle of structure which can be abstracted from the combination of linguistic elements in a literary text." The final aim of all criticism is to affirm that the text achieves "coherence" and that it is thus "meaningful."

A critic who adopts this neutrally analytic stance might seem to have escaped from any necessity of committing himself to substantive propositions about the nature and function of literature and its relation to the personal and cultural circumstances in which it is produced and interpreted. But even a formalist must still pose questions as to which "linguistic elements" are worth considering and what relation they bear to one another within the larger system of meanings from which they are drawn. In order to make certain that literary texts are subjected to no extrinsic explanatory structures, Ellis repudiates all system in the selection and organization of formal elements. "The structural properties of highly valued texts may be many and various and must be sought empirically, not speculated about." To seek empirically is to treat each text as a unique set of combinations from an unlimited pool of possible elements. To speculate would be to limit and organize the elements in the pool. In *Literature Lost*, Ellis continues to affirm that "the diversity of theme, content, and viewpoint found in literature is of the essence."

As a form of resistance to the crude impositions of political preoccupations, appeals to "variety" and "diversity" have a clear corrective value. As theoretical propositions about the "essence" of literature, they are patently incoherent. They lead by logical necessity to the repudiation of all general observation, all classification, and even all comparison. Ellis accordingly declares that any meaningful statement about a literary text "focuses on the particular qualities" of that text. With each text, the critic should be concerned primarily with "its unique stamp, the individual meaning that makes it unlike any other work." In practice, of course, no critic avoids all generalization and comparison, and the reality of practice in this case gives decisive evidence as to the inadequacy of the theory.

Formalists never actually succeed in avoiding all substantive propositions about the relation of literature to human nature and society. They only avoid explicitly formulating their assumptions as hypotheses and taking intellectual responsibility for them. In the place of explicit theoretical hypotheses, they deploy ad hoc notions from the field of educated commonplace—a hodge-podge of general information, common sense, and odd bits of popularized science, religious beliefs, political convictions, and literary or philosophical versions of sociology and psychology, versions that are often obsolete.

The targets of Ellis's antagonism are highly vulnerable to criticism based on common information and common sense. For instance, he delineates a standard feminist version of women's history as a tale of gratuitous suppression and passive endurance from which women have only recently and inexplicably awakened to a sense of their wrongs. To illustrate this version, Ellis cites a large array of feminist writings, including works by such prominent figures as Catherine MacKinnon, Peggy McIntosh, Andrea Dworkin, Sandra Harding, Catherine Stimpson, and Marilyn French. Taking to heart the historicist dictum "always historicize," Ellis describes the material conditions of women's lives in earlier times, noting the constraints imposed by life expectancy, childbirth and infant mortality, nursing, and other factors. Commenting on the Marxist basis of radical political criticism, he incisively identifies the labor theory of value as a central feature of the Marxist conception of economic relations, and he invokes the failure of communist economies as evidence for the fallacy of this theory. For this topic, rather than citing an array of examples, Ellis offers an intensive survey of the works of one critic, Fredric Jameson. As Ellis rightly says, Jameson is "arguably the most influential of all American literary critics," and can thus serve as a representative case. In a chapter devoted to the conflict between political activism and disinterested research, Ellis patiently explains the destructive consequences of erasing the boundaries between these two areas and illustrates his arguments with instances from the history of modern totalitarianism. In a chapter on the characteristic logical techniques of political correctness, he lucidly analyzes the sophistical device through which various polar opposites are turned into absolutes and then collapsed into one another: law and force, reason and power, objectivity and subjectivity, consensual sex and rape. In this chapter, the general theoretical arguments are brought into focus through succinct and penetrating critiques of two major theorists, Michel Foucault and Stanley Fish.

From his broadest historical perspective, Ellis argues that radical repudiations of the Western tradition depend on utopian ideals affiliated with "Rousseau's fantasy of a blissful state of primitive innocence before the ravages of civilization." This insight provides him with an excellent analytic angle on the politics of the academic left, but he does not recognize that his own alternative vision of man and nature is equally partial and equally susceptible to empirical criticism. "Rousseau," he tells us, "had things backward." Man is not good and civilization bad. Quite the contrary. Man is bad and civilization good. Close your Rousseau; open your Hobbes. Or, if you would prefer more recent antecedents, go to J. S. Mill's essay "Nature," T. H. Huxley's "Evolution and Ethics," or the ethical essays of contemporary sociobiologists such as Richard Alexander, Richard Dawkins, George C. Williams, or Donald Symons. Ellis himself cites none of these antecedents, and he thus gives us to suppose that his own anthropological myth is merely the voice of educated reason.

Whenever Ellis can identify a historical antecedent and declare that radical critics are unaware of it, he seems to feel that he has made a decisive point against them. As a theoretical refutation, the gambit is weak, but against a theorist, such as Ellis himself, who disclaims all theoretical preconception, it would have considerably more force. If Ellis were to acknowledge the hypothetical character of the theory of human nature and society under which he is himself operating, he would realize that this hypothesis has to be defended against alternative concepts, not just against Rousseau's fantasies, but also, and with more difficulty, against Darwin's argument that human beings have evolved as social animals and that their principles of morality and justice are grounded in innate psychological characteristics. (Among the more recent expositions of this thesis, James Q. Wilson's *The Moral Sense*, 1993, can be recommended as one of the most accessible and satisfactory.)

Ellis treats all contemporary criticism as exclusively or predominantly political in character. Deconstruction comes in only as a facilitator of radical politics, and Freudianism is shunted off to the side as "never more than a minority cult within the larger profession." A student who tried to take Ellis's book as an introduction to current criticism would therefore be sadly bewildered by the arcane intertwinings of these three doctrinal lines. Ellis has reduced current criticism to that aspect he can most easily comprehend and oppose, and this reduction perhaps helps to explain why he does not mention other important critics of postmodernism, like M. H. Abrams and Frederick Crews, who are not primarily political in orientation.

Ellis does not himself recognize the need for an explanatory framework independent of any particular text, and he fails to realize that in their combined effect the three chief elements of current criticism—deconstruction, Marxism, and Freudianism—constitute a comprehensive explanatory system. Freudianism provides an explanatory apparatus for individual identity and sexual and family relations, Marxism for social history, and deconstruction for the cosmic nature of things. Together, these three forms of explanation cover the whole field of human experience, and each also promises to provide a key to deep forces that have been repressed and disguised—for the sake of psychic economy, class interest, or rational order. They seem to offer access to a secret interpretive code, and they thus constitute a functional facsimile of a critical perspective.

I agree with Ellis that "what now passes for theory is a degraded and corrupt shadow of what theory should be." But if we are to move beyond this shadow, we shall have to do more than try to embarrass critics into turning back to the "cheerfully disorganized" paradise of traditional literary study. We shall instead have to provide an explanatory framework that incorporates more adequate versions of psychology, social history, epistemology, and natural philosophy.

5

Literary Study and Evolutionary Theory

A Review of Books by Alexander Argyros, Walter Koch, Karl Kroeber, Robert Storey, Frederick Turner, and Mark Turner

Books under review:

Argyros, Alexander J. *A Blessed Rage for Order: Deconstruction, Evolution, and Chaos.* Ann Arbor: University of Michigan Press, 1991.

Koch, Walter A. *The Roots of Literature.* Bochum, Germany: Universitätsverlag Dr. Robert Brockmeyer, 1993.

Kroeber, Karl. *Ecological Literary Criticism: Romantic Imagining and the Biology of Mind.* New York: Columbia University Press, 1994.

Storey, Robert. *Mimesis and the Human Animal: On the Biogenetic Foundations of Literary Representation.* Evanston, IL: Northwestern University Press, 1996.

Turner, Frederick. *Natural Classicism: Essays on Literature and Science.* Charlottesville: University of Virginia Press, 1992. (Originally published by Paragon House, 1985)

Turner, Mark. *Reading Minds: The Study of English in the Age of Cognitive Science.* Princeton, NJ: Princeton University Press, 1991.

Darwin's impact on literature, and particularly on the naturalistic fiction of the later nineteenth century, is a long-established and still active field of research. Lionel Stevenson's *Darwin Among the Poets* appeared in 1932, and in 1996, Bert Bender published *The Descent of Love: Darwin and the Theory of Sexual Selection in American Fiction, 1871–1926.* Bender tacitly accepts the validity of Darwin's naturalistic orientation, but in this respect, among contemporary literary scholars, he is something of an anomaly. From an ideological angle virtually opposite to that of Bender, and more fashionable, other recent studies have attempted to characterize Darwin, with perverse ingenuity, as a forerunner for the irrationalist antirealism of such contemporary authorities as Jacques Derrida and Michel Foucault. Signal instances include Gillian Beer's *Darwin's Plots: Evolutionary Narrative in Darwin, George Eliot, and Nineteenth-Century Fiction* (1983) and George Levine's *Darwin and the Novelists: Patterns of Science in Victorian Fiction* (1988). Whether naturalistic like Bender, or postmodern like Beer and Levine, historians have tended to take their theoretical frameworks as something given, not requiring original constructive effort. They devote their attention instead to influences or parallels among specific writers.

The books here under review represent a new and different kind of evolutionary literary study. Most contain illustrative instances of literary interpretation, but their purposes are primarily theoretical, not critical. Their authors are preoccupied with formulating new ways to think about all historical and interpretive literary topics. Literary theory is itself of course an ancient pursuit, but only one previous theorist has ever made a serious and sustained effort to incorporate the idea of evolution. In his immense *History of English Literature* (1879), Darwin's contemporary Hippolyte Taine took organism, environment, and heredity as central organizing principles. Taine has now been largely and undeservedly forgotten. None of the authors here under review cites him. If only by default, then, the current authors are all pioneers in what is, to them, a virgin wilderness.

It is the fate of pioneers to suffer and struggle mightily, to endure high rates of mortality, and after all their heroism still to produce settlements that, though monuments to their own industry and courage, make but a shabby impression on the eye of the touring cosmopolite. In his voyage on the *Beagle*, Darwin was shocked and disgusted by the squalor of New Zealand and Australia, and he was heartily glad to get back to England (1845). Our own generation of literary scholars has no such refuge as that to which Darwin returned. As we head into the wilderness, we leave behind no mature and refined society, no mellow landscapes, picturesque towns, and genial networks of zealous fellow workers. Our situation is rather more like that of the Pilgrims fleeing persecution, the Israelites escaping from Egyptian bondage, or Lot and his family turning their backs on the corruption of Sodom and Gomorrah. The flagrant and frivolous unreality of currently established literary doctrines—on which all these authors comment—leaves us no alternative but to make what order we can with the rough tools at our disposal.

For literary scholars with Darwinian sympathies, or for Darwinian social scientists sympathetic to humanistic study, most of the books reviewed here are likely to cause disappointment. To my own mind, only one of the books, Robert Storey's *Mimesis and the Human Animal*, makes any substantial progress toward establishing the foundations of a Darwinian literary theory that can produce progressive findings in close company with the biologically grounded human sciences. To say this need cast no skeptical light on the prospects for a Darwinian literary theory, because the central problem with all the books, except Storey's, is precisely that they are not Darwinian. They either do not understand or do not accept the full logic of the adaptationist program. All the books claim some sort of affiliation with biology, but (with the exception of Storey's) they adopt various marginal conceptions of biology, and they evade the central premises of sociobiology, evolutionary psychology, and human ethology.

Apart from the present reviewer, one other author of book-length studies, Ellen Dissanayake, joins Storey in assimilating to humanistic inquiry the information and logic of these disciplines. I have not included her work in the review only because her books, *What Is Art For?* (1988), and *Homo Aestheticus: Where Art Comes From and Why* (1995b), are oriented to the more general problems of art and aesthetics, not to the problems specific to literature.

The number of genuinely adaptationist studies will probably soon increase. (This essay was originally published in 1998.) Several capable scholars and critics have become alert to human evolutionary studies and are giving conference papers and writing articles and reviews. The more satisfactory studies that are still to come will not, however, instantly and automatically supplant the strange species that have begun to proliferate in the borderlands between biology and literary theory. For a good while yet, we shall need to be making distinctions between mainstream Darwinian thinking and the various misshapen offspring of the vagrant literary fancy.

Of all the authors in this set, Karl Kroeber is the only one who has an almost exclusive preoccupation with the literature of a specific historical period. He credits himself with having introduced the term "ecology" into Romantic scholarship, and his book, *Ecological Literary Criticism: Romantic Imagining and the Biology of Mind*, distills decades of research into his historical subject. In order to use his period specialization as the basis for theoretical construction, Kroeber must invoke the Romantics as models and precursors for what is, in his view, the most advanced and enlightened contemporary ideology: the eco-feminism of Evelyn Fox Keller and a few other like-minded theorists. The Romantics, we are told, believed that humankind belonged in "the world of natural processes." They were thus "proto-ecological" (p. 5). Current "ecologically oriented sciences" continue the Romantic revolt against the rationality of the Enlightenment, and they thus join with the eco-feminists in questioning the "'principle of rationality'" associated with a "'male-oriented' science" (pp. 6, 7). By associating the eco-feminists and Romantics with the affirmation of Nature, Kroeber can set them in diametrical opposition to the antinaturalism of deconstruction and its historicized successors.

Kroeber's alliances and oppositions involve him in several distortions. In order to make the Romantics suitable as models, Kroeber both colludes with Wordsworth's sentimental concept of Nature as wholly beneficent and denies, dogmatically and implausibly, that Romantic metaphysics are transcendental. In order to make postmodern theorists into suitable foils for his Romantic eco-feminism, Kroeber reduces their worldview to the repudiation of Nature. He thus overlooks the irrationalism through which they are intimately affiliated with Kroeber's own feminist antirationalism. Kroeber has little insight into the origins or underlying logic of contemporary literary theory—he attributes it to "a Cold War mind-set" (p. 3)—and the logic of his oppositions leads him into the absurd notion that "most contemporary criticism" has a "'scientific' foundation" indistinguishable "from that favored by the most brutally oversimplifying scientists of the later nineteenth century" (pp. 20–21).

In *Higher Superstition: The Academic Left and Its Quarrels with Science* (1994), Paul Gross and Norman Levitt have complained bitterly about humanists who venture to issue lofty opinions on sciences about which they are profoundly ignorant. Kroeber is highly vulnerable to criticism of this sort. He makes sweeping, grandiose claims about "recent biological research," "contemporary biological conceptions," and "contemporary ideas of evolution" (pp. 1, 2, 111), but he knows the least possible amount about these subjects. He has read a good deal in the history of ecology, but his reading in biology seems to consist of little more than a single book by Ernst Mayr, some Stephen Jay Gould, a few eco-feminists, and Gerald Edelman's "neural Darwinism." On the basis of this research, he feels himself authorized to declare that irrationalist eco-feminism has produced a rethinking of "fundamental presuppositions of biological science" (p. 8). Of research into sociobiology, evolutionary psychology, and human ethology, he seems to know essentially nothing. He roundly characterizes the idea of a universal incest taboo as a "myth" (p. 117), but he cites none of the important findings that have appeared on this topic in the past thirty years. More generally, he supposes that all human universals have now been revealed "to be no more than generalizations of Western European modes of thought" (p. 141), but he cites none of the dozens of studies in the annotated bibliography in Donald Brown's *Human Universals* (1991).

Although he has updated his rhetoric with a little anti-adaptationist biology, Kroeber's basic critical and theoretical approach is quite old-fashioned. His readings of the major Romantic poets operate almost exclusively in the medium of plodding thematic commonplace—he reduces all their work to dull thesis statements—and his larger theoretical formulations operate in the medium of Romantic metaphysics. The following instance will illustrate the quality of his style in his more exalted, metaphysical moments. Rejecting "the deadly mechanicalness" of "limited regularities"—that is, actual causal mechanisms like those of natural selection—he proposes a biological vision based on a teleology of the ecosystem (p. 106). "What if one conceives of life as diverse processes striving to sustain what we call ecosystems, complexes of interactivity that enhance the power and endurance of their vitality through a cooperative interplay of self-transforming individualities?" Such comically bloated bits of inane abstraction are endemic to philosophical literary criticism.

Kroeber's readings of the Romantic poets form the bulk of his book, and these readings can have little interest for anyone not specializing in the period. Indeed, they will probably provide no very lively stimulus even to specialists. Kroeber has some good things to say on the relation between Spinoza and Darwin and on the evolutionary themes in Keats's *Hyperion* poems. The strongest part of the book is the annotated bibliography embedded in the notes. Specialists will benefit from the decades Kroeber has spent judiciously sifting through the scholarship on the period.

Kroeber locates the moving power of nature at the level of the ecosystem. The next three books to be considered, those by Frederick Turner, Alexander Argyros, and Walter Koch, all take in a still larger scope. For all three, the specifically biological principles of evolution are merely special cases within evolution at the level of the cosmos or universe. With a speculative enthusiasm animated by creative license, and nowise diminished by the absence of any causal mechanism, the universe at large is credited with dynamic formal principles that transcend and sometimes suspend the workings of natural selection. As with Kroeber's teleology of the ecosystem, all such notions involve a regression to metaphysical, pre-Darwinian conceptions.

Frederick Turner is the son of Victor Turner, the cultural anthropologist. He is an English professor and a poet, and he has an intimate familiarity with contemporary literary culture. He also has a profound appreciation for his father's work on the cultural functions of ritual, and he is among the first of current critics to have made substantial use of new empirical information about neurophysiology. *Natural Classicism: Essays on Literature and Science* was first published in 1985, before the recent flood of studies in human evolution, and especially before the advent of "evolutionary psychology." Substantial work was already available under the rubric of sociobiology, but Turner makes almost no use of sociobiological theory, and his pronouncements on sociobiology are thoroughly equivocal.

Turner has strong spiritual aspirations, and like Kroeber he fears the concept of a determinate causal order that is essential to science. He uses anthropology and neurophysiology to illuminate aesthetic experience, but he also proclaims that the creative imagination transcends any "material" causality. "Matter and mind," he believes, "are different arrangements, the latter much more complex than, and subsuming, the former" (p. xiv). If mind is given the lead in the causal chain, the ultimate mysteries of nature are to be sought in mental experience, not in physiology and physics. "If we wish to understand the animating drives of nature, we can go to no better place than ourselves" (p. 169). The "driving force and inner principle" in "nature's own spontaneous creativity" is "self-awareness." The "process of creation" is an expansion of the universe and a continuation of the work of evolution" (p. xvi). Linking up this spiritualistic belief with the idea of "performative" utterances, from J. L. Austin's philosophy of speech acts, Turner attributes to literature the power of creating "a new reality by verbal fiat." This is a giddy creed. All things are connected, and the inspiration of the humanistic imagination is at the very source of universal creativity. The style appropriate to such a creed, Turner feels, is an "inspired amateurishness" (p. xii). What this means, in practice, is to envelop popularized science in an atmosphere of mystical rapture and to carry it forward on a stream of rhapsodic prose. A style of this sort can provide no firm foundations for the development of explanatory structures.

Turner is himself of two minds about the value of developing explanatory structures integral with those of science. In his boldest mood, he vigorously and succinctly lays out the unifying effect Darwin's evolutionary theory had upon the diverse branches of biological studies, draws suggestive parallels between these branches and those of traditional literary scholarship, and proposes to seek "an equivalent unifying idea" for literary scholarship (p. 4). Still further, he proposes that biology itself provide this unifying idea. "Obviously, any attempt to provide a scientific basis for the study of aesthetic phenomena must take the royal road through biology: the perception of beauty is first and foremost a capacity belonging to living organisms" (p. 240). This is well and truly said. If Turner had been able to sustain this conception, his book could have gone much further toward integrating biology and literary scholarship. He does not sustain it, and the invocation of Darwin as a model invites a comparison through which we can identify a basic weakness in Turner's habit of mind.

The Origin of Species is, as Darwin himself recognized, "one long argument" (2003, p. 379). It is a wholly unified, connected set of propositions and evidentiary expositions, all of which bear upon a tightly interlocked sequence of primary causal theses. There is in all this, apart from the depth of insight and the sheer magnitude of information accumulated, an instinct for the integrity of an argument. This instinct is something like the mental equivalent of a characteristic of personality, and it is a quality in which Turner is signally deficient. There are no sustained arguments in *Natural Classicism*. Instead, there are flashes of insight that are sometimes elaborated in a swirl of repetitive embellishments and sometimes diffused and canceled by contradictory propositions and equivocal reservations. After describing "a view of literature which sees it as continuous with all other kinds of reality," Turner backs off and says "that whole of which I speak" is "not easily scanned, expounded, or even described by a single line of argument" (p. xiii). Immediately after invoking evolution as an "analogy of a unifying paradigm in a natural science," he cautions, "Perhaps, indeed, the analogy should not be taken too far" (p. 5). Poised indecisively over the attractions of "rational virtues" and humanistic inspirations, Turner tilts the balance by reconceiving biology as itself a subjective, inspirational pursuit.

> Surely literary criticism should never be an exact quantified science. But then by the same token neither should biology: life, after all, is itself a survival strategy of finesse against the cold numbers of entropy. . . . Evolutionary theory did not falsify by reducing the complex and qualitative richness of the biosphere: rather, it helped us to reveal it. (pp. 5–6)

There is an elementary fuzziness here that will hardly yield to correction. The complexity of a subject is no argument against quantitative analysis. From the subjective, experiential standpoint, life has "qualitative" aspects, but as a subject of scientific study life can nonetheless be reduced to a distinct set of causal, explanatory hypotheses. In historical fact, Darwin's theory, like all successful scientific theories, did reduce the complexity of phenomena to underlying regularities, though it did not thereby "falsify" or deny the complexity. Biology is in fact an exact quantified science, though with varying degrees of exactitude in its various branches. Certain aspects of literary criticism involve taste and personal value. In the nature of things, expressions of taste and value are not statements of scientific fact, but expressions of taste and value can themselves be subject to psychological analysis, and psychology looks forward, with good reason, both to increasing unification through the reduction of complexity to underlying regularity and to a correspondent increase in exact quantified knowledge. In its objective aspect, as a topic of scientific study—a topic embedded in psychology, anthropology, and sociobiology—literature is intrinsically no less susceptible to scientific understanding than life itself.

Turner's treatment of sociobiology and human ethology is of a piece with his treatment of biology in general. On the one hand, he concedes that these disciplines "offer promising opportunities for research" into the biological basis of aesthetics (p. 242), and on the other hand he repudiates "the genetically hard-wired robot of the sociobiologists" (p. 62). Seeking a "third position" somewhere midway between genetic determinism and cultural relativism, he concedes that certain cultural universals "indicate a shared biological underpinning," but "unlike the genetic determinists" he does not "regard this shared inheritance as a constraint" (p. 80). If genes do not constrain, what is it that they could possibly do? In tacitly answering this question, Turner tries to make evasive equivocation sound like witty paradox. "Humankind has a nature; that nature is cultural" (p. xv). Or, in more discursive form, "Humankind *does* have a nature; there are cultural universals. But this nature is neither a limitation nor a totally protean adaptiveness. Rather, it is a system of neurobiological and developmental rules which make possible an immensely productive and infinitely versatile, but characteristically mammalian and human *generativeness*" (p. 222). Such formulations seek to split all differences by simultaneously affirming and denying identical propositions under slightly different words. Human nature is not a "limitation," but it is a set of "rules"; it is not "totally protean" but is nonetheless "infinitely versatile." Despite the yearning for an irrational compromise, Turner's culminating emphasis on "*generativeness*" slides inexorably toward cultural relativism—the idea that our genes gave us a creative brain and an aptitude for culture and then left the rest up to us. Accordingly, Turner suggests that culture "is now taking over the central genetic tasks of our species" (p. 215).

Turner's equivocal hostility to sociobiology seems to arise in part from his spiritual aspirations. He wishes to affirm the autonomy and indeed the supremacy of "the 'higher pleasures' of creative mental effort, of beauty, of goodness, of truth" (p. 14). He rejects the idea that these supposedly higher faculties are "merely perverted or sublimated versions of sexual or nourishment drives." Recent information about the chemical reward system reveals, he thinks, that the motive force of the higher faculties is "potentially much greater than that of hunger or lust." In order to reach this conclusion, he associates the "higher" faculties with endorphins, "the internally generated brain rewards," and sets these chemical rewards in contrast to "the conventional motivators proposed by crude materialists and behaviorists." The fallacy built into this argument should be apparent. It might well be the case that the appreciation of beauty and the pursuit of truth have satisfactions peculiar to themselves, not reducible to other animal satisfactions, but all satisfactions, "higher" and "lower," have evolved as adaptive mechanisms that are mediated through the chemical reward system. The pleasures derived from the satisfaction of hunger and lust cannot be set in contrast to the pleasures derived from "the internally generated brain rewards."

The peculiarity of a biologized aesthetics that deprecates hunger and lust can be underlined by Turner's effort to bring Darwin into close proximity with Thoreau. Both writers, he tells us, were "naturalists," and he suggests that Thoreau could serve as an anthropological guide to nineteenth-century New England, "though he has intriguing and significant omissions, such as kinship and sexuality" (pp. 202, 179). These are not, needless to say, omissions in Darwin's *Descent of Man*. A "naturalism" without kinship and sexuality is like a liquid without wetness. Turner's enchantment with endorphins, and his desire to segregate them from the fulfillment of common human needs, seem to reflect a paradoxical peculiarity of temperament: at once hedonistic and effete, sybaritic and ethereal.

Turner's book can be divided into two distinct parts, four essays devoted to theoretical topics, and three chapters of interpretive literary criticism. The chapters of criticism look as if they have been written up from lecture notes for seminars on English Renaissance literature, Shakespeare, and Thoreau's *Walden*. The readings are presented as examples of a "participatory" form of criticism. In practice, this means a sympathetic exposition of primary texts. The weakness of this method is that it offers no external standpoint, no independent critical perspective, so that one misses a chief merit of good criticism—the sense of what the literature means for some one particular mind. With all its limitations of conceptual order, the theoretical part of the book gives a much more decided impression of a distinct literary personality.

In *A Blessed Rage for Order: Deconstruction, Evolution, and Chaos*, Alexander J. Argyros presents himself as an acolyte of Frederick Turner. Like Turner, he propounds a philosophy of cosmic evolution, and again like Turner he takes a fundamentally equivocal stance toward sociobiology. The central principle in his scheme of cosmic evolution is that of an inner force driving the cosmos to "increasing complexation" (p. 149). In one part of his book, he uses Lumsden's and Wilson's work on gene-culture coevolution as his main guide, but he warns the reader that his "defense of Lumsden and Wilson is only a defense of those aspects of their work that support" his own "nonreductionist version of sociobiology" (p. 354). Being non-reductive apparently means taking refuge in a range of verbal equivocation that suspends all determinate conceptions. Argyros says he would defend "a progressive kind of sociobiology that pays homage to our evolutionary past while respecting the central importance of culture in determining the world of human beings." This sort of sociobiology is compatible, he thinks, with "a view of the natural and social worlds that situates them in a softly teleological and endlessly innovative continuum" (p. 7). For hard problems such as "the enlargement of the neocortex in advanced prehominids," Argyros offers this soft cosmic teleology as a source of solutions more satisfactory than those of "traditional Darwinian explanations" (p. 285).

Despite their considerable agreement at the level of large general ideas, Argyros and Turner make a very different impression on the imagination. They work in different contexts, with a different range of references and different styles. Turner has been genuinely impressed with information from anthropology, neuroanatomy, and neurophysiology, and he has brought this information into close proximity with an acute appreciation of specific literary structures, especially poetic meter. Argyros makes theoretical appeal to the general field of empirical science, and he takes literature as a point of reference for his philosophical disquisitions, but he begins and ends in metaphysical abstraction. His main-source science is chaos theory, and this he assimilates at the level of metaphysics. He has assimilated virtually no empirical information about anthropology, human ethology, or psychology. Although he uses Lumsden and Wilson as a guide, he refers to only one book by them. Generally, his bibliography is rather slight. His ample pages spin a very little matter into a very thin tissue of theoretical meditation. Of all the writers in this review, he has the least literature. He seldom cites a literary text, and he shows very little interest in the problems specific to literary productions. His prose reaches its culminating moments in formulations similar in style to those of Kroeber. For instance, "I conjecture that the universe is a dynamical, evolving system describing a vector of increasingly complex and self-reflexive information-processing technologies set against the background of ballooning entropy" (p. 325).

Argyros belongs to a generation of literary scholars who as graduate students were immersed almost exclusively in the deconstructive philosophy of Jacques Derrida. Deconstruction constitutes the chief topic and primary point of reference for his book, and with respect to Derrida's works Argyros's bibliography is very full. The first of the three parts of the book is devoted to a critique of Derrida. The second part consists in an exposition of a theory of cosmic evolution worked out by the philosopher J. T. Fraser. The third part offers an exposition of chaos theory and integrates this theory with Fraser's ideas. In the second and third parts, Derrida serves sometimes as a foil and sometimes as another component in the theoretical mix put forth as an alternative to an exclusively deconstructive philosophy.

Argyros's critique of Derrida is consistently intelligent, but it is not consistent in point of view. His position is something like that of the protagonist in the film *Little Big Man*, a story of a white man who as a boy was captured by Indians and then spent the rest of his life wandering between the two cultures, riding sometimes with the cavalry, and at other times slipping across the border and rejoining his native companions. At times, Argyros poses science as a frame of reference that could contain and discredit Derrida, but at other times he declares that deconstruction "cannot be evaluated in traditional philosophical or scientific ways (since it disputes the kinds of truths these disciplines purport to yield)" (p. 75). In his guise as a scientific rationalist, Argyros stoutly repudiates Derrida's central thesis, the idea that there is nothing outside the text, that writing is the universal substance. "Derrida's belief that hierarchies are metaphysical hypostatizations of an underlying unhierarchical bed of arche-writing is simply wrong" (pp. 119–120). As he begins to cross over the boundary into the opposing culture, Argyros hedges, suggesting that "Derrida has erected an ontological and epistemological hypothesis that is, if only partially, in error" (p. 89). Speaking from within the opposing culture itself, he regards Derrida's writing as "hyperlucid" and "a magnificent narrative" (pp. 61, 1). One way of resolving such perplexities is simply to abandon the project of a unified worldview, to set up alternative orders of reality, and to assign each culture to its proper sphere. The physical world can be given over to science, and the world of mental experience, the arts and humanities, can be yielded up to postmodernism. "In fact, it is here that Derridean deconstruction, Wittgensteinian skepticism, and Foucauldian historicism appear to be fruitful epistemologies" (p. 191).

For his critique of Derrida, Argyros might be recommended to readers who feel frustrated at never having been able to grasp the elementary principles of deconstruction. He might help them to inhabit, even if only for a moment, the state of mind in which it seems meaningful to declare that everything is made of words and that all things are contradictory. Despite his cautious reservations and equivocal disavowals, he does not, I think, achieve a perspective adequate to his subject. A more adequate perspective would both lay out the inner logic of deconstruction, as Argyros does, and also register the sheer absurdity and monstrosity of this whole way of thinking. One should be at least a little shocked at the spectacle of an entire generation of academic intellectuals who have given themselves over to perverse preciosity. To get one's mind around this phenomenon, one needs to have the satiric sense—an ability to recognize charlatanism, and an instinctive revulsion against it.

In attempting to identify readers for the other two parts of the book, for the exposition of Fraser and of chaos theory, one runs into a difficulty that is common among the books under review. Argyros is giving a secondhand account of matters in which he has no primary expertise. He is neither a professional philosopher, like Fraser, nor a professional mathematician. Comparing his exposition of chaos theory with that of N. Katherine Hayles—a dignitary among postmodern theorists of science—Gross and Levitt say that his exposition is "far more systematic and coherent, although it is far from flawless" (1994, p. 270). This is perhaps the least damning of their assessments of literary scholars who have ventured to offer critical commentaries on specialized scientific topics. Nonetheless, if one is chiefly interested in obtaining an introductory exposition of chaos theory, one would probably be better advised to read books written by people who have an assured mastery of the topic.

Literary scholars have no choice but to make use of information from other fields, but a distinction can be drawn between two ways of dealing with this information. One way is merely to give an amateur exposition of a specialized scientific topic—of brain structure, neurochemistry, sociobiology, anthropology, chaos theory, philosophy, or the psychology of personality and emotions. The other way is to assimilate information from any of these fields and to incorporate it into primary, independent constructs in the field of literary and cultural studies. Argyros makes little effort to formulate sustained arguments about problems specific to literature and culture, and his ventures into other fields necessarily remain at the level of the amateur.

In *The Roots of Literature*, Walter A. Koch operates on a scale that makes most other books seem very modest in their pretensions. Like Argyros, he conceives of evolution as a cosmic process in which the central driving force is a tendency toward "complexation" (p. 12), but unlike Argyros, he aims to survey the whole range of this process. He projects a philosophical and historical system that would "reach from cosmogenesis to recent human behavior" (p. 42), and he sketches out the whole saga, from the big bang through the earliest stages of life on earth, the gradual evolution of proto-human primates, the beginnings of civilization, and the major phases of Western cultural history. To connect all this information, he offers preliminary formulations for "the scientific development of an all-encompassing dynamics of form." In accordance with this faith in the scientific character of "the dynamics of form," he identifies his own school of thought as that of "evolutionary structuralism" (p. 190). His background is that of old-fashioned German philology updated, several decades ago, by the structuralist linguistics of Roman Jakobson. In his handling, such dynamics sometimes deteriorate to a pseudo-technical doodling that recalls the manner of medieval and Renaissance alchemical texts—a blending of scholastic philosophy and prescientific conceptions of the natural order. The following passage gives a fair impression of how a philosopher in the fifteenth century might have formulated the concept of kin selection:

> "Isologies" of every kind are a characteristic first step in any cognitive process: the **comparandum** (a new item for the neurognostic system) can only be approached through a **comparans** which is more or less firmly stored in the brain. . . . The vehicle for sameness is supplied in the form of the "tertium comparationis." This short-term craze for **sameness** (instead of for long-term

differences) is of course in tune with precognitive, biological short-term goal-directed behavior which lasts at best for the lifetime of an individual and which also favours sames, namely, in the form of "kin." (p. 12)

This passage invokes Koch's single most comprehensive structural conception, that of a simple tripartite balance. "Evolution developed living systems in which different states of different portions of sameness (stability) and of difference (instability) tend toward mutual equilibration" (p. 194).

Although his basic conceptual system is structuralist, not Darwinian, Koch has assimilated a good deal of naturalistic research into his cosmic chronicle. He argues that "part of the subliminal structuring of literature is due to neurognostic forms that are 100 million years old or even older" (p. 154). Like Frederick Turner, though with considerably less precision, he argues that certain literary structures are "somehow coded in our nervous systems (including the limbic system)" (p. 157), and he looks into animal ethology, paleoanthropology, and archaeology for forms of behavior that can be identified as "proto-narrative, proto-ritual and proto-art" (p. 161). He associates structuralism with Jungian archetypes as a form of genetically encoded human universals, and such formulations bring him into theoretical proximity with evolutionary psychology.

Koch has a passion for schematization but very little sense of underlying conceptual order. The two most prominent sources for his many diagrams are Karl Popper's scheme of "three worlds" and various linguistic schemas of Roman Jakobson. There are supplementary schemas from Freud, Tinbergen, Jung, Foucault, Toynbee, McLuhan, von Bertalanffy, and others. None of these fragmentary principles of order is analyzed with respect either to its place within its original context or to its compatibility with the other principles. The whole is merely a patchwork of descriptive diagrams scattered almost randomly across a universal temporal grid. There are interesting bits of information and even suggestive insights all along the way, but no usable structure of ideas. Reading the book is like visiting a large and disorganized intellectual antique shop. One wanders dispiritedly through rooms of oddly assorted materials, much of it little better than junk, but occasionally finding amid the clutter half-buried pieces of real value and interest. Among the more noteworthy finds, one could mention the analysis of hierarchy in medieval thought (p. 113), the distinction between "matrixing" and "mapping" as dichotomous forms of understanding (pp. 104, 116), and the contrast between medieval and modern attitudes (pp. 122–137).

Of all the writers considered here, the one who has been most fully acknowledged within mainstream literary study is Mark Turner. He has coauthored work with the cognitive linguist George Lakoff and has absorbed much from the cognitive scientist Mark Johnson, who is himself one of Lakoff's coauthors. He takes a tactfully critical stance toward the nonempirical orientation of contemporary literary theory, and he addresses himself smoothly to the concern for disciplinary status that has very largely motivated this theory. He writes in a polished, urbane manner, and he has a nice precision in the analysis of metaphoric structures—a field that is vital to literary meaning and that legitimately combines contemporary cognitive linguistics with traditional literary analysis.

Darwinian literary critics are likely to be enticed but ultimately frustrated by Turner's *Reading Minds: The Study of English in the Age of Cognitive Science*. He concisely formulates an ethological conception of literature, the idea that "acts of language, including literature" are "acts of a human brain in a human body in a human environment which that brain must make intelligible if it is to survive" (pp. vii–viii). This formulation is frequently repeated but never developed. Turner wishes to make cognitive linguistics central to literary study, and he posits the adapted mind as a locus for the development of language, but he does not then posit any evolved structure of human motives. He makes no use of ethology, sociobiology, or evolutionary psychology. At one point, pursuing a line of thought in Mark Johnson's work, he declares, "A brain is part of a body and in operation is inescapable from it. Evolutionarily, the brain exists only in order to serve the reproductive and metabolic body of which it is a part, and it is deeply and ineradicably invested with the nature of its body" (p. 36). This is strikingly said, but the only categories actually stipulated for the physical nature of experience are those of spatial organization, "discovery," and "pain" (p. 39). For the rest, Turner maintains that "we receive a tacit cultural education" in how to imagine "the body" and "the human person" (p. 40). There is nothing here of the intuitive evolved apprehension of inner life as it has been described by Donald Brown (1991), J. Q. Wilson (1993), and Steven Pinker (1997b). Instead, the whole of substantive human motivation has been relegated to "conventional cultural and conceptual structures" (p. 21). Ultimately, even the domain of spatial organization proves too substantive for Turner's conventional belief in the autonomy of conventions, and his ethological principle fades timidly into equivocal disavowals of epistemological realism. A purely formal concept of the relation among categories would, he feels, liberate us from "arguments about how literal language refers to the world" (p. 142). Indeed, there would be "no direct relation between language and the world."

Turner argues that "we organize knowledge around mental models" (p. 128). This proposition is, I think, both true and potentially important. To realize its potential, though, we have to stipulate what these models are, offer causal explanations for them (why precisely *these* models?), and organize them systematically within a total structure of human motives and values. Turner evades these larger tasks and tries to take a shortcut directly into the routinized technical analysis of normal science. Late in the book, he offers a random list of categories that he calls "conceptual domains": eating, dress, learning, buildings, travel, combat, and plants (p. 199). He makes no effort to correlate these domains with the concept of domain-specific modules in evolutionary psychology, nor does he provide any other rationale or organizing principle for the list. Instead, he offers tedious analyses of formal relations among poorly distinguished and weakly rationalized "levels" of metaphoric categories: "basic level" and "generic level" metaphors.

Turner defines literature as "the highest expression of our commonplace conceptual and linguistic capacities" (p. 4), and he accordingly seeks to reorient literary study to the analysis of such commonplace capacities. He repeatedly urges us to take little account of the exceptional aspects of literary usage and instead to find a deep interest in what we normally take for granted. As a general exhortation, this proposal has some merit, but in Turner's own performance it is not well vindicated. He does not demonstrate how we are to pass through the commonplace to achieve deeper levels of causal explanation or systematic connection. His minutely detailed analyses of common ideas lead him to no larger conclusions. If we collect some of his major findings, we discover that the mind has evolved both to make categories and to recognize differences (chapters 2 and 6); that originality consists in deviations from a common ground (chapter 3), that symmetry is an important principle of formal organization—a thesis that spreads into the tautological proposition that "pattern" is an important principle of formal order (chapter 4); and that arguments are figured in terms of opposing physical forces (chapter 5). It is on conclusions of this magnitude that Turner proposes to reconstruct the field of English studies. Never was revolutionary manifesto more inoffensively bland.

Frederick Turner's idea of drawing a parallel between current literary study and pre-Darwinian biology was prefigured at mid-century by Northrop Frye (1957), one of the greatest of modern literary theorists. In *Mimesis and the Human Animal: On the Biogenetic Foundations of Literary Representation*, Robert Storey quotes the *locus classicus* from Frye's *Anatomy of Criticism*: "'Criticism seems to be badly in need of a coordinating principle, a central hypothesis which, like the theory of evolution in biology, will see the phenomena it deals with as parts of a whole'" (p. xvii). Like Frederick Turner, Storey proposes that biology itself provide this central coordinating principle, and his formulations sound at times very similar to the ethological formulations of Mark Turner. Storey differs sharply from both Turners in that he understands clearly the implications of the biological idea and follows them out with a rigorous consistency. In opposition to Frye and to all theorists who propound the autonomy of literature, Storey argues that neither criticism nor literature "ever needed a conceptual universe of its own" but rather that "each is explicable only in terms of the natural world that the human being shares with the rest of terrestrial phenomena" (p. xvii). Still more directly, and in terms that display his commitment to the modern, gene-based understanding of natural selection, Storey affirms, "Far from having left biology behind," human beings "have simply exfoliated their cultures from its genetically productive heart" (pp. 13–14).

In important ways, Storey's book is a model of what to leave out and what to include in a biologically oriented study of literature. He leaves out all fanciful fringe conceptions of biology. There are no forays here into cosmic evolution or the teleology of the ecosystem, no hints of an autonomous inner dynamics of form, no idyllic sentimentalizations of a beneficent natural order, and no self-unfolding of the inner reflexivity of the human self-consciousness. He locates the concept of evolution at the right level—the level of living things—and he identifies the central principle of biology as the evolution of adaptive structures by means of natural selection. While excluding the metaphysical chimeras that have charmed the fancies of the other theorists under discussion, Storey has excluded also the whole metaphysical cast of mind—the naive humanistic faith in the supreme efficacy of grandiose abstractions, the credulous susceptibility to "Big Words." He has placed his confidence instead in the cumulative and self-correcting body of empirical information. He has made use of most of the kinds of information the various other theorists have used, and some they have not. His largest conceptual frame is that of sociobiology, and he makes extensive use of information from ethology, evolutionary psychology, developmental psychology, the study of emotions, cognitive psychology, the neurosciences, and anthropology. Along with this empirical information, he has a good familiarity with traditional literary theory, and he has made a particular study of scholarly works devoted to the specific literary topics to which he gives attention: to the theory of narrative, reader response, and the genres of tragedy and comedy. The empirical information is brought to bear directly on the kinds of problems specific to literature. Genre, for example, is largely a matter of feeling—tragedy is sad, and comedy happy—and it makes obvious sense to connect formal studies of generic structure with psychological research into human emotions. And finally, Storey does not fail to include literature itself in his development of literary theory. Unlike many of the younger scholars who have been trained in departments dedicated largely to postmodern philosophy, or "theory" as it is familiarly called, he has read widely in world literature. He sprinkles illustrative examples and allusions throughout the theoretical chapters of his book, and in the final chapter, for the purpose of comparing conscious authorial intent with intuitive naturalistic perception, he offers a detailed reading of a novel by Iris Murdoch. A long intimacy with great literature seems virtually indispensable for producing the sensitivity and tact necessary to keeping literary theory within the bounds of good sense, and it can also have beneficial effects on prose style. Storey writes with humor, wit, and felicity of phrasing.

Storey divides his book into two main parts. The first part summarizes the findings of recent evolutionary study and thus generates what Storey calls a "'biogrammar' of the species" (p. xviii), that is, an outline of the evolved human architecture, with a special emphasis on those aspects of sociality, elemental motives, and mental functions that are most relevant to literature. Part 2 is devoted to specifically literary problems. In both parts, Storey develops his constructive argument in opposition to the views that currently prevail in literary study. For instance, sketching out a biologically based idea of the individual human identity, he declares that the human "subject," as the individual person is know in literary circles, "is a seeker and maker of meaning first of all—not because it is a bourgeois capitalist, or a hegemonic sexist, or even a benightedly retrograde humanist, but ultimately because it is a gene-driven organism that has evolved to live by its wits" (p. 101). Taking up the structuralist and poststructuralist belief that meanings are generated by arbitrary and infinitely variable cultural "codes," Storey affirms that all such conventional structures are "bound up intimately with both the social dynamics and the cognitive practices that are more or less common to all human beings" (p. 123). A formulation like this enters the empirical arena in which propositions can be tested by reference to steadily accumulating empirical findings, and it sets itself firmly in opposition to the culturalist beliefs evinced, with varying degrees of consistency, by Kroeber, Argyros, Frederick Turner, and Mark Turner.

The challenges facing theorists and critics who take up an empirical program can seem all but overwhelming. Out of the vast and constantly increasing mass of specialized knowledge, what does one select? Not just particular books and articles, but what whole disciplines does one choose as relevant to literary study? At what level of generality or popularization does one absorb specialized knowledge? How loosely or speculatively does one hold by propositions that, in the very nature of empirical study, are necessarily provisional, subject to correction or falsification? Storey is fully aware of the risks he has taken, and he expresses an appropriate humility. He describes his effort as "a starting point only," a "provisional answer to the question I have posed myself: What does it mean to say that art imitates life" (p. xvii)?

Although Storey's book is, to my mind, by far the most satisfactory of those under review, it does not escape unscathed from the risks it has assumed. The exposition of sociobiological theory cannot avoid the problem of secondhand exposition. The distinction between the two main parts of the book is not maintained very clearly, and the separate chapters sometimes seem to be almost arbitrary divisions in what is one continuous, but not always consequent, stream of argument. In attempting to absorb and synthesize large amounts of information from a wide variety of disciplines, there is a danger of becoming distracted by local problems, of losing the thread while becoming disproportionately preoccupied with details, or of responding in a reactive, too passive way to the structure of ideas in some source. Synthesis is the right goal, but it is not a goal always to be reached. Ideas that have independent force and some obvious association with one another might fail to cohere as an explanatory unit. For example, in the theory of the functions of narrative, it might be true that emotions precede language, that language splits the world into a repressed "shadow" and a social persona, that narrative mediates ambiguously between the two, and that narrative is primarily about social relations, but the total set of these propositions does not, as it seems to me, penetrate to the heart of the issue or constitute a complete and coherent theory of narrative meaning. Similar kinds of reservations might be put forward with respect to the theories of tragedy and comedy, though on all these topics much is said that is suggestive and illuminating.

To say that Storey's book is, as he himself describes it, a "starting point," is by no means to damn with faint praise. As other efforts indicate, it is all too easy to wander off into byways and down dead ends, from whence no start could ever be made. From the point at which Storey has left us, where do we go? The one main thing Storey's book does not do, and cannot even attempt to do, is to provide empirical verification for its many speculative hypotheses. If we are ever to proceed beyond the range of mere speculation, bridges will have to be built between falsifiable empirical research and literary theory. All of the books under review have made some effort, and some have made a considerable effort, to assimilate new empirical information. This is a bridge built half-way, from one direction. To complete the bridge, constructive efforts will also have to be made from the other side. If we are to incorporate literary study fully within the community of empirical science, we shall have to have a collective effort that includes experimental research by practitioners in psychology, anthropology, and the other human sciences. Storey, especially, has formulated falsifiable propositions about the production and reception of literary meaning. These formulations need to attract the attention of empirical scientists who could devise experimental situations through which these propositions can be falsified, qualified, or developed.

By accumulating a body of provisionally valid empirical propositions about the production and reception of literary meaning, we can begin to construct a framework within which to conduct rational discussions about the interpretation of individual texts and authors and of whole literary periods. E. O. Wilson has proposed the nucleus of a theory of culture, based on "culturgens" or units of cultural meaning that are derived from genetically encoded and neurologically identifiable components of human nature (1996, p. 115). The analysis of literary meaning should be an integral part of the development of any such theory. It can offer important information both about human universals and about the psychology of individual differences. The problems are immense, but the prospects are also real and exhilarating. For literary scholars, the only alternative is to continue in an essentially frivolous line of activity—to filter literary texts through the arbitrary idioms of fashionable schools of thought, and to rationalize this process as the inevitable consequence of the purely conventional character of all meaning.

6
Pinker, Dickens, and the
Functions of Literature

In *How the Mind Works* (1997b), Steven Pinker offers a splendidly fluent and lucid survey of evolutionary psychology. Pinker propounds the view that the mind has evolved under the shaping pressure of natural selection and that it has developed a number of mental "modules"—chunks of cognitive software—designed to solve specific adaptive problems. Apart from the sense organs, these postulated modules include adaptations for understanding arithmetic, logic, language, physical objects and forces, natural kinds (plants and animals), other human minds, kinship, social status relations, sexual behavior, parent-child relations, and the sense of individual identity. Evidence for the existence of such modules derives from an overlapping array of disciplines, from theoretical biology, behavioral genetics, cognitive and developmental psychology, comparative anthropology, animal ethology, experimental psychology, neurobiology, and endocrinology. Though he is not himself an original thinker—only a popularizer of an unusually high order—Pinker organizes all this information into an impressively coherent body of ideas.

The inexorable logic of the adaptationist program requires that evolutionary psychology assume the position of a matrix discipline within the field of liberal education. From the adaptationist perspective, psychology is rooted in biology, and all cultural studies, including both the social sciences and the humanities, are rooted in psychology. Pinker formulates this logic with characteristic concision:

> The geneticist Theodosius Dobzhansky famously wrote that nothing in biology makes sense except in the light of evolution. We can add that nothing in culture makes sense except in the light of psychology. Evolution created psychology, and that is how it explains culture. (p. 210)

Pinker's voluminous bibliography gives ample evidence that a large cadre of evolutionary scientists are already striving to make good on such claims for a wide range of topics in the social sciences. Within the humanities, far fewer people have been at work and the program of research has been less clearly laid out. Drawing a parallel with the colonization of North America at the time of the Louisiana Purchase, we can identify the social sciences with the populous eastern seaboard and the humanities with the far western territory. However manifest the destiny, the continent remains to be mapped. (This essay was originally published in 1998.)

Pinker's disciplinary home base is in cognitive psychology and linguistics. To illustrate and decorate his text, he has collected a substantial number of relevant quotations from literature, but there is no evidence that his familiarity with most of the works he quotes extends very far beyond the quotations. His literary taste and judgment seem those of an undergraduate who is extraordinarily bright but who is much more sensitive to computers than to poems, plays, or novels. Nonetheless, conscientiously seeking to vindicate the scope of his title, Pinker ventures to situate literature, theoretically, within the general map of evolutionary psychology.

Pinker poses a question that is basic for all mental operations within the evolutionary framework—the question of adaptive function. Displaying an excellent intuitive capacity for seizing on apposite commonplace, he identifies two obvious purposes of literature: instruction and entertainment, the *utile et dulce* of Horatian lore. The first of these, he supposes, might have some genuine adaptive value. Literature, like social gossip, teaches us about the games people play and prepares us to enter into such play. "Life is like chess, and plots are like those books of famous chess games that serious players study so they will be prepared if they ever find themselves in similar straits" (p. 542). Knowledge might be adaptive, but the pleasure afforded by art, Pinker thinks, is merely a nonadaptive exploitation of adaptive sources of pleasure. The arts respond to "a biologically pointless challenge: figuring out how to get at the pleasure circuits of the brain and deliver little jolts of enjoyment without the inconvenience of wringing bona fide fitness increments from the harsh world" (p. 524). In this respect, literature and the other arts would work in the same way as alcohol, drugs, and rich deserts. Hence Pinker's suggestion that "music is auditory cheesecake, an exquisite confection crafted to tickle the sensitive spots of at least six of our mental faculties" (p. 534). The pleasure afforded by literature is of a similar kind:

> Now, if the intellectual faculties could identify the pleasure-giving patterns, purify them, and concentrate them, the brain could stimulate itself without the messiness of electrodes or drugs. It could give itself intense artificial doses of the sights and sounds and smells that ordinarily are given off by healthful environments. We enjoy strawberry cheesecake, but not because we evolved a taste for it. We evolved circuits that gave us trickles of enjoyment from the sweet taste of ripe fruit, the creamy mouth feel of fats and oils from nuts and meat, and the coolness of fresh water. Cheesecake packs a sensual wallop unlike anything in the natural world because it is a brew of megadoses of agreeable stimuli which we concocted for the express purpose of pressing our pleasure buttons. Pornography is another pleasure technology. . . . [T]he arts are a third. (pp. 524–525)

Despite the concession to the utility of fiction as a model for moves in the game of life, Pinker's wider exposition makes it apparent that like Freud he regards literary representation as largely a matter of pleasurable fantasy. It is different from pornography only in that the pleasure buttons it pushes are not those literally and concretely of sexual activity.

Pinker's hypothesis about the pleasure of art reflects a prejudice common to evolutionary psychology—the idea that only those functions that evolved in the distant evolutionary past have any particular adaptive status. We can call this prejudice the bias for the EEA ("environment of evolutionary adaptedness"). Evolutionary psychologists tend to regard the EEA as a relatively static condition in which the human mind was fixed and finished sometime before the past 100,000 years or so. An important correction to this prejudice has been proposed in Steven Mithen's *The Prehistory of the Mind* (1996). Mithen is a cultural archaeologist. He has fully assimilated the idea of "the modular mind," but he has also broken free from the premature concretization of the EEA. He describes the cultural revolution that took place about 40,000 years ago and that introduced complex multipart tools and the elements of higher culture, including art, religion, and more complex forms of social organization. How to account for this explosion of creative activity? Mithen postulates an organically based cognitive development in which the previously separate domains of the mind became accessible to one another. He argues that the domains devoted to technical understanding, social interaction, and natural history blended together, and that out of this blend there emerged an entirely new range of creative cognitive activity. Mithen describes this new capability as "cognitive fluidity," and he argues cogently that it is the basis for all our more imaginative, inventive cultural achievements.

Now, art, music, and literature are not merely the products of cognitive fluidity. They are important means by which we cultivate and regulate the complex cognitive machinery on which our more highly developed functions depend. Because he does not understand the necessity of such cultivation, Pinker believes that we could do without music and undergo no significant loss in our capacity to function. "Compared with language, vision, social reasoning, and physical know-how, music could vanish from our species and the rest of our lifestyle would be virtually unchanged. Music appears to be a pure pleasure technology, a cocktail of recreational drugs that we ingest through the ear to stimulate a mass of pleasure circuits at once" (p. 528). If we compare the effects of music with those of recreational drugs, we can begin to understand the mistaken direction Pinker's theory has taken. Drugs are disorienting and demoralizing. If young people use them habitually, they become incapable of adapting to the demands of a complex environment. Music has no such deleterious effect. More importantly, it seems very likely that people raised with no exposure to music, art, or literature would be psychologically and emotionally stunted—that they would be only marginally capable of developing in normal ways. They would probably have great difficulty learning to deal with their own emotions or to relate to other people with any sensitivity and flexibility.

Their capacity for responding in creative ways to the demands of a complex and changing cultural environment would probably be severely impaired.

If we shift from the metaphor of drugs to that of cheesecake, we find similarly misleading implications. Rich deserts offer a purely sensual stimulus. They appeal only to the taste buds. They have no intrinsic emotional or conceptual content, and they convey no information from one mind to another. In contrast, art, music, and literature embody emotions and ideas. They are forms of communication, and what they communicate are the qualities of experience. Someone deprived of such experience would have artificially imposed on him a deficiency similar to that which is imposed on autistic children through an innate neurological defect. (See Baron-Cohen, 1996.) Unlike autistic children, a child deprived of all experience with art and literature would still have innate capacities for social interaction, but these capacities would remain brutishly latent. The architecture of his or her own inner life and that of other people would remain dully obscure. In the place of meaningful pattern in the organization of emotions and the structure of human needs and purposes, such a child would perhaps scarcely rise above the level of reactive impulse. It is not difficult to imagine an inner life consisting of large desolate tracts of restless confusion sporadically traversed by violent and incomprehensible storms of fear and desire. When we speak of civilization as a form of salvation, it is from such conditions that we envision ourselves being saved.

The argument I've been making for the vital role of art in the healthy development of human beings is a central didactic theme in the works of one of our most psychologically astute novelists. In his great novel, *Bleak House*, Charles Dickens presents us with a case that we can compare with Pinker's notion of human beings who are musically deprived but who are nonetheless perfectly healthy, happy, and wise. As a foil for the full humanity and achieved civilization of his protagonists, Dickens depicts a family of misers, the Smallweeds, who are wholly practical in orientation. The family is one of Dickens's most vividly conceived set of grotesques. Grandfather Smallweed is paralytic, cunning, and venomous. He subdues the expression of his spite toward those from whom he would extract wealth, but he consoles himself by flinging pillows and imprecations at his senile wife, who breaks imbecile silence only to chatter in incoherent phrases about money. The young male heir to the house, Bartholomew Smallweed, is "a weird changeling" with "an old, old eye." He "drinks and smokes, in a monkeyish way" and "is never to be taken in; and he knows all about it, whatever it is" (1956, chapter 20). Bart's sister Judy "never owned a doll, never heard of Cinderella, never played at any game." Judy cannot laugh and is incapable of playing with other children. She is "a pattern of sordid age" (chapter 21). Dickens explains that in its exclusive fixation on gain, this family has "discarded all amusements, discountenanced all story-books, fairy tales, fictions, and fables, and banished all levities whatsoever. Hence the gratifying fact that it has no child born to it and that the complete little men and women whom it has produced, have been observed to bear a likeness to old monkeys with something depressing on their minds" (chapter 21).

The Smallweeds are constitutionally predisposed to this grotesque withering of their humanity. In *Hard Times,* a more schematically didactic presentation of the same theme, there are again two children who have been deprived of all imaginative cultivation, Tom and Louisa Gradgrind. Unlike the Smallweeds, these children are potentially normal, and they do not take happily to the imaginative desolation that has been imposed on them. Their father is a utilitarian ideologue. Convinced that art and literature are a waste of time and an influence corrupting to mental discipline, he eliminates all such influences from their carefully controlled curriculum. As a consequence of his educational policy, his children are morally and emotionally impaired, and the action of the plot flows from these impairments. As adults, the Gradgrind children can neither achieve personal fulfillment nor function as responsible citizens. Louisa proves incapable of developing a healthy marital bond, and Tom degenerates into common crime as a means of financing his vices.

Pinker's manner is rather different from that of Gradgrind, but the difference is not all in Pinker's favor. He is charming and witty, but he is too easily pleased with himself at having said something he deems provocatively clever, and he has not thought through the implications of his bright idea. Gradgrind is dull and oppressive, but he pursues his mistaken ideological convictions in a serious and determined way. When the consequences of his policy become apparent, he is capable of achieving a tragic recognition of his mistake. Pinker's tonal range does not include the capacity for tragic recognitions. He is unfailingly pleasant and self-possessed. Within the even tenor of his style, the closest approximation to grief and anguish would be a momentary compunction at having failed to pass up a dessert tray.

For Dickens, the period of childhood is a highly sensitive and vulnerable stage in which the whole personality can be forever stunted and impoverished by inadequate imaginative stimulus. From Oliver Twist through Pip, his books are full of stories of children who have been abused and neglected and who are threatened with lifelong degradation. Some, like Smike in *Nicholas Nickelby* and the crossing sweeper Jo in *Bleak House,* do not survive this treatment. Those who do, like David Copperfield and like Esther Summerson, the protagonist of *Bleak House,* do so because they create an imaginative world of their own, and within this world they fashion an environment that is adequate to their needs of self-development. To create an imaginative world in which to develop is not the same thing as merely fulfilling a fantasy of pleasure. Esther is raised in a household devoid of affection, under the shadow of an obscure religious condemnation, but through conversations with her doll she creates a small imaginary space for human affection. Within this space, she can keep her own emotional nature alive until her aunt dies and she is removed to a more genial environment. The conversations she has with her doll are not fantasies of pleasure; they are desperate and effective measures of personal salvation. (For more on Esther, see the second section of part 1, chapter 8.) As a small boy, David Copperfield is tormented and abused by his vicious stepfather, but close to his own room he discovers a neglected store of old books, including *Tom Jones, Humphrey Clinker, Don Quixote,* and *Robinson Crusoe.* What David gets from these books is not just a bit of mental cheesecake, a chance for a transient fantasy in which all his own wishes are fulfilled. What he gets are lively and powerful images of human life suffused with the feeling and understanding of the astonishingly capable and complete human beings who wrote them. It is through this kind of contact with a sense of human possibility that he is enabled to escape from the degrading limitations of his own local environment. He is not escaping from reality; he is escaping from an impoverished reality into the larger world of healthy human possibility. By nurturing and cultivating his own individual identity through his literary imagination, he enables himself to adapt successfully to this world. He directly enhances his own fitness as a human being, and in doing so he demonstrates the kind of adaptive advantage that can be conferred by literature.

7
Wilson's *Consilience*
and Literary Study

For students of the humanities, and especially of literature, E. O. Wilson's *Consilience: The Unity of Knowledge* (1998) presents an extraordinary challenge. For Wilson, the humanities are the last frontier of science. He believes that "the greatest enterprise of the mind has always been and always will be the attempted linkage of the sciences and humanities" (p. 8). Because the physical sciences and the humanities constitute polar points in the field of knowledge, and because the products of human genius constitute the most complex objects in nature, Wilson considers this linkage as the ultimate test of "consilience," his term for the unification of all knowledge. The term is taken from the Victorian philosopher of science William Whewell, and it signifies "a 'jumping together' of knowledge by the linking of facts and fact-based theory across disciplines to create a common groundwork of explanation" (p. 8). Wilson's own background is remote from the humanities, but he makes a heroic effort to meet the challenge he has set. He formulates a hypothesis about the evolutionary origin and function of the arts, and he draws a connection between human nature and the design of the arts. He argues that the arts serve to fill the gap between animal instinct and the "vastness of new contingent possibilities revealed by high intelligence" (p. 225), and he maintains that "even the greatest works of art might be understood fundamentally with knowledge of the biologically evolved epigenetic rules that guided them" (p. 213). His theory of art emphasizes the depiction of human behavior, and it thus implicitly makes fictional representation the central instance of art.

I think Wilson's hypothesis about the evolutionary origin and function of art is basically right, and it is far superior to aesthetic theories that have been formulated by other sociobiologists and evolutionary psychologists. As he would himself acknowledge, his aesthetic theory is little more than a sketch or an outline. The outline needs to be corrected in some important ways, and the whole larger design must still be filled in. These challenges will be my main concern in the latter part of this commentary. Before turning to them, I shall assess Wilson's achievement, examine his main themes, and consider a representative sampling of the critical responses that reject his larger theoretical program.

Wilson contrasts two kinds of intellectual achievement. "Discovery" is the supreme merit of scientific enterprise (p. 56). "Scholarship" and "wisdom" are the hallmarks of humanistic study (p. 39). The two kinds of achievement are so uncomplementary that "many accomplished scientists are narrow, foolish people," and "many wise scholars" are "considered weak scientists" (p. 57). The difficulty of combining these kinds of achievement gives some measure of Wilson's intellectual magnitude, for he has won singular distinction in both kinds. He is a world-class scientist, and his specific discoveries have led him steadily onward toward ever more encompassing reflection.

Wilson's areas of scientific expertise form a nested set that exemplify his core belief in causal explanation across diverse levels of organization. He is an entomologist, a naturalist, an ecologist, and a sociobiologist. He discovered pheromones, the chemical signaling system in ants—a discovery that opened an immense field of research for other naturalists. In collaboration with Robert MacArthur, he invented the science of island biogeography, and he thus brought ecology within the scope of the exact sciences. In *Sociobiology: The New Synthesis* (1975), he integrated population genetics, ethology, and evolutionary biology in such a way as to constitute a distinct new discipline, now the matrix or frame for a vast research program into the social evolution of all animals, including humans. In the final chapter of *Sociobiology* and in *On Human Nature* (1978), Wilson turned his own attention to the evolved basis of human behavior, and then, in collaboration with Charles Lumsden, he pioneered the theory of gene-culture coevolution. In the past two decades, he has become a leading authority in biodiversity and world ecology. Now, with the publication of *Consilience*, he has consolidated and extended the reach of all his previous study, and he has established a strong claim to be considered the most important general theorist of intellectual culture in his generation. *Consilience* is not the relaxed rumination of a senior scientist enjoying his retirement from the rigors of primary research. It is the bold and strenuous culmination of a lifetime's effort at exploring and mapping the natural world, and for Wilson the natural world includes the human world of culture and intellect. His deepest intellectual conviction is that nature forms an unbroken chain of causal sequences, and he supports this conviction by assimilating and integrating knowledge from the whole array of disciplinary domains—from physics and other hard sciences, from the many subfields of biology, and from the social sciences, intellectual history, and the humanities.

Wilson's lucid, easy style should make the book accessible to most educated people, but this is not "popular" science writing in the usual sense. Wilson is not merely retailing intriguing bits of information in an engaging manner. He has a powerful mind, and on any of twenty or thirty areas of specialized expertise, he penetrates to the heart of the matter, seizes on the central issues, and offers in condensed form an authoritative account of the best understanding in that area. All of this information is used to illustrate Wilson's larger themes and arguments, but if one were to read the book even in the most casual way merely as a smorgasbord of popular science, it would still be richly rewarding.

An illustrative selection of such nuggets of popular science would include expositions of quantum electrodynamics, the electromagnetic spectrum, nanotechnology, pheromones, neuroanatomy, the neurophysiology of dreaming, complexity theory, chaos theory, enzymes, artificial intelligence, color vision, language and communications in humans and chimpanzees, behavioral genetics, population genetics, modern economic theory, cave art, and world ecology. Along with these bits of scientific information, Wilson offers a summary account, extending over several chapters, of modern intellectual history. He begins with the Enlightenment and the Romantic reaction, and he includes the main phases of modern social theory and of the modernist and postmodern movements in the humanities. At the highest level of philosophic concern, he gives an extended exposition of the conflict between the materialist and transcendental worldviews, including their ethical ramifications. Major problems in the philosophy of science, especially the integration of science and the humanities, form recurrent themes. The final chapter, on world ecology, is surely the most masterful and authoritative such exposition available to a lay public. In all of these areas, Wilson displays the ingenuous enthusiasm of the naturalist delighted with his finds, but he is also deeply concerned with the philosophical principles that bind one piece of information to another and that bind all together into a seamless web of causal relations.

Wilson's public standing reveals an interesting split between the educated reading public and the academic left—to use the designation made familiar by Gross and Levitt (1994). Wilson first emerged into wide public recognition with the controversy over *Sociobiology: The New Synthesis*. His main role in this controversy was to serve as a target for the violent hostility of Marxist pressure groups such as Science for the People. The Marxist establishment, prominently represented by Steven Jay Gould and Richard Lewontin, tried to bully Wilson into recantation or silence, but he neither succumbed to intimidation nor allowed the bitterness of his enemies to sour his own temper. Instead, he steadily expanded the scope and strengthened the framework of his own positive formulations. As a result, he has emerged now, twenty-five years later, as a cultural hero and a national celebrity. He has won two Pulitzer Prizes, national and international awards for scientific achievement, and teaching awards at Harvard, and his expression of kindly humor and genial intelligence has been widely publicized in magazine photographs. He embodies some of the best qualities in the public idea of science—honesty, energy, a delighted absorption in sustained research, and a considered optimism about the power of the human mind to penetrate the mysteries of nature. Moreover, his concern for the environment and for biodiversity reflects a mature appreciation for the human and ethical dimensions of science. For all these reasons, he has become virtually an icon of the benevolent scientist, a benign double or counter-image to the image of the scientist as sinister genius—as Dr. Frankenstein or Dr. Strangelove.

Wilson's stature as a cultural celebrity can be indicated by the immense publication campaign accompanying the appearance of *Consilience*. Preview articles for the book appeared in a number of journals, including *Science, The Wilson Quarterly, Atlantic Monthly,* and *Academic Questions,* and the book itself instantly garnered a wide and enthusiastic readership. Nonetheless, reviews in the more prominent journals have been weighted toward the negative. Symposia in *The Wilson Quarterly* and *Academic Questions* had a balanced mix of positive and negative responses, but *The New York Review of Books, The New Republic,* and *Science* all gave the book to hostile reviewers. Wilson has continued to run directly counter to the ideology of a powerful academic class responsible for directing public opinion, and this class is itself largely out of touch with the best instincts and the freshest currents of thought in the educated reading public. The situation is something like that of a nation in which an official body of priests has fallen a generation behind the public movement of mind but still retains possession of the official pulpits.

The ideological antagonism to Wilson's work has taken three main forms: a Romantic belief in the autonomy of the human spirit, a postmodernist epistemological nihilism, and a traditional humanistic belief in the irreducible singularity of all artistic productions. Each of these forms constitutes a major position in the spectrum of current humanistic opinion, and the proponents of each form rightly regard themselves as fundamentally threatened by Wilson's vision—his conviction that the human spirit is an integral part of the causal web of nature, that science can obtain reliable knowledge about the structure of nature, and that human art, like all other objects in nature, can be reduced to underlying regularities and submitted to scientific understanding. Wilson's three sets of antagonists would find much to squabble about among themselves, but they join together in insisting on the separation of physical science from all matters of humanistic interest, and they find a common theme in repudiating a central sociobiological concept that links science and human affairs: the concept of human universals.

Tzvetan Todorov, writing in *The New Republic,* exemplifies the Romantic opposition to the causal determinacy of the naturalistic vision. Todorov affiliates his claims for spiritual autonomy with Rousseau and Kant, and he supports the idea of freedom by a predictable pattern of waffling. Since causal antecedents can be readily identified for any definite characteristic of human beings, anyone who would invest these characteristics with autonomy can scarcely avoid equivocation. Todorov identifies "culture" and "freedom" as the defining peculiarities of the human species, and he identifies culture itself as "a collective freedom" (1998, p. 30). Culture frees man from biology, he fancies, but then he bumps into the problem that culture itself becomes "a determining cause." There is no escape open, and Todorov can only disguise his logical *cul de sac* by appealing inappropriately to qualifications of degree, accompanied with rhetorical gestures. People are capable of detaching themselves even from culture "up to a point," but no, the human species is "not entirely free." Still, "it knows the motions of liberation" (p. 30). Rhetorical procedures of this sort are motivated by a sentimental attachment to spiritual feelings, and they nullify their own conceptual content.

Wilson's own thinking on the problem of human freedom displays his characteristic incisiveness, and it is embedded in one of his most inventive and potentially fruitful conceptions—the idea of human consciousness as a series of "scenarios." Wilson's exposition of this idea constitutes the bulk of a chapter entitled "The Mind," and it is boldly presented as a turning point in the way to do philosophy of mind. "Much of the history of modern philosophy, from Descartes and Kant forward, consists of failed models of the brain" (p. 96). This formulation is not meant merely to be provocative. It is a serious diagnosis, and Wilson offers an evolutionary explanation for the diagnosis. Previous philosophers have worked too exclusively from "introspection," and since the brain was designed by evolution not to achieve self-knowledge but "to survive," introspection is inadequate. Reliable models of mental activity can be produced only through scientific investigation. Responses to Wilson like those of Todorov are motivated not only by ideological animus but also by a desire to remain within the methodological boundaries of purely discursive philosophy—to cling to Kant and Rousseau rather than to negotiate the new and difficult terrain of neurophysiology and cognitive psychology.

Scenarios are "coding networks" of sensory impressions, memories, and imaginative projections (p. 109). "Consciousness consists of the parallel processing of vast numbers of such coding networks," and "decision-making" consists in "the competitive selection among scenarios" (p. 115). Selection is determined by emotion. "The winning scenarios are those that match goals preprogrammed by instinct and the satisfactions of prior experience" (p. 113). We make decisions as the consequence of the relative weight of emotional force behind alternative scenarios, and this emotional force is not wholly available to conscious thought. "Circuits and determining molecular processes exist outside conscious thought. They consolidate certain memories and delete others, bias connections and analogies, and reinforce the neurohormonal loops that regulate subsequent emotional response" (p. 119). This theory of decision making provides a straightforward solution to the supposed enigma of human freedom. "The hidden preparation of mental activity gives the illusion of free will. We make decisions for reasons we often sense only vaguely, and seldom if ever understand fully."

Critics of sociobiological theories alternate between indignantly repudiating them and superciliously dismissing them. John Dupré, Richard Rorty, and Susan Haack all exemplify the line of indignant repudiation. They all object to the standard sociobiological theme that average human sex differences are rooted in the evolutionary logic of reproduction, but their complaints offer no serious theoretical challenge to Wilson. They consist only of straw man oppositions between totalized environmental or genetic determinacy (Dupré,

1998), contentions founded on ignorance of the relevant literature (Haack, 1998, p. 67), and efforts at political blackmail (Rorty, 1998, p. 36). The other line of attack, supercilious dismissal, is more theoretically interesting. Steve Jones, writing in *The New York Review of Books*, exemplifies this approach. He offers a bland and sketchy list of sociobiological propositions, scoffs at the notion that they are "new revelations in human understanding," and maintains that "most human sociobiology is a restatement of the obvious in biological language" (1998, p. 15).

The merit of complaints like those of Jones can be assessed against the test case offered by Wilson's theory of mind. The idea that "we make decisions for reasons we often sense only vaguely" is indeed commonplace, but it is a commonplace that has stimulated myths of divine inspiration and demonic possession, that has teased the minds of dramatists and novelists for centuries, that has motivated elaborate and incoherent philosophies of moral autonomy, and that has generated major systems of modern psychology. The systems of Freud and Jung were created in the old-fashioned humanistic way. They are discursive and introspective, and they are enmeshed with fancies like that of the collective unconscious and the Oedipal complex. Jung's notion of the collective unconscious is a hodge-podge of Darwinism, Lamarckism, and mysticism, and it has produced some illumination but also much confusion. The Oedipal theory, in contrast, has been proven to be fundamentally wrong—the theory of incest avoidance is one of the showpieces of sociobiological research—and it has seduced generations of humanists into phantasmagoric error. (See Buss, 1999, pp. 217–219; Daly and Wilson, 1990; Degler, 1991, pp. 245–269; Easterlin, 2000; Sugiyama, 2001c.)

The common observation that "we make decisions for reasons we often sense only vaguely" is a fact to be explained. The efforts to explain this fact in the literary, philosophical, and psychological traditions have been wildly divergent, and these divergent explanations form parts of radically different systems of thought. On the basis of a considered hypothesis about intellectual history, a hypothesis that is itself rooted in the deep history of the adapted mind, Wilson discards obsolete dogmas and antiquated fancies, and he reformulates the common observation as an empirical problem within the conceptual framework of cognitive and emotional psychology. Like all empirical formulations, and unlike those of the humanistic tradition, Wilson's theory is a working hypothesis, provisional and amenable to improvements in scientific knowledge. Within the current framework of available information, he develops a model of decision making, and he uses this model to offer cogent solutions for problems that still mystify most humanistic writers.

The idea of consciousness as a set of scenarios should have a wide utility in the social sciences and the humanities. It should prove particularly useful for a theory of fictional representation, and I shall return to it later in this commentary. For now, it is enough to register that the seemingly "obvious" character of

Wilson's observation is an illusion produced by confusing levels of fact and theoretical explanation. The fact that seems so obvious is part of a theory of the mind that is only now being developed; it offers a parsimonious explanation of this fact; and the theory that explains the fact is itself embedded in a still deeper, well-established theory about biological evolution and the evolution of the mind. The two larger theories are themselves "consilient," and they produce broad and deep interconnections or "consilience" among diverse fields of knowledge; they are subject to falsification and development through empirical research, and they enable us to correct serious and long-standing errors from other, competing hypotheses. All these aspects of the theory exemplify the kinds of criteria that Wilson identifies as characteristic of scientific thinking (pp. 53, 198). They are largely alien to the set of mind exemplified by most of his critics.

Of all possible responses to *Consilience*, those informed by postmodernism are the most antithetical to Wilson's way of thinking, and he is himself aware of this irreconcilable antipathy. In the historical chapters, he identifies himself as a proud heir to the Enlightenment, especially to Bacon, and he declares that "postmodernism is the ultimate polar antithesis of the Enlightenment" (p. 40). Unlike his expositions of scientific topics, Wilson's excursions into intellectual history are the work not of a distinguished primary observer but of a talented and industrious amateur. Nonetheless, he seizes effectively upon the central features in this historical polarity. "Enlightenment thinkers believe we can know everything, and radical postmodernists believe we can know nothing" (p. 40). The postmodernists repudiate the idea of a "'real' reality" and hence of "objective truths" (p. 40). For them, science is not "demonstrably the most powerful instrument hitherto created by the human mind" (p. 190), but only "another way of looking at the world" (p. 214). Wilson's genial and impersonally objective manner, a product of his scientific cultivation, tends very little toward emotionally charged personal characterizations, but the postmodernists provoke an unusually angry and contemptuous response from him. He describes them as "a rebel crew milling beneath the black flag of anarchy" (p. 40).

Richard Rorty quotes Wilson on the postmodern view of science and concedes the justice of the description. "I do indeed think that science is just another way of looking at the world" (1998, p. 38). For Rorty, reality is a nonconcept. In its place, he postulates a heterogeneous set of incommensurable "vocabularies," each with its own peculiar charm, none with any particular claim to greater relative validity (p. 30). Wilson declares that Rorty's views "would drain much of the power and joy from scholarly inquiry," and he protests that Rorty's unwillingness to link discoveries by causal explanation "lazily" devalues intellect (p. 190). In response, Rorty only lifts his shoulders in a languid Gallic shrug. These are not concerns he can share. Rorty does not argue against the grounds of Wilson's beliefs. He merely disclaims any personal receptivity to them. One could illustrate the standoff between the two philosophers by reference to Wilson's descriptions of animal senses that humans do not possess. Human beings cannot feel what the sensation of an eel's electromagnetic field is like. Within the human range, one might compare the case with that of a moralist trying to awaken the tenderness of a sociopath. There is simply no mental organ to register the appeal. In parallel, a philosopher who has no interest in truth or reality could never be argued into feeling what he does not feel.

Despite his antipathy to the irrationality of the postmodernists, Wilson seeks to turn their provocations to the good by casting them in the role of antagonists in a productive dialectic. He divides the intellectual world into "those who upon viewing disorder try to create order, and those who upon encountering order try to protest it by creating disorder" (p. 43). The tension between the two, he thinks, "is what drives learning forward." Wilson is stimulated by skepticism about the unity of nature and of knowledge. He responds to this stimulus by recurrently seeking to formulate the conditions of a total explanatory network—an unbroken chain of causation from the simplest elements of nature to the most complex, from subatomic particles through the mind of Mozart. Wilson's terminology in these meditations is not always consistent, but the basic theory is fairly simple. *Consilience* moves in two directions. In one direction, it moves toward "reductionism," the "dissection and analysis" of complex phenomena (p. 54). This movement is "the cutting edge of science." In the other direction, it moves toward "synthesis and integration." Wilson characterizes this second purpose as "predictive synthesis" (p. 125) or "total consilience," but he refers to it also, confusingly, as a "deeper" form of "reductionism" (p. 55). The purpose of this second movement is to predict all the phenomena of the universe from the simplest elements in it. Wilson lucidly expounds the almost inconceivable complexity that rapidly emerges from even the simplest interactions of subatomic particles, and he acknowledges the daunting difficulty of predicting the emergence of new principles of organization within the scale of natural hierarchies—from physics through chemistry and molecules, and up to organs, organisms, and superorganisms. Though unreachable within any currently imaginable condition of knowledge, predictive synthesis is "the ultimate goal" of science (p. 125). (At one point, the idea of predictive synthesis as the "ultimate goal" is conflated with the idea of ordinary synthetic reassembly of analytically separated parts [p. 211].) The kind of science that can yield practical results proceeds mainly through ordinary analytic reduction and reassembly. Consilience at this level is a common conception in the rationalist philosophy of science, and it is at this level that the theory of consilience must meet the challenge of irrationalist critics.

The third major form of antagonism to Wilson's theory of consilience is that of a traditional humanistic dualism—the belief that the physical sciences and the humanities occupy irreducibly distinct ontological territories. In this vision, the physical world and subjective experience are radically distinct kinds of stuff. The physical world is subject to quantitative formulation and reductive causal analysis, and the mental world consists of unique and irreducibly qualitative moments of subjectivity. Roger Shattuck holds this belief, but he formulates his argument against Wilson in an epistemological rather than an ontological way. Shattuck declares that "the arts, in contrast with philosophy and science, deal with individuals and their particular actions, thoughts, and feelings in contingent situations that we find pertinent. The arts and the humanities do not look primarily for universals and general laws: they seek out the revelation and uniqueness of individual cases" (1998, p. 59). (For similar formulations, characteristic of the New Criticism, see Brooks and Warren, 1949, pp. 33–39, 1976, pp. 6–7; Ellis, 1997, pp. 34–35.) If we were to take this proposition at face value, we would be unable to make any generalizations about or comparisons of literature. We would be unable to identify commonalities of period, of style, or of genre. We would forbid ourselves to notice common themes or motifs, or to register similar situations depicted in different literary works. In practice, no one does or could observe such restrictions. They serve only as a makeshift barrier against systematic empirical understanding. Their purpose is to preserve the humanistic domain exclusively for traditional belle-lettristic practice—for eclectic or theoretically opportunistic response at the level of common language.

The repudiation or deprecation of human universals necessarily constitutes the main bastion of defense against Wilson's proposal to integrate science and humanistic study. Universals are underlying regularities that render human experience susceptible to scientific generalization, and the universals identified by sociobiology situate these regularities within a well-established scientific theory of deep causal processes. Wilson's proposal depends fundamentally on the idea that there is "a scientifically constructible map of human nature from which the deep meaning of texts can be drawn" (p. 214). That map would depict a species-typical goal structure, and it would provide a pattern that would enable social scientists and humanists to engage in valid reductive analysis and reliable prediction about human behavior, including artistic behavior. The crudest form of defense is simply to deny that any regularities exist. Todorov, for instance, declares that "the uniqueness of human events means that they cannot be generalized" (1998, p. 31). This claim is grossly and demonstrably false, so it could have effect only with humanists operating theoretically at the level of creationists and flat-earthers. A more subtle defense, exemplified by Rorty (1998, p. 36) and Jones (1998, p. 14), is to acknowledge some regularities but to dismiss them as trivial or banal.

Wilson identifies the underlying regularities of human nature as "epigenetic rules," defined as "the hereditary regularities of mental development that bias cultural evolution in one direction as opposed to another, and thus connect the genes to culture" (p. 164). Sociobiological propositions about human nature are neither trivial nor banal, but at this point in their development they are still, to use Wilson's own word, "rudimentary." He acknowledges that "the central weakness of contemporary human behavioral genetics and human sociobiology is that only a small number of the relevant genes and epigenetic rules have been identified" (pp. 154–155). The problems are "conceptual, technical, and deep," but they are also "ultimately solvable" (p. 173). Solutions will come through "the further expansion of biology and its coalescence with psychology and anthropology." Wilson's concessions about the still rudimentary character of sociobiology as a science reflect both his integrity as a scientist and his confidence in the ultimate success of his research program. Such statements are remote from the language of dogmatic certitude and partisan self-promotion common to manifestoes in humanistic cultural theory, but social scientists and literary scholars have no need to be discouraged by Wilson's candid appraisal of the historical condition of research in his field. The map of human nature has some firm outlines, and within these outlines there is a substantial and steadily growing body of specific findings.

Wilson devotes one main chapter, "The Fitness of Human Nature," to systematically delineating a sociobiological theory of human nature. At the beginning of the chapter, about two-thirds of the way through his book, he summarizes all the examples he has used so far as illustrations, and the list is an apparent hodge-podge: dreaming, fear of snakes, taste, mother-infant bonding, facial expressions corresponding to the basic emotions, cognitive tendencies toward conceptual reification and dichotomization, and color vision. This opening list and the more structured account of human nature that follows can illustrate an important difference between evolutionary psychology and sociobiology, two doctrinal labels that Wilson himself presents as virtually synonymous. Random lists like the one that opens the chapter are characteristic of essays that adopt the label of evolutionary psychology. The items in such lists are designated "cognitive domains" or "domain-specific modules." (See Pinker, 1994, p. 420; Tooby and Cosmides, 1992, p. 113.) Evolutionary psychology presents itself as a successor to sociobiology and distinguishes itself from its origin by emphasizing "proximate" mechanisms of motivation that are sometimes remote from the "ultimate" regulative principles of inclusive fitness. Inclusive fitness consists in successfully passing on one's genes, and proximate mechanisms are the evolved physical and behavioral structures that mediate inclusive fitness. As evolutionary psychology moves away from the sociobiological emphasis on inclusive fitness as a direct and proximate motive, it approaches more closely to cognitive psychology as a matrix discipline, and in this move it tends to eliminate the underlying motivational principles that would provide structure to randomly assorted lists of cognitive mechanisms.

For theorists like Wilson who take sociobiology as the matrix discipline, the deepest level of organization is that of the elementary principles of survival and reproduction. Richard Alexander (1987, pp. 40–41) identifies these principles as the somatic and reproductive motivational domains common to all organisms, and Wilson describes "greater longevity and a secure, growing family" as "the universal bottom line of Darwinian genetic fitness" (p. 252). Since human beings are social animals, somatic and reproductive concerns are deeply enmeshed in principles of social interaction. These three categories— survival, reproduction, and social interaction, provide the nucleus for standard efforts to organize sociobiological principles into distinct behavioral systems. For example, McGuire and Troisi identify four basic behavioral systems: survival, reproduction, kin assistance, and reciprocation (1998, p. 68); and Buss (1999), in a textbook of evolutionary psychology, surveys the whole field of evolutionary psychology within a sequence of book sections devoted to survival, sex and mating, parenting and kinship, and group living. In his chapter on "The Fitness of Human Nature," Wilson breaks sociobiology down into a similar list of categories and summarizes the well-established findings in each category. The categories directly concerned with reproductive success include kin selection, parental investment, and mating strategy. The categories concerned with social interaction include status seeking, territorial expansion and defense, and contractual agreement—this latter a peculiarly human feature of social organization dependent on the capacity for higher cognitive organization and long-term planning. Each of these categories breaks down into a number of specific regulative principles, and the combination or interaction of these principles within differing environmental circumstances provides a strong network of elements capable of achieving substantial structural complexity. For example, mating strategies involve an array of evolved sex differences in motivational structures and cognitive predispositions, and parenting and kinship include the whole field of developmental psychology—the problems of growing up—and of family dynamics. To gain some sense of the scope of these principles, consider that the vast bulk of fiction consists in personal interactions constituted primarily by combinations of motives involving mating strategies, family dynamics, and social strategies devoted to seeking status and forming coalitions.

In concentrating on behavioral systems directly connected to survival and reproduction, sociobiologists sometimes forget to include the higher cognitive functions in their repertory of motivational systems. Although the random list of examples with which he begins his chapter on human nature includes specifically cognitive functions (namely, reification and dichotomization), Wilson fails to include higher cognitive functions in his general exposition of sociobiological categories. These functions nonetheless form a major part of his larger exposition. (Also see Barkow, 1989, pp. 109–110; Brown, 1991, pp. 130–141.) His Enlightenment credo itself suggests that the desire for knowledge can be a primary life purpose (p. 44), and in a later chapter he declares that "what really matters" to people are "sex, family, work, security, personal expression, entertainment, and spiritual fulfillment" (p. 268). Personal expression and entertainment fall within the domain of artistic activity, and spiritual fulfillment consists in the need to envision a humanly meaningful order within the total order of nature. With respect to this latter need, to which he devotes a whole chapter, Wilson hopes that the quest for knowledge, combined with a reverential and morally responsible awe before the powers of nature, will ultimately supplant the illusions of religious myth. More importantly, for the purposes of literary study, Wilson's thesis about the evolutionary origin of the arts implies that they both depict epigenetic rules and are themselves regulated by such rules. They have an adaptive function and form part of the species-typical goal structure. In this respect, Wilson's views can be contrasted with those of other sociobiological theorists who have either treated the arts in a rather unintelligently reductive way as a form of sexual display or have discounted them as parasitic byproducts of other adaptive functions. (See Buss, 1999, pp. 407–410; Constable, 1997; Miller, 1998a, 1998b; Pinker, 1997b, p. 534–543.)

Wilson's chapter on the arts is not among the strongest chapters in *Consilience*, but the limitations in his specifically aesthetic and literary formulations can be corrected through appeal to the principles available within his own wider exposition. The four main limitations in his exposition are (a) the reduction of artistic purposes to the communication of emotion; (b) the failure to include scenario-building as one of the behavioral systems represented in literature and the other arts; (c) a too simple conflation of epigenetic rules with a quasi-Jungian conception of "archetypes" (and a correspondingly inadequate conception of the roles both of behavioral ecology and of individual psychology in the analysis of literary themes); (d) and a failure to envision the integration of substantive epigenetic themes (such as mating strategies or cheater detection) with specifically formal aesthetic and literary structures.

The limitations in Wilson's formulations about literature and the other arts are due in good part to one of those evolved cognitive propensities he himself describes so astutely—the tendency toward simple dichotomization: dark and light, in-group and out-group, good and evil. The dichotomy that in Wilson's case supplants precise analysis is the standard opposition between feeling and thought, an opposition that carries over into a rigid opposition between art and science. "The defining quality of the arts is the expression of the human condition by mood and feeling, calling into play all the senses, evoking both order and disorder" (p. 213). To emphasize the function of feeling in the arts, in contrast to the exclusion of feeling in scientific formulations, is perfectly reasonable, but if the contrast is made absolute it becomes invalid and misleading. In a formulation to which Shattuck (1998, p. 19) rightly takes exception, Wilson declares that artistic productions "are meant to be delivered directly to the sensibilities of the beholder without analytic explanation" (p. 213). In this supposed renunciation of explanation, "the arts are the antithesis of science" (p. 218). On the face of it, this proposition is false. Virtually all literature, even drama, contains some explanatory, meditative, essayistic content. Consider Hamlet's speech on the function of drama as holding the mirror up to nature. Some literature, like the poetry of Wallace Stevens or the novels of George Eliot, Tolstoy, or Conrad, are highly philosophical and contain immense efforts to explain themselves and everything else—the cosmos, history, the nature of civilization.

Literature does not restrict itself to the depiction of people operating out of instinctive motives—seeking sex and power—though these motives do in fact constitute a deep core of literary representations. Both the authors of fictional representations and the characters depicted in them are sentient agents. A significant part of their activity is interpretive activity. They are trying to make sense of the world, to construct usable models or scenarios. They often and even usually bias these constructions toward their own interest or vanity (see Sugiyama, 1996), but they also construct normative models of the kind of communities in which they wish to live—or alternatively they construct satiric and dystopic models of the kinds of communities they find antipathetic (See Cooke, 2002).

The meaning systems created by authors depend very largely on the relation among at least three sets of interpretive models or scenarios: the author's own (generally privileged) version of truth and reality; the versions formulated by the characters depicted, and the version implicitly attributed to the putative audience. The putative audience usually consists in the author's own community, though it can also consist in the larger audience of humanity in general. The versions of reality presented by the characters usually conflict among themselves, with each character or set of characters offering competing versions of the dramatic interactions in which they are mutually involved. The author negotiates with the meaning systems of his characters and negotiates simultaneously with the expectations, values, sympathies, and antipathies of his or her putative readers. (See Storey, 1996; and in this vol., see part 2, chapters 3, 5, snd 6.) No theory of literature that eliminates "explanation" can adequately account for such complex interactions, and without them the interpretation of "meaning" remains rudimentary. The theory of scenarios is one of the triumphs of Wilson's book. He has merely failed to incorporate it adequately into his theory of literary representation.

The failure to incorporate the idea of scenarios is closely linked with the failure to integrate substantive epigenetic themes with formal literary structures—with techniques of narrative, point of view, and genre, or with matters of style and specifically aesthetic properties. One excellent example of such integration appears in an essay by Brian Boyd, who connects the development of free-indirect discourse with the evolved psychological propensity toward cheater detection (1998, p. 22). More generally, one could argue that irony is a fundamental and pervasive literary device designed for the purpose of detecting and

exposing hypocrisy and deceit. Such detection is a major part of the sociobiological theory of social evolution. As Wilson himself notes, "More than error,
more than good deeds, and more even than the margin of profit, the possibility
of cheating by others attracts attention. It excites emotion and serves as the
principal source of hostile gossip and moralistic aggression by which the integrity of the political economy is maintained" (p. 172). All formal literary
structures are prosthetic developments of evolved cognitive structures that
serve adaptive functions. So long as theorists think of literature as purely emotional and expressive, they will be impeded in the effort to analyze the cognitive
mechanisms and sociobiological functions of formal literary structures.

One of the most serious deficiencies in standard versions of evolutionary psychology is the commitment to a model of the brain consisting exclusively of domain-specific modules—the "Swiss army knife" model of the brain. The reason
for this bias is easy to understand. In opposition to standard social science, the
evolutionary psychologists, like Wilson, wish to affirm the idea of an "adapted
mind" or structured human nature. Since standard social science attributes all
psychological structure to some external social or cultural force, it is committed
to the idea of the brain as a blank slate or all-purpose computer. Succumbing to
the instinct for partisan dichotomization, evolutionary psychologists have rejected the idea of the all-purpose computer, and along with it they have sometimes rejected all domain-general intelligence. (See Chiappe and MacDonald,
2003; MacDonald, 1990, 1998a, 1998b; Mithen, 1996, 2001; D. S. Wilson, in press;
and in this vol., see the introduction; part 1, chapter 6; part 2, chapter 6.) To deny
all general intelligence is to run counter to common observation, and this is not
an error that Wilson makes. On the contrary, he affirms that "the most distinctive
qualities of the human species are extremely high intelligence, language, culture,
and reliance on long-term social contracts" (p. 224). In reconstructing the evolution of mind, Wilson presents general intelligence as a major advantage but also
as major problem—as a source of confusion and disorientation—and he argues
that the arts evolved as a means for counterbalancing this confusion:

> There was not enough time for human heredity to cope with the vastness of new
> contingent possibilities revealed by high intelligence. . . . The arts filled the gap.
> Early humans invented them in an attempt to express and control through
> magic the abundance of the environment, the power of solidarity, and other
> forces in their lives that mattered most to survival and reproduction. The arts
> were the means by which these forces could be ritualized and expressed in a
> new, simulated reality. They drew consistency from their faithfulness to human
> nature, to the emotion-guided epigenetic rules—the algorithms—of mental de-
> velopment. (p. 225)

By building models of reality, the arts link all contingent and particular circumstances to the deep structure of elemental motives. They make psychologically
meaningful connections between elemental motives and the peculiarities in

specific configurations of culture and of individual experience. The arts thus consist neither in the representation of differences and unique moments, as Shattuck, Todorov, and others would have it, nor in the representation of common or universal human experiences, as the neoclassical theorists believed. The arts can be more accurately conceived as consisting in something like the combination of the two, but even this idea of a combination of universals and particulars needs to be qualified. A species-typical goal structure is a statistical aggregate, and any given person has an elementary motivational structure that varies, in however infinitesimal a degree, from the statistical average. In certain cases, the differences are substantial. For instance, the hierarchy of motives in homosexual writers is likely to differ substantially from that in the heterosexual structures taken as normative by sociobiological theorists. The motivational structure of men differs on average from that of women. The concerns of the old are not identical to those of the young, and each strongly marked personality type has its own distinct structure of goals and satisfactions. (See Buss, 1990, 1995; MacDonald, 1995b; Segal and MacDonald, 1998; D. S. Wilson, 1994; Wilson, Near, and Miller, 1998.) In all these cases, peculiarities of individual identity and personal experience make some difference. The commonalities of human nature make it possible for people to communicate across such differences, but when writers negotiate scenarios among themselves, their characters, and their audiences, such differences are a vital part of the total meaning system.

Wilson himself notes the interaction of "human nature," "historical circumstances," and "idiosyncratic personal experience" (p. 218). Moreover, in his exposition of scenarios, he identifies "the self" as "the key dramatic character of the scenarios" (p. 119), and he thus rightly implies the necessity of a psychology that pays due attention to the peculiarities of individual identity. His commentary on literature is nonetheless heavily weighted toward the universal aspects of fictional representation, and these aspects are conceived too simply as a set of static archetypal motifs—"the widely recurring abstractions and core narratives that are dominant themes in the arts" (p. 218). Drawing on Joseph Campbell and others, Wilson lays out a standard set of supposed archetypes, but these mythic themes are restricted largely to tribal and barbarian conditions of culture. All such formulations lack an adequate conception of adaptive flexibility. The epigenetic rules, as Wilson himself understands in his general psychological theory, are a set of potentials with a wide range of possible phenotypic expressions. (See Griffiths, 1997.) As sociobiology and evolutionary psychology become mature sciences, they will become increasingly capable of accounting for the complex interactions of epigenetic rules and specific environmental conditions—conditions that display significant historical and cultural differences. As sociobiological literary study progresses in tandem with sociobiology, it will leave behind the idea of fixed themes and unvarying archetypal images.

Sociobiology has made major advances in providing a map of elemental human motives rooted in our evolutionary history, and Wilson has been one of the most creative and influential figures in this movement. The program I am propounding here is fully in accord with the tenor of his larger argument in *Consilience*. I am urging that sociobiology become fully consilient with all standard psychology, including the psychology of development, the theory of individual differences in personality, and the interaction of instinctive biases and general intelligence. By integrating this more circumspect set of theories with concepts from traditional theories of cultural history, sociobiologists would achieve a mature theory of cultural ecology. I am urging further that sociobiological literary analysis become consilient with the best theory available from the traditional study of literature. This study includes both the techniques of formal analysis made available by the New Critics and their successors and the categories of historical analysis made available in studies of genre and period. Sociobiological literary study must incorporate terms such as "realism" and "symbolism," "tragedy," "comedy," and "satire." It must offer cogent sociobiological explanations for techniques of narrative, point of view, and style. It will have achieved consilience and will have mastered its subject when it can integrate the sociobiological theory of inclusive fitness, the theory of proximal mechanisms from evolutionary psychology, and the most subtle insights of traditional interpretive criticism. Within the total body of knowledge envisioned by Wilson, literary study is a specialized area of research, but as he rightly says, it is a crucial test case for the validity of his vision of a unified total body of knowledge. If we can formulate a theory and a methodology that links our deep evolutionary history, our evolved psychological structures, our cultural history, and the formal structures of literary texts, we shall have made a major contribution to the advancement of scientific knowledge. This is a goal worth working toward, and it is within our reach.

8
Ecocriticism, Cognitive Ethology, and the Environments of Victorian Fiction

For other comments on ecocriticism, see "Organism, Environment, and Literature" (in this vol., part 2, chapter 4).

In the past ten years or so, ecological literary criticism—that is, criticism concentrating on the relationship between literature and the natural environment—has become one of the fastest growing areas in literary study. Ecocritics now have their own professional association, their own academic journal, and an impressive bibliography of scholarly studies. Ecocritical scholars divide their attention between "nature writing" and ecological themes within all literature. That is, some scholars write on Thoreau, John Muir, Aldo Leopold, and Annie Dillard; others write on topics such as the representation of nature in Romantic poetry, the American West as a symbol, metaphors of landscape, or Dante's Inferno as a polluted ecosystem. Ecocritics have a distinct subject matter, and they share in a certain broad set of attitudes, values, and public policy concerns, but they do not yet have a firmly established framework of commonly accepted theoretical principles. In the absence of any overarching theory, ecocritics have usually sought to incorporate their ecological subject matter within other, already established theoretical schools: feminism, Bakhtin's dialogism, Lacanian psychology, or the idealist philosophy of English Romanticism and American transcendentalism. Most commonly, ecocritics have affiliated themselves with the standard contemporary blend of Foucauldian ideological criticism—a blend that is vaguely Marxist and Freudian, generally radical, and strongly tinctured with deconstructive irrationalism and textualism. (For a representative sampling of the theoretical range, see the essays in Glotfelty and Fromm, 1996; for Darwinian perspectives on ecocriticism, see, see Fromm, 1996, 1998, 2001; Love, 1998a, 1998b, 2003, and in this vol., see part 2, chapter 6, and the critique of Kroeber in part 1, chapter 5.)

Given their specialized themes and topics and their ready affiliation with the standard theoretical blend, ecocriticism might seem little more than a special topic area within the general field of contemporary literary study. But ecocritics do not see themselves in that way. They share in a feeling of being at the

forefront of critical response to an urgent practical problem of world-historical magnitude: the prospect of irreversible environmental devastation. They
thus have a strong sense of a political mission, and they often feel that the ur-
gency of their environmental concerns should sanction realigning the canon
to give much greater prominence to nature writers and to the study of ecological themes. In their view, the natural world claims a special status as the ultimate ground and frame of all existence. It is an object of peculiar veneration
and of primary experiential importance.

The special conceptual status of ecology as a theme and a topic necessarily
raises a question about its theoretical import. If the subject of ecocriticism is
the relation of literature and the natural world, and if this relation is more important and more elemental than any other concern, does it not follow that
ecocriticism should identify itself as a matrix for all literary study? To put the
question operationally, in what way could ecology, as a subject matter and a
concept, generate a theory of literature? Since the relation between organisms
and natural environments is a necessary precondition of all experience, one
could reasonably argue that the special topic of ecocriticism is more elemental
than the topics of feminism, Marxism, or any other form of political criticism,
and that the basic physical conditions of organic life take conceptual precedence over semiotics and theories of "culture" and "discourse."

I shall argue that ecology cannot by itself generate a theory of literature or
serve as the basis for a theory of literature, but I shall also argue that responsiveness to the sense of place is an elemental component of the evolved human
psyche and that it thus can and should be integrated into a Darwinian literary
theory. E. O. Wilson's notion of "biophilia" provides a Darwinian alternative to
the ecological transcendentalism of "deep ecology," and the evolutionary epistemology of Konrad Lorenz provides a Darwinian rationale for locating the
human psyche within its physical world. In constructing a bridge between
the evolutionary epistemology of Lorenz and the idea of place within verbal
narrative, I shall make use of a new branch of Darwinian aesthetics, Joseph
Anderson's "ecological" version of "cognitive film theory."

In order to illustrate the ways in which setting can be integrated into a Darwinian literary criticism, in the latter part of this essay I shall discuss the varieties and functions of setting within British fiction of the nineteenth century. I
shall argue that setting or physical place is an elemental condition of human experience and that it is consequently an elemental component of literary meaning. I shall argue also that setting is enmeshed with other aspects of experience
and meaning, with the themes of sexual identity that preoccupy most evolutionary psychologists, but also with themes of individual development, cultural
criticism, and cosmic order that these psychologists sometimes overlook.

In *Biophilia*, E. O. Wilson has an imaginatively arresting passage formulating the relations among different levels of biological analysis. He fixes on a
specific scene of two men walking and talking together, and he invites us to re-

gard them within differing temporal and spatial contexts—from the microseconds of biochemical reactions to the millennia and eons of evolutionary time. All of life is dependent on biochemical reactions, but they operate at a temporal scale far below the threshold of ordinary human perceptions. Moving toward the other end of the temporal scale, Wilson observes that within ecological time, "biochemical events have been compressed beyond reckoning. Organisms are no more than ensembles defined by the mathematical laws of birth and death, competition, and replacement" (1984, p. 43). For evolutionary time, the threshold interval is about a thousand years, and on this scale "individuals lose most of their relevance as biological units" (p. 44). The scale of time and space on which this exercise begins—the scale of two men walking and talking together—is that of the individual organism. Parceling out biological disciplines in accordance with this temporal scale, Wilson locates organismic biology between the extremes of molecular biology, measured in microseconds, and evolutionary time, measured in millions of years. Time in organismic biology can be measured in seconds, minutes, days, seasons, and lifetimes. These are the units of time in which we organize our behavior and in which we recollect our experience. As Wilson puts it, organismic biology "explores the way we walk and speak" (p. 44). It is worth lingering over this observation. Human feeling, motivation, and thought occur only in individual minds. The individual mind is the locus of experience and meaning, and it is, consequently, on this level that we must seek the organization of meaning in literary texts.

Literature is produced by the psyche, not the ecosystem, and the psyche has been produced by natural selection. The direct causal force that creates complex cognitive structures is not an ecological principle of community, of sustainable growth, or of the stable interchange of energy within a biosphere. The direct causal force that creates complex adaptive structures is natural selection. Individuals interact with their environments, and natural selection always operates within the constraints of a specific ecological context, but ecology is itself neither the locus of meaning nor the ultimate regulative principle within the total set of biological relations. The locus of meaning is the individual psyche, and the ultimate regulative principle is inclusive fitness, the differential transmission of genes.

Before turning to the question of how environmental responsiveness can be incorporated into a Darwinian psychology and a Darwinian literary theory, we should briefly consider an ecologically based alternative to Darwinism—the utopic ecology of Joseph Meeker's *The Comedy of Survival: Literary Ecology and a Play Ethic.* This book was first published in 1974 but has been substantially rewritten in two subsequent editions, most recently in 1997. So far, Meeker's book is the only sustained effort to found a theory of literature on concepts that are specifically ecological in character. Meeker has a background in both comparative literature and animal ethology (he studied with Konrad

Lorenz), and in the most recent edition of his book he has incorporated reference to prominent works of sociobiology and evolutionary psychology. Despite these putative ethological and evolutionary affiliations, Meeker's theory is only loosely and impressionistically associated with sociobiology and evolutionary psychology. Meeker makes no empirically conscientious effort to identify a structure of human motives and cognitive mechanisms that have evolved through an adaptive process of natural selection. Instead, he projects his own ethical and aesthetic values onto evolution, and he then employs his own vision of evolution—a vision that is more akin to Rousseauistic fantasy than to Darwinian science—as a sanction for those very values he has projected onto it. Meeker likes comedy and dislikes tragedy, so he maintains that "comedy grows from the biological circumstances of life" and is "unconcerned with cultural systems of morality" (1997, p. 15). Tragedy, in contrast, is purely cultural, that is, unnatural, and it is specifically Western. By developing a sense of self, by engaging in goal-oriented behavior, and by making moral judgments, tragic protagonists disrupt the blissful quietude of the natural order and make themselves vulnerable to "strong emotions" (p. 15). The emotions of comedy, Meeker feels, are not strong but playful, and they arise from exactly the same playfulness that characterizes evolution. In both evolution and comedy, play is governed by a set of "ground rules" that can guarantee an emotionally successful outcome. "Organisms must adapt themselves to their circumstances in every possible way, must studiously avoid all-or-nothing choices, must seek alternatives to death, must accept and revel in maximum diversity, must accommodate themselves to the accidental limitations of birth and environment, and must prefer cooperation to competition, yet compete successfully when necessary" (pp. 20–21). By taking evolutionary biology as a guide, ecological literary critics can escape from tragic sensations, restore the joyous quietude of nature, and make objectively correct judgments of tonal value.

In *The Descent of Man* (1981), Darwin attributes human morality to the capacity to compare present action with the past and the future and hence to assess the consequences of our acts in the light of our evolved feelings of social sympathy. We feel sympathy for conspecifics, and in this respect we are like other social animals, at least among the mammals, but moral judgment is a complex and peculiarly human phenomenon depending on our highly evolved intelligence. By repudiating goal-oriented behavior and moral judgments, Meeker tends toward eliminating the specifically human from his aesthetic organon, and in this respect he affiliates himself with the school of ethical philosophy known as "deep ecology." Deep ecology is a form of radical biotic egalitarianism that locates value not in human beings but in ecosystems. Deep ecology defines itself primarily through its opposition to "anthropocentrism" or human-centered systems of value and meaning. Ecocritics who wade into deep ecology are wont to say things like "there exists not one scrap of evidence that humans are superior to or even more interesting than, say, lichen"

(Manes, 1996, p. 22). Or, as another critic puts it, "The most important challenge to traditional hierarchies in ecology is the concept of biocentrism—the conviction that humans are neither better nor worse than other creatures (animals, plants, bacteria, rocks, rivers), but simply equal to everything else in the natural world" (S. Campbell, 1996, p. 128). (Devall and Sessions, 1985, are a standard source for deep ecologists.)

As a form of radical egalitarianism, deep ecology reverses the ethical content of traditional social Darwinism, but it shares the basic category error of social Darwinism. Both social Darwinists and deep ecologists formulate a general concept of some cosmic natural process, and they wrongly use this concept as a model or pattern for human ethical norms. Both the social Darwinist and deep ecological conceptions of nature—as the arena of ruthless individualism and the Edenic abode of utopic egalitarianism—are partial and inadequate. In emotional quality, one is cynical and the other is sentimental, but both fail to take account of the evolved structure of motivations that are specific to human beings; and both erroneously invest the whole natural order with moral characteristics that are appropriate only within the human sphere.

Deep ecologists adopt a stance more radical than that of the standard postmodern blend. Standard radicals declare their wish only to subvert the hegemony of white male European heterosexuals of the ruling classes and to champion the cause of nonwhites, women, non-Europeans, homosexuals, and the proletariat, but it has not occurred to them to seek to subvert the hegemony of human beings in general and to champion the cause of lichen, bacteria, and rocks. If the deep ecologists were quite serious in their anti-anthropocentrism, they would of course be quite mad. But deep ecology is not a serious philosophy or a serious basis for a literary theory. It is only another and yet more decadent form of radical posing. Manes does not seriously wish to read novels that feature lichen as protagonists, nor does Campbell seriously propose to regard rocks and bacteria with the same respectful concern for their sensibility that she expects them to show to hers. Meeker does mention that he compelled a small boy to apologize to a rock the boy had kicked (1997, p. 111), but this is not serious, and Meeker most certainly does not seriously reject all goal-directed behavior. If nothing else, writing and publishing three editions of a book involves very extensive goal-directed behavior. Nor does he seriously repudiate all polarization of good and evil. Indeed, he rejects goal-directed behavior precisely because he considers it evil, and he celebrates an ethic of play precisely because he considers it good. As Warwick Fox observes, in a sympathetic account of the movement, "Deep ecology has been elaborated within a philosophical context rather than a sociological or political context" (1989, p. 24). Armchair radicalism need fear nothing from the consequences or inconsequentiality of the stances it adopts. (On sentimentalism in deep ecology, see Fromm, 1998; Ridley, 1997, chapter 11. For a serious discussion of ecological problems, see E. O. Wilson, 1992, 1998, chapter 12.)

Deep ecology is not serious, but a passionate responsiveness to the natural world is a real and important part of the human psyche. In order to incorporate this psychological reality into our understanding of literary theory, we need make no appeal to transcendental or mystical values invested in the ecosystem. We can appeal instead to the evolved structure of human motives. The desire to come into close contact with the natural world, and the satisfaction that contact gives, make themselves most apparent in nature writers—in Thoreau and Muir, Leopold and Abbey. In them, the feeling for nature has been isolated, concentrated and refined, but the same feeling, diffused and intermixed with other feelings, is part of the universal human experience, and it is a universal aspect of literary representation. E. O. Wilson isolates the biotic aspect of this experience and seeks to bring it within the range of empirical psychological study. He calls it "biophilia," and he defines it as "the innately emotional affiliation of human beings to other living organisms" (1993, p. 31). Elaborating on this hypothesis of an innate desire for contact with nature, Stephen Kellert proposes that "much of the human search for a coherent and fulfilling existence is intimately dependent upon our relationship to nature" (1993, p. 43). He argues that biophilia is universal, that it has adaptive value, and that fulfilling it might "constitute an important basis for a meaningful experience of self" or personal identity (p. 60).

Biophilia does not appear in most of the standard lists of basic motives compiled by sociobiologists and evolutionary psychologists. They tend to concentrate on motives directly pertaining to survival and reproduction, and much more to reproduction than to survival. Books on mating strategies are proliferating rapidly, but there have been no recent books that take as their subject the psychological structures keyed specifically to survival. This emphasis on reproduction perhaps reflects the fact that in evolutionary terms survival is subordinate to reproduction. As the male praying mantis could attest, the crucial requirement of natural selection is not that one survive indefinitely but only that one survive long enough to reproduce. Even so, in order for human beings to reproduce effectively—to produce offspring and raise them to maturity—they must survive quite a long time, say a minimum of twenty or thirty years—and they must do so in a difficult and dangerous world. The preoccupation with mating psychology and the relative neglect of motives appertaining to survival probably reflects a prejudice or distortion resulting from the conditions of health and security in the modern world. These are the conditions in which evolutionary psychologists themselves live, but they are very different from the Pleistocene conditions in which humans evolved.

The conservationist and nature writer Aldo Leopold says that in the wilderness he is "back in the Pleistocene" and that outdoor recreations are "essentially primitive" and "atavistic" (1987, pp. 148, 181). In Leopold's own experience, those recreations prominently involve hunting, fishing, providing fire, securing shelter, and managing elementary technologies that minister to animal needs.

Throughout most of our evolutionary history, an alert attentiveness to the natural world would have been crucial to our survival, and the latent emotional responsiveness that attends this adaptive function has not disappeared with the advent of controlled climates and supermarket foods.

At the present time, the immediate problems of shelter, hunger, and physical danger are less pressing, at least for those of us in the affluent West, but we are all rapidly becoming conscious of great potential danger from a catastrophically degraded natural environment. In this respect, the effects of mismatch have come full circle. That is, modern industry and technology have at first detached us from our close and immediate dependence on the natural world, though without eliminating our sense of emotional connection to it, but they have then also created new dangers, and these dangers have fueled the growing concern for environmental conservation. At no point in this sequence has nature become emotionally and imaginatively unimportant to us.

No organism can be understood except in its interactive relations with its total environment. An organism is never an isolated thing. By definition and in brute reality the world that an organism inhabits is part of that organism. The organism carries that world embedded and molded into every inmost fold of its physiology, its anatomy, and its psyche. Ecology is not a matrix category that can serve as a transcendent sanction for normative literary values or as a source for foundational concepts of literary structure. It can be linked to literary theory only through the intervening medium of human nature, but human nature can itself be understood only in its adaptive relationship to its environment. Writers—especially great writers—vividly apprehend the fundamental conditions of experience, and they make these conditions part of their total imaginative structures. The felt quality of experience within a natural world is one of those fundamental conditions of experience. It should also be one of the fundamental categories of literary analysis.

Up to the present time, literary theorists and critics who have attempted to incorporate Darwinian theory into their conceptual apparatus have tended to concentrate heavily on sexual and social interactions, and especially on sexual interactions. In this trend they have no doubt been influenced by the preoccupations both of evolutionary psychology and of mainstream literary theory. (Deleting from the *MLA Annual Bibliography* all entries oriented to feminism, gender studies, and psychoanalysis would reduce the publication from the size of a large book to that of a thin pamphlet.) There are good reasons for such preoccupations. Problems of human identity, motivation, and feeling are the central topics of literary representation; reproduction is elemental for all organisms; reproductive relations form the basis for human social organization; and all aspects of reproduction are necessarily saturated with the emotional forces that regulate behavior. All of these emotionally intensive aspects of personal life are nonetheless contained within a broader physical reality, and they can be adequately understood only when we take account of that reality.

Konrad Lorenz—one of the founders of modern ethology and also a seminal figure in evolutionary epistemology—concisely formulates the larger context within which we need to situate the motivational concerns of evolutionary psychology. "All human knowledge derives from a process of interaction between man as a physical entity, an active, perceiving subject, and the realities of an equally physical external world, the object of man's perception" (1978, p. 1). Sense organs and the central nervous system have evolved so that organisms can "acquire relevant information about the world" and can "use this information for their survival" (p. 6). The Darwinian developmental psychologist John Bowlby follows Lorenz on this crucial point, and he argues that cognitive maps "can be of all degrees of sophistication from the elementary maps that we infer hunting wasps construct to the immensely complex world-picture of an educated Westerner" (1982, p. 80).

In *The Reality of Illusion: An Ecological Approach to Cognitive Film Theory*, Joseph Anderson does not cite Lorenz or Bowlby, but he constructs an ethological argument for cognitive adaptation very similar to theirs, and he uses this argument as the basis for an incisive analysis of the techniques of cinematic representation. Human beings have always been participants in the "life-and-death struggles" that pervade nature, and spatial orientation is necessary for survival (1996, p. 104). "While moving around, continually shifting our own position we are keeping track of where we stand in and amongst the objects we are looking at" (p. 104). Cinema constructs narratives through the framing and cutting of discrete visual scenes—that is, discrete segments of space extending through time. The scope of these segments parallels that which Wilson identifies as the "organismic" scale. "Spatially, we can perceive things as small as a grain of sand or as large as a mountain, and our sense of time ranges from about a tenth of a second to perhaps three generations of our family" (p. 97). Given his emphasis on the evolution of adaptive structures oriented to survival, Anderson might well have labeled his theory "ethological" or "evolutionary." By calling it "ecological," he signifies that "as meaning-seeking creatures we are not outside the environmental system looking in at it. We are inside the system, part of it, affecting and being affected by the environment" (p. 44).

By expounding the evolved, adaptive character of audiovisual orientation, Anderson seeks to explain why movies are so accessible, so universally intelligible, and so compelling in their effects. In this explanatory purpose, he joins with film theorist Noel Carroll, who suggests that movies rely on cognitive aptitudes that are more natural or "biological" than verbal narratives. Carroll argues that movies "rely on a biological capability that is nurtured in humans as they learn to identify the objects and events in their environment," and he maintains that "the rapid development of this picture-recognition capacity contrasts strongly with the acquisition of a symbol system such as language" (1988, pp. 140, 139). People learn to watch movies more quickly and easily than they learn to read. True enough, but the implications of this observation can be stretched to cover a false proposition: the idea that verbal narratives operate on a cultural plane that is somehow disconnected from innate and evolved characteristics of human beings. "Insofar as movies are constituted of a mode of representation connected to biological features of the human organism, they will be generally more accessible than genres in other media, such as the novel, that presuppose the mastery of learned conventions, such as specific natural languages" (p. 143). As Derek Bickerton (1990) and Steven Pinker (1994, 1995, 1997b) explain, language acquisition develops reliably and spontaneously, and it depends on evolved cognitive aptitudes. Since it is a peculiarly human acquisition, it is a late development in the phylogenetic sequence. And of course, in the development of cognitive skills, decoding written verbal narratives takes us yet one step further beyond decoding oral narratives. Ontogenetically, language acquisition develops more slowly than the capacities for spatial orientation that humans share with other animals, and the acquisition of written language more slowly still, but language is for all that no less natural or "biological" the visual perception. Once humans have acquired language, they use spatial orientation and language interdependently to comprehend how they are situated in the world.

Filmed and verbal narratives form a continuum. Filmed narratives give a more direct and vivid apprehension of immediate physical reality—of what we can see and hear. Verbal narratives provide easier access to abstract reflection and hence more flexibility in the handling of complex conceptual and temporal relationships. But movies are not devoid of conceptual relations or the superposition of temporal phases, and verbal narratives do not take place in a physical void. (See Beja, 1979; Bluestone, 1957; Boyum, 1989; Cardwell, 2000; Giddings, Selby, and Wensley, 1990; M. Turner, 1996; Whelehan, 1999.) The quality and intensity of responsiveness to the physical and biotic world varies from writer to writer, but virtually any writer worthy of serious attention will register it in some significant fashion. In what remains of this essay, I shall be speaking primarily about British fiction of the nineteenth century— arguably one of the most cultivated and domesticated tracts in all of literature—and one main claim I shall make is that in all these novels nature is a vital and integral part of the total imaginative structure.

A few prominent works of ecocriticism concern themselves primarily with British literature, but there is a strong general bias in the field toward American literature, and among the Americans—with the major exception of Thoreau— toward the literature of the American West. Ecocritical treatments of British literature have gravitated toward the Romantics. (For prominent examples on American and British literature, see Bate, 1991; Buell, 1995; Kolodny, 1975; Kroeber, 1994; Marx, 1964; Nash, 1982.) These canonical predilections reflect a tendency to divide writers into two groups. Those in the favored group are deemed particularly responsive to nature. All the rest are relegated to the realm of purely personal and social preoccupations. For instance, Scott Russell Sanders quotes D. H. Lawrence's appreciative commentary on the presence of the natural world in the fiction of Thomas Hardy, and he says that "while Lawrence's account seems to me largely true of Hardy, it does not apply to the mainstream of British fiction" (1996, p. 183). Sanders mentions a representative sampling of major British novelists, including Defoe, Fielding, Austen, Dickens, and Eliot, and in all these writers he maintains that "the social realm—the human morality play—is a far more powerful presence than nature" (p. 183). He tacitly identifies nature with "wilderness," and he argues that wilderness is more adequately represented by American than by British writers.

British writers of the later nineteenth century lived in a long cultivated, densely populated, and heavily industrialized country, but world exploration, colonial expansion, and the still fresh scientific revelations about geological time and evolutionary transformation offered a wide field for imaginative exploration into wild places. More importantly, there is a deep fallacy in the idea that the world can be simply divided into wild and cultivated tracts, that "nature" can be identified with wilderness, and that all cultivated territory can thus be regarded as somehow outside of nature. (See Fromm to this effect, 1998.) In what follows, I shall first describe some of the more prominent British depictions of wild nature, and then consider the ways nature enters into the cultivated tracts of British domestic fiction.

H. G. Wells ranges, chronologically and geographically, across the whole spectrum of possible human environments. In "A Tale of the Stone Age," he credibly recreates the environment of Paleolithic humans. Many of his short stories are set in remote and exotic regions of the world, and in his science fiction he explores the variety and plasticity of natural environments. In *The Time Machine*, the time traveler goes forward almost a million years, to a world that has been cultivated into a perfect garden but in which humans have degenerated into divergent subhuman species of predators and prey. In his second voyage, the time traveler advances billions of years to witness the final decay of the sun into a red giant and the imminent extinction of all life on earth. In *War of the Worlds*, Martian invaders use advanced technology to devastate the cultivated landscape of England, and this landscape begins rapidly to revert to wilderness, but the Martians are themselves subject to "the action of natural selection" (1978, chapter 6). They are trapped and destroyed by the ecological network of earthly microbes. Along with physical devastation, they leave behind them a new and permanent sense of the fragility and vulnerability of the human world. In *After London*, Richard Jefferies constructs a compelling futuristic fantasy of an England that has been devastated and depopulated by industrial pollution and that is then covered over, in a matter of decades, with forests inhabited by savage tribes. A similar social world, evoked in realistic detail, appears in the novels about the Scottish highlands by both Scott and Stevenson. In some of his later historical stories, Kipling evokes the

primitive tribal phases of British culture, and in his contemporary English stories he retains a sense of the land as the enduring basis of human life. In his
early work, Kipling had made the landscapes and culture of India intimately
familiar to his English audience, and in *The Jungle Books* he creates a fantasy
that recuperates the sensations of savagery. *The Second Jungle Book* also contains a powerful naturalistic story ("Quiquern") about the hunting people
who inhabit the polar regions. In *She* and *King Solomon's Mines*, H. Rider Hag-
gard combines tales of fabulous adventure with realistic topographic and
ethnographic descriptions of Africa. Much of Conrad's early fiction is set in
the jungles and seas of the Malay Archipelago. In *Nostromo*, Conrad powerfully evokes a vast and varied South American topography; and in *Heart of
Darkness*, he broods over the spirit of the African wilderness. Journeying into
the wilderness takes him into the prehuman past. "'Going up that river was like
traveling back to the earliest beginnings of the world, when vegetation rioted
on the earth and the big trees were kings'" (1995, chapter 2). Marlow tells this
tale of the wilderness to a group of modern British professionals, sitting on a
yacht in the mouth of the Thames. To point up the relevance of his story, he
begins it by reminding his listeners that the place in which they sit has also
been "'one of the dark places of the earth'" (chapter 1). As in most serious literature, the natural world is a symbol of Nature. The African wilderness is
"'something great and invincible, like evil or truth'" (chapter 1). It is a primary,
literal reality, but it is also the concrete image of a metaphysical conception
about the ultimate character of the universe.

Robinson Crusoe is probably the most frequently referenced antecedent in
all British fiction, and Crusoe serves as a mythic archetype for the lone individual coming to terms with a wilderness. Dickens's world includes both the
country and the city, but his stories most often and memorably lodge themselves within the labyrinthine and historically layered topography of London.
Dickens nonetheless alludes to *Robinson Crusoe* in every one of his novels until
the last few. In the American section of *Martin Chuzzlewit*, he exploits the experience of his own American travels to depict the miseries of life in an American swamp, but one could plausibly argue that the wildest places in all of
Dickens are the strange holes and corners of the urban world—the slums, pris-
ons, refuse shops, cellars, sealed rooms, gated graveyards, and garbage dumps
evoked in novels such as *Oliver Twist, The Old Curiosity Shop, David Copperfield, Bleak House,* and *Our Mutual Friend.* For Dickens's protagonists, London
is often a dangerous and bewildering wilderness, full of dark lairs that house
monstrous, subhuman predators. The opening lines of *Bleak House* evoke the
setting of Chancery as a sort of primeval chaos predating the human world by
millions of years:

London. Michaelmas Term lately over, and the Lord Chancellor sitting in Lincoln's Inn Hall. Implacable November weather. As much mud in the streets, as if

the waters had but newly retired from the face of the earth, and it would not be wonderful to meet a Megalosaurus forty feet long or so, waddling like an ele-phantine lizard up Holborn Hill. Smoke lowering down from chimney-pots, making a soft black drizzle, with flakes of soot in it as big as full-grown snow-flakes—gone into mourning, one might imagine, for the death of the sun. (1956, chapter 1)

Conrad also thinks of London as another kind of wilderness, a man-made "heart of darkness." In *The Secret Agent*, he turned to London from the South American setting of *Nostromo*, and in his introduction to the later novel he de-scribes his meditation over the transition in settings:

> One fell to musing . . . of South America, a continent of crude sunshine and bru-tal revolutions, of the sea, the vast expanse of salt waters, the mirror of heaven's frowns and smiles, the reflector of the world's light. Then the vision of an enor-mous town presented itself, of a monstrous town more populous than some continents and in its man-made might as if indifferent to heaven's frowns and smiles; a cruel devourer of the world's light. There was room enough there to place any story, variety enough there for any setting, darkness enough to bury five millions of lives. (1990, pp. 40–41)

Like most great English novelists, Conrad is a moralist; that is, in assessing all human behavior, he gives a predominating weight to its moral (or immoral) as-pect. But morality does not present itself to him as an arena of purely personal action separated from nature. Morality is part of human nature, and human na-ture is only the strangest and most exotic growth in the natural world.

What of writers like Fielding, Austen, the Brontës, Gaskell, Thackeray, Trol-lope, Meredith, and Eliot—writers who take predominantly domestic subjects within the human moral comedy? In all of these novelists, place is intimately associated with personal identity. In Fielding, Austen, Thackeray, and Trollope, the place is often an estate, but the estate is never merely an abstract calcula-tion of social status and monetary value. It is a set of buildings in a park, usu-ally surrounded by farms, and it is situated in a district that has woods and fields, towns and villages, farms and manufactures. Characteristically, this whole setting is described in minute topographic detail, and it is not merely described and then set aside as the novelist gets on with the plot; it is kept vividly before the reader's eyes, with all its attendant changes of season and weather, as an essential aspect in the quality of experience.

Plots in the Victorian novel are most often stories of growing up and stories of marriage, but such stories, in real life and in fiction, depend heavily on where and how people live, how they are molded by the weather and the hills and fields around them. We can take Austen as a test case, since one thinks of her as among the most interior and domestic of all writers. In all of her novels the characters are situated in a minutely realized physical place that deeply in-fluences the quality of their feelings. *Sense and Sensibility* offers a representa-tive instance. Early in the novel, the Dashwood ladies have lost their estate through inheritance and are forced to move. They have come down in the world and are obliged to accept the charity of a relative who offers them a cottage. Here is Austen's description of their approach to the cottage:

> The first part of their journey was performed in too melancholy a disposition to be otherwise than tedious and unpleasant. But as they drew towards the end of it, their interest in the appearance of a country which they were to inhabit overcame their dejection, and a view of Barton Valley as they entered it gave them cheerfulness. It was a pleasant fertile spot, well wooded, and rich in pasture. After winding along it for more than a mile, they reached their own house. A small green court was the whole of its demesne in front; and a neat wicker gate admitted them to it. . . .
>   The situation of the house was good. High hills rose immediately behind, and at no great distance on each side; some of which were open downs, the others cultivated and woody. The village of Barton was chiefly on one of these hills, and formed a pleasant view from the cottage windows. The prospect in front was more extensive; it commanded the whole of the valley, and reached into the country beyond. The hills which surrounded the cottage terminated the valley in that direction; under another name, and in another course, it branched out again between two of the steepest of them. (1998, vol. 1, chapter 6)

It is quite true that Austen never roamed over the Canadian Rockies or even tramped through the highlands of Scotland, but it is also true that physical place is a fundamental condition of life in all her novels, and that it is integral with the dramas of mate selection that form her central subjects. *Pride and Prejudice* offers a familiar example. Elizabeth has rejected Darcy's proposal of marriage, and then, as a result of his epistolary explanations and her own later reflections, softened in her feeling toward him. She has not, however, yet actively regretted her rejection of his proposal. While she is touring with her aunt and uncle, they decide to stop by and visit Darcy's estate, on the understanding that he is himself away: Austen describes the approach and the lay of the land in a fashion similar to that in her description of Barton Cottage, and then registers Elizabeth's response. "Elizabeth was delighted. She had never seen a place for which nature had done more, or where natural beauty had been so little counteracted by an awkward taste. They were all of them warm in their admiration; and at that moment she felt, that to be mistress of Pemberly might be something!" (1993, vol. 3, chapter 1). In the peripeties of plot that follow, moral behavior and sensibility have their due place, but neither Elizabeth nor the reader ever again thinks of Darcy without feeling that the qualities of his personal identity—not just his status but his character and temper, his ethical code, his personal manner, and the style of his speech—are inextricably bound up in the physical character of his home.

Austen belongs to the world of neoclassical decorum. Nature is important, but it is nature cultivated and consonant with all the ceremonies of genteel life. Emily Brontë and Thomas Hardy stand at the other end of a scale in style and manner—mingling Romantic passion and naturalistic hardness in a way that escapes the bounds of ceremony. The plot of *Wuthering Heights* works itself out in an alternation and opposition of two locations: on the one side the Grange, situated in a pleasant, sheltered valley and inhabited by the Lintons, who are civilized and cultivated but also weak and soft; and on the other side Wuthering Heights, rough and bleak, exposed to violent winds, and inhabited by the Earnshaws, who are crude and violent but also strong and passionate. The characters are like natural growths from the ground they inhabit. Describing her connection with the earth, Catherine Earnshaw tells Nelly Dean she once dreamed she was in heaven, "'but heaven did not seem to be my home; and I broke my heart with weeping to come back to earth; and the angels were so angry that they flung me out, into the middle of the heath on the top of Wuthering Heights; where I woke sobbing for joy'" (2003, chapter 9). The plot of this story, like that of so many Victorian novels, turns on conflicts between class and romantic attraction. Catherine plans to marry Edgar Linton because he is of a higher class than Heathcliff, but she herself recognizes that class is for her a relatively superficial distinction of personal identity. "'My love for Linton is like the foliage in the woods. Time will change it, I'm well aware, as winter changes the trees. My love for Heathcliff resembles the eternal rocks beneath—a source of little visible delight, but necessary'" (chapter 10). Catherine does not merely use images from nature as metaphoric descriptions of a personal identity and a romantic bond that exist independently of the natural world. In her thinking, personal identity and romantic bonding are constituted out of the very substance of the place in which they are formed. This interpenetration of person and place is so complete that after their death the spirits of Heathcliff and Catherine Earnshaw continue to walk the moors, like spectral emanations of the ground.

Hardy's sense of the interdependence of place and person is as passionate as Brontë's, but he has more feeling for ecological flexibility. Characters in his novels take on the coloring of the country they inhabit, blending insensibly into the landscapes they traverse. After the wretched experiences of a childhood spent with shiftless parents, followed by an episode of seduction and betrayal, Tess Durbeyfield removes to the lush dairy country of the Var Vale, and there she finds herself happier than she has ever been. "She was, for one thing, physically and mentally suited among these new surroundings. The sapling which had rooted down to a poisonous stratum on the spot of its sowing had been transplanted to a deeper soil" (1991, chapter 20). As with Catherine Earnshaw's description of her feelings, this interpenetration of person and place is not simply a fanciful metaphor. The sense of place and season enters into the hormonal and neurological substrate of feeling. "Amid the oozing fatness and warm ferments of the Var Vale, at a season when the rush of juices could almost be heard below the hiss of fertilization, it was impossible that the most fanciful love should not grow passionate. The ready bosoms existing there were impregnated by their surroundings" (chapter 24).

Hardy is an almost exclusively rural writer, but England in the nineteenth century was transforming itself from a primarily agricultural economy into a manufacturing economy. The contrast between the salubrious life of the country and the squalid, unwholesome life of the towns forms a distinct topic in the fiction of the period, and in its most specialized manifestations this topic constitutes something like a subgenre: the Victorian industrial novel. Signal instances include Gaskell's *Mary Barton* and *North and South*, Disraeli's *Sybil or the Two Nations*, Dickens's *Hard Times*, and Eliot's *Felix Holt*. The plots of these novels contain the usual stuff of moral drama—childhood, education, parenting, seduction, betrayal, courtship, marriage, work, status-seeking, friendship, inheritance, theft, and murder. In the stories, as in reality, people struggle to create fulfilling or at least decent lives for themselves, and success or failure in that struggle depends vitally on the kind of place in which they live. Victorian novels commonly conclude in marriage, and the resolution of happy comedy often involves an escape from urban squalor into some garden location—as in the creation of a second Bleak House at the end of that novel, or in Dinah Morris's ultimate retreat from the harsh coal country to a pleasant agricultural region in *Adam Bede*. At other times, as in *North and South* or *Felix Holt*, the choices of vocation lead the protagonists to resign themselves to the sadder, grimmer life of the towns. In *Bleak House*, the two Rouncewell brothers go their separate ways, socially and geographically, one to the independence and wealth produced by his ironworks in the scarred and dirty landscape of the industrial North; and the other to the gracious parklands of the South, and thus also to the traditions of servitude to aristocratic power. Social class and personal character diverge and articulate themselves within their distinct topographies, but brothers are brothers still, and their divergence also symbolizes Dickens's sense of a civil tolerance in the deep economic and political divisions of the country.

The interpenetration of character and place has its necessary correlatives in literary style, and style registers meaning at the highest level of philosophical theme in a novel. *Bleak House* will serve for the illustration. *Bleak House* is a multilayered novel, with more than fifty characters, dual narrators, multiple plots, and themes that range across the whole spectrum of human concerns, from intimate problems of personal identity and mate choice, through social and political conflicts, and ultimately to philosophical visions about the ultimate nature of things. One main story, that of the first-person narrator Esther Summerson—provides a nexus of unifying themes for this complex fictional assemblage. Esther is illegitimate and has been raised by a stern and unloving aunt. The central problem in her story is not inheritance or even marriage—though her plot ends in marriage. The most important challenge she faces is that of personal development. While operating under circumstances that would in most cases permanently cripple a personality, she succeeds in creating a coherent sense of personal identity that realizes her potential for emotional fulfillment. She is surrounded by characters who fail to achieve an adequate development—who have never been children or who have never grown up—and all along the way, she is herself threatened with a loss of identity or with deforming substitutions in her social persona. In the midst of a large gallery of characters who are diseased, stunted, or deformed, she constitutes a nucleus of strength and emotional health. Dickens registers her existential success through the testimony of other characters, but he also registers it directly through her relation to nature. In one elaborately staged scene, she is walking in the grounds of Sir Leicester Deadlock, is caught in a thunderstorm, and takes refuge in a lodge. This is her description of the storm:

> The lattice-windows were all thrown open, and we sat, just within the doorway, watching the storm. It was grand to see how the wind awoke, and bent the trees, and drove the rain before it like a cloud of smoke; and to hear the solemn thunder, and to see the lightning; and while thinking with awe of the tremendous powers by which our little lives are encompassed, to consider how beneficent they are, and how upon the smallest flower and leaf there was already a freshness poured from all this seeming rage, which seemed to make creation new again. (1956, chapter 18)

We do not learn much in detail about Esther's education, but a scene like this conveys all the information we need about its effects. We learn here that Esther has not only read Wordsworth but has absorbed his lyricism into her own style, and that along with the lyricism she has fully assimilated his Romantic religion of a beneficent natural order. From this one passage, we know as much as we can be told about the quality of Esther's literary imagination and the largest scope of her philosophic vision. The power of her imagination has preserved her from the deforming accidents of her personal and social circumstances, and that power registers itself in her literary style.

Dickens still participates in a Wordsworthian vision of nature as a beneficent force. Wells, Hardy, and Conrad all share a post-Darwinian sense of natural force that dwarfs all merely human measures of good and evil. Philosophical differences of this magnitude have a major impact on the largest generic and thematic structures in a work of fiction, but in no work of fiction is character ever divorced from physical place. As the evolutionary epistemologists and cognitive ethologists tell us, the necessities of survival have adapted us to find our way in the world, and as both E. O. Wilson and the nature writers remind us, those adaptations carry with them an instinctive sense of emotional connection to the world. The writers of fiction have always intuitively understood that connection. In one aspect, they are like ethologists reporting on the behavior of animals in their natural habitats. They present us not simply with social and moral agents acting out plots but rather with human organisms intricately enmeshed in their environments. The challenge for theorists and critics is to formulate explanatory concepts and interpretive methods that are adequate to account for these primary observations.

Part 2
Adaptationist Literary Studies:
Theory and Practical Criticism

1
The Deep Structure of Literary Representations

Steven Mithen and Michael Gazzaniga make statements that represent complementary extremes in our current evolutionary understanding of the human mind. Mithen declares that "when thoughts originating in different domains can engage together, the result is an almost limitless capacity for imagination" (1996, p. 71). Gazzaniga poses a rhetorical question "What Are Brains For?" The answer is "Sex" (1997, p. 157). Both statements are correct, more or less, but neither by itself provides us with enough structure to build a usable model of literary representations. If we try to go directly from these statements to literary representation, we end up either with too little constraint, or with too much. If we take Mithen's statement alone, we end up with unlimited combinations of images that could only be cataloged seriatim. And if we take Gazzaniga's statement alone, we end up with some version of the simple proposition that all literary works are ultimately about sex, that they are written out of sexual motives, that they represent sexual relationships, and that they are read for the purpose, direct or indirect, of sexual gratification. Neither statement alone provides adequate structure, but if we combine them and mediate between them, we shall find that we now have the means for analyzing literary representations and for understanding the psychological functions of literature.

Throughout this paper, the term "literature" will be used as a shorthand term signifying both oral and written forms of narrative, verse, and dramatic enactment. Writing is an extension of oral communication. Literacy is less than 10,000 years old, and it should be clear that no claim is being made here that literacy and its offshoots are themselves adaptations. When I speak of the adaptive functions of literature, I mean to signify the adaptive functions of the oral antecedents of written stories, poems, and plays. The same arguments that apply to these oral forms will be understood as extending also to their counterparts in written language.

Mithen has assimilated and revised a central concept of evolutionary psychology—the idea that the human mind contains a rich array of innate structures that have evolved through the adaptive process of natural selection. Some of the most prominent evolutionary psychologists (Tooby and Cosmides, Pinker) conceptualize evolved psychological structures as "modules"

103

dedicated to specific domains or adaptive tasks, for example, to visual cognition, mate selection, and predator avoidance. Drawing on recent work by cognitive scientists, mainly psychologists and philosophers, Mithen argues that between 100,000 and 30,000 years ago, the human mind underwent a crucial phase of evolutionary development (1996, p. 194). The modules dedicated to hitherto separate domains became permeable, and the mind began to make analogical connections among them. This reflexive capacity, which Mithen calls "cognitive fluidity," is a necessary precondition for the production of modern culture—for complex technology, science, art, and religion (p. 71).

The concept of cognitive fluidity brings evolutionary psychology into partial alignment with a set of ideas that has already been long-established in a field sometimes called cognitive linguistics or cognitive rhetoric. The seminal text in this field is Lakoff and Johnson, *Metaphors We Live By* (1980). Lakoff and Johnson have published subsequent work independently, and Lakoff has coauthored a book with literary scholar Mark Turner, who has himself published various independent works. Lakoff and Johnson argue that "our ordinary conceptual system . . . is fundamentally metaphorical in nature" (p. 3), and further, that we habitually use constructs from one "domain" of experience to talk about corresponding concepts in other domains (p. 52; and see Johnson, 1987, pp. xiv–xv). Lakoff and Johnson are making a claim not just about the logic of specific figures of speech, as decorations or elaborations of isolated concepts, but about the elementary structures of whole conceptual systems. Propositions of this sort hold out the promise of situating literary analysis within some stable, empirically grounded and philosophically rationalized system of general knowledge. To connect literary study with cognitive science would be to render it thus far scientific—objective, progressive, and technical.

In the nearly two decades since Lakoff and Johnson made their argument, this promise has not been realized. The central problem the cognitive rhetoricians have failed to solve is that of grounding the concept of "domains" within some larger concept of human experience and cognition. In the work of Lakoff, Johnson, and Turner, the concept of domains remains nebulous and variable. They propose to establish order by identifying hierarchies of metaphors, but these hierarchies are themselves grounded in no larger or deeper set of regularities and can provide no stable basis of causal or systematic connection. The closest Turner gets to a systematic order is an apparently random list of categories that he calls "conceptual domains": eating, dress, learning, buildings, travel, combat, and plants. He makes no effort to correlate these domains with the concept of domain-specific modules in evolutionary psychology, nor does he provide any other rationale or organizing principle for the list. He says only that these categories are "basic source domains, grounded in our forms of life" (1991, p. 199).

The failure of cognitive rhetoric is one of the most encouraging developments in the literary theory of the past decade. It is encouraging because the cause of failure is easy to diagnose, and the diagnosis points us very clearly in the direction we need to take. The one crucial element missing in cognitive rhetoric is an ordered system of domains; the necessary precondition for this system is a structured concept of human nature; and the source for this concept is the study of the adapted mind—that is, the study of the evolved structure of the human psyche. One of the best pieces of evidence for this diagnosis can be found in the work of the cognitive rhetoricians themselves. Their own logic leads them inexorably to invoke the adapted mind as the site of metaphoric domains. They simply fail to carry through on their own logic. Johnson titles a book *The Body in the Mind: The Bodily Basis of Meaning, Imagination, and Reason* (1987). Lakoff affirms that "our conceptual systems grow out of bodily experience" (1987). He grounds all "*cognitive models*" in "experience"; and he grounds experience in "the internal genetically acquired makeup of the organism and the nature of its interactions in both its physical and its social environments" (pp. xiv, xv). Together Lakoff and Johnson declare that "our conceptual systems grow out of our bodies" and that "meaning is grounded in and through our bodies" (1999, p. 6). Turner follows these leads. He insists on the bodily basis of meaning and stipulates, "A brain is part of a body and in operation is inseparable from it. Evolutionarily, the brain exists only in order to serve the reproductive and metabolic body of which it is a part" (1991, p. 36; and see M. Turner, 1996, p. 25). Similarly, attempting to integrate cognitive psychology with literary analysis, Spolsky appeals to "the evolutionary history of the species" and to "the genetically inherited architecture of the brain" (1993, pp. 5, 12). Once one has made any such appeal as this, the obvious and inescapable next step is the step toward human ethology or human sociobiology, and it is a step that each of these writers fails to take. Their bibliographies contain almost no titles of books or articles on the evolution of human sexuality, human sociality, or human behavior of any kind. Their emphasis on "the body" has restricted itself largely to concepts of physical direction or orientation—concepts like up and down, and front and back. (On the physical constraints of human existence, also see Barrow, 1995.)

In recent work, Lakoff and Johnson (1999) identify the idea of physical well-being as the source domain for concepts of morality and the idea of family structure as the source domain for concepts of political orientation. These concepts do not form part of a comprehensive conception of a species-typical motivational structure. On the contrary, Lakoff and Johnson reject the concept of a relatively stable set of species-typical characteristics. They argue that in biology, cognitive science, and neuroscience "human nature is conceptualized rather in terms of variation, change, and evolution, not in terms of a fixed list of central features" (p. 557). Given the relatively slow pace of evolutionary change, one cannot legitimately invoke evolution as an antithesis to the idea of a distinctly structured set of species-typical characteristics. The question is whether evolution has produced any such set of characteristics in human beings. The answer from evolutionary psychology is that it has.

In one broad and obvious sense, the problem presented by the failure of cognitive rhetoric is easy to solve. It is simply a matter of expanding one's reading to take in as much information as possible about the evolved structure of the human psyche. Lakoff, Johnson, and Turner are by no means wrong to emphasize the body and even to insist on the primacy of a few directional concepts that regulate physical existence, but we hardly need stop there in defining the architecture of human experience. We already have a large amount of well-documented information about the species-typical structure of human motives and concerns. (For further commentary on cognitive rhetoric, see Carroll, in press; and in this vol., see section 2 of the introduction, and the critique of Mark Turner in part 1, chapter 5.)

The problem that presents itself to us is this: how do we connect our current understanding of species-typical motives with the concept of domain-specific cognition, and further, how do we use these combined concepts for the purposes of literary analysis? The first thing to consider is the actual current status of our understanding of domains and modules.

At first sight, the theory of domains presents a jumbled array of possibilities, a mere disparate list of specialized cognitive mechanisms. For example, Tooby and Cosmides (1992, p. 113) offer a list of special modules for the following functions: face recognition, spatial relations, rigid object mechanics, tool use, fear, social exchange, emotion perception, kin-oriented motivation, effort allocation and recalibration, child care, social inference, sexual attraction, semantic inference, friendship, grammar acquisition, communication pragmatics, theory of mind, "and so on." This is the sequence they themselves give, and the "and so on" signifies an open-ended series. Pinker (1994, p. 420) offers a similar list containing fifteen items. For someone who is concerned with analyzing the imaginative structure of literary texts, lists of this sort would probably not seem very helpful. Taking such a list as a guide, the critic could do little more than catalog metaphors, a practice that would not take us beyond the kind of random analysis of metaphoric structures practiced by the cognitive rhetoricians. It takes us scarcely beyond the unlimited field of metaphoric particularities that has been thoroughly tilled by old-fashioned literary critics since the early decades of this century.

Faced with any such random list, the natural impulse is to start grouping items into larger categories. Among cognitive psychologists concerned with domain-specificity, there is still substantial controversy about the definition, number, and organization of cognitive domains, but there is also a fair degree of consensus about some of the main categories in which to group domains. The starting point for domain-specific reasoning has been the purely sensory modules, like that for visual perception, and the concept of a language module, derived from Noam Chomsky. Beyond these heavily studied modules, there is widespread agreement on the existence of at least three main cognitive domains: the domains of physics, biology, and psychology. (See Carey and Spelke, 1994, p. 171; Cosmides and Tooby, 1994, p. 102; Mithen 1996, p. 51; Pinker 1997b, p. 352; Sperber, 1994, p. 42.) The psychological domain is sometimes called the "theory of mind module," and it consists in the recognition of feelings and thoughts in other minds. The domain of physics is the area in which we can locate the directional metaphors (up-down, etc.) that preoccupy the cognitive rhetoricians. By adding biology and psychology to the purely spatial sphere, the cognitive evolutionary psychologists bring us much closer to the range of subjects and motives that constitute the substance of most literary texts.

Assuming for the moment that there is adequate empirical support for the provisional grouping of domains into a few major categories, how does that advance the case for literary analysis? In order to make use of cognitive domains as categories of literary analysis, we have to correlate domains with some specific structure of human motives and concerns and locate the functions of literary representation within this structure of motives and concerns. Literature represents human motives and concerns, and it is written and read because it satisfies human needs. If evolutionary psychology can give a comprehensive explanation of motives and concerns, it should both provide a taxonomy of themes in literary representation and also explain why people read and write and how literature affects them.

To begin with, how does a list of four or five major cognitive domains translate into a structure of human motives and concerns? At this point, we should recall the question by Gazzaniga. What are brains for? If we reformulate the answer in a less rhetorically striking way, we can say that the function of the brain is to promote *inclusive fitness*. The differential transmission of genes depends on the organism surviving long enough to reproduce, and in human beings it involves also parenting, collateral nepotism, and the successful negotiation of a social environment. These basic requirements result in behavioral mechanisms oriented to solving problems within a limited range of concerns. McGuire and Troisi (1998, p. 61) identify four basic behavioral systems: survival, reproduction, kin assistance, and reciprocation. Following the same logic, Buss (1999) surveys the whole field of evolutionary psychology within a sequence of book sections devoted to (in this order): survival, sex and mating, parenting and kinship, and group living.

Evolutionary psychologists emphasize proximal mechanisms of adaptation, and in this respect they distinguish their method from that of sociobiological thinkers who place a greater emphasis on the direct and immediate pursuit of reproductive advantage. (See Barkow, 1989, p. 296; Betzig, 1991, p. 140; Pinker 1997b, p. 44; Symons, 1992, p. 151; Tooby and Cosmides, 1992,

p. 54.) Evolutionary psychologists nonetheless recognize that all proximal mechanisms can have evolved only under the regulative force of inclusive fitness. Features of living organisms that are physiologically expensive and that display complex functional organization can have evolved only if they enabled the organism to pass on its genes more effectively than other, competing organisms. Thus, Cosmides and Tooby, taking issue with the purely epistemological preoccupations of cognitive psychology, argue that "cognitive mechanisms capable of acquiring knowledge evolved solely because they subserved a larger cognitive architecture that regulated behavior" (1994, p. 105).

The more closely any motive impinges on the elementary principles of inclusive fitness, the deeper it goes into the regulative structure of species-typical motives. The two behavioral systems that most directly impinge on inclusive fitness are survival and reproduction. Discussing a broad range of research into human motives, Buss observes that "power and love emerge consistently and cross-culturally as the two most important dimensions of interpersonal behavior" (1995, p. 21). Kinship relations outside the reproductive nucleus of mates, parents, and children have diminishing levels of affective force, and more remote social relations have still less. In the grouping of domains into four or five major categories, this whole primary set of concerns falls within the basic categories of "psychology" or "social interaction." Reproductive interests—sex, parenting, and family—form a clear and distinct subset of these categories. There is ample evidence for evolved cognitive structures that regulate these specific motives and concerns.

Alexander explains that biologists divide the expenditure of effort in the life cycle into two basic forms of life effort—the somatic and the reproductive (1987, pp. 40–41; and see Geary, 1998, pp. 11, 199; Low, 1998, pp. 138–40; MacDonald, 1997, 1998a; McGuire and Troisi, 1998, pp. 58–59; Ridley, 1999, pp. 12, 127–128). Somatic effort is all the effort an organism expends on gaining resources for its own survival and development. Reproductive effort is all the effort expended on mating, parenting, and aid to kin. These two forms of effort overlap; they are seldom wholly separate. For instance, food-gathering, building shelters, and negotiating a position in a social group all contribute both to our own individual support and to the support of our children and kin. If we accept the idea of modules for social activity and for cognition of the physical and natural world, these modules would be hierarchically subordinate to somatic and reproductive effort.

In order to make any hierarchical principle of human motivation usable for literary analysis, we must stipulate that there is a fundamental parallel between the structure of human motives and concerns and the organizing principles of literary representation. Human beings living in a real physical world and interacting both with their physical environment and with other human beings form the central topic of all literary representation. Cognitive rhetoric emphasizes metaphorical relationships, but this elementary configuration presents us with a primary, literal order of representations. Metaphors are diverse, but they have meaning and force only in the degree to which they reflect the elementary structure of human motives and concerns.

In literature the most frequent and important themes are those that concern individual identity, sexual romance, and the family. Survival is the basis of all adventure stories, and by far the largest proportion of stories that are not strictly oriented to survival are organized around the mating game, the concerns of parents for children, and family relations generally. On the basis of such observations, we can propose a large generalization about the primacy of adventure, personal success, and romance within the themes of world literature, and this kind of generalization can in fact yield hypotheses that are testable through large-scale cross-cultural analyses of literary subjects. (See Fox, 1995; Gottschall, in press; Nettle, in press; Whissel, 1996.)

Both social and cognitive activity are a significant part of what is actually represented in literature, and they are intertwined with themes of personal power and reproductive success, but in literary texts they will almost always have less structural importance than the more primary levels of somatic and reproductive effort. That is, most plots will be grounded more deeply in issues of personal power and love than in problems of social antagonism, social affiliation, and the pursuit of knowledge about the physical and natural world. The broader biological and physical environments that constrain personal and social interaction have their own affective values, and these values are registered in nature poetry and the description of setting. Much of the metaphoric elaboration of intimate human relations derives from images of the natural world. And conversely, virtually all direct representations of the natural world are intertwined and suffused with the images and affects of intimate personal relations.

Literature itself has until recently been the only great repository of information about human nature. Empirical psychology is scarcely a hundred years old, and much of the psychological theory in this century has foundered amidst the sensational and distorted speculations of Freud and the barren reductions of behaviorism. Throughout the greater part of our history, our best psychologists have been playwrights, poets, and novelists. When Hamlet tells the players that the purpose of the poet is to hold "the mirror up to nature" (1963, act 3, scene 2), it is human nature he has most in mind. Literary authors have intuitively understood that the subject matter of literature is human experience, that experience is grounded in common natural motives and feelings, and that sympathetic response to the depiction of experience in texts depends on the common shared experience among authors, the characters depicted, and the audience. Understanding the inner workings of the mind has been the heart and soul of the literary tradition, as it no doubt was the heart and soul of the oral traditions that are the ancestors of all literate cultures.

Any psychological system could become the basis for an associated school of literary analysis, but only a Darwinian conception of the evolved and adapted character of the human mind can provide an understanding of human nature that is sufficiently profound and incisive to correspond with the intuitive understanding embodied in the literary tradition. In the middle decades of this century, literary critics sometimes used Jungian ideas of innate "archetypes" as categories for the analysis of universal human themes, and these categories can be partially but very imperfectly correlated with the themes of evolutionary psychology. (See Carroll, 1995, p. 155–56.) At present, overwhelmingly the most influential version of psychology in literary studies is the Freudian version. Literature itself appeals to a sense of human nature truer and deeper than Freudian doctrine, and evolutionary psychology has already corrected basic elements in the Freudian scheme of analysis. (See Buss, 1999, pp. 217–19; Daly and Wilson, 1990; Degler, 1991, p. 245–269.) Freudian readings of literary texts almost inevitably introduce distorting ideas of incest and castration anxiety, and a form of literary analysis that appeals to evolutionary psychology rather than Freudian psychoanalysis will have a vastly improved access to the deep structure of literary representations. (See Carroll, 1995, p. 44, 410–417, 442–445; Storey, 1996.)

Brown (1991) argues that the idea of the self or of individual persons is a human universal, and Pinker (1997b) includes it as one of the "modules" or cognitive domains. Among human beings, the sense of individual persons is the conscious correlative for the biological concept of the organism, and this concept is an essential precondition for the organization of behavior in goal-directed ways and for the interaction of individuals in social groups. In literary structures, the idea of an individual self is indispensable to the organization of literary meaning. Characters in poems, plays, and stories are individuals, and authors necessarily present their stories from some distinct point of view. All emotion and cognition is organized within the individual mind, and the response of audiences to literary works is thus necessarily lodged in individuals, even when the response is collectively experienced, as in the audience of a play. For these reasons, the study of individual psychology is integral both to the Darwinian conception of human beings and to literary analysis.

The modern study of Darwinian psychology has tended to concentrate on the idea of human universals, and within the Darwinian community itself there has been controversy over the adaptive significance of individual variations. Theorists who believe that individual variations are not adaptively important argue that adaptations display complex functional structure and that any such structure must be common to the species as a whole. (See Tooby and Cosmides, 1990.) Other theorists seek to explain the adaptive value of variation within a given ecology. (See Barash, 1997; Buss 1995, p. 20, 1999, pp 393–398; MacDonald, 1990; Wilson, 1994.) For the purposes of identifying a species-typical human psychological design, the crucial point to be made is that human universals and individual variations are not mutually exclusive concepts. The dimensions through which individual identity is structured and in which it necessarily varies are themselves universals. These dimensions are part of the evolved structure of human nature.

Tooby and Cosmides (1992, pp. 73–77) argue that evolutionary psychology must work both backward and forward, from hypotheses about ancestral environments to predictions about evolved structures, and from observation of evolved structures to speculations about ancestral conditions. Any information on universal features of the human design, even if they have been studied by scientists indifferent to evolutionary psychology, provide substantive empirical data that can be used by evolutionary psychologists.

One of the most important set of structures for individual identity are the five factors of personality. (See Ashton et al. 1998; Bouchard, 1994; Digman, 1990; McCrae, 1992, MacDonald, 1995b.). These five factors—extraversion/introversion, agreeableness/antagonism, neuroticism/security, conscientiousness/carelessness, and curiosity/dullness—can be used for the comparative analysis of characters, authors, and audience response. Each of these factors can be described in ways that correlate with a biologically based understanding of human motives and concerns. The extraversion/introversion scale involves the elementary biological terms of organism and environment, measuring whether the organism is more responsive to external stimuli or, alternatively, more attuned to internal processes. In literary terms, the concept of organism and environment correlates with the concept of character and setting, and it is thus an indispensable dimension for assessing literary situations. Agreeableness and antagonism identify the two possible extremes in social interaction. They thus reflect basic principles in the hierarchy of elementary regulative principles for human behavior. Neuroticism involves an array of traits that respond to danger and that are thus signals of threat to survival both of the organism and of his/her kin and social affiliates. Conscientiousness is a quality of character that is essential to personal success and to authority within a social group. Openness or intellect is a measure of responsive sensitivity to the whole range of environmental conditions, physical and social. These latter two factors, conscientiousness and openness, form the basis of the theory of moral psychology worked out by Darwin in *The Descent of Man*, and they remain basic parts of Darwinian ethical psychology. (See Arnhart, 1998; J. Q. Wilson, 1993.)

Individuals vary in the degree to which they are extraverted or introverted, emotionally stable or insecure, intellectually open or dull, friendly or antagonistic, and conscientious or careless, but variations in these dimensions can be likened to variations in other adaptive features of the human design—for example, in keenness of eyesight or hearing, intelligence, physical strength, and sexual attractiveness. (See D. S. Wilson, 1994, p. 233.) The observation of such differences is part of the common experience of everyday social interaction, and evolutionary psychologists have now begun to make reasonable conjectures about the ways in which such differences can be integrated into other fundamental features of the human motivational system. For instance, Ashton et al. (1998) correlate differences of agreeableness and emotional stability both with sex differences and with differential dispositions to kin altruism and reciprocal altruism. (Also see MacDonald, 1995b.)

Buss argues that the dimensions of personality in the five-factor system "summarize the most important features of the social landscape that humans have had to adapt to" (1995, p. 22). (Also see Eysenck and Eysenck, 1985, p. 44; Pinker, 1997b, p. 448). If Buss is correct, and if it is also correct that literary texts reflect an intuitive psychological understanding of human nature, we can anticipate that literary representations will depict the way humans perceive individual differences and integrate their perceptions into elemental motives such as mate-selection strategies. For the sake of illustration, I shall cite here one specific kind of individual difference that enters into stories of female mate selection. Jane Austen's *Pride and Prejudice* can serve as the main example. At the level of sociobiological themes of mate selection, we can see that the heroine, Elizabeth Bennet, marries a male, Darcy, who is higher in status than herself, and that he demonstrates his suitability as a mate in part by extending protection to her endangered kin (her sister Lydia). At the level of resolution appropriate to personality theory, Elizabeth undergoes a process of sorting through the personality factors, learning to make allowances for the qualities of manner attendant on Darcy's introversion, and learning through her experience with Wickham the relatively small reliance to be placed on agreeableness when it is not accompanied by conscientiousness. In the largest thematic structure in the book, she rearranges her whole psychic economy to detach herself from her father, who is cultivated but careless, and to attach herself instead to the ethos of responsibility represented by Darcy. This psychological reorientation plays itself out in dialogue that is concerned with the functions of satire and humor, and thus with the tonal, literary dimensions that correlate with the psychological dimensions. All of the characters in the narrative play the mating game, in accordance with sociobiological rules, but they also form a carefully constructed array of personality types within a psychological economy dominated by the lead couple, and they self-consciously assess one another on the basis of verbal and imaginative styles that reflect their specific psychological constitutions.

Similar kinds of intuitive psychological depictions are integral parts of the meaning system of most fictional narratives. The specific pattern used as the elementary structure of plot in *Pride and Prejudice* is by no means universal but is certainly very common. It appears also, for example, in Hardy's *Far from the Madding Crowd*, Trollope's *Can You Forgive Her?*, and Tolstoy's *Anna Karenina*. In all of these cases, personality dimensions are not alternatives to sociobiological themes of mate selection. They are the more finely nuanced perceptions through which appropriate sexual choices are made. (For literary analyses that integrate sociobiological themes with assessments of personality and locate both within specific cultural contexts, see Boyd, 1998; Carroll, 1995; Jobling, 2001a; Nesse, 1995; Storey 1996; and in this vol., see part 1, chapters 6 and 8; part 2, chapters 3, 5 and 6. For literary analyses that tacitly limit consideration to basic mate selection strategies, see Whissel, 1996; Thiessen and Umezawa, 1998.)

The one configuration of personality characteristics I have given as an example could be supplemented with a wide range of configurations. To give just one more example, sociopathy is a prominent feature of personality analysis. Though it is a characteristic in which individuals display a high degree of variability, it has been conceptualized within the framework of evolutionary psychology. (See Mealey, 1995; J. Q. Wilson, 1993; and on the related topic of Machiavellianism, see Wilson, Near, and Miller, 1998.) The sociopath presents a serious challenge to all human social groups, and it is thus to be expected that literary authors would seize upon this character type as a means of focusing on the problems of social integration. And as it happens, a survey of the antagonists in prominent English novels presents a whole gallery of sociopaths: Blifil in *Tom Jones*, Becky Sharp in *Vanity Fair*, Heathcliff in *Wuthering Heights*, Bill Sikes in *Oliver Twist*, and Ferdinand Lopez in Trollope's *The Prime Minister*. The list could be extended almost indefinitely.

Personality factors can be used in the analysis of characters, authors, and readers. They provide points of entry into the values and sensibility of any given author and a means for assessing the evaluative response of audiences to any given author. For instance, Fielding and his protagonists are robust and good-natured, sensual but friendly and open, outgoing but a little lax in their moral fiber. Rather than attempting to locate this configuration within some supposedly absolute standard of literary merit, we can instead understand that certain kinds of critical temperaments will respond to Fielding with genial warmth, and that others, more neurotically sensitive, withdrawn, and antagonistic, will find him an uncomfortable companion. Pater, in contrast, is introverted, sensual, and narcissistic. He has evoked a narrower range of sympathetic response, but he has a small, distinct cadre of like-minded readers—readers for whom words such as "aestheticism" and "decadence" evoke no unpleasant connotations.

The use of personality factors as categories of analysis need not pretend to be exhaustive. These factors can be combined with any array of significant traits—for instance, of sex or gender, age, social class, national or ethnic identity, and cultural period. (See Sugiyama, 1996, pp. 406–411.) But if personality dimensions are in fact part of the evolved structure of the human psyche, they provide us terms that are in themselves important and that can serve as stable points of comparison.

Pinker observes that "cognitive scientists think of people as Mr. Spock without the funny ears" (1997b, p. 315), and a similar observation could be made of the cognitive rhetoricians. If we accept the stipulation that the organizing principles of literary representation run parallel to the structure of human motives and concerns, we must also accept an implication that takes us outside the range of conceptual analysis in cognitive rhetoric and brings us into the psychology of emotion. Motives and concerns are mediated not, in the first place, by conceptual patterns or metaphoric systems. They are mediated most directly by feelings or affects, by desire and fear, by pleasure and pain. Ekman argues that "the commonalities in the antecedent events that call forth each emotion are the product of our evolution and reflect the most important or frequent events our ancestors encountered" (1994, p. 147). Motives and emotions evolved together. Both have to be understood within the framework of evolutionary psychology.

Metaphors have imaginative and specifically literary value only if they are able to engage and evoke the subjective quality of experience. Feelings are the basis of tone in literary texts, and tone is the basis of generic structure. Working out from a concept of the evolved structure of human motives and concerns, we can derive a reasonable framework for analyzing both the subjects of literary representation and the emotional affects that give subjective value and meaning to represented events. To give value and meaning is to impose shape; it is to define what, subjectively, constitutes an "event."

In the study of emotions, as in the study of cognitive domains and personality factors, there is a good deal of controversy over the identification of the specific units of analysis and the larger categories within which they are grouped. There is nonetheless a fair consensus on certain core emotions, particularly on the seven emotions identified by Ekman as having distinct facial expressions that are recognizable across diverse cultures. These seven basic emotions are joy, sadness, fear, anger, disgust, contempt, and surprise. All of these emotions are essential components in the tonal and generic structures in literary texts. Sadness is the basis of elegy and tragedy; and happiness the basis of comedy. Surprise is essential to suspense, and anger, contempt, and disgust are the animating sentiments of satire. (On universal, species-typical emotions, see Brown, 1991, p. 134; Ekman, 2003; Pinker 1997b, p. 366.)

The main plot structures in literary representations map simultaneously onto elementary human motives and basic emotions. The story of growth from childhood to adulthood, the adventure quest, the romantic comedy love story, the saga of revenge, the drama of jealousy—all have their place in the structure of elemental human motives, and they each have their characteristic set of emotions. The reading audience characteristically participates in the emotional experiences of the characters, sympathizes with them, experiences anxiety and hope as their fortunes vary, and finally experiences satisfaction or disappointment at the outcome of the action.

The basic emotional trajectory of any plot can be modulated through any combination of other emotions. The joy and anxiety of a romantic comedy plot like that of *Pride and Prejudice*, for example, can be modulated by anger and disgust, fear, remorse, shame, defiance, gratitude, and compassion. The main plot structure nonetheless follows a primary emotional trajectory, and this trajectory serves as the principle around which all the other emotions are organized. In this respect, the emotional trajectory of a literary work is parallel to the representation of motives. That is, the array of incidental motives in any representation is brought into subordinate order to the elemental motives that determine the primary plot structure. Elemental human motives and emotions provide the deep structure of literary representations, and this deep structure serves to organize subordinate motives and subordinate emotions.

Recall for a moment Mithen's appeal to cognitive fluidity: "When thoughts originating in different domains can engage together, the result is an almost limitless capacity for imagination" (1996, p. 71). The range of metaphoric combination is limitless, but combinations become meaningful only by being integrated with the elemental structure of human motives and human emotions. Even the most fanciful and phantasmagoric literary texts—for example, George MacDonald's hallucinatory allegories of spiritual experience, *Phantastes* and *Lilith*—speak to us and move us because their fantasies give metaphoric form to elemental passions and universal concerns—to themes of life and death, personal identity, sexual desire, parental affections, and to the love of friends and the hatred of enemies.

The question of the adaptive function of literature is at present highly controverted. Literary theorists who take fitness maximization as a direct motive speculate that the writing of literature is a form of social manipulation or of sexual display. (See Constable, 1997; Miller, 2000; Sugiyama, 1996.) From this perspective, writing is a means of attracting attention, enhancing prestige, and thus advancing one's reproductive prospects. The question of function is reduced directly to "ultimate" function, and the psychological functions specific to literature are simply passed over. Pinker (1997b, pp. 534–543) follows the traditional division of literary function into two parts—use and pleasure, or instruction and entertainment. As instruction, he says, literature serves an adaptive function because it provides us with models for situations we might meet with in our own lives. As a form of pleasure, literature is a nonfunctional byproduct of higher cognitive processes. In describing the pleasures specific to literature, Pinker, like Freud (1959, pp. 146–147), suggests that literature is mainly a means of fantasy fulfillment. (Also see Buss, 1999, pp. 407–410.)

The argument I am making for the way literature grounds itself in elemental motives and basic emotions suggests a different hypothesis about its psychological function. Literature is satisfying—moving or disturbing—not in the degree to which it fulfills fantasy expectations—though it can do this—but in the degree to which it provides a sense of psychological order. It provides order by depicting the particularities of time and place—of cultural context, individual circumstance, and personal character—and by integrating these particularities with the elemental structures of human concerns. Through literature and its oral antecedents, we recognize the elemental structures of human concerns in our own lives and in those of others. We filter out the trivial and the tangential aspects of experience and see into the deep structure of our nature. And we not only "see"—not only understand objectively. Through stories and verse and dramatic enactments—whether written or oral—we realize our deeper nature in vividly subjective ways. Through such realization, we situate ourselves consciously within our environments and organize the feelings and thoughts through which we regulate our behavior. Literature produces pleasure, but it is not merely a "pleasure technology" equivalent to recreational drugs (Pinker, 1997b, p. 528). It is one of the primary means through which we regulate our complex cognitive machinery. It contributes to personal and social development and to the capacity for responding flexibly and creatively to complex and changing circumstances. (See Boyd, 1998; Dissanayake, 1995b, 2000; Storey, 1996; and in this vol., see part 1, chapters 6 and 7; part 2, chapter 6.)

As Pinker argues, literature presents simulated situations through which we can model our own behaviors, but it does not only provide game plans for specific situations. It integrates emotional processes with elemental motives in highly particularized circumstances that we might never encounter—for example, the circumstance of being stranded on an island like that of Robinson Crusoe. The utility of reading about such experience does not depend on duplicating it in literal terms. Readers register the qualities of character through which Crusoe sustains himself in solitude, and they integrate these perceptions with the repertory of their psychological potentialities. Moreover, imaginatively assimilated experience serves not only to guide our own behavior but also to assist us in assessing the experience of others. In this latter regard, literature is a medium for cultivating our innate and socially adaptive capacity for entering mentally into the experience of other people. (See Brown, 1991, p. 135; Buss, 1995, p. 17.)

The predominant forms of literary study at the present time offer unqualified assent to a "historicist" belief that all experience is determined by autonomous and historically unique cultural processes. (See Carroll, 1995; Dissanayake, 1995b; Storey, 1996.) Such beliefs are parallel to the belief in cultural autonomy that distinguishes the Standard Social Science Model. (See Brown, 1991, pp. 1–38; Degler, 1991; Fox, 1989, chapters 3 and 4; Freeman, 1992, 1999, pp. 17–27; Tooby and Cosmides, 1992, p. 28.) Evolutionary psychology can revise such views by demonstrating that elemental, species-typical motives constrain all specific cultural forms. Of all competing theoretical alternatives, evolutionary psychology gives the most access to the elemental structure of human concerns. It thus offers the best available framework for understanding the psychological functions and represented content of literature. As a framework for literary study, evolutionary psychology can best fulfill its promise by integrating the basic principles of inclusive fitness with models for the analysis of personality and emotion.

2
Universals in Literary Study

From the time of Aristotle until the late eighteenth century, most literary theorists believed that literature represented universal realities or gave expression to universal truths. The belief in universals has been based on two distinct philosophical orientations, the naturalistic and the transcendental. Transcendental theorists postulate absolute spiritual realities—ultimate forms of beauty and truth—and argue that literary works gain access to those ultimate realities. Naturalistic theorists postulate a common human nature—a structure of motives, cognitive processes, and emotions that are common to all people—and they argue that literary works represent that common human nature. The naturalistic conception of universals has had the deepest and most widespread influence on literary theory, and it is almost inescapably implied by literary practice. In respect to the idea of a common human nature, naturalism and transcendentalism are not necessarily incompatible, and transcendental theorists have sometimes also been, in this respect, naturalistic. At present, naturalism is the only orientation in which theorists are actively developing the theory of literary universals. Most contemporary proponents of literary universals are Darwinians. They argue that the universal characteristics of human nature have been produced by an adaptive process of natural selection, and they seek an understanding of human nature in evolutionary disciplines such as ethology, sociobiology, and evolutionary psychology.

Two main schools of thought have challenged the idea of literary universals: philosophic particularism and historicism. Philosophic particularism is the belief that every moment of perception is unique and irreducible, and that the only regularity is flux. This belief has roots both in ancient Heraclitean philosophy and in the empirical English philosophy of the eighteenth century, but it became a major component of literary theory only in the late nineteenth century. Philosophic particularism enters into the closely related literary movements of aestheticism, decadence, and symbolism, and through these movements it had a major impact on modernist literature in the first half of the twentieth century. (See E. Wilson, 1931, pp. 20–21.) Historicism is the belief that human experience and literary expression can be radically modified by differences of cultural context. The historicism that arose in the later eighteenth century and that pervades nineteenth-century cultural theory is largely developmental and progressivist. The order of cultural change is sometimes attributed to the developmental design of human nature, and in this form historicism is itself a theory of a universal human design. The "New Historicism" that has emerged in the past twenty years, and that currently dominates Anglophone literary theory, repudiates human universals. The New Historicists subscribe to the deconstructive doctrine that all experience is wholly constituted by verbal forms and cultural constructs, and they treat all historical change as discontinuous and nonprogressive. (See Carroll, 1995, pp. 3–5, 38–40, 154–155.)

In the first part of this article, I shall give some illustrative instances of naturalistic universalism, transcendental universalism, philosophic particularism, and historicism. In the second part, I shall examine the effort to make sense of universals within the Darwinian framework.

Universalists, Particularists, and Historicists

Aristotle is the chief classical exemplar of a naturalistic conception of literary universals. In his *Poetics* he maintains that both the impulse toward literary representation and the represented content of literature are universal. Representation is a form of "imitation," and the impulse toward imitation is "rooted in human nature" (1982, p. 47). In a passage that has been very frequently quoted as a defense of literary meaning, he contrasts the literal particularity of historical writing with the typical or representative character of literature. Literature, he claims, "is a more philosophical and a higher thing than history, in that poetry tends rather to express the universal, history rather the particular fact" (p. 54).

The writers of the neoclassical period in Europe and England—the later seventeenth century and most of the eighteenth century—refine and complete the classical version of the naturalistic conception of literary universals. The import of their work can be exemplified by a passage from Samuel Johnson. Probably the single most frequently cited formulation of a neoclassical aesthetic creed is that which Johnson gives to his spokesman, the poet Imlac, in the philosophical novel *Rasselas*. Johnson's creed is both naturalistic and transcendental. That is, he appeals both to human nature and to a divinely sanctioned order of moral truth. Imlac declares that "the province of poetry is to describe Nature and Passion, which are always the same" (1990, pp. 39–40). The poet's purpose must be "to examine, not the individual, but the species; to remark general properties and large appearances: he does not number the streaks of the tulip, or describe the different shades in the verdure of the forest" (p. 43). Johnson recognizes that the forms of experience are modified by changes of time and cultural circumstance, but he believes that beneath all variations the same motives and passions are at work. The poet must "estimate the happiness and misery of every condition; observe the power of all the passions in all their combinations, and trace the changes of the human mind as they are modified by various institutions and accidental influences of climate or custom" (p. 44). The elementary passions and motives are essential components of a universal design; changes of culture and climate are merely "accidents," that is, superficial or adventitious modifications of the design. Thus far, Johnson's formulation closely parallels the views of evolutionary psychologists, but Johnson has no suspicion of the evolutionary basis for the species-typical human design, and his classical naturalistic conception orients itself instead to a transcendental morality. The poet, Imlac says, "must divest himself of the prejudices of his age or country; he must consider right and wrong in their abstracted and invariable state; he must disregard present laws and opinions, and rise to general and transcendental truths, which will always be the same" (p. 44).

In Johnson's thinking, the elementary human passions are closely connected with moral realities that are universal and accessible to enlightened reason. In another form of transcendental theory, the passions and the senses are taken to be part of the lower, animal nature of humanity, and this lower nature is set in stern opposition to the supposedly divine powers of reason and will. If, within this dualistic conception of human nature, the theorist associates literature with the lower nature, the senses and feelings, he will regard literature with deep moral suspicion. It is thus that Plato chooses to banish poets from the ideal republic, and similar motives animated the English Puritans in shutting down the Elizabethan theaters. Plato believes in beauty and good as absolutes, but he does not believe that literature, concerned as it is with flux and the surface of things, can gain access to this absolute good (1937, vol. 1, p. 865).

In contrast to Plato, transcendental writers of a Romantic bent take literature and the literary imagination as the central means of access to absolute beauty or good. Percy Bysshe Shelley, for instance, declares that "to be a poet is to apprehend the true and the beautiful, in a word, the good. . . . A poet participates in the eternal, the infinite, and the one" (1969, pp. 123–124; also see Blake, 1965, p. 637; Schiller, 1965, letter 12, pp. 64–67). In Romantic theorists, transcendentalism is often combined with a naturalistic appeal to a common human nature. Thus, Shelley argues that poetry represents actions in accordance with "the unchangeable forms of human nature"(p. 128). William Wordsworth argues that poetry traces "the primary laws of our nature," and especially "the essential passions of the heart" (1965, p. 447). Wordsworth thinks that poetry both represents and appeals to "our elementary feelings" (p. 447). Though the Romantics emphasize fervor of composition and response rather than objectivity of representation, formulations of this sort recall the neoclassical formulations of Samuel Johnson, and they anticipate Victorian reaffirmations of a classical universalism. The most prominent Victorian literary theorist, Matthew Arnold, simultaneously invokes Aristotle and echoes Wordsworth. He declares that the purpose of dramatic poetry is to depict actions, and he identifies the most excellent actions as those "which most powerfully appeal to the great primary human affections: to those elementary feelings which subsist permanently in the race, and which are independent of time" (1979, p. 4).

In the twentieth century, the most prominent theorist of literary universals has been Northrop Frye. Like his Romantic predecessors Frye invokes both transcendental and naturalistic versions of universals. The best known aspect of Frye's literary theory is the cyclical seasonal taxonomy of genres in *Anatomy of Criticism* (1957). Frye associates each of four major genres with a season: spring with the romance quest, summer with romantic comedy, fall with tragedy, and winter with irony and realism. Frye links each of these phases with a set of character types, plot situations, and tonal perspectives. Each type has mythic antecedents or archetypes, and the types serve to categorize both specific individual works and whole cultural periods. Frye's sources include Jung's theory of psychological archetypes as innate mental forms derived from inherited ancestral experience, but the most comprehensive framework for his theory is a Platonic conception of transcendent ideal forms. He argues that at the highest level, the "anagogic" or spiritual level, all of the archetypal forms merge into a single spiritual absolute, "a single infinite and eternal verbal symbol" (p. 121).

In the mid-century period, Frye was widely esteemed the most creative and authoritative contributor to modern literary theory, but his prestige has now faded. Archetypal myth criticism flourished in the 1960s and 1970s but has had very few recent proponents. From the 1940s through the 1960s, a large proportion of Anglophone literary critics cherished beliefs, similar to Frye's, about the transcendent nature of the poetic symbol, but the Derridean deconstructionists who came into prominence in the 1970s gleefully repudiated transcendentalism, and the general ideological temper of recent theory has been subversive, not reverential.

In both its transcendental and naturalistic forms, the idea of literary universals sets itself in opposition to the idea of literary particulars. This opposition can be conceived either invidiously, as a contrast between the better and the worse, or as a complementary relationship between interdependent poles of representation.

Invidious oppositions can favor either universals or particulars, though the proponents of universals have been more numerous. Invidious universalist conceptions are apparent in the contrast that Aristotle makes between poetry and history, and in the contrast that Johnson makes between the essential structure of unchanging human passions and the merely accidental variations of climates, and customs. Invidious proponents of particularity include advocates of "realism" in fiction. Ian Watt, for instance, identifies the novel as the paradigmatic realist form, and he presents it as an integral part of "that vast transformation of Western civilisation since the Renaissance which has replaced the unified world picture of the Middle Ages with another very different one—one which presents us, essentially, with a developing but unplanned aggregate of particular individuals having particular experiences at particular times and at particular places" (1957, p. 31). Watt's historical vision consists in a simple progression from Platonic transcendentalism through British empiricism. The one British writer who most forcibly articulates an extreme philosophic particularism, critic and novelist Walter Pater, offers a more complex account of philosophical history. Pater sets his own vision in contrast to that of Plato, but he also affiliates himself with the ancient Heraclitean and Epicurean philosophy (1910). Pater's particularism is both ultra-individualistic and ultra-atomistic. He speaks of each "individual in his isolation," and he insists that "those impressions of the individual mind to which, for each one of us, experience dwindles down, are in perpetual flight; that each of them is limited by time, and that as time is infinitely divisible, each of them is infinitely divisible also; all that is actual in it being a single moment, gone while we try to apprehend it" (1980, pp. 187–188).

Pater's particularism takes extreme form only in his earlier work. In his later work, he offers a more balanced account of the complementary interaction between particulars and universals, and in this more balanced account he rejoins the mainstream of modern European literary theory. Schiller's distinction between "naïve" and "sentimental" poetry (1966) offers an exemplary instance of this mainstream tradition. Assimilating previous formulations of the distinction between ancient and modern literature, Schiller holds that "naïve" poetry, associated with pagan antiquity, is objective, sensual, concrete, action-oriented, and particularistic. "Sentimental" poetry, associated with modern Europe, is subjective, reflective, abstract, meditative and synthetic. Schiller's theory had a direct influence on the literary theory of Carl Jung (1966), who invokes Schiller's dichotomy and links it with extraversion and introversion, the primary polar terms of his theory of personality. Northrop Frye follows in the same tradition and adapts it to a generic distinction between the novel, which is supposedly realistic and extraverted, and the romance, which is symbolic and introverted. "The romancer does not attempt to create 'real people' so much as stylized figures which expand into psychological archetypes" (1957, p. 304). Robert Browning formulates a dichotomy similar to Schiller's and fashions it into a dialectic intended to describe the laws of development in all literary traditions (1981). In one phase, Browning argues, poets seek new material from the concrete particulars of contemporary reality, and in a succeeding phase they organize this new material within a total imaginative synthesis. The dialectic progresses as an expansive spiral, not merely cycling through the phases of the dialectic but using it to increase the range of poetic representation.

In the later eighteenth century, cultural historians began attempting to take account of the differences of imaginative life in differing periods of history. Before the publication of Darwin's *Origin of Species* in 1859, none of these accounts had access to a vision of cultural change rooted in ecological conditions and the evolved structure of the human mind. The theory of natural selection is mechanistic and nonteleological. Species change through a mechanical process of adaptation that leads to no necessary culmination. As a paradigm of large-scale change, this conception is radically different from the Aristotelian idea of a teleological organic process, and Aristotle's idea was the most naturalistic conception available within a pre-Darwinian worldview. Whether transcendental or naturalistic in orientation, most early historicists conceived of change as progressive and teleological. Among the German cultural theorists of the classical and Romantic period, Johann Gottfried von Herder, Gotthold Ephraim Lessing, and G. W. F. Hegel all construct teleological versions of cultural change. Herder and Hegel seek some inherent principle of necessary progression within culture itself, and Lessing fashions a theory of change based on a parallel between the "education" or development of individual people and the education of the human race as a whole. In contrast to the German cultural historians, the French Positivists and their English acolytes—for instance, Auguste Comte and John Stuart Mill—do not seek to rationalize or justify earlier phases of culture. They operate instead from within the Enlightenment perspective exemplified by Voltaire—a perspective from which all cultural change appears as a relatively simple progression from barbarism and ignorance to rationality, civilization, and positive or scientific knowledge.

Most historicists presuppose some continuity in the ground-plan of human nature. They tacitly allow for some level at which basic cognitive and emotional processes and basic social interactions can be compared. In their programmatic statements, however, they tend to emphasize the differences between their own views and the more strongly universalist bias of neoclassical writers. Hippolyte Taine offers an instructive instance. Taine is a naturalistic historicist who was influenced by Darwin and by the whole climate of biological thought in the middle of the nineteenth century. Celebrating the historicism of his own time, he sets it in sharp contrast with the supposedly ahistorical vision in the writers of the preceding century:

> They thought men of every race and century were all but identical; the Greek, the barbarian, the Hindoo, the man of the Restoration, and the man of the eighteenth century, as if they had been turned out of a common mould; and all in conformity to a certain abstract conception, which served for the whole human race. They knew man, but not men; they had not penetrated to the soul; they had not seen the infinite diversity and marvelous complexity of souls; they did not know that the moral constitution of a people or an age is as particular and distinct as the physical structure of a family of plants or an order of animals. (1879, p. 5)

In practice, the historicists do in fact give more sensitive attention to the peculiarities of period and culture, but at the level of theoretical formulation, Taine's contrast is too sharply drawn. Recall the representative neoclassical formulation of universals in Samuel Johnson's *Rasselas*. Johnson declares that

"Nature and Passion" are "always the same," but he also argues that the poet must "trace the changes of the human mind as they are modified by various institutions and accidental influences of climate or custom." Moreover, Taine himself compares various distinct cultures by analyzing differences in the way certain common motives and cognitive processes operate among different races and at different periods.

In the twentieth century, the teleological progressivism of historicist cultural theory has remained alive in its Marxist versions, but the effort of writers like Herder and Hegel to construct a comprehensive rationale, intrinsic to the historical process, for every phase of cultural history, has long been abandoned. The Darwinian vision of biological change in evolutionary time as a mechanical process directed to no particular end has discouraged large-scale transcendental conceptions. The sentiments and assumptions animating Victorian visions of a necessary progress leading to "the solidarity of mankind" and "the perfection of our race" (Eliot, 2000, chapter 61) were dissolved and scattered in the cataclysm of the First World War. In the last two decades of the nineteenth century and the first decade of the twentieth, many social thinkers and literary artists assimilated the Darwinian vision, particularly the social Darwinists and the naturalists. Presumably, a biologically based social science would eventually have had further ramifications in literary theory, but after the first decade of the twentieth century the social sciences turned sharply against any association with Darwinism. The idea of cultural autonomy became the cornerstone of standard social science, and until the 1970s Darwinism essentially disappeared from professional social theory. (See Buss, 1999, part 1; Degler, 1991; Fox, 1989, chapters 3 and 4; Freeman, 1992, 1999; Tooby and Cosmides, 1992.)

In the "new historicism" that emerged under the auspices of French cultural historians, and especially of Michel Foucault, the idea of cultural autonomy reached a culminating extreme. Foucault and his followers not only deny that humans share a common set of psychological structures; they claim that even the idea of "humanity" itself is the relatively recent invention of a specific cultural moment. "Before the end of the eighteenth century, *man* did not exist. . . . He is a quite recent creature, which the demiurge of knowledge fabricated with its own hands less than two hundred years ago" (1973, p. 308). As reference to Aristotle or almost any ancient writer will demonstrate, such claims do not stand historical inspection, but they have nonetheless enjoyed considerable popularity among literary theorists. (See Abrams, 1995.)

Literary Universals and the Adapted Mind

In the past two decades, evolutionary thinkers in the human sciences have reaffirmed the elementary Darwinian idea that human beings, like all other animals, have evolved through an adaptive process and that consequently they display an innate, species-typical structure of cognitive and behavioral characteristics. They have reaffirmed, that is, the primary tenet in the naturalistic theory of literary universals—the idea that there is in fact such a thing as "human nature." Literary theorists sympathetic to Darwinian thinking must now confront two basic questions: what precisely is this species-typical or universal structure, and what bearing does it have on literary representation? Beyond these basic questions, there are other problems that are familiar in the history of literary theory and that now must be reformulated within the context of Darwinian social science. What is the relation of literary universals to cultural difference—differences of ethnic and national identity, socioeconomic organization, and historical periods? And further, within any given culture, what is the relation of literary universals to individual differences among authors—differences of sex or gender, race, social class, temperament, personality, and quality of mind? Theories of literature have often broached the question of function or purpose, and most formulations have adhered to the ancient idea that literature is both useful and pleasurable—*utile et dulce*. To give just one example, in a seventeenth-century dialogue on dramatic poetry, John Dryden's spokesman defines a play as "a just and lively image of human nature, representing its passions and humours, and the changes of fortune to which it is subject; for the delight and instruction of mankind" (1970, p. 25). The question of function on this level must now be situated, at a deeper level, in relation to the problem of biological or adaptive function.

Systematic and empirically grounded psychology did not begin until the latter part of the nineteenth century. Darwin's *Descent of Man* (published in 1871) is itself one of the first scientifically grounded texts of analytic psychology, and in the psychology that dominated the twentieth century, Darwin's fundamental insights into the evolved and adapted structure of human nature were forgotten or rejected. Only in the past few decades has psychology begun to reestablish itself on a solid adaptationist foundation. In all the millennia preceding this adaptationist revolution, the best psychological insight available to educated people was the intuitive understanding of poets, novelists, and playwrights. Literary writers are by nature strong in empathy—in the sympathetic understanding of the inner workings of other minds. Since those minds are themselves governed by the common, elemental human passions, literary writers have always had the best direct access to human nature.

Literary writers are concerned to describe behavior in particular circumstances, delineate individual characters, and evoke the felt quality of experience. They are not much concerned with the systematic reduction of psychology to empirically falsifiable principles capable of progressive development. That sort of work is more appropriate to the methodology of the social sciences. Now that this methodology is being integrated with an adaptationist understanding of human nature, we have, for the first time, a situation in which the intuitive understanding of literary writers can converge effectively with the findings of empirical psychology. A wide array of social scientists and a few literary theorists now accept the basic Darwinian premise of the adapted mind—a mind imbued with a rich and complex structure of innate dispositions and developmental programs. Literary Darwinians make the necessary extension from this premise to the claim that literary texts are themselves organized in close correlation with the elementary structures of the adapted mind. Working out from this premise, how much else is actually known? What specific features of human nature can be identified, what organization can be discerned among them, and how do they translate into the formal characteristics of verbal order and literary representation?

Two main schools of thought have directed the development of contemporary Darwinian theory about human motives: sociobiology and evolutionary psychology. The sociobiologists formed the first wave in the resurgence of Darwinism in the 1970s. They went to the root of Darwinian thinking, the idea of "inclusive fitness" as the ultimate regulative principle of evolution. Inclusive fitness is the differential success in the transmission of genes, and sociobiological psychologists, geneticists, and anthropologists have tended to concentrate their attention on the elementary biological processes of survival and reproduction. One result of this concentration is a tendency to regard "fitness maximization" or the maximization of progeny as a direct and primary motive in human behavior. Seeking to avoid this result, a younger generation of Darwinians, the evolutionary psychologists, distinguish between fitness maximization, as an ultimate regulative principle, and the proximal mechanisms through which fitness is mediated. (See Alexander, 1979, 1987, 1990; Barkow, 1990; Betzig, 1986, 1998; Chagnon, 1979; Chagnon and Irons, 1979; Irons, 1990, 1998; MacDonald, 1995a; Symons, 1989, 1992; Tooby and Cosmides, 1992; Turke, 1990.) Evolutionary psychologists maintain that these mechanisms—the structures of cognition and motivation—are the actual evolved content of the adapted mind. Some of the most influential evolutionary psychologists integrate Darwinian theory with cognitive psychology, and they identify the elementary components of the adapted mind as "cognitive domains" or "modules." (See Cosmides and Tooby, 1994, Pinker, 1995, 1997b; Symons, 1992; Tooby and Cosmides, 1992.) These modules are conceived as genetically transmitted mechanisms that are designed through natural selection for the purpose of solving specific adaptive problems. They display complex functional structure and have anatomical components, physiological processes, or neural circuitry dedicated to the execution of their purposes.

The theory of cognitive domains is a large-scale research program, not an established body of confirmed fact. The identity and number of specific domains remains an open question, and lists have been compiled that vary from three or four to fifteen or sixteen. (See Carey and Spelke, 1994, p. 171; Cosmides and Tooby, 1994, p. 103; Mithen, 1996; Pinker, 1994, p. 420, 1995, p. 236, 1997b, pp. 128, 315; Sperber, 1994, p. 42; Tooby and Cosmides, 1992, p. 113.)

Much of the controversy in such matters, like that in the study of personality factors, consists in the problem of how to group specific items in larger categories. Beneath such uncertainties, there is a good deal of agreement on some of the most important large-scale components of human nature. Steven Pinker summarizes a view common among cognitive psychologists that "innate intuitive theories or modules for the major ways of making sense of the world" include "modules for objects and forces, for animate beings, for artifacts, for minds, and for natural kinds like animals, plants, and minerals" (1997b, pp. 314–315). Pinker adds that this list, reflecting the limited concerns of cognitive psychology, "is surely too short." A more realistic inventory would include "modes of thought and feeling for danger, contamination, status, dominance, fairness, love, friendship, sexuality, children, relatives, and the self" (p. 315).

Similar lists can be found in the work of Darwinian anthropologists concerned with typical goal structures or universal human attributes. Jerome Barkow, for instance, compiles a list of common goal structures that includes maintaining physiological well-being, engaging in sexual and family relations, being a member of a social group, and constructing cognitive maps of one's environment, including the social environment (1989, pp. 109–110). In an anthropological study that offers an extensive and carefully considered treatment of human universals from within the Darwinian framework, Donald Brown constructs a composite portrait of "the universal people," and in this portrait he includes the idea of the self and of other persons as beings actuated by beliefs and feelings, a set of basic emotions and facial expressions (happiness, sadness, anger, fear, surprise, contempt, and disgust), a dimorphic organization of sexual identity that involves division of labor and differential reproductive strategies, the elementary forms of kinship organized around the four components of the nuclear family (father, mother, son, daughter), some basic forms of social interaction, such as reciprocal exchange and status recognition, the formulation of worldviews, and some basic forms of proto-literary (oral) expression, including narrative, metaphor, metonymy, onomatopoeia, and poetic meter (1991, pp. 130–141.). (On ethical universals, see also Arnhart, 1998; Frank, 1988; J. Q. Wilson, 1993; on aesthetic universals, see Barrow, 1995; Eibl-Eibesfeldt, 1989.)

Brown (1991) argues that the idea of the self or of individual persons is a human universal, and Pinker (1997b) suggests it is almost certainly one of the evolved "modules" or cognitive domains. Among human beings, the sense of individual persons is the conscious correlative for the biological concept of the organism, and this concept is an essential precondition for the organization of behavior in goal-directed ways and for the interaction of individuals in social groups. In literary structures, the idea of an individual self is indispensable to the organization of literary meaning. Characters in poems, plays, and stories are individuals, and authors necessarily present their stories from some distinct point of view. All emotion and cognition is organized within the individual mind, and the response of audiences to literary works is thus necessarily lodged in individuals, even when the response is collectively experienced, as in the audience of a play. For these reasons, the study of individual psychology is both integral to the Darwinian conception of human beings and to literary analysis. As Taine understood, within both biology and literary analysis, the concept of an organism necessarily involves a complementary concept of an environment. Character and setting are thus elementary and inescapable components of all literary representation, and the principles that apply to all biological interaction must be taken as the larger context for all depicted action in literary texts. We now have a steadily growing body of empirical findings about the organization of individual organisms—psychological, cognitive, emotional—and the interactions of individuals with their social and physical worlds, and all of this information can be used as a framework for the critical analysis of literary depictions of human nature.

The modern study of Darwinian psychology has tended to concentrate on the idea of human universals, and within the Darwinian community itself there has been controversy over the adaptive significance of individual variations. Theorists who believe that individual variations are not adaptively important argue that adaptations display complex functional structure and that any such structure must be common to the species as a whole. (See Tooby and Cosmides, 1990.) Others seek to explain the adaptive value of variation within a given social ecology. (See Bailey, 1997, 1998; Barash, 1997; Buss, 1995; Eysenck, 1980; MacDonald, 1990, 1995b, 1998a, 1998b; Segal, 1997, 1999; Segal and MacDonald, 1998; D. S. Wilson, 1994, 1999.) For literary study, the vital point to be made is that universals and individual variations are not mutually exclusive concepts. The dimensions through which individual identity is structured and in which it necessarily varies are themselves universals. These dimensions are part of the evolved structure of human nature.

Two of the most important patterns through which individual identity is structured are personality factors and emotions. The five major factors of personality—extraversion/introversion, friendliness/hostility, neuroticism/security, conscientiousness/carelessness, and curiosity/dullness—can be used for the comparative analysis of characters, authors, and audience response. The universal human emotions are essential components in the tonal and generic structures in literary texts. (See Damasio, 1994; Ekman, 2003; Ekman and Davidson, 1994; Ledoux, 1996; MacDonald, 1995b; Panksepp, 1998.) Sadness is the basis of elegy and tragedy; and happiness the basis of comedy. Surprise is essential to suspense, and anger, contempt, and disgust are the animating sentiments of satire. All individuals experience some measure of such emotions, and all individuals experience some of the affects that attend on the polar terms in the factors of personality. But individuals vary a great deal in the degree to which they experience any given emotion, for instance, anger or fear, and in their characteristically open or self-enclosed relations with the outside world. (See Bouchard, 1994; 1997; Buss, 1990, 1995; Costa and Widiger, 1994; Digman, 1990; Eysenck and Eysenck, 1985; McCrae, 1992; MacDonald, 1995b, 1998b; Pervin, 1990, 2003; Pervin and John, 1999; Segal and MacDonald, 1998; Wiggins, 1996.)

The most important general structure available for the hierarchical analysis of motivating concerns within narrative and dramatic texts is the study of motives or lifegoals. Motives vary in the depth and intensity of the concern they evoke. Some motivations have more fundamental structural significance than others. Brown observes that some universals "are deeply meaningful to humans," and he specifies "the attachments of family members, the grief they will feel at loss, the anguish at betrayal; bonds of loyalty among members of a group; pleasure in music and dance; distinguishing between true and false," and "recognizing the morality in reciprocity" (2000, p. 169). Generally, the closer one comes to the elementary principles of inclusive fitness—the closer to survival and reproduction (including family relations)—the deeper and more compelling the concern. Evolutionary psychologist David Buss notes that "power and love emerge consistently and cross-culturally as the two most important dimensions of interpersonal behavior" (1995, p. 21). They emerge also as the two most important motivating concerns in the plot structures of dramatic and narrative texts. Not all texts follow precisely the same structure of species-typical values and concerns, but the species-typical concerns provide the larger context within which all variation takes place, and they thus provide a common framework of analysis and comparison. (For examples of literary criticism that use this common framework, see section 3, "Contributions to Adaptationist Literary Study," in the introduction to this volume.)

Evolutionary psychologists have thus far reached no consensus about the adaptive functions of literature. Geoffrey Miller argues that art and other forms of higher mental activity are merely forms of sexual display (2000). Steven Pinker suggests that art conveys useful information but that in its pleasurable aspect it is merely a nonfunctional byproduct of higher cognitive processes (1997b, pp. 534–543, 2002, pp. 405–407). Other theorists have argued that art and literature serve an array of adaptive purposes, including emotional and personal development, the integration of higher cognitive faculties with the elementary motivational structures, social bonding, social subversion, and cognitive mapping or the construction of models that can organize the complex and emotionally rich features of subjective life. (See Carroll, 1995; Dissanayake, 1988, 1995a, 1995b, 2000, 2001, in press; Storey, 1993, 1996; and in this vol., see part 1, chapters 6 and 7; part 2, chapters 1 and 6.) Theorists who argue for some distinct adaptive value of art note that it is a universal feature of human life, that it consumes large quantities of energy and attention, and that it displays complex functional structure. These theorists maintain that the arts are forms of understanding and communication, and they conclude that, at the very least, the arts participate in the adaptive value that attaches to all understanding and communication.

3
Human Universals and Literary Meaning
A *Sociobiological Critique of* Pride and Prejudice, Villette, O Pioneers!, Anna of the Five Towns, *and* Tess of the d'Urbervilles

Reproduction is central to the logic of evolution, and as a result, it is central to human motivational systems. Any given culture organizes reproduction in a way specific to that culture, but evolutionary anthropologists and psychologists have identified certain sex differences that hold good across diverse cultures, and they cogently argue that these "human universals" reflect species-typical motivational structures. In all known societies, males are dominant. Males engage in the preponderance of all combat, and females take primary responsibility for the care of the young. In seeking mates, males tend to give priority to youth and beauty (signals of reproductive potential), and females tend to give priority to wealth and social status (indications of an ability to provide for her and her offspring). Males are more open to casual, promiscuous sex, and females tolerate sexual infidelity in their mates more easily than males. Males are sexually jealous and possessive; females are more jealous of emotional commitments. Broad characteristics such as these provide a common foundation for the way any given culture organizes reproductive relations. (See Brown, 1991; Buss, 1994, 2000; Daly and Wilson, 1983; Geary, 1998; Goldberg, 1993; Low, 2000; Symons, 1979.)

Literature reflects and articulates the vital interests of human beings as living organisms. Because reproduction is central to human motivational systems, it is central also to the organization of meaning in literary representations of human behavior. That is, literary representations commonly organize themselves around problems of reproduction, especially mate selection and family relations. Accordingly, critics who have attempted to link literary study with sociobiology or evolutionary psychology have tended to concentrate on the depiction of reproductive behavior. Understandably, they have also frequently conceived of their task as that of examining literary texts in order to identify the representation of sociobiologically typical behavior. (See Barash and Barash, 2002; Cooke, 1995, 1999d; Fox, 1995; Gottschall, 2001; Jobling, 2002; Nesse, 1995; Sugiyama, 2001c; Thiessen and Umezawa, 1998; Whissel, 1996). Cooke explains the logic of this approach:

Sociobiological research often begins by examining phenomena which are statistically non-random, such as the greater age of husbands over that of their wives, the huge disproportion between the numbers of polygynous and polyandrous societies, and the differing roles played by the two sexes. Literary scholars can begin by looking at these same phenomena and then by searching for their occurrences in fictive texts. (1995d, p. 185).

Similar reasoning enters into three projects recurrently undertaken by sociobiological critics: (a) to summarize the basic findings of evolutionary psychology (Boyd, 1998; Roele and Wind, 1999); (b) to delineate a "biogrammar" or "deep structure" of human behavior (Storey, 1996; and in this. vol., see part 2, chapter 1); and (c) to identify some basic set of human universals correlative with symbolic "archetypes" or common themes and story patterns (Cooke, 1999c; Wilson, 1998; and in this vol., see part 2, chapter 2).

Identifying species-typical forms of behavior offers a reasonable starting point for sociobiological literary study, but it is not in itself sufficient to account for literary meaning. Literary texts do not limit themselves to representing species-typical behavior, and literary representations are never merely transparent revelations of behavior. Literary representations are interpretive models that are mediated through the perspectives of the authors who fashion them. Each individual author is necessarily limited by the horizon of his or her own values and perceptions, and these values and perceptions are crucially influenced by individual temperament, by the accidents of personal experience, and by the thoughts and feelings available within the cultural order to which the author belongs. Homer cannot think and feel just as Virginia Woolf thinks and feels. Their temperaments, social positions, and sexual orientations are different, and the values of the cultural orders within which they operate are also different.

If meaning is constrained by differences both of individual identity and of cultural context, how can critics make use of those statistically nonrandom phenomena that sociobiologists and evolutionary psychologists seek to identify? What relevance do human universals have for the interpretation of specific literary texts? All behavioral norms consist in some particular organization of elemental biological dispositions. Examples of such dispositions include the need for social interaction, the desire for sexual intimacy, the drive toward dominance, the desire for wealth and status, the love of one's own children, the creation of social coalitions, the demand for justice, and the creation of cognitive order through such means as religion, myth, philosophy, literature, art, and science. (See Arnhart, 1998; Brown, 1991; Buss, 1999; Damasio, 1994; Griffiths, 1997; McGuire and Troisi, 1998; Mithen, 1996, 2001; Pinker, 1997b; Tooby and Cosmides, 1992, E. O. Wilson, 1998.) By definition, universals or species-typical behaviors are those behaviors that are common to all cultures; they are the core of every cultural norm, but all forms of cultural organization involve conflict, and all cultures elaborate their values in ways that create tension among elemental dispositions.

Authors make use of species-typical norms as a common framework of understanding, and they define their own distinct identities in relation to these norms. They are sometimes sympathetic to species-typical norms, and sometimes alienated from them, and they are sometimes sympathetic and sometimes hostile to their own cultural orders. Often, but not always, they align themselves with some particular set of species-typical norms, under the rubric of "human nature," and they use these norms as a means of adopting a critical perspective on the conventions of their own cultures. By appealing to elemental dispositions that answer to their own idiosyncratic psychological organization, they can adopt a critical perspective on species-typical norms, on their own cultures, or on both.

In order to integrate the idea of interpretive models into the analysis of individual texts, we need always to pose two questions. First, what is the relation between the represented subject matter and the author's own interpretive vision? And second, what is the relation between the reader's point of view and that of the author? To codify these questions, I shall use two special phrases. I shall say that when we answer the first question, about the author's interpretive vision, we identify "the total structure of meaning" in a literary text. When we answer the second question, about the reader's critical assessment of that vision, we identify "the total meaning situation." (Similar distinctions appear in Hirsch, 1967, 1976.) I shall elaborate briefly on these special phrases.

Meaning in literature is always meaning for some specific person, from some specific point of view. Characters behave, but they also think and feel. They interpret their own behavior and that of others, and authors frequently give us to understand that these interpretations are partial, incomplete, biased, or distorted in some fashion. Characters offer differing and sometimes conflicting interpretations of the same events, and authors create total structures of meaning that encompass the thoughts and feelings of all the characters in their works. Authors mediate among the characters, often aligning themselves with some characters and distancing themselves from others. Within his or her own total structure of meaning, each author is necessarily dominant; he or she constitutes a supreme authority.

Authors negotiate with the meaning systems of their characters, and they negotiate simultaneously with the expectations, values, sympathies, and antipathies of their putative readers. A literary text is a communicative act. The author can control the organization of meaning within his or her own story, but he or she can only partly control the way readers will respond to what he or she has written. In the degree to which an author is astute, persuasive, and charming, or to which a reader is impressionable or passive, the reader's viewpoint, at least while he or she is reading, converges with that of the author, and this convergence, this willing submission to the "authority" of the author, is part of the total meaning situation. In the degree to which the author excites suspicion or disbelief, the reader's separate and distinct sense of meaning becomes part of the total meaning situation. Readers' beliefs, feelings, and values often conflict with those of the author. The total meaning situation for any literary text thus consists of two parts—the author's communicative act, and the way this act is received and interpreted by the reader. The reader is an integral part of the larger communicative event, and thus part of the total meaning situation.

In order to give a comprehensive sociobiological critique of a literary text, we must take account of the total meaning situation, and to do this we must analyze the relations among elemental dispositions, species-typical norms, cultural norms, and individual structures of meaning. To illustrate the sort of analysis I have in mind, I shall compare the depiction of normative heterosexual couples in five novels: Jane Austen's *Pride and Prejudice*, Charlotte Brontë's *Villette*, Willa Cather's *O Pioneers!*, Arnold Bennett's *Anna of the Five Towns*, and Thomas Hardy's *Tess of the d'Urbervilles*. Four of these novels are British and one American, and all were written in the nineteenth or early twentieth century. All five depict the personal development of a female protagonist, and in all five cases the problems of personal identity culminate in the question of choosing a mate. All five display prominent instances of the kinds of sexual motivations and situations sociobiology teaches us to expect. Strong men of high status gain sexual access to young and beautiful females. In three of the novels, Hardy's *Tess*, Bennett's *Anna*, and Cather's *O Pioneers!*—sexual competition leads to lethal violence. Such matters are the bread and butter of fictional representation, and these novels are in this respect perfectly commonplace.

Why consider these specific novels? The first four—Austen's *Pride and Prejudice*, Brontë's *Villette*, Cather's *O Pioneers!*, and Bennett's *Anna of the Five Towns*—occupy points on a scale in the author's treatment of the normative heterosexual couple. The scale runs from the simple and straightforward to the complex and problematic. In the fifth novel, *Tess of the d'Urbervilles*, Hardy's stance toward the normative heterosexual couple is not itself problematic, but Hardy does not share Austen's confidence in the normative authority of the traditional cultural order. To create a structure of meaning adequate to his story, Hardy must make explicit appeal to elemental biological dispositions and set them in contrast to the cultural conventions of his time.

Pride and Prejudice provides a base of comparison for the treatment of the normative heterosexual couple. The emotional interest of the author and reader are directed toward a successful courtship leading to a happy marriage—the standard form of "romantic comedy." In Brontë's *Villette* and Cather's *O Pioneers!*, the weight of emotional interest shifts away from the normative heterosexual couple, and the authors use the novels to fulfill their own idiosyncratic emotional needs. *Villette* enacts a process in which emotional energy is deflected from erotic fulfillment and concentrated in the narrower sphere of self-affirmation, and *O Pioneers!* centers its emotional interest in the relations of a sociobiologically atypical couple. Bennett's *Anna of the Five*

Towns also depicts atypical sexual psychology, and both Cather and Bennett leave explanatory gaps that require the reader to fill out the total meaning structure with speculative interpretation. In the case of Bennett's novel, interpretive speculation does not ultimately close the gap between the author's depiction of female sexual psychology and the expectations of readers.

These five novels present an emotional range extending from cheerful romantic comedy in *Pride and Prejudice* to tragic anguish in *Tess*. The protagonist of *Pride and Prejudice* marries her ideal mate and thereby achieves wealth and status; the protagonist of *Tess* is reduced to harlotry and then executed for murder. Cather's *O Pioneers!* has two main stories, one a tragedy and the other a romantic comedy, and both *Villette* and *Anna of the Five Towns* conclude in an emotionally ambivalent way. Given the evidence of these novels alone, it should be clear that the pleasure specific to literature does not limit itself to vicarious participation in fantasy fulfillments. As obvious as this point should be, it remains theoretically uncertain both in traditional Freudian criticism and in some of the theoretical commentaries of evolutionary psychologists. (See Buss, 1999a, p. 410; Freud, 1959, p. 146; Pinker, 1997b, pp. 539–540, 2002, p. 406.)

Pride and Prejudice and *Tess of the d'Urbervilles* occupy a canonical position much higher than that of the other three novels. Comparing these novels thus offers an occasion for considering the issue of literary merit or the evaluation of quality. Sociobiological critics have only begun to consider the question of evaluation, and as with the analysis of themes, the considerations thus far have focused on the presence of universal themes or sociobiologically typical behaviors. (See Cooke, 1999c; F. Turner, 1992; E. O. Wilson, 1998.) Turner (p. 26) suggests that value can be correlated with the sheer number of such themes, and Cooke (p. 55) identifies literary merit with the representation of conflicting biological predispositions. Countering the emphasis on universals, Easterlin argues that "many factors" come into evaluation and that the presence or absence of "biologically based" content or form does not "predict or determine the value of a given work" (1999a, p. 247). Wilson, Turner, and Cooke are right in seeking sources of power in universal themes, but Easterlin is also right in insisting that aesthetic value does not consist in represented content alone.

The multitude of factors that enter into evaluative judgments can be grouped into three main categories: the significance of the represented action, the mind and temper of the artist, and formal aesthetic organization. The represented action consists not just of elemental or universal themes but also of circumstantial conditions—including both natural and social environments—and the individual identities of characters. The significance of a represented action depends on the integration of all three aspects of the action: elemental themes, circumstantial conditions, and individual identities. All represented action is mediated through the mind and temper of the author and manifests itself as a quality of experience. Style and form make the quality of experience available to the imagination of a reader, and they also satisfy intrinsic cognitive needs—needs we identify as "aesthetic." (See Barrow, 1995; Dissanayake, 1995b, 2000; Eibl-Eibesfeldt, 1989.)

Of these five novels, only *Pride and Prejudice* and *Tess of the d'Urbervilles* are likely to be familiar to an educated general audience, and the details of all novels grow dim in memory over time. Bearing this in mind, I'll summarize the stories as necessary.

Pride and Prejudice presents a classic instance of romantic comedy. It is in various ways a highly sophisticated novel. In its integration of individualized personalities and universal motives within a vividly particularized set of social conditions, in its fine meshing of style and theme, and in the elegant economy of its narrative, *Pride and Prejudice* displays a mastery amounting to rare genius. But in the relation of the author to her subject and to her implied audience–the audience created by the writer's expectations of response—*Pride and Prejudice* is ingenuously simple and straightforward. The central perspective within the represented action is that of the protagonist Elizabeth Bennet. Austen frankly likes Elizabeth and expects us to like her and to wish her well. The beliefs, values, feelings, and perceptions of the author and her protagonist are very similar. The few differences that Austen registers are mainly those of inexperience on Elizabeth's part, and one can chart the course of Elizabeth's development by assessing the way in which her own perspective comes gradually into a near perfect convergence with that of her author. Austen has no detectable ulterior purposes. The central interest of the novel is the love story between Elizabeth and Darcy, and the principal satisfaction Austen proposes, for herself and for the reader, is to participate vicariously in the satisfactory resolution of their differences.

The marriage of Elizabeth and Darcy embodies and reaffirms the normative principles within their whole cultural order, and the satiric humor directed at other characters registers deviations from those normative principles. Austen confidently anticipates that her readers will recognize her ironies and participate in her implied judgments. The story thus culminates in a harmonious concord among all the factors within the total meaning structure and the total meaning situation: the protagonist, the author, and the implied audience are brought together in a single community of discourse. The protagonists satisfy normative sociobiological expectations and at the same time embody the normative virtues of their own culture. The fulfillment of their happiness thus strongly suggests an ideal concord between their specific cultural order and the elemental aspects of human experience.

Readers who fall under the spell of this novel tacitly accept the idea of this concord, at least while the spell lasts. (See Bradley, 1929; C. L. Johnson, 1988; Lewes, 1859; Litz, 1965; Tanner, 1986; Van Ghent, 1953; Woolf, 1953.) Readers who are hostile to Austen's cultural order or to the idea of any normative heterosexual romance must either distance themselves from Austen's perspective or find some way of interpreting her perspective that makes it seem more alienated than it actually is. (See Ahearn, 1987; I. Armstrong, 1990; N. Armstrong, 1981, 1987; Auerbach, 1978; Belsey, 2002; Brownstein, 1988; Fraiman, 1989; Handler and Segal, 1990; Harding, 1940; Litvak, 1992; Mudrick, 1952; Newman, 1983; Newton, 1981; Poovey, 1984; Smith, 1993, 2000; Wylie, 2000.) Postmodern criticism—the established ideology of academic literary criticism since the 1980s—is programmatically radical in its orientation. It seeks to render all meaning indeterminate and adopts an automatically hostile stance toward all forms of normative order—political, social, and sexual. Austen's own ideology is conservative, and her structure of meaning is exceptionally clear. Her work thus exercises a strong constraining force on the distorting pull of postmodern ideology. The obligatory postmodern efforts to radicalize and problematize all literary texts tend, in Austen's case, to lack force and conviction, and the degree of consensus among her critics has remained very high. The postmodern formulas are often recited in a perfunctory way, and the main body of the critical expositions follow the outlines of meaning so firmly and cleanly drawn by Austen herself. The largest parts of most interpretations of Austen, from her own time to the present, are overlapping and complementary. (For a more detailed account of *Pride and Prejudice* and of the criticism on it, in this vol., see part 2, chapter 6.)

Austen herself never married, but her fiction betrays little personal frustration. Her generosity of feeling, buoyed by her humor, enables her to rise above her personal situation and to identify with the fulfillment of a normative heterosexual relationship. Charlotte Brontë, like Austen, was a spinster (she married in her late thirties, in the last year of her life). She was physically unattractive, socially obscure, and financially insecure. Unlike Austen, she had little sense of humor. She suffered intensely from her sexual marginalization, and her frustrated yearning fundamentally constrained the kind of fiction she wrote. She had a despairing need of intimate sexual affection, and she was at the same time fiercely proud. She was, as a result, egoistically self-preoccupied and absorbed in defensive self-affirmation. These are all characteristics shared by the protagonist of *Villette*.

If we were to approach *Villette* looking only for examples of normative heterosexual couples and illustrations of sexual psychology concordant with sociobiological expectations, we would find what we were looking for, but we would also fail to identify the total meaning structure of the novel. To identify this structure, we have to ascertain what kind of psychological function the novel fulfills for its author. The emotional center of the novel is the narrator and protagonist whose personal characteristics and circumstances are taken from Brontë herself. Like Brontë, the narrator goes to teach in a Belgian school for girls, and then, for the next few hundred pages, nothing happens. That is, nothing happens to her. She sits and watches quietly, largely unnoticed, while two love stories are played out around her. The male protagonist of these love stories is a young doctor who attends the girls at the school. He first falls in love with a frivolous and worldly flirt, and then is fortunate to have his attention drawn instead to a young lady who fits the pattern of Victorian heroines. This second girl is beautiful, cultivated, feminine, modest, discreet, and devoted. The doctor succeeds in making an appropriate sexual choice, and the flirt gets her just deserts by marrying a degenerate for the sake of his aristocratic rank. The plot thus fits the pattern of a standard romantic comedy, but almost no reader would call this novel a romantic comedy. The love stories I have described do not constitute the center of interest in the novel. The center of interest is lodged instead in the quiet, neglected narrator. She is herself secretly in love with the doctor, and her story, for several hundred pages, is mainly an experience of passionate, lonely suffering and intense self-suppression. If she were merely a passive sufferer, the story would be unbearable, but the protagonist has a sustaining purpose, that of affirming or validating her own sense of identity, and it is this purpose that forms the central organizing principle in the story. The normative heterosexual romance that she observes provides her with an occasion of psychological self-discipline, relatively easy in the first phase, when she can scorn the flirt and pity the doctor, difficult and even heroic in the second phase, when she must acknowledge the value of a romantic norm from which she herself will forever be excluded. This part of the story constitutes a process of psychological adjustment to a painful reality. Through her fiction, Brontë enacts a process that it is psychologically necessary for her to complete.

In the final phase of the novel, the protagonist accepts the attentions of an older man who is, like herself, sexually marginalized. The protagonist-narrator makes a clear distinction between the normative heterosexual romance from which she is excluded and the kind of relationship that emerges at this lower level of romantic interest. She says that "the love, born of beauty was not mine; I had nothing in common with it," but affirms her readiness for "another love, venturing diffidently into life after long acquaintance ... this Love that laughed at Passion" (chapter 39). Even at this lower level of romantic interest, the protagonist is denied sexual fulfillment. The older man dies before the marriage can take place. The appended story of a successful courtship nonetheless seems to vindicate Brontë's potential for some sort of intimate sexual bonding.

The protagonist of *Villette* is not a heroine in a normative romance, but she is a figure with which most readers can sympathize and even identify. Her motives are clearly recognizable within the framework of our common human nature. She yearns for intimacy, seeks to sustain her dignity, has to come to terms with diminished expectations, and then ultimately must renounce even those expectations. She defines her own position in relation to a normative model of romance, but she also provides in herself a model for the affirmation of personal integrity in the face of insuperable obstacles to happiness.

The critical tradition has adequately grasped the characteristic features of Brontë's mind and art, in respect to both its merits and its limitations. George Eliot's husband, G. H. Lewes, Brontë's contemporary and one of her most astute early admirers, understood that one of her main sources of strength, her emotional intensity, is complementary and interdependent with one of her chief weaknesses—the deficiency in her sense of humor. Commenting on her dislike of Austen, Lewes observes that "those who have little sense of humour, or whose passionate and insurgent activities demand in art a reflection of their own emotions and struggles, will find little pleasure in such homely comedies. Currer Bell [Charlotte Brontë] may be taken as a type of these. She was utterly without a sense of humour, and was by nature fervid and impetuous" (p. 107). Virginia Woolf's father, Leslie Stephen (1990), also reflects on the narrowly self-absorbed intensity of Brontë's work, and that perception has been reiterated in modern commentary (Carlisle, 1979). Brontë's friend Harriet Martineau (1990) was alert to the neurotic quality of Brontë's character, and in more recent commentary Heilman (1991) and Tanner (1979) have seconded Martineau's observations. John Maynard draws attention to the intensity of frustrated sexual passion that drives the fantasy structures in Brontë's fiction. The feminist critics have not, of course, been terribly keen to acknowledge frustrated heterosexual desire as a predominating theme or motive in the work of a great female novelist, but their predictable and often distorting preoccupations have nonetheless cast a bright light on another important aspect of Brontë's character—her affirmation of individual female identity. (See Gilbert and Gubar, 1979; Millett, 1970; Silver, 1983; Yeazell, 1991.)

The narrator's relation to her subject in *Villette* is fairly complex, but there is little uncertainty about the total structure of meaning. The emotional development in the narrator's point of view follows a clear causal trajectory, and the meaning of that trajectory is available to both the narrator and the reader. In the next novel I shall consider, Cather's *O Pioneers!*, the meaning structure is much less determinate. Cather was a exceptionally masculine woman, and in all likelihood a lesbian. The influence of her sexual orientation appears in the relation between two main love plots. Cather does not explain and perhaps does not consciously understand the emotional logic in the relation between these two plots. Consequently, the reader must fill a gap in Cather's structure of meaning.

I shall summarize the story. The protagonist is Alexandra, a strong, masculine woman who has inherited her father's farm in the closing years of the nineteenth century. While growing up, Alexandra has a tender attachment to a boy who is sensitive, artistic, and effeminate, and who is several years her junior. His family returns to the east, and she loses touch with him for a number of years. When he comes back to Nebraska, he forms an adult attachment with Alexandra, but then again leaves to make his fortune. For most of her adult life, Alexandra's emotions have been focused on educating a younger brother.

Like the boy who moved away, the brother is artistic and intellectual. Alexandra sends her brother to the university, but while on vacation at home he falls in love with a neighbor's wife. The woman's husband is violently possessive and jealous. He finds his wife and Alexandra's brother together and murders them both. The sensitive and artistic man Alexandra loved in the past then returns once more, and they decide to marry. Alexandra vows to seek a pardon for the man who murdered her younger brother.

The central dramatic event in this sequence, the jealous murder, is not the emotional culmination of the novel. The emotional culmination is the belated, middle-aged romance between a masculine woman and a younger, effeminate man. This atypical romance has no clear causal link with the romantic tragedy that precedes it. The two stories seem like separate and discrete lines. Beneath these lines, though, there is an emotional logic that connects them. The love triangle that ends in murder represents normative heterosexual love, and within the logic of Cather's own emotional economy, the death of Alexandra's brother and his lover removes this kind of love from the imaginative landscape of the story. It is as if Cather has to eliminate the normative heterosexuals in order to make way for the kind of romance that satisfies her own imagination—the romance of the middle-aged, sexually equivocal protagonists. If this is the case, it would help explain why Alexandra forgives the man who murders her brother. He is merely an instrument in her own fantasy structure. In murdering her brother, he is doing work necessary to the fulfillment of Cather's own psychological needs.

Although Alexandra's love story does not appeal simply and directly to sympathetic identification with a normative heterosexual romance, the emotional structure of the novel nonetheless depends on Alexandra's relation to a normative heterosexual couple. Moreover, while Cather reverses the typical sex roles in her protagonist's own romance, the roles are themselves familiar within the framework of normative heterosexual expectations. A dominant personality in command of worldly resources forms an intimate domestic partnership with a person who is younger, more sensitive, more delicate, and dependent. Beneath her participation in this common form of an intimate dyadic relationship, Alexandra shares the common human need for intimate bonding with another person. Her griefs and fulfillments remain intelligible within the framework of a common human nature.

Criticism on *O Pioneers!* is less voluminous than that on *Pride and Prejudice*, or even that on *Villette*. And it is also less firm and distinct in its results. Cather's lesbianism was not overt, and some of her critics have been diffident in affirming what, from the biographical data, should be obvious. They have felt a delicacy in identifying the lesbian orientation, and they have thus been reluctant to pursue the implications of Cather's sexual identity. (See Acocella, 2000; Lee, 1989; O'Brien, 1987; Wagenknecht, 1994.) Sexual identity is central to personal identity, no matter what one's gender orientation might be—

whether robustly heterosexual like Austen's, equivocal like Henry James's, or decidedly homosexual like Oscar Wilde's or Gertrude Stein's—and personal identity shapes every aspect of an artist's work. Art is personal in a way that science, say, or even historical scholarship, is not. Sexual identity enters into theme and tone, and it can shape the plot to fulfill the psychological needs of the author. The failure of criticism to come to grips with Cather's sexual identity thus forestalls adequate comprehension even of her formal organization. In the case of *O Pioneers!*, the problem of formal analysis is exacerbated by the fact that the novel was cobbled together out of two preexisting stories (See Stouck, 1992). Some critics (Cooper, 1984; Daiches, 1951) have argued that the two parts of the novel are heterogeneous and unintegrated. Others have sought to vindicate the unity of the work by delineating various archetypal configurations (Baker, 1982; Charles, 1965; Moseley, 1985) or various thematic formulas (Murphy, 1984; O'Brien, 1978; Stouck, 1992). If the total meaning structure of this novel has the determinate order I have identified—or any determinate order at all—there is a clear gap between that total meaning structure and the public understanding of the work.

The atypical sexual psychology in Alexandra's love story makes sense in terms of Cather's own sexual psychology. Arnold Bennett's *Anna of the Five Towns* presents another instance of atypical sexual psychology, but Bennett was unequivocally heterosexual, and the peculiar psychology of this story requires a different sort of explanation. I shall again quickly summarize the story. The protagonist Anna, a young woman of marriageable age, is a severely repressed Methodist who has been raised by a cold, tyrannical father. She is courted by and accepts a man who is an alpha male—confident, poised, successful, charming, reliable, and even kind—but at the very end of the novel we are told that she harbors a secret amorous passion for an ultra-low-ranking male (an "omega" male), a young man who is timid, awkward, submissive, and generally hapless. After his father falls into disgrace and commits suicide, the young omega male, Willie Price, decides to leave the country. Before he departs, Anna kisses him once, revealing her passion, but she still marries the alpha male, ostensibly out of a respect for her prior commitment.

From within the framework of our evolved sexual psychology, Anna's supposed passion for Willie Price is aberrational. Bennett does not prepare the reader for this strange sexual turn, nor does he offer any overt explanation of it. Not surprisingly, critical responses to the novel have been divergent and confused. The strongest response is that of one early reviewer who expressed frank skepticism about the sexual psychology depicted in the novel. "Pity suddenly turns into an overwhelming love, not, be it remembered, in an unoccupied heart. We refuse to believe. The tragedy is not according to nature, but according to art" (review of *Anna of the Five Towns* [anonymous], 1981). Other critics have registered similar disbelief but have articulated it less completely. James Hall (1959) remarks that pity is the only love of which Anna is capable, but he still does not find her feeling for the omega male convincing. John Lucas remarks that "Bennett is rarely able to deal convincingly with sexual passion" (1974, 51). Margaret Drabble recognizes that Anna's supposed love for the omega male is psychologically abnormal, but she tries to explain away the problem by declaring that Anna "mistakes" pity and guilt for love (1974, 95). Bennett himself gives no signals indicating that Anna has made a "mistake." Stone (1983), Anderson (1988), and Bauer (1992) perceive a link between Anna's sexual unresponsiveness to the alpha male and her passive resistance to the tyranny of her father.

A critic determined to make sense of Anna's behavior could fabricate some sort of psychological explanation for it. One could argue that Anna suffers from a severe psychological dissociation. She behaves sexually in a sociobiologically normal way—that is, she marries an alpha male—but her imaginative and emotional life have, one could argue, become disconnected from her behavior. She associates the alpha male with the patriarchal oppression represented by her tyrannical father, and her need for self-affirmation manifests itself as an affirmation of her own ethos of maternal pity. That self-affirmation might somehow channel sexual responsiveness toward the object of her pity.

This psychological explanation seems forced and labored. There is no evident reason that maternal pity and self-affirmation would become a channel for sexual passion, and the dissociation between this supposed passion and Anna's actual behavior—marrying the alpha male—remains an anomaly, poorly rationalized by the idea of prior commitment. The solution is strained, and the strained solution has to be weighed against the brute shock of disbelief produced by the late, sudden revelation of Anna's secret passion.

Why would Bennett be led into an implausible depiction of Anna's sexual nature? As an alternative to the hypothesis of simple psychological incompetence on Bennett's part, I would suggest the possibility that psychological verisimilitude has been sacrificed to another motive. To identify the motive, we should look for the governing forms of meaning—some thematic or tonal structure that gives shape to the narrative.

The largest structure of meaning in the story consists in a gendered thematic opposition between two worldviews, one Christian and female, the other quasi-Darwinian and male. Anna achieves a sense of her own personal identity in epiphanies of Christian maternal sentiment, and her feelings for Willie Price, the omega male, are almost wholly those of maternal pity, though these feelings briefly mingle with erotic expressions in the climactic scene of the novel. When Anna is sent by her father to demand payment of a debt from Willie Price's father, she has an interview with Willie, and his haplessness evokes her religious fervor:

> His tone was so earnest, so pathetic, that tears of compassion almost rose to her eyes as she looked at those simple naïve blue eyes of his. His lanky figure and

clumsily-fitting clothes, his feeble placatory smile, the twitching movements of his long red hands, all contributed to the effect of his defencelessness. She thought of the text: "Blessed are the meek," and saw in a flash the deep truth of it. . . . Blessed are the meek, blessed are the failures, blessed are the stupid, for they, unknown to themselves, have a grace which is denied to the haughty, the successful, the wise. (chapter 6)

The Alpha male to whom Anna is engaged speaks slightingly of Willie, but the effect is only to reinforce her maternal attachment. "How was he to know that in misprizing Willie Price before her, he was misprizing a child to its mother?" (chapter 12).

In contrast to Anna's own imaginative visions of Christian maternal passion, Bennett evokes and tacitly adopts a male perspective that is quasi-Darwinian, brutal, and violent. He associates Christianity with maternal sentiment, and quasi-Darwinian naturalism with male sexuality. Brutal male sexuality directs itself against a feminized Nature, and the English pottery district becomes the local embodiment of this elemental, archetypal conflict, a conflict between dominating, violating males, and supine, alienated females:

Nothing could be more prosaic than the huddled, red-brown streets; nothing more seemingly remote from romance. Yet be it said that romance is even here— the romance which, for those who have an eye to perceive it, ever dwells amid the seats of industrial manufacture. . . This disfigurement is merely an episode in the unending warfare of man and nature, and calls for no contrition. Here, indeed, is nature repaid for some of her notorious cruelties. She imperiously bids man sustain and reproduce himself, and this is one of the places where in the very act of obedience he wounds and maltreats her. . . . (chapter 1)

The entire landscape was illuminated and transformed by these unique pyrotechnics of labour atoning for its grime, and dull, weird sounds, as of the breathings and sighings of gigantic nocturnal creatures, filled the enchanted air. It was a romantic scene, a romantic summer night, balmy, delicate, and wrapped in meditation. But Anna saw nothing there save the repulsive evidences of manufacture, had never seen anything else. (chapter 6)

Bennett himself is clearly responsive to the sexual charm of male domination in nature and in industry, but Anna is not, and her unresponsiveness to the romance of industry associates itself, in Bennett's own mind, with her sexual unresponsiveness to the successful industrialist she is to marry. The breathings and sighings of gigantic nocturnal creatures strike no responsive sexual chord in her. She is primarily maternal in character, and the releasors for maternal passion—the signals or stimuli that activate that passion—are weakness and helplessness.

What has happened here, I would suggest, is that Bennett has been captured by the charm of a dichotomy—the dichotomy between male sexuality and female maternity—and he has allowed this dichotomy to distort his understanding of human nature. He has condensed two phases of female reproductive psychology—the mating phase and the maternal, parenting phase—into the single maternal phase. It is not just that Anna is sexually unresponsive but maternally responsive; that would be a common and plausible female profile. Anna is in fact sexually responsive, but her sexuality is elicited by the same releasors that elicit her maternal impulses. Her sexuality and her maternity have been strangely and perversely blended. The responses of critics, confused, dissatisfied, or weakly rationalizing, register the effect of this distorting simplification in Anna's psychology.

In both *O Pioneers!* and *Anna of the Five Towns*, the protagonists and narrators suffer lapses into blankness that have to be filled in by interpretative speculation. In *Pride and Prejudice, Villette,* and *Tess of the d'Urbervilles,* the structure of meaning is more complete. Of these three novels, *Tess* has to meet the greatest challenge in achieving a structure of meaning adequate to its subject. In *Villette,* the protagonist serves as a fictive extension of the author's own personal concerns, and the imaginative purposes of the story restrict themselves to the problems of her individual identity. In *Pride and Prejudice,* the marriage plot serves to affirm the normative principles within a traditional cultural order. Unlike Brontë, Hardy concerns himself with problems of nature and civilization that extend beyond his own personal preoccupations, and unlike Austen and her protagonists, Hardy and his protagonists must undergo a conscious struggle to construct an interpretive model of their world. Hardy's characters have shattering experiences in areas of elemental concern: sex, birth, death, betrayal, and abandonment. They must overcome philosophical confusion and replace conventional values, and they must meet these challenges while suffering from sustained emotional distress.

The story of *Tess,* as Hardy presents it, has exceptional beauty and power, but the basic plot of the novel, starkly summarized, is sordid and painful. One challenge for a sociobiological critique of the novel is to account for the beauty and power. The protagonist is a young peasant girl, descendant of a long decayed aristocratic family. She is raped by a wealthy cad, her employer, dallies with him a few weeks, and then leaves him. She has his baby, and after the baby dies she goes to work at a dairy. There she meets and falls in love with an educated and high-minded young man studying to be a farmer. She hides her past, and they marry, but on her wedding night she reveals her secret. Because her husband is fixated on a conventional conception of female chastity, he leaves her, and more than a year later, destitute and desperate to help her family, she returns to her former lover. When her husband eventually comes back to her, she murders the former lover. She and her husband flee and have a week of happiness before she is caught and hanged.

What makes this a great novel? Both the characters and the author in *Tess* have to confront the sordid facts I have described, and the significance of the action depends on the qualities of mind and character evoked by this confrontation. The protagonists in *Tess* are sensuous, passionate, and reflective, but they find themselves in circumstances that are always a little in advance of their capacity to comprehend and control them. In response to the stress of these circumstances, they are ultimately forced to look past cultural conventions and to probe the elemental, instinctive basis of human nature. To rise to the challenge of their situation requires extraordinary qualities of generosity, tenderness, and compassion. Hardy himself has these qualities of mind and temper, and his characters also ultimately attain them, but only through the experience of events that destroy their chances for happiness. The emotional process of the story culminates in a sensation of a noble pathos. That is the sensation appropriate to tragedy, and experiencing that sensation satisfies an imaginative need as real and definite as the needs satisfied through the happier affects of comedy.

Hardy's own qualities of mind and temperament are a central component in the total effect of his work, but to give them full value he must fashion a style and a symbolic order adequate to his subject, and in this respect *Tess* is singularly successful. In all the phases of his characters' lives, from romantic intoxication to tragic despair, Hardy evokes their experience with an extraordinary lyric power. Almost every scene is sensuously vivid. Hardy envisions the characters always as living organisms closely intermeshed with their concrete physical environments, and he gives a detailed evocation of the topography of each distinct geographic region of the story. (For further comments on Hardy's sense of physical place, in this vol., see part 1, chapter 8.) In the close physical correlation of organism and environment, Hardy is affiliated with the "naturalistic" school, but he does not, like the more narrowly naturalistic writers (Zola or Norris), reduce his characters to bestial mindlessness. His characters have rich inner lives, and they take on large symbolic value for each other and for Hardy as well. This symbolic value is not merely "archetypal" or universal. As symbols, the characters simultaneously combine the elemental or universal aspects of experience with the sense of a unique moment of cultural history. In their elemental aspects, the dairy maids, and especially Tess, constitute mythic embodiments of primal nature. "She was no longer the milkmaid, but a visionary essence of woman—a whole sex condensed into one typical form" (chapter 20). And conversely, to the dairy maids, the young man embodies all higher culture, the sphere of the mind and of gentlemanly chivalry. "To her sublime trustfulness he was all that goodness could be, knew all that a guide, philosopher, and friend should know. She thought every line in the contour of his person the perfection of masculine beauty; his soul the soul of a saint; his intellect that of a seer" (chapter 31). As symbols of a unique historical moment, the characters dramatize the transition from a simpler, more naive culture to a cultural phase Hardy characterizes in the famous phrase, "the ache of modernism" (chapter 19). What Hardy means by "modernism" is the historical moment—his own moment—at which thoughtful people shake off traditional religious beliefs and find that they must take individual responsibility for organizing new systems of meaning and value.

Altogether, the elements of Hardy's distinctive vision—his tenderness of feeling, his poetic sensuousness, his naturalistic immediacy, and the scope and depth of his symbolism—form a dense medium through which the reader experiences the events of the story. The total structure of meaning in the story emerges from the successful integration of all these elements.

The simplicity and clarity of outline in Austen's work have a classical grandeur distinct from the lush sensuousness and Romantic passion in Hardy's novel, and romantic comedy places less stress than tragedy on the powers of imaginative response. At least partly for these reasons, the challenge presented by Austen has proved easier for criticism to master. No one critic seems so fully to have commanded the phenomenon of *Tess* in the same way that the better critics have mastered the challenge of *Pride and Prejudice*. Virginia Woolf (1960) gives a perspicacious account of Hardy's mythic scope—the way in which he envisions elemental human passions cast against a primal landscape. Katherine Anne Porter (1940) catches well the nuances of his moral temper. Tony Tanner (1968) powerfully evokes the artistic congruity of image, tone, and philosophic vision in *Tess*. Gose (1963), Meisel (1972), Johnson (1977), Robinson (1980), Beer (1983), and Morton (1984) all discuss Hardy's use of Darwinian themes, but only Robinson makes very good critical use of this topic. He registers the integration of Darwinian naturalism and tender poetic sensitivity in Hardy's works, and he perceptively assesses the relations among mythic images, social stereotypes, and individual identities in *Tess*. Taken collectively, these various critical responses are adequate to the novel, and the total impression produced by this collective effort is very different from that of simple confusion arising from the indeterminacy of its object, as in the case of Bennett, or, in lesser degree, the case of Cather.

All five of these novels create distinctive structures of meaning and at the same time make at least tacit appeal to elemental dispositions. *Pride and Prejudice* is simply and classically normative in the harmonious concord it establishes between the author's identity, her cultural order, and species-typical behavioral norms, but that concord is itself a rare and distinctive characteristic. Hardy has no such sense of concord, but by appealing to an order of nature outside the conventional values of his time, he creates an alternative cultural community with his readers. In both *Tess of the d'Urbervilles* and *Villette*, the pathos and dignity of the protagonists' experience derive from the way they respond to the frustration of their desire to participate in a normative romance. The protagonists of *O Pioneers!* and *Anna of the Five Towns* define their own sexual identities in contrast with sociobiologically typical expectations, but the protagonists are nonetheless motivated by the need for sexual intimacy and for the affirmation of individual identity. Cather's Alexandra reverses typical sex roles but still seeks intimacy within typical forms of a dyadic relationship. Bennett's Anna deviates from typical female mate preferences, but, as Bennett conceives her, she fashions her own idiosyncratic sexual identity through her elemental maternal nature. The elemental dispositions of human nature provide a common basis for understanding what is intelligible in these novels and also what—as in the case of Anna—is confusing or unsatisfactory.

These novels have not been equally valued by readers. *Pride and Prejudice* and *Tess of the d'Urbervilles* hold an unequivocal position in the highest rank of English novels. They appeal to common and basic motivational structures, create clear, complete, and coherent structures of meaning, display extraordinary stylistic felicity in the evocation of their subjects, and treat their characters with a rich and magnanimous generosity of fellow human feeling. *Villette* has a dedicated but narrow audience. Its verbal artistry alone assures it continued appreciative attention among aficionados of prose, and its preoccupation with the self-affirmation of an intelligent, sensitive, but socially and sexually marginalized woman has always tapped a certain vein of sympathetic response—a response heightened if sometimes distorted by the feminist preoccupations of the past few decades. The quality of defensive, self-absorbed egoism that assures exceptional personal identification with some readers also virtually guarantees that the novel will never have the kind of broad appeal displayed by *Pride and Prejudice* or *Tess of the d'Urbervilles*. For these reasons, *Villette* holds a secure position on a second canonical tier. *Anna of the Five Towns* and *O Pioneers!* drop below that tier. They have both garnered some serious academic attention, but neither has stimulated a wide and enthusiastic responsiveness among the generally literate public. They are not favorites of "the common reader," and the common reader has her reasons. Both novels have eccentric motivational structures, and, partly as a result of this eccentricity, their total structures of meaning are obscure, latent, or confused. The novels thus present interesting puzzles for critical analysis, but they also leave a sense of dissatisfaction. They have imperfectly mastered their subjects and have as a result incompletely satisfied the reader's desire for cognitive order. The greatest literary works most completely satisfy that desire, and for this reason they can and should serve as a central point of reference for our understanding of human nature.

4
Organism, Environment, and Literature

This essay was adapted from a talk given at a meeting of the Association for the Study of Literature and the Environment, Flagstaff, Arizona, June 2001.

For further commentary on ecological literary criticism, in this vol., see part 1, chapter 8.

For the past decade or so, I have been working to integrate Darwinian thinking with literary study. I have written a book on the topic and a number of articles and reviews. Here, I am first going to describe some of the main features in the theoretical terrain I have crossed and then assess the relations between evolutionary literary theory and ecology.

I am sometimes asked how I came to take up Darwinism. My graduate training, in the 1970s at Berkeley, was in comparative literature. I spent a lot of time in language study and gave particular attention to the history of ideas. I subscribed, uncritically but sincerely, to what Meyer Abrams identifies as the traditional humanistic paradigm—the idea that "the site of literature is the human world, and a work of literature is the product of a purposive human author addressing human recipients in an environing world" (1997, p. 115). In order to provide a governing frame for my own scholarly and critical work, I adopted no one particular theory. Instead, I depended on what I took to be the common understanding of educated people. The Darwinian theory of evolution, I assumed, was one of the largest and most important elements within that common understanding. In the introduction to my first book, *The Cultural Theory of Matthew Arnold*, written twenty years ago, I made tacit appeal to this Darwinian element. I said that "Arnold bases his system of culture on two assumptions that most of us no longer make. He comes to believe in the existence of objective, universally valid laws, and to believe that these laws have been progressively revealing and developing themselves throughout the history of Western culture" (1982, p. xiv). Arnold was Darwin's contemporary, but Arnold never assimilated the cultural and metaphysical implications of Darwin's thinking. Unlike Darwin, Arnold envisioned history as an immanent spiritual dynamic leading to a culminating condition of human cultural "perfection." In his belief in teleological progressivism, Arnold was typical of Victorian cultural theorists.

When I spoke of "assumptions that most of us no longer make," I was presupposing that "most of us" had assimilated the larger implications of Darwin's understanding of evolutionary processes. I myself had not yet read much of Darwin, but I understood the basic theory and held it as an axiom that all organisms are the product of an interaction between their innate biological characteristics and their environmental influences. The naturalism of this axiom seemed integral to the Enlightenment belief in reason and nature, and I regarded that Enlightenment belief as the central current in our modern intellectual heritage. Over the next decade, throughout the 1980s, it gradually became apparent to me that in invoking this common heritage, I had been hasty and naive.

In the mid-century period, the traditional humanistic paradigm of which Abrams speaks had accommodated a hodge-podge of ideologies, philosophies, and religious beliefs. Within the culture of literary study, the Enlightenment belief in reason and nature had never achieved clear dominance, and post-Darwinian naturalism had had very little influence. Several of the major literary theorists of the twentieth century were traditional Christians. Others were Romantic mystics. From the 1930s into the 1970s, the core ideology for academic literary study was the New Criticism, and the core belief of the New Criticism was a mystical sacralization of the literary artifact. This aestheticist credo was compounded from sources that had no affiliation with Darwinian naturalism: from Kantian aesthetics, Coleridgean metaphysics, the Arnoldian transvaluation of religion as poetry and poetry as religion, and the formalist aspects of Paterian aestheticism.

In the late 1970s and early 1980s, a theoretical and ideological revolution occurred in literary studies. The new poststructuralist paradigm eliminated both the aestheticist idolatry of the New Criticism and the ethos of reason and nature that had subsisted uneasily alongside it. The 1980s were a period of swift transition. By 1990, most practicing literary critics had subscribed, however grudgingly, to the new poststructuralist paradigm. There are two essential elements to the poststructuralist paradigm: textualism and indeterminacy. Textualism is the belief that language or culture constructs the world according to its own internal principles, and indeterminacy identifies all meaning as self-contradictory. Within the poststructuralist world view, signs determine the shape of reality, and all sign systems necessarily subvert themselves.

Sometime in the late 1980s, a friend of mine, lodged happily in the bosom of the new theoretical establishment, remarked in a complacent way, "We are all deconstructionists now." No, I thought, not quite all of us. There is at least one of us who is not. To me, the philosophical rationale for the new paradigm seemed wholly unconvincing. I saw nothing in the propositions of textualism and indeterminacy that even remotely approximated to the axiomatic force of the basic biological proposition that organisms are the product of an interaction between their innate characteristics and their environmental influences. But it was not possible simply to ignore the new paradigm and proceed with specialized scholarship. For scholars to register with other scholars that they were initiated members of a professional discipline, it had became obligatory that every formulation couch itself within the codes of textualism and indeterminacy. In order to continue to speak about literature as an act of communication between individual people in an environing world, it had become necessary to formulate an explicit philosophical justification for each of those terms.

My first effort to formulate a theoretical system as an alternative to poststructuralism was descriptive and schematic. I designed a set of concentric circles that were meant to constitute a map of all possible categories of experience. The innermost circle, at the center of the set of concentric circles, was the individual person. The outermost circle was the universe—the whole world to the furthest glimmer of light filtering in from the Big Bang 15 billion years ago. Between these two points, I located a series of nested categories. These categories were, I said, the major terms through which human beings organize their experience. Starting from the individual, the next category was the sexual dyad, the couple, and I noted that love stories—stories about the romantic and sexual relations between two people, usually a man and a woman—constitute the overwhelming preponderance of all literary plots. Beyond that, the next circle—the next major category through which human beings organize their experience—was the family, that is, a social group consisting of parents and children, of sisters and brothers, and then of other kin. It is within the family that individuals develop and define themselves personally and socially, and few love stories take place without some reference to family relations. Moreover, the family is the basis for the generational ethos, and thus for dramas, epics, and myths in which the sense of connection and consequence extends beyond the lifetime of a single individual. The next category was that of the whole social world—the world of communities, occupations, classes, nations, political organizations, and political ideologies. For most contemporary critics and humanists, this is the last substantive category. All experience defines itself exclusively in terms of particular social configurations. But in this respect most contemporary theorists part company with most literary authors. Beyond the limits of any particular social order, most authors make some appeal to "human nature," that is, to a set of motives and cognitive dispositions that are specifically human and that appear in all cultures. The category of human nature is itself contained within the still larger category of nature—the world of living things and their physical environment. For me, this last category, that of the physical environment, was coterminous with the outermost sphere on my map. There is no larger or more inclusive category. For many other people, the outermost sphere would be defined not in terms of the physical universe but in terms of spirit or divinity. This outermost sphere is thus the sphere of metaphysics, the sphere in which one identifies the ultimate stuff or matter of the universe.

Every person has a worldview, and all literary representations articulate the worldviews of their authors. The individual person at the center of this set of categories can be an author of a literary representation, and he or she can also be a character in a literary representation. That is, all authors and all characters are individual persons. Characters are passional agents, animated by the common human passions and motives, but they are also perspectival agents. They struggle to make sense of the world, to interpret actions in ways that answer to their own needs and values, and to impose their reading of events on other characters. In the degree to which authors themselves wish to influence the behavior of others through their works, they are themselves passional agents, but their primary role is that of perspectival agents. They enjoy a special privilege of exercising interpretive authority over the stories they themselves tell.

The relations of comparison and contrast among the viewpoints of characters and between the viewpoints of authors and characters is one of the most important dimensions of meaning in literary texts. Characters struggle with one another to tell the story in their own terms, and the author constantly mediates among characters, aligning himself or herself with one or another, and distancing himself or herself from others. Each distinct point of view involves a distinct meaning system, and the total meaning structure derives from the interplay of competing or collusive meaning systems within any given text. It is for this reason that the analysis of irony, as a central tonal medium for registering differences in point of view, occupies a position of singular importance in the interpretation of literary meaning.

Every text has a total meaning structure, that is, an at least hypothetically recoverable set of meanings, but even when we have gone so far as to establish a category as portentous-sounding as that of "the total meaning structure," we have not yet exhausted the problems and potentials in point of view. The viewpoints of readers need not converge precisely with those of characters or authors. The total meaning *situation* of any literary text thus involves more than the total meaning *structure* of the text. The total meaning situation involves the relation between the total meaning structure of the text—with all its interacting points of view—and the point of view of any reader or set of readers. When we interpret the larger meaning situation of a text, we at least tacitly include the response of various readers, and in this respect, interpretation presents the prospect of an endless regress—new readers reading previous readers reading the text. Lest this formula sound dizzyingly abstract, consider that in any ordinary introduction to a paperback edition of a classic literary text, we are almost certain to hear an account of the historical reception of that text, and at the end of the introduction, if it is even ordinarily competent, we shall find a "guide to further reading." Each of the books and articles in any such bibliographic list embodies a distinct way of organizing the main categories of human experience.

The purpose of the map I have described was to provide a set of common, neutral categories that could provide a basis for the comparison of world-views. Different people and different cultures give different definitions to the various categories of the map. From my own naturalistic perspective, the figure at the center of the map, the individual person, is an organism, and the whole set of circles surrounding that organism is the environment. The human environment is both social and natural; it includes other people as well as land, sea, and sky, plants, and animals. For a Christian, in contrast, the circle at the center might well be the individual soul, and the whole set of intervening circles a series of challenges and temptations lying between the soul and God, who occupies the outermost circle. For someone participating in the post-modern paradigm, the inner circles of individual, the sexual couple, and the family, would be defined through textualized Freudian terms such as those available in Lacan; the social world would be defined through textualized Marxist terms such as those available in Althusser, Foucault, and Jameson; and the outermost circle would be defined through the deconstructive linguistic philosophy derived from Derrida.

By constructing a set of conceptually neutral categories for the comparison of worldviews, I had provided myself with a framework within which to compare the competing paradigms of poststructuralism and the traditional humanistic paradigm, but I had not yet constructed a rationale for the naturalistic content that I myself wished to give to the categories in this map. This was the point to which I had come, about ten years ago, when I first sat down to read two of Darwin's major works, *The Origin of Species* and *The Descent of Man*. The immediate occasion for reading Darwin was simply to participate in a conference panel as part of my ongoing scholarship in the field of Victorian prose. The effect of reading Darwin was immediate, massive, and decisive. It did not so much transform my worldview as unfold and illuminate it. Darwin's own vision of evolutionary history has a simple grandeur and power that comprehends the whole natural world, including the human world, over all of geological time. Set beside the scope and comprehensive force of the Darwinian worldview, the sophistical verbal formulas and tortured encodings of poststructuralism appear trivial and irrelevant. Up to this point, my own naturalistic convictions had been stubbornly but passively held intuitions. Now I began to formulate them as active theoretical propositions about human nature, the adaptive functions of the mind, and the nature of literature as a biological phenomenon.

While formulating these propositions, I was reading intensively in the current research on the biological basis of human behavior, and I was able to locate my own Darwinian efforts within the larger historical trajectory of evolutionary thought. The general outlines of that trajectory are now well known. Darwinism had been an active force in social and even in literary theory until about the end of first decade of the twentieth century. In the following decade, an anti-Darwinian ideology arose and took command over the social sciences. The chief tenets of this ideology were that culture has supplanted biology and that human nature is infinitely plastic and malleable— that there are no evolved genetic constraints on human behavior. (See Brown, 1991, pp. 1–38; Buss, 1999, part 1; Degler, 1991; Fox, 1989, chapters 3 and 4; Freeman, 1992, 1999, pp. 17–27; Tooby and Cosmides, 1992, p. 28.)

In the mid-century period, Konrad Lorenz and Karl Popper took up where Darwin had left off in the adaptationist study of human cognition, but "evolutionary epistemology" does not directly concern itself with specifically human motivational structures and it thus did not mount a direct challenge to the theory of cultural autonomy that dominated the social sciences. The first widely recognized challenge to the theory of cultural autonomy came in 1975, with the publication of E. O. Wilson's *Sociobiology: The New Synthesis*. Wilson had collected all the available information on the evolution of social behavior in animals, and by including humans in this category he violated an ideological taboo. As a result, he was violently and repeatedly attacked by Marxist ideologues—most prominently by Stephen Jay Gould and Richard Lewontin, but his work also became a rallying point for a newly emerging movement in Darwinian social science. That movement first gained major ground in anthropology and then spread quickly into psychology, political science, linguistics, ethics, and aesthetics. (See Alcock, 2001; Chagnon and Irons, 1979; Segerstråle, 2000; E. O. Wilson, 1994, chapter 17).

Within the past decade or so, a scattered group of literary theorists and critics has begun to take account of all this information. At the time I started working on a Darwinian literary theory, I assumed that I was working alone. But there were several other people who had also responded to evolutionary theory and were actively developing ways of applying it to literary study or to the wider field of aesthetics. Like me, most of these people started in isolation and only gradually became aware that they were part of a rapidly expanding common effort. (In this vol., see the introduction, section 3, "Contributions to Adaptationist Literary Study.")

From my reading in Darwinian studies of human behavior, I abstracted four large principles that I used to organize my understanding of literature: (a) the relation between organism and environment is a matrix concept prior to all social, psychological, and semiotic principles; (b) the human mind is organized through innate psychological structures (motivational and cognitive) that have evolved through an adaptive process of natural selection; (c) inclusive fitness is the ultimate regulative principle that has governed evolutionary adaptations; (d) literature is a form of cognitive mapping. All four of these principles work simultaneously to repudiate the textualist indeterminacy of poststructuralism and to affirm the naturalist conviction that literature reflects and articulates the vital motives and interests of human beings as living organisms.

From the evolutionary perspective, human beings are only a late and special instance of primate evolution; primates are late and special instances of mammalian evolution; and mammals themselves are relatively recent branches on the tree of animal life. The peculiar cognitive, linguistic, and cultural developments of human beings have done nothing to liberate them from the elemental constraints of all animal life—the necessity of nourishment, of water and air, a certain range of temperature, of protection from physical harm, and of successful reproduction. The evolution of all specifically human adaptive structures has proceeded within biological conditions that are larger, broader, deeper, and older than any specifically human characteristics. Humans are social mammals, and the consequences of that broader set of conditions are fundamental to their motivational and affective lives. Live birth, the suckling of young, and the organization of individuals within a larger community shape and constrain our deepest needs. Upright posture and a large brain—our two most important specifically human adaptations—have produced innate motivational characteristics that fundamentally constrain sexual identity, human mating, and childhood development. The combination of a large brain and an upright posture produce a narrow birth canal. Humans are born premature, more helpless for longer than any other animal. Human babies are totally dependent on mothers, and as a result, throughout all of human evolutionary history, successful human reproduction has involved some kind of female dependence on male support. (In this respect, humans differ from the majority of other animals, including mammals and primates, but not from most birds.) The common characteristics of human sexuality—the specificity of male and female identity and the often conflicted interdependence of men and women—flow directly from these biological realities.

The human brain has evolved to subserve all these more elemental needs and characteristics. In opposition, then, to the textualist creed of poststructuralism, I invoke the central principle of evolutionary epistemology, the idea that "all human knowledge derives from a process of interaction between man as a physical entity, an active, perceiving subject, and the realities of an equally physical external world, the object of man's perception" (Lorenz, 1978, p. 1). From this perspective, literature itself is only a special case of the cognitive activity aimed at orienting the organism to its environment—an environment that is in the first place physical. Literature distinguishes itself from other forms of knowledge in subject and method. Its subject is human experience, and its method is to evoke the subjective, felt quality of that experience by integrating conceptual understanding with the senses and the emotions.

While I was writing *Evolution and Literary Theory* (1995), one of the main challenges I saw in front of us, both for evolutionary psychology and for evolutionary literary study, was that of giving more precise and definite content to the second heuristic principle identified above, the idea that the human mind is organized through innate psychological structures (motivational and cognitive) that have evolved through an adaptive process of natural selection. Which structures, organized in what way? I wished to use biologically based and empirically derived information about human nature as a framework for discussing the depiction of human behavior in literary texts, and for discussing the motives and identities of authors. Where to start? We needed detail, specific ideas.

The seminal thinkers within evolutionary psychology also recognized the need for detail, and they responded to it with the theory of "domain specific cognitive modules." Merging the ideas of adaptive mental structures with the findings of cognitive psychology, evolutionary psychologists identified cognitive modules as something like "mental organs," hard-wired bits of neural anatomy that have evolved to solve specific adaptive problems. (See Buss, 1999; Cosmides and Tooby, 1994; Pinker, 1994, 1997b; Tooby and Cosmides, 1992.) By identifying such modules, evolutionary psychologists were able to repudiate an idea that they saw as central to the Standard Social Science Model (SSSM) they wished to overthrow—the idea that the mind is a blank slate or general, all-purpose computer in which all particular cognitive structure is supplied by culture. In what has become the single most influential theoretical essay in evolutionary psychology, John Tooby and Leda Cosmides offered a list of special modules for the following functions: face recognition, spatial relations, rigid object mechanics, tool use, fear, social exchange, emotion perception, kin-oriented motivation, effort allocation and recalibration, child care, social inference, sexual attraction, semantic inference, friendship, grammar acquisition, communication pragmatics, theory of mind, "and so on" (1992, p. 113). The list is random and open-ended. Steven Pinker (1994, p. 420) offered a similar list containing fifteen items. The metaphor that became standard for signifying this conception of the mind was that of the "Swiss army knife," with each little corkscrew or snipping device standing for yet another specialized mental "organ." The research program required predictions of a series of discoveries; of hard-wired bits of cognitive neuroanatomy designed to solve specific adaptive problems in the Pleistocene. These discoveries would provide all the necessary structure to fill in a model of human nature.

The idea of cognitive modules has displayed important limitations both empirically and theoretically. The research program has never gotten past its original lists of supposed modules, and random lists of modules, while they meet the need for specificity, do not meet the need for structure at higher levels of organization. To meet that second need, one must construct a bridge between the idea of cognitive domains and the elementary regulative principles of evolution by means of natural selection. In Darwin's own formulations, there are two elementary regulative principles of natural selection: in order to become part of the evolutionary process, organisms have to survive and reproduce. More precisely, they have to survive long enough to reproduce. As Richard Alexander explains, these principles serve for biologists as a basic dichotomy for the analysis of life effort in all organisms (1987, pp. 40–41). "Somatic effort" is the effort an organism expends in acquiring energy, in growing and sustaining itself. "Reproductive effort" is the effort the organism expends on mating and nurturing young: the risks males run and the time and energy they expend in seeking and defending mates, and the expenditure of bodily resources and often of time by female parents.

The vast majority of all organisms that come into life do not succeed in the basic evolutionary task of surviving long enough to reproduce. This is the sobering recognition to which his reading of Malthus drew Darwin's attention in a forcible way. (See Carroll, 2003b, pp. 47–49.) If the largest proportion of the offspring of any species were not doomed to destruction, that species would with astonishing rapidity overrun the planet. (We are now learning in very practical terms about how this principle applies to the human species.) If the message of the necessity of "much destruction" is a negative or sinister aspect of the evolutionary imperative (Darwin, 203, p. 135), there is an equally arresting positive aspect: every single organism alive at the present time, from the lowliest bacterium to the most gifted and talented human being, constitutes the most recent link in a success story that is billions of years old—a story of successful reproduction that stretches back without a single break to the very beginning of life on earth. Whatever else might be said about our ancestors, each and every one of them succeeded in the only two tasks that, from an evolutionary perspective, count at all.

To what degree are human motives reducible to the elemental regulative principles of evolution itself? This question lies at the heart of the controversy between the two main phases of modern evolutionary thinking in the human sciences. The first phase, dominated by biologists and anthropologists, was that of "sociobiology." In the late 1980s and early 1990s, the sociobiologists were gradually supplanted by the newer generation of "evolutionary psychologists." Sociobiologists focus on "fitness maximization" or the drive for reproductive success as the ultimate regulator of human behavior. Evolutionary psychologists acknowledge reproductive success or "inclusive fitness" as the ultimate regulator of adaptive change, but they also insist that inclusive fitness is mediated by "proximate mechanisms" that can be decoupled from direct reproductive motives. They argue that living things should be conceived not primarily as fitness maximizers but rather as "adaptation executors." At its extreme, proponents of this view argue that humans have no irreducible desire for progeny. What they desire instead is sex or mating. More broadly conceived efforts at organizing human motivations have made an allowance for parenting as one of the basic human behavioral systems.

In its more comprehensive formulations, Darwinian thinking about evolved human motives now recognizes at least four basic behavioral systems: survival, reproduction, parenting and kinship, and group living. (See Buss,

1999; McGuire and Troisi, 1998.) The single most important development in sociobiological theory since Darwin has been the clear recognition that "selection" proceeds primarily not at the level of individual organisms or groups of organisms but at the level of genes. (See Alexander, 1979, 1987; Dawkins, 1987, 1989; Hamilton, 1996, 2001; Trivers, 1972, 1985; William, 1966.) Humans share roughly half their genes with siblings. A human being who never reproduced but who sacrificed his or her own reproductive opportunities to benefit two or more reproductively successful siblings—say a maiden aunt who gave up the prospect of marriage in order to devote herself to the care of the orphaned children of her siblings—would thus have achieved reproductive success. The logic of selection at the level of the gene has shaped our motivational systems, and as a consequence sociobiologists and evolutionary psychologists now recognize "kin assistance" as one of the elementary human behavioral systems.

In order to account for social interaction beyond the kin group, evolutionary social scientists invoke the principle of "reciprocation" or "reciprocal altruism." This is simply the principle of mutual back-scratching. In the thinking of most sociobiologists, the logic of gene selection strictly prohibits the idea of true "altruism," of evolved proclivities to sacrifice one's own reproductive advantages for the advantage of others. But as Darwin himself recognized, social animals can often benefit themselves through cooperative effort with others. "When two tribes of primeval man, living in the same country, came into competition, if the one tribe included (other circumstances being equal) a greater number of courageous, sympathetic, and faithful members, who were always ready to warn each other of danger, to aid and defend each other, this tribe would without doubt succeed best and conquer the other" (1981, vol. 1, p. 162; and see Sober and Wilson, 1999; D. S. Wilson, 2002.). Arguing from a Darwinian perspective, James Q. Wilson (1993, p. 70) has proposed that the evolved human capacities for social interaction include the instincts for fair play—for reciprocity and equity—and E. O. Wilson also identifies an evolved human proclivity for contractual arrangements (1998, p. 171). All such orientations necessarily involve the cognitive capacity for monitoring compliance and noncompliance with social contracts—for cheating and for cheater detection. In cheating and the detection of cheating, some Darwinian social thinkers see an evolutionary arms race that is in large measure responsible for the rapid development of human intelligence. (For literary theorists, cheater detection offers a highly suggestive evolutionary basis for the development of irony.) Finally, all complex social organization involves the creation and recognition of distinctions in rank or status, and in this respect human social instincts are continuous with that of other social animals. Our predisposition for forming alliances and conducting elaborate programs for achieving collective dominance is continuous with that of our nearest evolutionary relatives, the chimpanzees. (See De Waal, 1996; Diamond, 1992.)

When we speak of basic human behavioral systems, we are speaking of human universals, and it is to the level of human universals that evolutionary psychology has directed the largest part of its attention. Identifying common human motivational structures is a necessary step in the whole program of repudiating the idea of cultural autonomy. In a more mature phase—often now only glimpsed in the work of evolutionary social scientists—Darwinian thinking about human behavior must also include at least two further levels of analysis: that of specific cultural configurations and that of individual personal identity.

Specific cultural configurations should be conceived as distinctive organizations of the common or universal human motives. One metaphor that might be helpful for envisioning this level of analysis is that of the kaleidoscope. The common elements are the bits and pieces of human nature, and the patterns are the way those bits and pieces fall into relation with one another in a given historical situation. The patterns include the forms of social and political organization, religious beliefs and practices, and artistic conventions. A still better metaphor is that of ecology—an economy of natural and biological forces that varies considerably from clime to clime but that operates always under the constraints of adaptive organization and of natural selection.

Individual differences of identity are of vital importance in our personal and social lives and are crucial to the construction of meaning in literary texts. The meaning in any text is informed by the identity of its author, and that identity is itself compounded of the peculiar characteristics of personality or temperament in interaction with the particular circumstances of his or her personal history. In this respect, the formula for what creates individual identity is only a special case of the larger formula that any organism is a product of the interaction of innate characteristics and environmental influences.

For the analysis of personality, some evolutionary psychologists have wisely assimilated the empirical work that is done in personality psychology. (See Buss, 1990, 1995; MacDonald, 1995b, 1998b; Segal and MacDonald, 1998; J. Q. Wilson, 1993.) The current paradigm in personality psychology recognizes five major factors or dimensions of personality: extraversion/introversion, neuroticism, conscientiousness, agreeableness, and openness or cultural curiosity. Extraversion/introversion speaks directly to the question about the degree to which any given organism orients itself receptively and actively to the environment—in the broadest sense of everything outside the organism—or, conversely, turns in on its own internal workings, absorbed in its internal processes. Neuroticism is a measure of anxiety or fearfulness; its polar antitheses are terms such as confidence and assurance. Conscientiousness is the capacity for making plans and commitments and carrying through on them—for regulating behavior in accordance with long-term objectives. It is a fundamental dimension of moral character. Agreeableness or likableness measures the disposition toward warm and positive social affiliation. Openness or cultural curiosity is a measure of intellectual and aesthetic liveliness or responsiveness—one of the basic measures we take of people when we assess whether they are "dull" or "bright." These five factors have convergent support from multiple sources, and they mesh very neatly with common observation and with the depiction of characters in literature. (In its beginnings a century ago, personality factor research used dictionaries as the source for terms about personality and character. See Pervin, 1990.) The consolidation of an empirical consensus about the major factors of personality can provide to literary analysis a common frame of reference for the description both of characters and of authors. By setting such terms in definite relation to other thematic and tonal elements—to philosophical, religious, and ideological views, to qualities of feeling and to literary conventions and stylistic characteristics—literary critics can make complex interpretive propositions that have a relatively stable point of contact with empirical psychological study.

One further set of terms derived from evolutionary psychology looks particularly promising for literary study—the theory of emotions, and especially of "basic" emotions. Paul Ekman (2003) identifies seven basic emotions that are recognizable from facial expressions across widely diverse cultures, from modern European sophisticates to preliterate peoples in New Guinea. Emotion combined with point of view is the source of "tone" in literature. Tone is a primary element in the larger emotional structures that, together with subject matter, constitute genre, and genre is a major literary category that operates at a level of generality roughly parallel to that of "species" in biology. Ekman's seven basic emotions are (1) joy, happiness, pleasure; (2) sadness, distress; (3) anger, excitement; (4) disgust; (5) contempt; (6) fear; and (7) surprise, interest. Joy and happiness are the governing emotions of festive comedy—all the happy love stories that end in marriage. Sadness is the governing emotion of tragedy and elegy. Together, anger, contempt, and disgust comprise the main emotional components of satire. Fear has its own special genres of terror and horror (ghost stories, for instance), but it is also an active component in the nearly painful suspense that is important to the reader's response to most plots. Surprise also is integral to suspense, and it operates almost independently at times, as a generic determinant of the special "twist" we require of mysteries and thrillers. These emotions can combine with one another and with various identity themes to produce more complex emotions such as "pride" and the sense of "honor." As with the five factors of personality, these terms can be useful for description and analysis both of characters and of authors, and they are also useful for describing audience response. Literary texts depict emotion, but they also stimulate and release it in their readers, and it is the putative quality of emotion in readers that determines the tonal element of genre.

All these psychological categories—cognitive domains, behavioral systems, the idea of cultural configuration as an economy of human universals, personality factors, and basic emotions—help give specificity to the idea of an evolved human nature. Much of this information is modern, most of it is still developing, and none of it was current before the middle of the nineteenth century. How then can it be relevant to literature of earlier periods or literature that is written from within worldviews different from the Darwinian? Milton is not a Darwinist, nor Shakespeare, nor Homer, nor Jane Austen. The answer to this question is that writers, and especially great writers, have an intuitive grasp of human nature and of the elementary realities of human experience. A modern, empirical understanding of human experience can provide us with a common conceptual order for assessing the meaning structure of any given literary text. We can assess how different cultures and ideologies organize the common elements of human nature into their own distinct cultural ecologies, and we can analyze the way in which individual authors make sense of the common human realities. We can examine the way in which literary conventions function within the economy of our needs and impulses, and we can analyze literary techniques as prosthetic extensions of evolved cognitive aptitudes—as when we treat of irony as a literary means for articulating our evolved propensity for cheater detection. Empirical study grounded in an evolutionary understanding of human nature provides a framework within which we can both interpret literary texts and also assess other interpretive paradigms such as those of psychoanalysis, Marxism, and Foucauldian discourse theory.

The elemental, universal motives recognized by evolutionary psychologists include the desire for sexual intimacy, the love of one's own children and kin, and the need for social interaction. To this list, I would add one further motive that, among sociobiologists and evolutionary psychologists, receives only spotty, fragmentary recognition: the need to create cognitive order. Because they do not recognize this need as a need distinct in itself, evolutionary psychologists have for the most part been able to make only clumsy efforts at providing an adaptive explanation for literature (or, more precisely, for its oral antecedents). Geoffrey Miller speaks of artistic activity as a form of sexual display (1998a, 1998b, 2000). Steven Pinker acknowledges that literature can provide models for behavior, like moves described in a chess book. To account for the pleasure of art, Pinker describes it as an exploitation of response systems evolved for other adaptive purposes. He presents literature as operating in parallel with pornography, rich foods, and recreational drugs (1997b, pp. 534–543). Most Darwinists in the humanities have an intuitive conviction about the inadequacy of this thesis, and at least one distinguished evolutionary biologist has formulated a better hypothesis. In reconstructing the evolution of mind, E. O. Wilson treats of general intelligence as a major advantage but also as a major problem—as a source of confusion and disorientation—and he suggests that the arts evolved as a means for counterbalancing this confusion (1998, p. 225).

The arts make emotionally meaningful connections between elemental motives and specific configurations of culture and of individual experience.

Literature presents simulated situations through which we can model our own behaviors, but it does not only provide game plans for specific situations. It integrates emotional processes with elemental motives in highly particularized circumstances that readers might never encounter. It helps us to regulate our complex psychological organization, and it helps us cultivate our socially adaptive capacity for entering mentally into the experience of other people. Literature produces pleasure, but it is not merely a "pleasure technology" (Pinker, 1997b, p. 528). It contributes to personal and social development and to the capacity for responding flexibly to changing circumstances.

From all that I have said so far, it should be apparent that evolutionary thinking and ecological thinking have large areas of overlap. In both conceptual fields, the relation between organism and environment takes a predominating role, and ecologists as well as biologists recognize that the relation between organism and environment is adaptive and has been produced by natural selection. Evolutionists are of necessity ecological theorists—they understand biological relationships as complex, systemic interactions within an ecosystem, and biologically oriented humanists often use ecological metaphors to describe psychological and social interactions. Much of Darwin's own specialized work was devoted to analyzing the coevolution of adaptive mechanisms among interdependent organisms, and he delighted in expatiating on the "ever-increasing circles of complexity" in ecological systems (2003, p. 140).

Ecology is integral to evolutionary thinking, but the concepts that are specific to ecology cannot by themselves provide a basis for a theory of literature. Human feeling, motivation, and thought occur only in individual minds. The individual mind is the locus of experience and meaning, and it is, consequently, on this level that we must seek the organization of meaning in literary texts. Literature is produced by the psyche, not the ecosystem, and the direct causal force that creates complex cognitive structures is not an ecological principle of community, of sustainable growth, or of the stable interchange of energy within a biosphere. The direct causal force that creates complex adaptive structures is natural selection. Organisms interact with their environments, and natural selection always operates within the constraints of a specific ecological context, but ecology is itself neither the locus of meaning nor the ultimate regulative principle within the total set of biological relations. The locus of meaning is the individual psyche, and the ultimate regulative principle is inclusive fitness, the transmission of genes.

Throughout most of our evolutionary history, an alert attentiveness to the natural world would have been crucial to our survival, and the latent emotional responsiveness that attends this adaptive function has not disappeared with the advent of controlled climates and supermarket foods. Responsiveness to the sense of place is an elemental component of the evolved human psyche. In this respect, ecocriticism and Darwinian literary study are reciprocal and interdependent. Darwinian humanists must take account of the organism's relation to the environment, and ecological humanists must take account of the evolved psychology that derives from our deep evolutionary past. Leading biologists and ecologists have both already shown us the way. E. O. Wilson identifies "biophilia" as "the innately emotional affiliation of human beings to other living organisms" (1993, p. 31), and Aldo Leopold, declaring that when he is in the wilderness he feels himself "back in the Pleistocene," describes outdoor recreations as "essentially primitive" and "atavistic" (1987, pp. 148, 181).

Evolutionary change proceeds very slowly. Its units of measure are tens and hundreds of thousands of years. In the past 10,000 years, since the introduction of agriculture, the human species has abandoned the hunter-gatherer form of life that dominated its evolutionary past. The rate of change in culture has vastly exceeded the rate of evolutionary change. Evolutionary psychologists have often speculated about a possible "mismatch" between the conditions of modern life and a psychological organization shaped in the Pleistocene. We evolved to meet the demands of a world in which we lived in small, closely affiliated groups, in much closer and more immediate contact with the natural world than we now usually experience. Much of our ancestors' energy was devoted to the direct pursuit of food, shelter, and safety. At the present time, in the industrialized nations, the immediate problems of hunger, the elements, and physical danger are less pressing, but we are all rapidly becoming conscious of great potential danger from a catastrophically degraded natural environment. In this respect, the effects of mismatch have come full circle. Modern industry and technology detached us from our close and immediate dependence on the natural world, but did not detach us emotionally. In all the phases of modern urban life, literary writers have in their images and metaphors brought us intimately into imaginative connection with the earth and sky, the weather, the sun and moon and stars. Now, industry, technology, and the growth of the human population have created new dangers, and our sense of affiliation with the natural world has become shadowed by alarm and dismay.

Each generation reinterprets the literary tradition in the terms of its own concerns, and in our own generation, we rightly give a new and urgent attention to the role of the environment. But the current and necessary preoccupations with problems of environmental degradation should not obscure the general theoretical significance of the environment in the biology of literary representation. Every aspect of an organism—its physiology, its anatomy, and its motivational structures—has been fundamentally shaped by the world its ancestors inhabited. We have lungs because the world has oxygen. We have eyes because the world has light. We instinctively recognize the motions of objects because the world of our ancestors, like our own, was governed by the laws of physics. And we instinctively classify plants and animals as members of a special category—as part of the living world—because recognizing the properties of living things was vital to the survival of our ancestors. "Human nature" has been shaped through natural selection so that it fits into the contours of the natural world. When we speak of "characters" and "setting" in literature, we need to bear in mind that those conventional categories reflect an elemental fact—the fact that all human beings are organisms within an environment. If we take one step further, and recognize that no organism can be understood apart from the environment in which it has evolved, we have made the necessary connection between ecological literary criticism and Darwinian literary study.

5

Adaptationist Criteria of Literary Value

Assessing Kurtén's Dance of the Tiger, Auel's
The Clan of the Cave Bear, *and Golding's* The Inheritors

The Elements of the Literary Situation

In a classic formulation, literary scholar and theorist M. H. Abrams (1986) identifies four basic elements in a literary situation: an author; an audience; a literary work; and a represented subject matter. At the level of common sense, this formulation has the force of an *a priori* maxim. Writers are people talking to other people about their shared experience in a common world. The written work—or the spoken work, in preliterate cultures—is the medium through which one person communicates with other people. The subject matter is almost always some sequence of human actions in a concretely specified setting. Abrams first expounded his scheme in 1953, in the introduction to *The Mirror and the Lamp: Romantic Theory and the Critical Tradition.* He used the four elements as categories within which to classify all theories of literature throughout history. He argued that expressive theories concentrate on the author; rhetorical theories on the audience; formal theories on the work itself; and "mimetic" theories on the represented subject matter. This study was rightly celebrated as a masterwork of historical scholarship, but the classificatory scheme that provided its theoretical underpinning did not become the basis for any new theoretical system. (Hernadi [1976] tried to develop the scheme but only obscured its classic outlines.)

In the late 1970s, the eruption of poststructuralist theory radically transformed the landscape of literary studies, and this transformation shattered the framework of common sense from which Abrams had abstracted his four elements. Poststructuralism totalizes "discourse" as the sole causal agency in the world, and it thus suppresses both persons and the world they inhabit. There is no "outside the text," Derrida tells us (1976, p. 158), and Jameson draws the inference that "nature is gone for good" (1991, p. ix). "Man does not exist prior to language, either as a species or as an individual" (1972, p. 135), Barthes declares, and the literary work, Foucault infers, "is not something written by a person called an 'author'"; the author is himself only "a function of discourse" (1977, pp. 118, 124). In his valiant efforts to counter the flagrant unreality of such declarations, Abrams has repeatedly reaffirmed the validity of the four elements in the literary situation, and he has identified these elements as the essential components of "the humanistic paradigm." Within this paradigm, "the site of literature is the human world, and a work of literature is the product of a purposive human author addressing human recipients in an environing world" (1997, p. 115).

Abrams believes that common sense is a foundation, a bedrock, and that literary theory cannot legitimately go deeper than that foundation. Poststructuralism deviated from common sense only by arbitrarily eliminating two components in the humanistic paradigm (people and nature) and totalizing a third component (language). What I propose, in contrast, is to locate all the elements of the humanistic paradigm within larger concepts deriving from Darwinian social science. Human beings—authors, audiences, and characters—are evolved organisms inhabiting environments to which they have adapted by a process of natural selection. Literary works can be understood as products of an adaptive need to make sense of the world in emotionally and imaginatively meaningful ways—to produce cognitive order. All the elements of the literary situation—the purposes of authors, the responses of audiences, the behavior, thought, and feeling of characters, and the formal properties of literary works—can be assessed and analyzed within the framework of adaptationist theory.

In this essay, I shall be particularly concerned with the question of evaluating literary quality. I shall formulate criteria of quality for each of the four elements of the literary situation: (a) the quality of authorial intentions and the quality of the author's mind and feeling; (b) the sort of response or effect a work is intended to have on a given audience; (c) the character of the represented subject matter; and (d) the formal character of the works themselves. I shall consider all of these criteria from within the conceptual framework of Darwinian anthropology, evolutionary psychology, cognitive ethology, and behavioral ecology. By using that framework, we can move beyond impressionistic and adventitious response, provide greater explanatory depth to our evaluative judgments, and connect these judgments with the whole larger network of empirical knowledge about human behavior and cognition.

In order to test and illustrate these evaluative criteria, I shall compare three works of fiction, each of which depicts encounters between Neanderthals and Cro-Magnons: Björn Kurtén's *Dance of the Tiger: A Novel of the Ice Age* (1995), Jean Auel's *The Clan of the Cave Bear* (1981), and William Golding's *The Inheritors* (1955). Such depictions directly confront the question of what it means to be "human," and they thus provide a peculiarly rich subject for the purpose of assessing depictions of human nature. In my view, Kurtén's and Auel's novels are both quite bad, and Golding's is a work of rare literary merit. Kurtén and Auel have ulterior purposes—Kurtén those of ideological manipulation and

Auel those of narcissistic fantasy—that diminish the seriousness with which they conceive their subjects, and the falsity of their representations forestalls any deep integration of formal elements. Golding immerses himself in his subject with extraordinary intensity, and through his handling of point of view and symbolism he fashions a thematically and tonally integrated work of art.

Values, aesthetic and moral, are grounded in emotion, and emotion is itself grounded in evolved systems of motivation. In an obvious sense, no value is "right" or "wrong" in the way that factual propositions are right or wrong. It is an objectively ascertainable fact that on a certain day in the first century B.C. the emperor Julius Caesar was stabbed to death by republican conspirators. When one states that fact, one is "right." But if one then goes on to declare that Caesar was either "right" or "wrong" in assuming dictatorial power, or that Brutus was "right" or "wrong" in assassinating him, that second statement is clearly of an order different from saying that these events took place. The question as to whether an act is good or bad in an ethical or political sense is a matter of subjective judgment based on personal value. So also, it is "right" to say that William Shakespeare wrote a play about Julius Caesar, but if one goes on to say that the play is good or bad, a masterwork of art or a hack piece of political propaganda, those judgments are not "right" or "wrong" in the same sense that a statement of fact is right or wrong. Judgments of value are relative to the motivational and emotional dispositions of individual readers.

In what sense, then, can we invoke evolutionary psychology, or any scientific information, in our judgments of literary value? Values cannot be justified by an appeal to fact, but values are themselves facts. They are psychological phenomena, and as such they are subject to analysis and explanation. We cannot claim that any of our own literary judgments are objectively correct in the sense that they are grounded in some system of values independent of personal feeling, but we can nonetheless identify the basis for our judgments; we can generalize the principles on which they are founded; and we can correlate these principles with the characteristics of our evolved psychology. We cannot justify our values, but we can explain them, and those explanations are part of the total body of knowledge relevant to literary criticism.

One of the chief qualities of any literary representation is the specifically human capacity for "theory of mind." (See Baron-Cohen, 1996; Baron-Cohen, Tager-Flusberg, and Cohen, 2000; Carruthers and Smith, 1996.) In common language, we can call this capacity the power of "empathy," and it translates often into the feeling of "compassion." An author who is strong in this characteristic has a strong intuitive understanding of the internal psychological coherence of the depicted characters. And the author has also a strong intuitive understanding of the way the thoughts and feelings of those characters are enmeshed within a specific environment. The idea of internal psychological coherence is parallel to an anatomical principle first enunciated by the great

French naturalist Frederic Cuvier—the principle that all the parts of an organism are functionally integrated—teeth, claws, skeleton, digestive tract, brain. (See Mayr, 1982; Young, 1992.) The idea of the integration of organisms within a specific environment is a founding principle of ecology. Both principles guided Darwin's thinking about natural selection and remain central to all adaptationist theory.

The degree of internal coherence in a represented organism, and the degree of coherence in the fit between an organism and its environment, are distinguishing features in any literary representation. The degrees of internal and ecological coherence vary, and that variance offers us a measure of the author's own integrity in his or her conception of the represented subject. Shakespeare, to take an exemplary instance, characteristically displays a truly extraordinary degree of integrity in the conception of the represented subject matter. Each character forms a coherent, integrated set of characteristics, and each is an integral component of the world he or she inhabits. This is not a question of realistic accuracy; Shakespeare often writes in the mode of symbolic fantasy. It is a question of truth to human nature—to the verisimilitude of motives and feelings, to the internal coherence of characters, and to the fit between characters and their imagined worlds.

The integrity of the represented subject matter is a necessary precondition for the coherence of formal organization. Coherence and integration are themselves ultimate formal characteristics that satisfy an elemental cognitive need—the kind of need that is satisfied in logical conclusions about sequences of events, correct arithmetical calculations, musical harmonies, cogent propositions, balanced architectural designs, elegant scientific reductions, plots that constitute completed actions with a beginning, middle, and end, tonal sequences that constitute emotional progressions correlative to completed plot actions, and thematic organizations that bring divergent aspects of a subject into meaningful relation to one another. (On the integration of formal elements as a criterion of literary quality, see Arnold, 1979, pp. 5–7, 11; Brooks, 1947, pp. 18–20; Brooks and Warren, 1976, pp. 9–12; Coleridge, 1984, vol. 2, pp. 15–18; Wellek and Warren, 1977, pp. 24.)

The coherence of artistic organization—or its absence—provides clues about an author's motives and the quality of his or her mind. Truth of representation is in itself a motive, and in literature the truth of representation is closely associated with an imaginative sympathy for the inner lives of other people. Seriousness and honesty in the conception of a subject matter give evidence that both these motives—truth of representation and imaginative sympathy—are dominant features of an author's mind. In the absence of seriousness and honesty, some other motive can reasonably be assumed to be at work. If a representation does not hang together, if it does not make sense, the reader must ask what motive has deflected or distorted the truth of the representation. The reader's sense of an author's motives enters directly into his or her feeling about the imaginative quality of the literary work.

Dance of the Tiger

When I assess Kurtén's novel as a bad work of art, I am making a judgment based on the criteria I have outlined above. The representation of character in *Dance of the Tiger* is not true to human nature. The motives and feelings of its characters are not plausible. They are neither internally coherent nor integral with their environments. The plot is accordingly weak and dim, and the thematic structure is equivocal and indeterminate. All of these artistic features have been sacrificed to a prevailing didactic motive, and the quality of mind reflected in that motive is deficient in depth of feeling, in imaginative sympathy, and in simple honesty. All of these features have their correlative in the response of readers. No reader would heartily approve Kurtén's work unless he or she were both sympathetic to his didactic purpose and relatively indifferent to qualities of artistic integrity. Kurtén's work has won unqualified admiration from at least one prominent reader, Stephen Jay Gould. After giving a critique of the book, I shall consider Gould's defense of it.

Kurtén's protagonist is a young Cro-Magnon male, "Tiger," whose band is attacked and wiped out by another band. Like Hamlet, Tiger has a mission to kill the man who killed his father. It is a revenge plot, but the revenge plot lacks internal drive, in good part because Kurtén himself feels diffident about attributing to his protagonist any motive not in accordance with the values of an enlightened modern man of liberal sensibility. "His was not a vengeful nature. A happy boyhood and the friendly camaraderie among the Chief's men had made him an outgoing, pleasant young man" (1995, p. 70). How does one construct a revenge plot without invoking revenge as a motive? Kurtén takes refuge in hypocrisy. He translates morally suspect motives into those of an impersonal concern for the higher social good. Tiger "wanted redress, retribution. But the most important thing was to rid the land of this menace" (1995, p. 70). Redress and retribution have an ethical ring rather different from that of revenge, and even these relatively noble motives are subordinated to the larger, impersonal concern for the public welfare. Tiger is a shadow of a character, a facsimile created by an ethical formula. That shadow does not have the energy or conviction necessary to carry out an act of revenge, and the plot becomes murky and finally concludes in a long, talky scene in which all the characters suspend their threats of mutual mayhem so that they can justify their own ethical behavior and bemoan their existential plight. In the slow-motion sequences of violent action, repeatedly suspended for the sake of wambling introspection, this scene reaches something like a maximum in the nullity of its dramatic force. Given the author's inability to invest his characters with the power of definite action, the monologues in this climactic scene might well have gone on indefinitely, but a natural dam breaks, the antagonist is swept away by a convenient flood, and the protagonist climbs safely to a hill, with all his surviving friends, who live happily ever after.

Plot and character in *Dance of the Tiger* are subordinated to an ulterior didactic purpose. The main purpose of the novel is to create a model of peaceable interaction among distinct human populations—Cro-Magnon and Neanderthal—presumably with the hope and intention that the model will influence the ethical beliefs and motives of Kurtén's readers. After his natal band has been wiped out, Tiger is rescued by a band of Neanderthals. His feelings toward them, at first, are typical of his Cro-Magnon outlook. He regards them with contempt and disgust, almost with abhorrence, thinks of them as "Trolls," and refers to their males as "oxen" and their females as "bitches." Predictably, he learns that he has been blinded by prejudice and that the Neanderthals, though different in some ways from Cro-Magnons, have unique talents, lovable personal qualities, and rich cultural traditions. Indeed, in important ways they are altogether superior to the Cro-Magnons. For instance, they offer an early model for modern, postindustrial, gender relations. They are matriarchal, and polyandry is common among them. The women are more "forceful and interesting" than the men (p. 60). Both men and women hunt, and both also do domestic work. Tiger finds that once he has overcome his Cro-Magnon prejudices, he too takes real pleasure in doing work that in his own band would be considered "women's work." He enjoys sitting about the camp scraping hides and swapping tales (p. 54). In this guise, Tiger is only a vehicle for the transmission of a didactic message about being broad-minded and culturally flexible.

One main wrinkle in Kurtén's didactic structure is a carefully embedded set of clues about the reasons for Neanderthal extinction. He wishes not only to avoid the scenario of extermination but also to present an image of amicable interaction. He solves this problem by depicting the hybrid offspring of Neanderthals and Cro-Magnons as sterile. Cro-Magnons are socially dominant and more numerous. Cro-Magnon males interbreed more frequently with Neanderthal females than Neanderthal males breed with Cro-Magnon females, and the Neanderthals gradually, quietly, become extinct. In an author's note, Kurtén worries that this scenario might bear an unpleasant comparison to policies of sterilization, but he still prefers it to the scenario of extermination (1995, p. 255).

Kurtén's Neanderthals have gracious manners and advanced botanical knowledge. They take their names from the names of flowers and ornamental and medicinal plants, and they invariably speak to one another in the forms of high courtesy, with formal titles such as Mister Silverbirch, Mister Baywillow, Miss Woad, and Miss Silverweed. They have difficulty articulating all the sounds that characterize Cro-Magnon speech, but they nonetheless have highly developed vocal musical skills and elaborate traditions of oral narrative. Kurtén is a paleontologist, and he has been careful not to intrude any depictions that could be disconfirmed by archeological evidence. Names, manners, oral traditions, and vocal music do not fossilize, so who is to say this depiction could not possibly be true?

Before answering that question, I shall quote one passage to give the reader a feel for the tone and style of life among the Neanderthals. In this scene, the Neanderthal band has come across the corpses of Tiger's slaughtered band, which had been surprised and ambushed while they were hunting mammoths. In the last moment before the surprise attack, Tiger had been caught beneath a tree knocked over by a fleeing mammoth, and he had thus escaped the slaughter. The Neanderthals are occupied with salvaging meat from the dead mammoths, tending to the corpses of the Cro-Magnons, and looking after the injured boy. (The Neanderthals refer to Cro-Magnons as "Gods," hence the appellation "the young God.")

> "Would you be gracious, Mister Silverbirch, and look at the young God? Can you tell us how badly he is hurt?"
> The old man was already beside the boy. "We must get the tree off him, Miss Angelica," he said.
> "Please, Miss Woad, would you ask some of the men here to assist?"
> "With pleasure, Mother."
> Gently they lifted the tree and flung it aside, muttering, "Excuse me, Miss Woad," "Please, Mister Silverbirch," and other civilities. The tree had fallen on the boy's legs, which were badly bruised and bleeding; the left leg had an ugly twist.
> "He is alive, Miss Angelica," said the old man. "His leg must be straightened out. I should like to have some plantain for the wounds, but we have to go back to the coast for that. I will need a strong stick and some straps. Then we must make a litter...."
> The meat collectors went to work on the fallen mammoths.... "They must have departed in a hurry, Miss Silverweed," said Miss Rosebay. Miss Silverweed, wielding a big hand-axe and splattered with blood from head to foot, agreed. (1995, pp. 37–38)

Characters in the novels of Jane Austen frequently exchange "civilities," but then, they are not splattered from head to foot in mammoth blood, nor are they standing amidst the corpses of an alien species they regard with both terror and awe. Despite their civilities, Austen's characters operate in the high tension of a ruthless social world focused on status and mate selection. They are civilized, but they are not saccharine, and they are not fatuous. The tonality in the passage I have quoted would not be out of place in a tea party among the Teletubbies. It would be painfully jarring even in Austen's world, and it is ludicrously out of place in a world characterized by pervasive violence, constant, strenuous labor, and chronic physical discomfort. The brutality of conditions in this world could not conceivably produce or sustain the manner of mincing politeness that characterizes the speech attributed to the Neanderthals.

The question of the plausibility of conversational tone among Kurtén's Neanderthals involves a principle of the widest application in the reconstruction of Paleolithic life. The principle is that of coherence and integration in a coordinated suite of behaviors. Plausible reconstructions require not just the *absence* of contrary evidence on any one specific form of behavior; plausible reconstructions require positive evidence for behaviors that could reasonably be expected to accompany the behavior in question. Stringer and Gamble (1993, p. 198) identify a suite of archeological features that distinguish the moderns of the Upper Paleolithic (Cro-Magnons) from all ancient peoples, including Neanderthals. These features include structured living spaces, windbreaks, storage pits, fixed hearths, huts, bone tools, and art. The absence of these items indicates limited capabilities in three critical areas of cognitive performance among the Neanderthals: (a) complex spatial organization, (b) depth of planning, and (c) symbolic order (pp. 154–177, 195–218).

The issue of Neanderthal language provides a good test case for the principle of plausible inference from coordinated suites of behaviors. On the basis of anatomical evidence alone, the extent to which Neanderthals possessed the powers of complex, fully articulated language remains controversial. (See Mellars, 1996, pp. 387–391; Shreeve, 1995, pp. 271–276; Stringer and Gamble, 1993, pp. 89–90; Tattersall, 1999, pp. 170–173.) Most investigators agree that Neanderthal vocal tracts would have made them capable of only a limited range of sounds. (Some commentators argue that gestures and sign language could have compensated for limited vocal capacities [Shreeve, p. 274], but modern users of sign language have the full neurological equipment of modern speakers; their signing compensates for a simple physical disability.) Mellars weighs the evidence. "In terms of the archeological evidence, the most significant observation is the virtual lack of convincing evidence for symbolic behavior or expression in Neanderthal contexts. . . . There is a lack of well documented decorative or artistic items in Mousterian contexts; a lack of any obvious symbolic component in most Middle Paleolithic tools, and a lack of convincing evidence for ceremonial burials" (p. 389). Tattersall employs similar logic. "It seems improbable that the symboling properties that are basic to language would ever fail to express themselves in at least some of the complex features that are so conspicuously lacking at Neanderthal sites—and that are present in the upper Paleolithic" (p. 171). Stringer and Gamble grant that Neanderthals "could certainly communicate, as can all social animals, and they no doubt spoke, albeit simply and probably slowly," but they also argue that Neanderthals "lacked complex spoken language because they did not need it. We could not imagine life without it, but they did not have the social life to require it" (p. 217).

Kurtén, Auel, and Golding all take account of anatomical limitations in Neanderthal vocal tracts, but Kurtén and Auel sidestep this limitation—Auel by attributing extraordinary powers of fluent articulation to Neanderthal gestures and sign language, Kurtén by ignoring the way in which restrictions of sounds would also very likely restrict the development of complex vocabularies and sophisticated syntactic structures. (One advantage of oral language is that one can both talk and sew skins at the same time. Auel's loquacious Neanderthals carry out all the complex manual tasks their ecology necessitates while simultaneously conducting long, elaborate dialogues with their hands.) Both Auel and Kurtén fudge the evidence on symbolic behavior among Neanderthals, making too much of limited (and now largely discredited) evidence for ceremonial burial. Kurtén tacitly acknowledges some of the negative archeological evidence—the absence of the items listed by Stringer and Gamble—but he attributes to his Neanderthals complex forms of symbolic behavior that are wholly out of keeping with this negative evidence. Auel simply ignores the negative archeological evidence and invests her Neanderthals with forms of technological, social, and cultural organization that are equivalent in complexity to those of fully modern humans.

Integrity in art and integrity in science are closely related characteristics. The English translation of Kurtén's novel contains a laudatory introduction by Stephen Jay Gould, and Gould's critical response provides us with an opportunity to elaborate on this parallel. Gould is enthusiastically responsive to the bad art of Kurtén's novel, and he formulates a scientific theory in support of the art. The theory amounts to a vindication of dishonesty, and in its sophistical illogicality, the theory is itself thoroughly dishonest. Gould has made it his special mission to counter adaptationist reasoning in biology, and most particularly to discountenance adaptationist reasoning in respect to human nature. He is a Marxist and is committed to the idea of social construction—the idea that innate characteristics do not significantly constrain human behavior and that the main source of human behavior is social conditioning. He applauds Kurtén's novel for its political ideology, and specifically for Kurtén's "proper treatment of both Neanderthal and Cro-Magnon as people of fully human intelligence and feeling" (1995, p. xviii). The word "proper" in this context is ambiguous. It might seem to imply "scientifically correct," but that reading would beg many questions about what it means to be "fully" human in intelligence and feeling. The word "proper" more plausibly signifies "in correspondence with my ethical disposition to insist on equality among distinct human populations," and in that sense it is an ideological designation, not a designation about scientific fact.

The theory that Gould formulates in support of Kurtén's depiction makes appeal to his own famous deprecation of all adaptationist explanations as "just-so stories." By designating adaptationist explanations as an equivalent to Kipling's whimsical mythography, Gould implies that they are the products of fanciful speculation unconstrained by scientific evidence:

> Let me, as a scientist, make a claim that may seem curious. I believe that Kurtén's novel is a more appropriate place than the professional literature itself

for discussing many of the truly scientific issues that swirl about the Neandertal-Cro-Magnon debate. Evolutionary biology has been severely hampered by a speculative style of argument that records anatomy and ecology and then tries to construct historical or adaptive explanations for why this bone looked like that or why this creature lived here. These speculations have been charitably called "scenarios"; they are often more contemptuously, and rightly labeled "stories" (or "just-so stories" if they rely on the fallacious assumption that everything exists for a purpose). Scientists know that these tales are stories; unfortunately, they are presented in the professional literature where they are taken too seriously and literally. Then they become "facts" and enter the popular literature, often in such socially dubious form as the ancestral killer ape who absolves us from responsibility for our current nastiness, or as the "innate" male dominance that justifies cultural sexism as the mark of nature.

Yet these stories have a role in science. They probe the range of alternatives; they channel thought into the construction of testable hypotheses; they serve as tentative frameworks for the ordering of observations. But they are stories. So why not treat them as such, get all the benefits and pleasures, and avoid the wrangles that arise from their usual, inappropriate placement? (1995, pp. xvii–xviii)

The largest sophistical maneuver in this formulation is that of giving with one hand and taking with the other. We are told both that "stories" have a role in science, and also that they do not. They "have a role in science," but if they appear in science they are guilty of "inappropriate placement." Gould implies some vague distinction between "stories" that channel adaptive hypotheses and the adaptive hypotheses themselves, but that distinction is merely verbal, and it evaporates in his own examples. Arguments for "why this bone looked like that" or "why this creature lived here" would be adaptive hypotheses, not merely "stories." Such hypotheses are indispensable to all evolutionary science. Eliminating them would eliminate the interconnected explanatory power of paleontology, comparative anatomy, biogeography, ecology, embryology, and genetics. Real and important distinctions can be drawn about the relative weight of empirical support for any given adaptive hypothesis. Some are weak and fanciful (the aquatic ape theory); some are highly plausible (the functions of temperature regulation in the stocky construction of Neanderthal bodies); and some are so robustly supported that they approach to the condition of established fact (the functions of specific kinds of teeth as adaptations for specific diets, and the differences in the digestive tracts of carnivores and herbivores).

As a scientific proposition, then, Gould's formulation is transparently false. As aesthetic theory, it cannot be judged by the same criteria of truth or falsity. It must be assessed instead in accordance with the aesthetic values that are implied by the theory. We can paraphrase his argument as follows: "Adaptive hypotheses have a role in science, but not really. They are more appropriate in fiction, where the rules of evidence and logic don't count. In fiction, we can reject hypotheses we don't like (innate violence, male dominance) and entertain hypotheses we do like (matriarchy, social equality)." In opposition to this aesthetic proposition, I would argue that in fiction the rules of evidence and logic do count. They are important elements in the integrity of conception in the representation of the subject. Allowing ideological values and didactic purposes to violate the integrity of conception produces bad art. Gould himself does not object to the badness of Kurtén's art, but then, he does not object to bad logic in science theory, either. With respect to his proposition about the role of adaptationist hypotheses in evolutionary science, one can say that he is simply wrong. His statements are factually erroneous and logically contradictory. With respect to his proposition about using art as propaganda, those of us who disagree with him can say only that our own aesthetic values are different from his, and that for us, at least, integrity counts. (For further comments on Gould, in this vol., see part 3, chapter 2.)

The Clan of the Cave Bear

The Clan of the Cave Bear is the most prominent example of a popular genre, that of Stone Age fantasy. The novels in this genre tend to be published as massive pulp paperbacks with schlocky art on the covers. Such works can be clearly distinguished from serious efforts in the fictional reconstruction of Paleolithic life. The two seminal authors in this latter genre are H. G. Wells (1971a, 1971b), and J. H. Rosny (1985), both of whom combine naturalism of style with allegorical themes of human evolutionary history. Auel's chief antecedent is not the work of Wells or Rosny but the 1960s cartoon series *The Flintstones*. Fred and Wilma are just folks from the suburbs, like Dagwood and Blondie, who happen to use stone and wood as the materials with which they replicate the technology and culture of modern suburban America. There are important tonal differences between *The Flintstones* and *The Clan of the Cave Bear*. *The Flintstones* is a sitcom, and *The Clan of the Cave Bear* is a soap opera. Nonetheless, the kind of historical imagination involved in the two works is clearly the same. The task that Auel has tacitly posed for herself is to provide a detailed fictional answer to the following question: "What would life be like if I could take myself and all my friends, with all our values, sensibilities, customs, manners, forms of technological expertise, and social dispositions, and place them in a world in which the only materials with which we had to work were stone, wood, bone, and leather?" Auel has evidently done some research into conditions of life in the Upper Paleolithic, but the precision is all in the details, and the larger picture is absurdly wrong.

Ayla, the heroine, is a Cro-Magnon girl who is orphaned in an earthquake and then adopted into a Neanderthal band. She is taken into the home of a kindly brother and sister, a shaman and a medicine woman. The Neanderthals are genetically programmed for conservative behavior. Their minds—as is supposedly indicated by the "occipital bun" or bulge at the back of their skulls—

operate exclusively by means of inherited memory. Ayla, as a Cro-Magnon, is genetically programmed to be boldly innovative and creative. As a result, she perpetually disrupts the Neanderthal way of life. She even takes up hunting with a sling, a practice that is taboo for Neanderthal females and for which the stipulated punishment is death. The main plot conflicts turn on her struggle against a male Neanderthal who is politically reactionary and sexually abusive. Eventually, she leaves the group and sets out in quest of her own people. (There is a long series of sequels, presumably still in progress.)

Auel makes distinctions between the cognitive style of Neanderthals and Cro-Magnons, but like Kurtén she attributes to both essentially modern levels of cognitive complexity. Both species have "a richly developed, if dissimilar intelligence" (1981, chapter 6). The kinds of distortions that arise from treating the Neanderthals as just another variety of modern humans can be exemplified by their organization of living space. Two of the features that Stringer and Gamble identify as missing from Neanderthal sites are structured living spaces and fixed hearths. Ayla, the heroine of Auel's story, lives with the Neanderthals in a capacious cave, and in this cave, there is a place for everything, and everything is in its place. Food and herbs are neatly stored in wicker baskets, and each family has its own private hearth. Ayla, lacking the instincts of the Neanderthals, must learn not to let her eyes wander into the hearths of her neighbors—the sort of problem an inquisitive teenager might face when growing up in a crowded trailer park.

Auel's contributions to the genre of Stone Age fantasy are complicated by the ambition of investing her story with certain thematic structures and making use of archetypal symbolism, but the central motive that animates the story is the desire to engage in ego-fulfillment fantasies. As the jacket copy explains, Ayla is "a very special heroine." She is an ugly duckling, a truly superior creature planted in the midst of ordinary people who misunderstand her and only gradually come to recognize her unique personal gifts. She struggles against tyranny and emerges triumphant, psychologically unscathed and supremely confident of her own prowess. She performs marvels of skill and courage, displays extraordinary resources of resilience and wisdom, humbles her enemies, wins the devoted love of her friends, and gains universal admiration. As the jacket copy of one of the sequels describes her story, it is "the breathtaking saga of one magnificent woman who shaped mankind" (*The Valley of Horses*, 1983). At the modest cost of a cheap paperback, the reader is invited to participate vicariously in Auel's fantasy projections—and many millions of readers have accepted this invitation. The vulgarity of feeling and style displayed in such projections reflects on both the author and the audience.

The chief thematic structure in the story is the political dichotomy between conservatism and liberalism—between sticking with the ways of the past and adapting to changing conditions. This is an important political dichotomy, arguably one of the basic dimensions in the organization of all political life. (See Carroll, 1995, pp. 185–187; Eibl-Eibesfeldt, 1989, p. 15; Eysenck and Wilson, 1978.) Moreover, it is a dichotomy that is in fact central to the difference between all ancient hominid species, including the Neanderthals, and the modern humans who supplanted them. Auel grasps the basic idea, but translates it into a style more appropriate to partisan political rhetoric, or to advertising copy, than to serious reflection on the deep history of the human race:

> She had not had subservience bred into her for untold generations. She was one of the Others; a newer, younger breed, more vital, more dynamic, not controlled by hidebound traditions from a brain that was nearly all memory. Her brain followed different paths, her full, high forehead that housed forward-thinking frontal lobes, gave her an understanding from a different view. She could accept the new, shape it to her will, forge it into ideas undreamed of by the Clan, and, in nature's way, her kind was destined to supplant the ancient, dying race. (1981, chapter 10)

In contrast to Kurtén's Neanderthals, Auel's Neanderthals are profoundly patriarchal, and Auel works this idea into the logic of species succession. Throughout their evolutionary history, the Clan has executed any woman who touched a man's weapon or showed any disposition to hunt, and they are now paying the genetic price for this rigid differentiation of gender roles. "Over countless ages, only those with properly female attitudes and actions were left. As a result, the adaptability of the race—the very trait on which survival depends—was curtailed" (chapter 14). This application of the standard political dichotomy takes human universals from the wrong end. Auel does not use evolutionary history as a larger framework within which to consider the changing social roles of women in her own time. Instead, she takes the changing social roles of women in her own time as the conceptual frame within which to envision evolutionary processes over vast stretches of time in the deep past.

The problem of perspective that appears in Auel's use of sociopolitical themes appears also in her use of archetypal symbols. We can take an instance from a scene near the end of the novel. At a gathering of the clans, after a feast featuring multiple courses of finely dressed dishes (not neglecting the hot salad oil splashed at the last minute onto the bowl of mixed greens), the folk participate in a religious ceremony honoring their totem, the great cave bear. As he hands around bits of bear meat, the high priest intones, "You drank of his blood. Now eat of his body and be one with the Spirit of Ursus" (chapter 24). In this ursified Eucharistic ceremony, Auel is not recognizing the common humanity in local cultural practices but taking a local cultural practice, the Eucharist, as a universal. Again, this is taking human universals from the wrong end.

Auel's failure of historical imagination can be exemplified in its extreme form in the most full-blown evolutionary fantasy in the novel. During the meeting of the clans, Ayla takes a hallucinogenic drug and under its influence retraces the whole course of evolution. "She felt the individuality of her own cells and knew when they split and differentiated in the warm, nurturing waters still carried within her. . . . Another divergence, and she knew the pain of the first explosion of air breathed by creatures in a new element" (chapter 24). And on it goes, up to walking on two legs and the emergence of a fore-brain. This is good fun, no doubt, but it is hardly serious. Ayla feels herself as a single-celled organism, and then feels herself diverging into multicellular shape. That is, she actively experiences conditions that in the nature of the case are not accessible to self-reflexive awareness. Sensation and perception imply a highly developed nervous system, and single-celled organisms do not have such systems. The problem is parallel to that of recreating the mental conditions of Paleolithic people by investing them with all the reflective powers of modern humans.

The failures of imagination in both *Dance of the Tiger* and *Clan of the Cave Bear* make themselves felt within each of the four elements of the literary situation. The failures are in the first place failures in the authors' own minds—failures of insight, imaginative sympathy, and artistic integrity. They are lapses or deficiencies in the mental experience and cognitive performance of the artists themselves, and the responses of readers, positive and negative, reflect their own motives and qualities of mental character. The kind of appeal that is made to the reader is an appeal to share in or to collude with the mental experience of the author. With Kurtén, the reader is invited to replace real human sympathy with false and shallow sentiments that have been channeled by a local modern ideology. With Auel, the reader is invited to participate in a narcissistic fantasy that makes a false and sensationalistic use of sociopolitical themes and symbolic images. Writers and readers are always engaged in a social exchange, and in these two cases, the mental experience involved in the exchange is poor in quality.

The medium of social exchange in a literary situation is the literary work itself. It is in the quality of the work that the quality of the exchange makes itself felt. A key factor in the quality of the represented subject matter is the evoked inner life of the characters, and the quality of that evocation depends heavily on both the inner coherence of the characters and the way they are integrated—or not integrated—within their environments, both physical and social. Kurtén's characters have no genuine inner life, and Auel's heroine is merely an evocation of Auel's own sense of personal identity transplanted into a world in which it does not belong—like a Pomeranian dog or a Persian cat transplanted into a savage wilderness. These failures in ethological imagination have effects also in the formal dimension. In Kurtén's novel, weak perceptions of ethological integrity eventuate in weak plotting, feeble scenic construction, and misjudgments of tone. In Auel's novel, they eventuate in stylistic and tonal vulgarity and in absurd perspectival misconstructions.

The Inheritors

The purpose of this essay is not merely to say unpleasant things about two bad books but to bring the whole question of literary evaluation within the scope of Darwinian literary theory. The same criteria that have been used to register the artistic deficiencies in the books by Kurtén and Auel can also be used to register the merits of Golding's novel. I would myself identify *The Inheritors* as one of the great fictional works of the twentieth century. It is certainly the only work of Paleolithic fiction for which capable critics have made serious claims to that effect. (See Babb, 1954, p. 37; Everett, 1986, pp. 114–117; Hughes, 1986, p. 162; Kermode, 1962, pp. 205–207; Kinkead-Weekes and Gregor, 1984, pp. 81, 112, 117–118; Tiger, 1976, pp. 68–69, 89–90.) Golding's general reputation is very high. He won a Nobel Prize and holds a secure position among the canonical novelists of the twentieth century. *The Inheritors* has been much less popular than some of his other novels, especially *Lord of the Flies*, but Golding's best critics hold it in high esteem, and Golding himself considered it his finest work. (See Friedman, 1993, p. 49; Tiger, 1976, p. 91.)

The Inheritors has received a good deal of serious and respectful critical attention, but not the kind or amount of attention that has been devoted to the major works of Joyce, Lawrence, or Woolf. The relative and I think unmerited obscurity of *The Inheritors* can be accounted for in part by its genre. Paleolithic reconstructions are a specialized area of interest, like Westerns, science fiction, or detective novels. By their very nature, Paleolithic fictions do not engage a full and detailed array of modern social and psychological concerns. If they are any good at all, they do not portray their characters as possessing sophisticated modern minds. The minds they depict are rudimentary, the social order primitive, and the manners rough. The reader is not asked to participate vicariously in a refined social world graced by charming nuances of sentiment and wit. Good Paleolithic fiction creates a world of harsh conditions in which the characters are dominated by brute necessity, driven by elemental passions, and capable of only inchoate reflection.

Golding's narrative technique in *The Inheritors* presents special difficulties. He speaks from within the perspective, and often from within the idiom, of the Neanderthals, that is, of inarticulate and semi-human creatures who do not themselves fully understand the events they witness. This technique is essential to the success Golding has in evoking the inner life of his characters, but it presents a serious challenge to the competence of readers. Much of the story is hard to follow, and almost all readers have to read the novel at least twice to piece it all together. The sorts of readers who would be willing and able to meet such challenges have for the most part been less interested in the world inhabited by Neanderthals than in the worlds inhabited by Maggie Verver, Stephen Dedalus, and Mrs. Dalloway.

In *The Inheritors*, a small band of Neanderthals, eight in all—two old people, two adult couples, one child, and a baby—are making a seasonal migration to a rock shelter beside a high waterfall. There they encounter a Cro-Magnon band, a species hitherto unknown to them. The Cro-Magnons have broken away from their own parent band and are fleeing for their lives. They have encamped on an island at the foot of the waterfall and must make a portage of their canoes over the falls. The Neanderthals are pacific by nature and curious about the strangers. The Cro-Magnons are frightened and hostile. They regard the Neanderthals as forest devils and kill them one by one, until only two are left, an adult male and the baby. The Cro-Magnons have captured the Neanderthal child and baby, have eaten the child, Liku, and have kept the baby as a pet. The remaining adult Neanderthal, the protagonist Lok, falls into despair and lies down to die.

A major structural feature in the organization of the story is the manipulation of point of view. For all but the last two short segments, the story is told from the point of view of the Neanderthals, and especially of Lok. Events are narrated as he perceives them, and they are described only from within the concepts that are available to his limited intelligence and his restricted range of knowledge and experience. A few pages before he lies down to die, there is a sharp shift to a more objective perspective. He is then referred to as a "creature" and his movements are described without directly evoking his own perceptions and feelings. Lok has himself viewed the Cro-Magnons from this objectivized perspective, and up to this point in the story we have had no direct access to their point of view. We have not perceived events as they perceive them. We have very little idea what they think, and we do not know what their motives and purposes might be. In the final sequence, the Cro-Magnons have succeeded in crossing the falls; the new protagonist is an adult Cro-Magnon male, Tuami, and the narrative adopts his point of view. The final scenes are depicted as he sees them, and the main events of the narrative are his own thoughts and observations.

Dance of the Tiger also employs major shifts in viewpoint. The narrative first follows the protagonist Tiger; then shifts and tells the story of his antagonist, Shelk, from Shelk's point of view; and finally brings them together, in the same camp, and alternates between them. Since the plot in Kurtén's novel is inconsequential and the theme muddled, this device cannot be effectively integrated within a total artistic order. In *The Inheritors*, the manipulation of point of view is an integral part of the total artistic order. Golding's management of point of view (a) ministers to the represented subject matter, (b) reflects his motives and the quality of his mind, and (c) mediates the largest thematic design in the work. I shall take up each of these three aspects in turn.

Golding's mimetic or representational purpose is to evoke the character of experience in both sets of protagonists. The more unfamiliar set is that of the Neanderthals, and they occupy the bulk of the narrative. Many of the fictional

efforts to depict Neanderthals have been meticulous in registering the peculiarities of their anatomy, and especially the configuration of their skulls. (See
Asimov and Silverberg, 1992; Silverberg, Greenberg and Waugh, 1987.) To my
knowledge, no writer other than Golding has succeeded—or even made much
of an effort—to see what the world looked like from within those skulls. To
succeed in the effort to see the world from the perspective of the Neanderthals
requires not just arranging the furniture in the cave, as Auel does. It requires
(a) placing the organism in intimate cognitive relation to the physical and social conditions of its environment, (b) regulating the proportions of sensory
perception and abstract reflection in the stream of its mental events, (c) coordinating language use with the level of cognitive complexity, and (d) calibrat-
ing the horizon of temporal anticipation suitable to its behavior.

As Darwin himself understood, the scope of temporal anticipation is a key
structural feature in cognitive organization (1981, vol. 1, pp. 88–92). Using
archeological evidence to assess the scope of temporal anticipation among Neanderthals, Stringer and Gamble conclude, "It is clear that the Neanderthals could
plan, but only with limited depth and provision for the future" (1993, p. 168). In
the light of that observation, consider that on a regular basis once every several
years Auel's Neanderthals meet with other clans for feasts and rituals—a cultural
practice that would require a horizon of temporal expectation wholly modern in
its scope. In Golding's depiction, the main concern among the Neanderthals, before they encounter the Cro-Magnons, is the search for food. Once they have
enough food for two days, they have reached the limit of the range in which their
behavior can be actively regulated by conscious intent. They are aware, vaguely,
of larger temporal patterns such as the annual migration from the sea cave to the
waterfall, and when they approach a stream expecting to find a log bridge, and
see that it is no longer there, the old man, Mal, struggles to recall what was done
on a similar occasion in his youth. But the larger rhythms of behavior are matters
of habit prompted by seasonal signals not very different from those that prompt
the migrations of mammals and birds. Intentional behavior restricts itself to immediate physical needs. After they have found a dead deer and have eaten, "The
people were silent. Life was fulfilled, there was no need to look farther for food,
to-morrow was secure and the day after that was so remote that no one would
bother to think of it. Life was exquisitely allayed hunger" (chapter 3). When the
old man Mal has died from sickness and the dominant, smarter male Ha has
been killed by the Cro-Magnons, Lok is forced to assume leadership. In attempting to fulfill his new responsibilities, he makes a feeble bid to provide direction.
"'To-day we shall hunt for food'" (chapter 5). The response of the old woman reflects the incompetence of his effort. "The old woman wailed pitilessly. There was
still food piled in the recess, though little enough was left. What people would
hunt for food, when they were not hungry and there was food to eat?"

Our most recent information indicates that the Neanderthals were big game
hunters. Their diet consisted largely of meat (Richards et al., 2000). Golding

did serious research into paleoanthropology (Biles, 1970, pp. 106–107), and at the time that he wrote, the available information supported his supposition that the Neanderthals were a scavenging people. This whole issue was still controversial even in the 1990s. (See Mellars, 1996, pp. 220–244; Stringer and Gamble, 1993, p. 161.) Factual accuracy in historical reconstruction depends on the information available at the time of writing. The artist can work only with the materials at hand. For the purposes of art, what counts is not whether this information is factually correct but whether the initial premise is reasonable and whether the artist has succeeded in developing this initial premise in a coherent and meaningful way.

For an ecology of scavengers living in rock shelters, the rhythms of cognitive life would be very closely tied to the immediate sensory world. For a small band that is faced with a daily struggle to find adequate food and to defend itself against predators, the sense of collective, communal life would be very strong. In the passage below, Golding captures both these aspects of their mental life. The passage comes early in the story. The band has just arrived at the rock shelter by the waterfall and has built a fire. They are relaxing after the dangers and discomforts of the journey:

> The old woman moved softly, pushing in more wood so that the red spot [glowing coals] ate and the flame grew strong. The people watched, their faces seeming to quiver in the unsteady light. Their freckled skins were ruddy and the deep caverns beneath their brows were each inhabited by replicas of the fire and all their fires danced together. As they persuaded themselves of the warmth they relaxed limbs and drew the reek into their nostrils gratefully. They flexed their toes and stretched their arms, even leaning away from the fire. One of the deep silences fell on them, that seemed so much more natural than speech, a timeless silence in which there were at first many minds in the overhang; and then perhaps no mind at all. So fully discounted was the roar of the water that the soft touch of the wind on the rocks became audible. Their ears as if endowed with separate life sorted the tangle of tiny sounds and accepted them, the sound of breathing, the sound of wet clay flaking and ashes falling in. (chapter 2)

The delicacy of sensory evocation here is not that of a hypersensitive, post-Romantic poet. It is the delicacy appropriate to a people for whom finely discriminated sensory perception is an adaptive necessity. The quality of lyricism derives from the blending of perceptual intensity with the mood of comfort, peace, and communion that is appropriate to the occasion and that emerges out of the rhythm of the day's activities.

I shall offer one further example to illustrate Golding's evocation of the Neanderthals' perspective. In this passage, Lok is on guard at the rock shelter, before the Cro-Magnons have made their presence known, and while the Neanderthals are aware of no danger more serious than the recent presence of hyenas:

Lok squatted to one side and looked out over the dark waters. There had been no conscious decision but he was on watch. He yawned too and examined the pain in his belly. He thought of good food and dribbled a little and was about to speak but then he remembered that they were all asleep. He stood up instead and scratched the close curls under his lip. Fa was within reach and suddenly he desired her again; but this desire was easy to forget because most of his mind preferred to think about food instead. . . . His eyes considered the stars without blinking, while his nose searched for the hyenas and told him that they were nowhere near. . . .

The island dimmed, the wet mist stole towards the terrace, hung under the arch of the overhang and enveloped the people in drops that were too small to be felt and could only be seen in numbers. Lok's nose opened automatically and sampled the complex of odours that came with the mist.

He squatted, puzzled and quivering. He cupped his hands over his nostrils and examined the trapped air. Eyes shut, straining attention, he concentrated on the touch of the warming air, seemed for a moment on the very brink of a revelation; then the scent dried away like water, dislimned like a far-off small thing when the tears of effort drown in it. He let the air go and opened his eyes. The mist of the fall was drifting away with a change of wind and the smell of the night was ordinary.

He frowned at the island and the dark water that slid towards the lip, then yawned. He could not hold a thought when there seemed no danger in it. The fire was sinking to a red eye that lit nothing but itself and the people were still and rock-coloured. He settled down and leaned forward to sleep, pressing his nostrils in with one hand so that the stream of cold air was diminished. He drew his knees to his chest and presented the least possible surface to the night air. His left arm stole up and insinuated the fingers in the hair at the back of his neck. His mouth sank on his knees. . . .

There came a noise from the foot of the fall, a noise that the thunder robbed of echo and resonance, the form of a noise. Lok's ears twitched in the moonlight so that the frost that lay along their upper edges shivered. Lok's ears spoke to Lok.

"?"

But Lok was asleep. (chapter 2)

The rhythm of desire and impulse in this sequence is not much different from that in a modern mind, but there are no higher layers of temporal concern, no anxiety about distant events, no obtruding memories, no complicated tangle of reflections involving self-images, abstract concepts, goals, values, and calculations. Hunger and sexual desire are the only active sources of impulse. There is nonetheless a constant and vivid stream of mental events, consisting of sensory impressions cued to information relevant to potential dangers.

Nothing in Lok's experience is alien to us, except as a matter of degree—the intensity and subtlety of his sensory perceptions. (Lok's ears and nose are so highly developed in their operations that they function almost as independent agents. "Lok's ears spoke to Lok.") His effort to analyze the odors in the air warming in his nostrils remains at the level of pure sensory awareness, but it nonetheless follows a cognitive pattern instantly recognizable to anyone who has struggled to formulate an inchoate thought but then lost the thread and abandoned the problem as too faint and evanescent for solution. Even the absence of higher reflection is familiar to us as a local passage in the sequence of our own mental events. The sensations of locating one's self in a physical place, registering the presence of one's own people, scanning the environment for dangers, and feeling secure in the command of that environment—all those experiences are of such elemental importance that they place our own hypertrophic capacities for abstract reflection in perspective, reducing them in their proportions relative to the basic conditions of life.

In retrospect, the reader knows that the odor and sound from the island are indications of the Cro-Magnon camp and thus signs of the menace that will destroy the band, but as we read we are kept entirely within the pace and sequence of Lok's own perceptions and responses. The sense of a mortal danger almost glimpsed, and then lost, is as much a part of our experience as it is of Lok's. On this elemental level, Lok is one with the characters of Sophocles and Shakespeare, and Golding makes this connection possible without falsifying the actual scope of Lok's cognitive powers.

The total effect of the passage is to place us emotionally and cognitively inside Lok's skin, contracting its exposed surface to preserve warmth against the night air. As has often been remarked by Golding's critics, a performance like this is a tour de force of technique, an instance of dazzling virtuosity in narrative method. It is also an instance of a large and generous moral nature. Without preaching, without didacticism, simply by enabling us to share in his own achievement of imaginative sympathy, Golding gives new depth and breadth to our capacity for sharing in the experience of other creatures. He takes us outside the limitations of our own particular identities and our own local cultural values. He enables us to register our common nature not merely on the level of "human universals" but on the level of universals that extend beyond the characteristics of our own species.

When the point of view shifts to the Cro-Magnons, the whole cognitive landscape changes. It becomes more complex and sequential; there are layers of suppression and deceit, complex emotions of shame, embarrassment, and remorse, and the capacity for complex symbolic thought. All of this comes together in a single image at the end of the story, as the survivors of the Cro-Magnon band are floating across a lake in their canoe. Speaking of the "forest devils" from whom they feel they have escaped, the leader Marlan says, "'They live in the darkness under the trees'" (chapter 12). For the protagonist Tuami, this statement precipitates a moment of symbolic perception:

> Tuami looked at the line of darkness. It was far away and there was plenty of water in between. He peered forward past the sail to see what lay at the other end of the lake, but it was so long, and there was such a flashing from the water that he could not see if the line of darkness had an ending.

A symbol in literature is an image, often an aspect of the setting, that is an integral component of the represented action and that functions metaphorically to signify the thematic implications of that represented action. For both Tuami and Golding, the scene on the lake crystallizes itself into a symbol for the human condition. The darkness is a natural metaphor for evil—for objects of terror lurking out of sight, for horror and self-loathing. The flashing of the light is a metaphor of mental reflection, at times not illuminating the world but blinding us to it. The water with its flashing of reflected light is an image of the future, stretching out beyond the visible horizon. The flashing of light obscures perception and leaves the protagonist suspended in uncertainty, but it is also epiphanic, a visionary culmination in its own right. The tone is complex and divided: relief at the escape from the darkness behind, a sense of temporary security, and anxiety about what lies ahead. In this one symbolic image, Golding has compacted all the latent complexity of the modern mind, and the capacity to think symbolically is itself one of the defining features of that mind. (See Mellars, 1996; Mithen, 1996, 2001; Stringer and Gamble, 1993; Tattersall, 1999.)

Golding's handling of point of view serves as the medium for his absorption into the experience of his characters, and it thus reflects his creative motives and the quality of his mind. It reveals that one of his central motives is the relatively pure and disinterested desire to exercise the power of sympathetic insight into the experience of other sentient creatures. Neither the Neanderthals nor the Cro-Magnons function merely to reflect ideological values or to serve as vehicles for narcissistic fantasy. They are not idealized, sentimentalized, or glamorized. They are treated with respect as figures of inherent interest and value.

The Neanderthal protagonist Lok is foolish, easily distracted, often baffled, and ultimately helpless, but he is also vividly alert to the world around him, and he is warm and loving. He accepts his lowly place in the band without petty egoistic concern; and when he realizes that he must be the new leader, after the deaths of Mal and Ha, he struggles heroically, though ineffectually, to fulfill his mission. He has a lot of heart, and the depth and sincerity of his feeling for the band invest him with dignity. The new people "had tugged at the strings that bound him to Fa and Mal and Liku and the rest of the people. The strings were not the ornament of life but its substance. If they broke a man would die" (chapter 4). There is a deep pathos in Lok's ultimate solitude and defeat. That pathos is conveyed in the blankness of the sudden shift to an objectivized perspective as he lies down to die. After we have been so deeply immersed in his point of view, being taken out of it and being made to see him only externally, from the outside, as an alien creature, has the sensation of a death, of a sudden, final separation.

The Cro-Magnon protagonist Tuami is frightened and secretive, and his mind is weighed down with foreboding, suspicion, resentment, and guilt. His social world lacks the simple and instinctive bonding that distinguishes relations among the Neanderthals, but he has a dignity of a different sort—of the sort that is illustrated in the final moment of symbolic imagery on the lake. His world is complex and full of sinister mystery, but he is cognitively adequate to that world. He has helped Marlan, the leader, to steal a woman from their parent tribe, but he already plans to assassinate Marlan, and he secretly sharpens an ivory knife for that purpose. This anticipated act of treachery forms part of his sense of the darkness in his world. He is not morally obtuse. He is a tragic protagonist and not merely a villain. Like Macbeth, he is conscious of the evil he commits, and he suffers from that consciousness. He does not speak in soliloquies, but he articulates his experience, for himself, in symbolic imagery. In that imagery, he suppresses none of the conflicted elements of his moral consciousness, and he makes even his own confusion an integral part of the symbolic complex. Golding's sympathy for Tuami is not less than his sympathy for Lok. In the final words of the novel—"he could not see if the line of darkness had an ending"—Golding's own perspective and that of his Cro-Magnon protagonist converge into a single point of view. (On Golding's symbolism and the thematic significance in his manipulation of point of view, see Babb, 1954, pp. 53–61; Kinkead-Weekes and Gregor, 1984, pp. 110–118; Tiger, 1976, pp. 69–70, 74–75, 86.)

The interplay between the points of view of the Neanderthals and the Cro-Magnons provides a medium for articulating Golding's ambivalent vision of human nature, and it thus mediates the largest thematic purposes of the story. The Neanderthals are both entranced and horrified by the new people. By looking at the Cro-Magnons from the Neanderthal perspective, Golding evokes the strange and singular fascination of modern humanity, with all its ingenuity, its grotesque social and mental complications, and its cruelty. From the other direction, looking at the Neanderthals from the modern perspective, Golding conveys a sense of the simpler, more elemental realities of human life. In one scene in the final chapter, the Cro-Magnons collectively participate in this more humane perspective. The Cro-Magnons have taken the Neanderthal baby with them, and it has been adopted by a woman, Vivani, who has lost her own baby. The Cro-Magnons are both fascinated and repelled by the simian character of the baby:

> He sniffed, turned, ran at Vivani's leg and scrambled up to her breast. She was shuddering and laughing as if this pleasure and love were also a fear and a torment. The devil's hands and feet had laid hold of her. Hesitating and half-ashamed, with that same frightened laughter, she bent her head, cradled him with her arms and shut her eyes. The people were grinning at her too as if they felt the strange, tugging mouth, as if in spite of them there was a well of feeling opened in love and fear. They made adoring and submissive sounds, reached out their hands, and at the same time they shuddered in repulsion at the too-nimble feet and the red, curly hair.

Tuami already anticipates the time when the cute Neanderthal baby will be a fully grown male of an alien species, and he wonders "what sacrifice would they be forced to perform in a world of confusion?" Nonetheless, for a moment, the baby serves as a temporary point of collective emotional poise. The baby gets turned upside down in Vivani's hood, and as his rump waggles in the air, everyone laughs. The laughter releases tension and ill will, and for a moment the group is in harmony. "They were an answer, the frightened, angry love of the woman and the ridiculous, intimidating rump that was wagging at her head, they were a password." The cruelty of ritual sacrifice that Tuami anticipates is one answer to "a world of confusion." Another answer is that of comedy—the upturned rump, the human animal divested of its mystery and surrounded by human warmth.

What We Can Claim

The criteria I have invoked in assessing these three novels are universal in their application. All novels involve authors, readers, represented subjects, and formal structures. For all authors, quality of motive and quality of mind are critical factors in the social exchange between author and reader. Readers can be more or less adequate to an author's intentions, and they can refuse complicity with intentions that they feel are ignoble or degrading. The author nonetheless holds the initiative in this exchange. It is for him or her to propose some structure of meaning. Meaning in fictional narratives inheres in a represented subject— some sequence of actions by characters living in a world. Fantasy and symbolism often involve some deviation from simple realism, and the literal accuracy of a depiction is not a decisive factor in the quality of fiction. Seriousness and honesty in the conception of a subject, in contrast, are decisive factors, and for those factors, Darwinian social science can provide us with important conceptual measures. One measure is the internal organismic coherence of a represented subject, and another is the integration of an organism and its environment. Those measures hold good whether the subject consists in Neanderthals splattered with mammoth blood or gentlemen and ladies exchanging civilities in a drawing room. The formal features of a literary work—the plotting, scenic construction, thematic order, symbolic imagery, style, and tone—are all dependent on the integrity with which an author conceives of the represented subject. The ultimate formal properties are coherence and integration, and one classic criterion of literary merit is the degree to which an author in any given work succeeds in integrating all the elements of that work: the represented subject matter, the organization of the narrative, and the theme, tone, and style. We cannot claim any absolute, transcendent source for aesthetic values—whether those of motive and quality of mind, those of integrity in the conception of the represented subject, or those of formal integration. What we can claim is that certain specific qualities satisfy our own cognitive needs. We can hypothesize that the need for cognitive order is an adaptive response to "a world of confusion," and we can explain how certain works, for us, satisfy that need, or fail to.

6
Human Nature and Literary Meaning
A Theoretical Model Illustrated with a Critique of Pride and Prejudice

The Challenge to a Darwinian Literary Criticism

The common notion of what Darwinian literary criticism could or should do is that Darwinian critics should first look into evolutionary psychology in order to identify universal, basic forms of human behavior—human universals—and that they should then examine this or that literary text in order to demonstrate that the characters in that text behave in precisely the way that evolutionary psychologists predict people will behave. The method involved in this common notion is naïve and vulnerable to obvious objections. People in reality do not simply exemplify common, universal patterns of behavior. They have individuality that is distinguished by the peculiarities of their individual temperaments, their cultural conditioning, and their individual experiences. Cultures vary widely in the ways that they organize the common elements of the human motivational and cognitive system, and even within any given culture many people deviate drastically both from the behavioral norms that characterize that culture and from the deeper underlying commonalities of human nature. Moreover, characters in literary representations are not real, living people. They are fictive fabrications that reflect the notions and beliefs and purposes of individual authors, and individual authors are themselves constrained by their larger cultural context and by the traditions and conventions of literary representation that are available to them. To treat characters as if they were actual people is to ignore the whole concept of "meaning" in literature, and to ignore meaning in literature is something like ignoring the concept of "energy" in physics or the concept of "life" in biology. It is simply to miss the point.

The deficiencies in the common notion of Darwinian literary study can easily be corrected. There is no necessity that Darwinian literary critics muddle along doing a bad job with a naïve methodology simply because they have no notion of how to do a good job. The concepts necessary for integrating Darwinian psychology and literary criticism are neither hard to understand nor difficult to use. What I propose here is to lay out a necessary minimum of analytic concepts—five in all—that must enter into any reasonably competent literary analysis informed by a Darwinian understanding of human nature. The basic concepts are these: (a) human nature as a structured hierarchy of motives (within which the motive of constructing imaginative representations holds a prominent place); (b) "point of view," or the location of meaning within three distinct centers of consciousness—that of the author, the characters, and the implied or projected audience; (c) the use of human universals as a common frame of reference in relation to which authors identify their own individual identities and their own distinct structures of meaning; (d) a set of categories for analyzing individual differences in identity; and (e) the distribution of specifically literary meaning into three chief dimensions: (i) theme (conceptual content), (ii) tone (emotional coloring), and (iii) formal organization (a concept that ranges all the way from macrostructures like plot and narrative sequencing to microstructures like phrasing, word choice, and sequences of sounds).

In the course of laying out these concepts and explaining their relations, I shall also make arguments that should be of some interest to Darwinian social scientists, whether or not they care much about literature and the other arts. I shall argue that Darwinian psychology is on the verge of achieving a paradigm—that is, a consensus about the necessary minimum of conceptual elements that enter into an understanding of "human nature." This emerging paradigm does not consist merely of a list of common basic motives or "universals." It consists both of universals, the common human elements, and of the variations among those elements that we describe as "individual differences." And the paradigm also includes an understanding of how the specifically human pattern of life history—birth, development, reproduction, and death—responds with flexible but integrated strategies to the wide range of physical and cultural conditions in which it is possible for people to subsist. Among Darwinian psychologists, there is still disagreement in all these areas, and the currently dominant school of Darwinian psychology, the school most readily identified as "evolutionary psychology," has committed itself to dead ends and fallacies in its deprecation of both individual differences and domain-general intelligence. But Darwinian social science as a whole has a diverse array of intellectually independent investigators, from many convergent disciplines—paleoanthropology, life history analysis, behavioral ecology, behavioral genetics, personality theory, and the study of intelligence, among others. Given this array of investigators eager to make advances in their own fields and to integrate those fields within the larger logic of evolutionary theory, claims that are motivated by ideology and that lack both empirical support and internal consistency are not likely to survive for long. The necessary elements for a paradigm in Darwinian psychology are already virtually in place, and I am fairly confident that the energy of active research will in the near future sweep away the obstructions that have temporarily arisen from the premature consolidation of certain orthodox doctrines.

In order to make an argument about the structure of Darwinian literary criticism, then, I shall first need to make an argument about the current condition and future prospects of Darwinian psychology. I shall sketch out what I take to be the emerging paradigm for human nature, and I shall introduce one concept—the concept of a "cognitive behavioral system"—that is relatively unfamiliar but that is, I shall argue, indispensable to the formation of an adequate paradigm both in psychology and in literary study. Most evolutionary psychologists have paid slight attention to literature and the other arts, and some have argued that the arts have no adaptive function central to human life history goals. (See Miller, 2000; Pinker, 1997b, 2002.) Invoking the logic of the emerging paradigm in Darwinian psychology, I shall argue that literature and the other arts do indeed have an adaptive function and that understanding this adaptive function is a prerequisite to understanding our specifically *human* nature. The effort to construct a paradigm for Darwinian literary criticism and the effort to construct a paradigm for the broader field of Darwinian psychology are thus interdependent. They need each other. Fortunately, they are both within reach, and by reaching the one, we shall also reach the other.

The central challenge for a specifically Darwinian form of literary criticism is to connect the highest levels in the organization of human nature with the most detailed and subtle aspects of literary meaning. Can we connect the basic life history goals—survival, growth, and reproduction—with the finest nuances of theme, tone, and style in the organization of literary meaning in specific works? The answer to this question will determine the success or failure of Darwinian literary criticism, and the answer is "yes, we can." The elementary principles of life history analysis enter into the organization of all literary representations, and the manner in which any given author manages those principles is a defining feature in the character and quality of that author's work. In order to give a practical illustration of these claims, in the final section of this article, I shall offer a Darwinian critical commentary on a single novel, *Pride and Prejudice.* I have selected this novel because it is one of the most familiar of all novels; it is relatively short and simple; and it is so finely realized, as an artistic construct, that it offers a good test case for the challenge of demonstrating the integral relation between life history analysis and the finest components of literary meaning.

Let me emphasize that this choice of an illustrative text is in one sense arbitrary. Any work of literature, from any period or genre, could be chosen for illustrative purposes. Darwinists have written critiques of folktales, myths, plays, poems, romance novels, realist fiction, science fiction, operas, ballets, and movies. They have written interpretive studies of, among other writers, Homer, Shakespeare, Swift, Wordsworth, Pushkin, Tchaikovsky, Walter Scott,

Charlotte Brontë, George Eliot, Hans Christian Andersen, Willa Cather, Walter Pater, Zamyatin, and Dr. Seuss. There is no work of literature written anywhere in the world, at any time, by any author, that is outside the scope of a Darwinian analysis. In order to be susceptible to a Darwinian analysis, an author does not have to be a Darwinian. An author can be a pagan Greek, a Christian, a Moslem, or a Zen Buddhist. He or she can be a Brazilian tribesman, a European lady, a medieval Japanese warrior, or a Tibetan monk. He or she can be heterosexual, homosexual, bisexual, or celibate. He or she need not be average or typical, and he or she need not himself or herself embrace beliefs and attitudes that are similar to those of Darwinian psychologists or Darwinian literary critics. If Darwinism gives a true account of the human mind, and if the human mind produces all literary texts, all literary texts are susceptible to a Darwinian analysis. They are susceptible, that is, to an analysis of the constraining psychological structures that regulate the production of all imaginative artifacts.

Geneticists have often found fruit flies a convenient species for their experiments. But they do not believe or suggest that genetics applies only to fruit flies. I have written on *Pride and Prejudice* in various places, using it for various illustrative purposes. I want to be clear, then, that I do not consider *Pride and Prejudice* a particularly or specifically Darwinian text. I consider it the literary equivalent of a fruit fly. Various of my colleagues in Darwinian literary study are working on the literary equivalents of mice or nematode worms, but whatever the local subject of study, we are all contributing to the same larger field.

The Emerging Paradigm in Darwinian Psychology

The argument I shall make for what Darwinian literary critics can and should do will turn on the questions of individual differences and "domain-general" intelligence. The two main orthodox tenets of evolutionary psychology that have so far impeded the full development of a paradigm for Darwinian psychology are the repudiation or deprecation of the significance attaching to domain-general cognitive abilities and individual differences in personality and intelligence. "Evolutionary psychology" as a distinct school—and not just as a general term covering the whole field of Darwinian psychology—gives overwhelming, preponderating weight to "human universals," and it envisions the mind as consisting almost exclusively of "domain-specific" cognitive mechanisms, that is, "cognitive modules" that have evolved specifically for the purpose of solving adaptive problems within a Paleolithic environment. And that ancient environment is itself conceived as a set of statistically stable physical and social conditions, the "environment of evolutionary adaptedness" (EEA). The central tenets of evolutionary psychology as a distinct school, then, are these: (a) everyone has pretty much the same sort of mind and personality, not only in basic structures but in force or quality; (b) this one universal mind, the mind that is common to all people on earth, is "designed" (= adapted) exclusively to deal with a statistically stable environment that lasted for perhaps two million years but that in good part no longer subsists; and (c) all the significant adaptive features of that mind are "cognitive modules" designed to solve adaptive problems specific to the statistical regularities of this ancient environment; domain-general intelligence is not one of these adaptive cognitive features.

This characterization of evolutionary psychology is stark, stripped of qualifications and equivocations, and it is thus far a "caricature," but the merit of a caricature is that it brings into sharp relief the signal, defining features of a physiognomy. The oddly misshapen countenance that emerges from these three starkly defined tenets is in its main outlines a true portrait. (See Cosmides and Tooby, 1994; Pinker, 1994, 1995, 1997b, 2002; Symons, 1992; Tooby and Cosmides, 1992. Also see the textbooks by Barrett, Dunbar, and Lycett, 2002; Bridgeman, 2003; Buss, 1999; Gaulin and McBurney, 2001; Palmer and Palmer, 2002; Rossano, 2003.)

There are two reasons, I would suggest, that evolutionary psychologists have propounded this peculiarly distorted version of human cognitive evolution. The first reason is that they have been preoccupied with opposing the Standard Social Science Model (SSSM) of the mind as a blank slate or general, all-purpose computer in which all content is produced by external (social and cultural) influences (Tooby and Cosmides, "Psychological Foundation"). Domain specificity offers an alternative to domain generality. The second reason is that they have been frightened by the association of Darwinian psychology with social Darwinism, eugenics, and the exploration of individual and group differences in behavior (the field known as "behavioral genetics"), and especially differences in intelligence. The radical environmentalism or blank-slate model that dominated the social sciences in the twentieth century was itself largely motivated by the fear or rejection of social Darwinism, eugenics, and racial theory. By emphasizing universals and domain-specific mechanisms the evolutionary psychologists have sought to effect a compromise between Darwinism and the SSSM. They have reintroduced the notion of adaptive cognitive structure into psychology, but have done so without violating the ideological taboos against acknowledging the significance of individual and group differences.

The appeal of these two advantages has been so strong that it has, since the early 1990s, blinded many Darwinian psychologists to the fundamental disadvantages of the concepts that enable the compromise. The disadvantages are that this whole complex of ideas runs counter to gross and obvious features of common experience—to the vital importance both of individual differences and of general intelligence in everyday life—and that it runs counter also to the elementary logic in the theory of natural selection. In that theory, "selection" can only work on variation, that is, "individual differences." No variation, no selection. No selection, no adaptation, and thus no evolution "by means of natural selection" (Darwin, 2003).

Since the late 1990s, evolutionary psychology has achieved sufficient substance and stability to provide a big market for popular expositions and for textbooks—for summary expositions of common findings. In about the same period—in just the past few years—the psychological ideas that so quickly congealed into a premature orthodoxy have been under increasing pressure from new and genuinely innovative research into the single most important event in human evolutionary history—the "cultural revolution" that took place some 60,000 to 30,000 years ago and that produced the first evidence of complex technology, complex forms of socioeconomic organization, and sophisticated symbolic and artistic activity. This whole research area is fraught with controversy, but there is enough agreement about some basic facts so that a compelling new vision of human evolution has been emerging—a vision that contrasts sharply with the orthodox tenets of evolutionary psychology. In this new vision, the most distinctive feature of the specifically human mind—the feature that distinguishes it most from that of its primate cousins—is the emergence of a flexible general intelligence that enables humans to adapt to variations within an environment that is itself complex and unstable. (See Chiappe, 2000; Chiappe and MacDonald, 2003; Crawford, 1998; Foley, 1996; Geary 1998; Geary and Huffman, 2002; Irons, 1998; MacDonald, 1990, 1995b, 1997, 1998a, 1998b; Mithen, 1996, 2001; Potts, 1998; Richerson and Boyd, 2000; D. S. Wilson, 1999, in press; E. O. Wilson, 1998.)

It is a simple fact available to common observation that humans have evolved a truly extraordinary capacity to adapt to new and different environments—and to effect these adaptations while undergoing relatively little or no actual change in their anatomical or physiological characteristics. Humans can live everywhere from polar regions to deserts to tropical rain forests; they can organize themselves socially in groups that extend from small hunter-gatherer bands to tribes, hordes, nation-states, empires, and new world orders; and they can adapt to socioeconomic ecologies that stretch from hunting and gathering to agriculture, market economies, industrial cities, and vast metropolitan regions linked digitally to a total world culture. The one crucial feature of human nature that underwrites this adaptability is domain-general intelligence, and that intelligence, along with all the distinctive features of human temperament and personal character, varies from person to person and group to group. (See Bailey, 1997, 1998; Barash, 1997; Bouchard, 1994, 1997; Buss, 1990, 1995; Eaves, Eysenck and Martin, 1989; Eysenck, 1979, 1980, 1995; Herrnstein and Murray, 1994; Jensen, 1998; MacDonald, 1990, 1995b, 1997, 1998a; Rushton, 1995; Segal, 1997, 1999; Segal and MacDonald, 1998; Seligman, 1992; D. S. Wilson, 1994; 1999.)

In the new, emerging vision of human evolution and human nature, the idea of cognitive domains has not been discarded. It has been assimilated and integrated into the larger general structure of human cognition. Cognitive domains have their place and function; they subserve cognitive activities that track constant features of the environment. The eyesight that tracks the spatio-physical world is a prime example; and language aptitude that tracks the human physical and social environment is another. But these domain-specific aptitudes are only a part of the total human cognitive repertory. Another part is general intelligence, and general intelligence subserves the basic adaptive needs of human beings. The new vision does not fall back to the old blank-slate model. It does not assume that all human motives are simply fabricated by arbitrary cultural conventions. It identifies a distinct structure of human motives and cognitive dispositions that derives from the larger logic of inclusive fitness—the logic that regulates the adaptive structure of all life on earth. The distinct structure of human motives and cognitive dispositions is that which is appropriate to a primate species that is highly social and mildly polygynous, that displays concealed ovulation, continuous female receptivity, and postmenopausal life expectancy corresponding to a uniquely extended period of childhood development, that has extraordinary aptitudes for technology, that has developed language and the capacity for peering into the minds of its conspecifics, and that displays a unique disposition for fabricating and consuming aesthetic and imaginative artifacts. So long as we bear all this in mind, we need have no fear of falling back into the structural vacuum of the blank slate—a vacuum in which the mind evolved, the mind produced culture, and culture gave all content and structure to the mind.

In the 1990s, the most important theoretical conflict within Darwinian psychology itself was the conflict between "sociobiology" on the one side and "evolutionary psychology" on the other. In its simplest terms, this conflict turned on differing views of the human motivational system. Sociobiologists tended to regard humans as "fitness maximizers." As Irons formulates the idea, "Human beings tend to behave in such a way as to maximize their genetic representation in future generations" (1979, p. 257). In its most extreme form, as in the arguments produced by Betzig, fitness maximization is conceived simply in numerical terms as a matter of leaving the greatest possible number of progeny. Evolutionary psychologists, in contrast, committed themselves to the view that humans do not care particularly about reproductive success. In their view, humans are not "fitness maximizers" but rather "adaptation executers" (Tooby and Cosmides, 1992, p. 54). That is, humans are motivated exclusively by "proximal" motives like the desire for sex. In the EEA, such motives operated reliably to maximize fitness but did not, supposedly, require that reproductive success be an active motive in its own right. In the modern world, the argument goes, birth control neatly severs the link between the proximal motive of sexual desire and the "ultimate" regulative principle of inclusive fitness. People are designed only to push the pleasure buttons in their proximal motives, not to worry about the ultimate evolutionary or adaptive rationale that produced those buttons. (See Alexander, 1979, 1987, 1990; Barkow, 1990; Betzig, 1986, 1998; Chagnon, 1979; Chagnon and Irons, 1979; Irons, 1990, 1998; MacDonald, 1995a; Symons, 1989, 1992; Turke, 1990.)

In the currently orthodox version of evolutionary psychology, the idea of humans as adaptation executors has gained a decisive victory. In so far as this concept is set in contrast to the notion of counting offspring as a monolithic human motive, the victory has been legitimate, but the idea of pushing pleasure buttons is not in itself a satisfactory account of the human motivational system. We can formulate a better, more comprehensive account of the human motivational system by integrating two concepts: (a) the concept of human life history as a cycle organized around the distribution of effort between "somatic" and "reproductive" activities, and (b) the concept of "behavioral systems."

The central categories of life history analysis are birth, growth, death, and reproduction. The organisms of all species engage in two fundamental forms of effort—the acquisition of resources (somatic effort) and the expenditure of resources in reproduction. Birth, growth, and death are somatic activities. Mating and parenting are reproductive activities. (Not all individuals of all species engage in reproductive activity, but if reproductive effort were not part of the suite of characteristics in a species, that species would become extinct within a single generation.) All the main activities in the life history of an organism are integrated and interdependent. "What an organism spends in one endeavor cannot be spent in another. Life histories, the patterns of birth, growth, and death that we see, are thus the outcome of competing costs and benefits of different activities at any point in the life cycle" (Low, 1998, p. 131). Life history analysis compares the different ways in which the logic of inclusive fitness—the maximization of reproductive success—has regulated the interplay of these large-scale principles in different species. The organization of life history traits—of size, growth rate, life span, mating behavior, number and pacing of offspring, sex ratios of offspring, and parenting strategies—enters into every aspect of a species' characteristics: into its physiology, its anatomy, and its behavior. Life history theory can thus be regarded as the overarching theory for both a macroeconomics and a microeconomics of biology. (See Alexander, 1979, p. 25, 1987, pp. 40–41; Geary, 1998, pp. 11, 199; MacDonald, 1997, p. 328; McGuire and Troisi, 1998, pp. 58–59; Low, 1998, pp. 138–40, 2000, p. 92; Ridley, 1999, pp. 12, 127–128 ; Trivers 1972, pp. 168–174, 1985, pp. 311–314.)

The human species has a distinct form for the organization of its life history, and the logic of this organization enters into every facet of the human behavioral and cognitive order. Humans are highly social animals with pair-bonded, semi-monogamous mating systems and extraordinarily high levels of parental investment. They have upright posture, narrowed birth canals, and large brains. As a result, their reproductive economy necessarily involves motivational systems geared toward male-female pair-bonding, sustained family structures, extended kinship systems, and complex social organization. Their large brains entail long development as children so that they can acquire the information and skills necessary for successful life effort. Their long childhood requires intense child-parent attachment, male-female cooperative parenting, and extended kin networks. Their large brains present them with unique adaptive opportunities, both technological and social, and also with challenges and problems other species do not face.

The idea of "behavioral systems" has been formulated as a concept in Darwinian psychiatry, and it has emerged also, implicitly, half-consciously, as an organizing principle in orthodox versions of evolutionary psychology. In *Darwinian Psychiatry*, McGuire and Troisi define behavioral systems as coordinated suites of behavior subserving specific life goals. "The term *behavior system* refers to *functionally and causally related behavior patterns and the systems responsible for them*" (1998, p. 60). McGuire and Troisi themselves identify four specific systems: survival, reproduction, kin assistance, and reciprocation—with reciprocation serving as a generalized term for social interaction beyond the kin group. In the now numerous textbooks devoted to evolutionary psychology, very similar terms typically serve as the chapter titles for the whole sequence of chapters. For instance, in the first of the textbooks (1999), after introductory chapters on the history, theory, and methodology of evolutionary psychology, Buss has this sequence of main sections: "Problems of Survival," "Challenges of Sex and Mating," "Challenges of Parenting and Kinship," "Problems of Group Living." The organization of topics in Buss's textbook set the pattern for the subsequent textbooks, and the pattern itself tacitly underwrites the theory of behavioral systems. (Buss himself is alert to the importance of personality theory and to individual differences, and in a final section of his textbook he discusses this topic but also acknowledges that orthodox evolutionary psychologists have concentrated almost exclusively on human universals.)

By combining the idea of life history analysis with the idea of behavioral systems, we can formulate an alternative to the opposing notions of fitness maximization and adaptation execution. Despite the evidence of a few great sultans, humans are not typically motivated, in any very direct or active way, to maximize the number of their progeny. But neither are they merely puppets adequately fulfilled by the pushing of their pleasure buttons. People are neither fitness maximizers nor adaptation executors. They are highly integrated sets of behavioral systems that have been organized and directed by the logic of the human life history cycle. Human nature is organized in structured sets of behavioral systems, and these systems subserve the goals that are distributed into the basic functions of somatic and reproductive life effort. Fitness maximization is not itself an active motive, but the fundamental somatic impulses (surviving and acquiring resources, both physical and social) and the fundamental reproductive impulses (acquiring mates, having sex, producing and tending children, helping kin) are in fact direct and active motives.

The behavioral systems identified by McGuire and Troisi and by the textbook writers—survival, mating, parenting, kin relations, and social interaction—are built into the human organism. They are mediated by innate structures in the genetically conditioned features of anatomy, physiology, hormones, and neurochemistry. All of these mediating forces manifest themselves psychologically as emotions—the "basic" emotions identified by Ekman and others as universal motivating forces in human psychology (joy, sadness, fear, anger, contempt, disgust, surprise). (See Damasio, 1994; Ekman, 2003; Ekman and Davidson, 1994; Ledoux, 1996; Lewis and Haviland, 2000; MacDonald, 1995b; Panksepp, 1998.) The main behavioral systems that subserve the largest life history goals are sensitive to the appropriate stimuli, but they are latent in all conditions of life. Male sexual desire, for example, is activated by the sight of nubile females, but even a male raised in total isolation by machines would presumably have stirrings of confused sexual interest or sensation—a sense of vague, frustrated longing, accompanied by spontaneous erections and emissions, and I think it safe to predict that the first time any such hypothetically deprived male saw a nubile female, he would have a sudden and instantaneous conviction that THAT was what he had been wanting, had he only known. A woman raised in similar isolation would presumably not think to herself, "I wish to be inseminated, grow an embryo in my uterus, and produce a child, which I shall then suckle and nurture," but whatever her thoughts or longings might be, she would still grow breasts and undergo a menstrual cycle, and if she were inseminated by machines in her sleep, the growth and birth of a child, however terrifying to her ignorance, would have in it a certain natural, physical logic, and the effects would carry with them instinctive impulses and sensations. Language is an instinct (Bickerton, 1990; Pinker, 1994), but feral children can never gain fluency in speech. Maternity is an instinct, but female monkeys raised in isolation perform badly as mothers. Normal human development requires socialization, but socialization itself is channeled by innate dispositions. The behavior of a female raised in isolation is disorganized and dysfunctional, but it is not simply blank.

The total anatomical and hormonal organization of women is geared toward the bearing and raising of children. Even the massively conditioned women in Huxley's *Brave New World* feel a vague longing that can be satisfied only by a full course of hormonally mediated "pregnancy substitute." In the actual modern world, a world in which people can choose whether or not to reproduce, the overwhelming majority do choose to reproduce. Many couples who for physical reasons cannot have children go to astonishing lengths, in expense and effort, to adopt children. Evolutionary psychologists emphasizing the activation of proximal mechanisms point to the fact that not everybody wants to have children. True enough, but most people are equipped by nature with the physical and psychological attributes that are necessary to the bearing and raising of children, and the majority of people feel at some point a powerful need to activate those attributes and to fulfill the behavioral capacities they feel latent within them. If this were not the case, we would have a hard time explaining adoption and the nearly universal human practice of treating pet animals as surrogate children. (See Alcock, 2001, pp. 35–40.)

Childbearing and child-rearing are only an instance, though an important one. The larger principle is that in most cases people accede to the psychological force of the total set of motivational systems that have been implanted in them by the logic of human life history. More often than not, people have a compelling need to give full and integrated play to the whole suite of their behavioral systems. Exceptions and special cases abound, but it is a broad general truth about human nature that people have a need to activate the latent capacities of the behavioral systems that have shaped the largest features of their bodies and their minds. For most people, achieving satisfaction in life depends on the fulfillment of the emotional needs built into those systems.

The Cognitive Behavioral System

The textbook versions of evolutionary psychology are a little uncertain about what, if anything, to make of the various specifically cognitive aspects of human nature. Language can usually be inserted somewhere in the sections on social interaction, but it is less clear where one is to locate aptitudes for tool use, cognitive biases for the acquisition of organized information about plants and animals, and the production of cultural artifacts of no apparent utility, especially if these artifacts do not push simple pleasure buttons in the way that pornography does for many people. If we combine the idea of behavioral systems with a recognition of the peculiarly human attribute of domain-general intelligence, we can solve this puzzle. The human mind is an extraordinary, complex organ. It is both highly structured and flexibly responsive to contingent inputs. It solves an immense array of adaptive problems. Some of its processes develop in predictably universal ways, as in the acquisition of language, of colors, or of botanical and zoological categories. (See Atran, 1990; Brown, 1991; Cosmides and Tooby, 1994; Geary, 1998; Pinker, 1994, 1995, 1997b, 2002; Tooby and Cosmides, 1992.) Other processes develop with the combinatorial fluidity that we designate as "creative" or "inventive," as in the invention of new technologies and new arts, but all new inventions and discoveries work by extending and combining the elemental cognitive components that develop spontaneously and universally in human minds, as the product of an adaptive evolutionary history, and all cultural artifacts, no matter how complex or seemingly arbitrary, are constrained by the limitations of physical nature and are both prompted and constrained by an evolved human psychology. (See Barrow, 1996; Carroll, 1995; Chiappe, 2000; Chiappe and MacDonald, 2003; Darwin, 1871; Geary, 1998; Mithen, 1996; Geary and Huffman, 2002; D. S. Wilson, in press; E. O. Wilson, 1998; and in this vol., see part 1, chapter 6; part 2, chapter 1.)

The mind is a complex and integrated feature of human nature—sufficiently complex, structured, and integrated in its operations so that it answers to the criteria for what McGuire and Troisi identify as a "behavioral system." If we identify the mind in this way, we are adding it, as a specifically human characteristic, to the set of human behavioral systems. We identify it as having characteristic innate constraints and distinctive latent capacities elicited by appropriate releasors. The mate selection system arouses desire and fulfills it in successful coupling. The parenting system arouses concern for children and achieves fulfillment in the successful rearing of children. The social interaction system arouses desire for forming coalitions and finding a place within a status hierarchy, and achieving those goals offers pleasure and provides a sensation of satisfaction. The cognitive behavioral system arouses a need for conceptual and imaginative order, and that need fulfills itself and provides satisfaction to the mind through the formulation of concepts, the construction of religious, philosophical, or ideological beliefs, the development of scientific knowledge, and the fabrication of aesthetic and imaginative artifacts.

I have already argued that domain-general intelligence has an adaptive function; it facilitates a flexible response to a variable environment. That flexibility gives humans an advantage other animals do not have, and it presents them also with challenges and difficulties unique to the human species. Other species operate mainly by means of instinct, that is, by means of stereotyped behaviors that leave little room for conscious choice. Humans create elaborate mental models of the world and make decisions on the basis of alternative scenarios that present themselves within those models. (See E. O. Wilson, 1998; and in this vol., see part 1, chapter 7.) The materials available to the mind and imagination are vast, and the combination of those materials virtually infinite. The possibility for error, uncertainty, and confusion is an ever-present fact of human mental life. Because they have an irrepressibly active and unstable mental life, humans have a special need to fabricate mental maps or models that make sense of the world and provide behavioral directives that can take the place of instinctive behavioral patterns. For these mental maps or models to be effective in providing behavioral directives, they must be emotionally saturated, imaginatively vivid. Art and cultural artifacts like religion and ideology meet this demand. They fulfill a necessary adaptive function, that of regulating the human cognitive behavioral system. The arts provide emotionally saturated images and aesthetic constructs that produce a sense of total cognitive order and that help regulate the other behavioral systems. The arts make sense of human needs and motives. They simulate subjective experience, map out social relations, evoke sexual and social interactions, depict the intimate relations of kin, and locate the whole complex and interactive array of human behavioral systems within models of the total world order. Humans have a universal and irrepressible need to fabricate this sort of order, and satisfying that need provides a distinct form of pleasure and fulfillment. (See Boyd, 1998,

2001; Brown, 1991; Carroll, 1995; Cooke, 1999c, 2002; Dissanayake, 1995b, 2000, in press; Fromm, 2003a, 2003b; Love, 2003; Storey, 1993, 1996; Sugiyama, 2001b; E. O. Wilson, 1998.)

A Diagram of Human Nature

In order to clarify the hierarchical motivational structure of human nature I have been describing here, I shall construct a diagram, with inclusive fitness at the top, as the ultimate regulative principle (but not as an active and direct motive). Active and direct motive begins at the next level down, with the organization of life effort into somatic and reproductive effort. Through this hierarchical structure, I am suggesting that over and above their specific goals and motives, many people have a generalized but distinct desire to acquire resources and also to achieve successful reproduction. Not all people have an active desire for reproductive success, but such a desire is nonetheless, I would argue, a characteristic of the species as a whole. Young men do not think only, "I want to buy a red convertible so I can attract that girl there and have sex with her." They also often think, "I'd like to become prosperous, and I'd like to get married and have a family." And young women do not think only, "I'm impressed by that guy with the red convertible. I want to arouse his sexual interest and attach him to me." They also think, "I'd like to find a prosperous, reliable man, marry him, have children, and raise a family." It is these latter, generalized inclinations that I am identifying as the somatic and reproductive motives in their own right.

Below the level of generalized desire to acquire resources and succeed in sexual reproduction, I shall place the various behavioral systems that subserve both those general motive dispositions. The specific subordinate systems identified here are systems dedicated to survival, technology, mating, parenting, kin relations, social relations, and cognitive activity. Between the somatic and reproductive levels on the one hand and these specific behavioral systems on the other, I shall place the term "development" to indicate that these various systems are activated and distributed according to the developmental program appropriate to the human species. (The mating and parenting systems operate only at specific times in the life history of a human organism, and social dispositions vary in the course of the life cycle.)

In a box under each behavioral system, I have placed a few motivational goals or directives characteristic of that system. Thus, under "Survival," there is a directive "avoid predators." Under "Mating," there is a directive "avoid incest." Under "Social," a directive "build coalitions," and so on.

In the interest of completeness, I include one behavioral system—that of "technology"—that is not mentioned in the accounts by McGuire and Troisi and the textbook writers. The disposition to construct stone tools is one of the most ancient hominid adaptations, and our modern technology is continuous with the construction of complex, multipart tools that constitutes one of the distinguishing features of the "human revolution" from perhaps 100,000 to

30,000 years ago. In one of the most elaborate efforts so far to mediate between evolutionary psychology and the idea of a domain-general intelligence, Mithen (1996) identifies technology as an integrated area of cognitive activity. He calls it a cognitive domain, but the concept as he describes it is on a structural level equivalent to what I have been calling a behavioral system.

Specific cognitive modules would be activated within the relevant behavioral systems. For instance, the cognitive modules for vision—edge and motion detection, color, depth, etc.—would be activated within the technological behavioral system and the survival system. Kin-recognition modules would be activated within the kinship system. "Face recognition" modules would be activated within all interpersonal behavioral systems (mating, parenting, kin, social interaction). Modules for regulating social exchange or cheater detection would be activated in the mating system and in the social system, and so on. If, as seems likely, the brain has specific modules geared to the construction of narratives and the recognition of aesthetically pleasing verbal patterns, those would be activated within the cognitive behavioral system. (For lists of domain-specific cognitive modules, see Carey and Spelke, 1994, p. 171; Cosmides and Tooby, 1994, p. 103; Mithen, 1996; Pinker, 1994, p. 420, 1995, p. 236, 1997b, pp. 128, 315; Sperber, 1994, p. 42; Tooby and Cosmides, 1992, p. 113. For suggestions about cognitive predispositions to certain kinds of aesthetic order, see Barrow, 1995; Eibl-Eibesfeldt, 1989; Frederick Turner, 1992; M. Turner, 1996.)

One final feature of the diagram is that the box in the diagram containing behavioral systems has a list of Ekman's basic emotions at the bottom of the box, thus signifying that all behavioral systems are activated and mediated by emotion.

Meaning and Point of View in Literary Representations

Literary representation is first and foremost the representation of human behavior within some surrounding world. Creating such representations is itself a fundamental motive of human nature, and human nature is the fundamental subject of the representations. The "meaning" of a representation does not reside in the represented events. Meaning resides in the *interpretation* of events. And interpretation is always, necessarily, dependent on "point of view." "Point of view" in literary narrative is not just another technical feature in a catalog of formal literary devices. In its broadest sense, point of view is a term signifying "the locus of consciousness or experience within which any meaning takes place." Point of view is thus the term we use to designate the primary components in the social interactions constituted in and by a literary representation. There are three components in the social interactions of a literary representation: the author, the represented characters, and the audience. (See Abrams, 1986.) The primary locus of meaning for all literary works is the mind of the author. Whether consciously or unconsciously, the author provides whatever

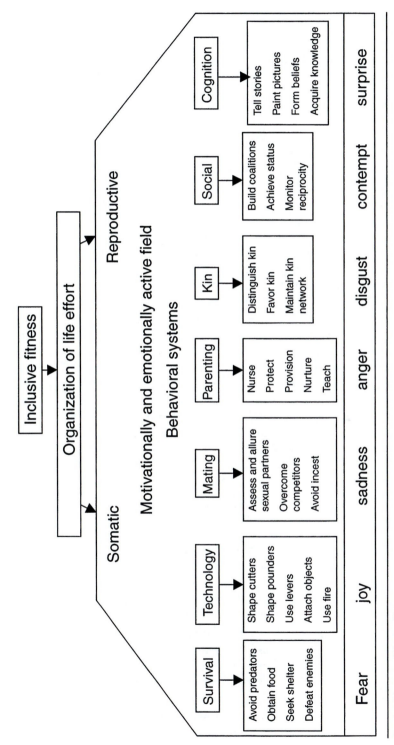

Fig. 1 A Diagram of Human Nature

determinate meaning resides in a work, but the author also negotiates among the competing points of view within the characters in the work, and negotiates further with the point of view he or she attributes to an audience.

Authors are people talking to people about people. Most stories are about people seeking resources and reproductive success—fortune and love. But they are also about people seeking to perceive meaning in or impose meaning on the events of their own lives and the lives of every person they know. All authors seek to dominate the meaning of the story they tell, and all the characters in a story have their own version of what happens. As a rule, these versions partially overlap both with one another and with the version presented by the author, but they also often conflict. The author has final say among his or her own characters, but to control the interpretation of the story as it will be registered by the audience, the author can only persuade, manipulate, cajole, wheedle, intimidate, solicit, insult, flatter, bully, harangue, coax, shame, or otherwise appeal to or provoke the readers. (See Booth, 1996; Leaska, 1996, Sugiyama, 1996; and in this vol., see part 2, chapters 3 and 5.)

It is important to grasp the foundational significance of this set of simple axioms about point of view. These axioms provide a distinct, finite, and manageable set of analytic categories for the analysis of meaning in a literary representation. There are *three specific components* in the social interactions of a literary representation. There are *always* three components. There are *only* three components. The members of each of these three categories organize the meaning of represented events in some distinct way. One of the chief analytic procedures a critic needs to perform in assessing any literary representation is to assess the relations between the author's point of view, the point of view of the characters, and the point of view in the audience that is implied or projected by the author. At the highest possible level, the meaning of a literary representation consists in the interaction among the points of view of author, characters, and implied audience. That interaction is largely controlled by one of those three distinct sets, the author.

It might be objected that in this exposition I am thinking only of narrative, not of theatrical representation, and it might be argued that in theatrical representations there is no author but only a transparent and unmediated action taking place on stage. The absence of an author from the stage in a theatrical representation is, I think, altogether an illusion. A play sets into motion an array of forces—of human passions and motives, desires and fears. There is a mind that governs and organizes this array of forces—the mind of the author. The author's mind is the one mind that is most nearly adequate to understanding the full array of forces within the play. A leading character can sometimes approximate to the level of an author's own adequacy of comprehension—as in Hamlet's soliloquies—but it is not possible for an author to depict a character whose comprehension of the total set of forces at work in a representation exceeds the comprehension of the author. Any level of comprehension the author can depict is, by definition, within the scope of the author's own understanding.

Human Nature, Human Universals, Culture, and Individual Differences

Almost all authors explicitly invoke "human nature" as their ultimate referent and the source of their authority. The term "human nature" signifies a set of elemental motives and dispositions—what MacDonald (1990) calls "evolved motive dispositions." The diagram of human nature sketched out above suggests the sorts of motives that are usually contained in the common conception of human nature—motives like self-preservation, sexual desire, jealousy, maternal love, and the desire for social status—and these substantive motives are elaborated by the ideas that enter into the folk understanding of ego psychology: the primacy of self-interest and the prevalence of self-serving delusion, manipulative deceit, vanity, and hypocrisy. Authors understand that each elemental disposition varies in quality and degree from person to person; they know, for instance, that some people are more fearful of death, more sexually passionate, more maternal, or more ambitious than their neighbors. And they understand further that each of these dispositions, variable in itself, can be combined in different ways with the other dispositions so as to produce the distinct configurations of individual identity. A woman might be both terrified of death and intensely protective of her children, but have little sexual desire and little social ambition—or be exactly the reverse, bold and fearless, coldly indifferent to her offspring, sexually ardent, and passionately determined to achieve high social rank. And yet again, she might be fairly bold, typically maternal, moderately amorous, and modestly ambitious.

Human universals or species-typical norms of behavior are merely behavioral patterns so firmly grounded in the logic of human life history that they are characteristic features of all known cultures. For instance, all cultures have marriage, rites of passage, social roles defined by age and sex, religious beliefs, public ceremonies, kin relations, sex taboos, medical practices, criminal codes, storytelling, jokes, and so on. (See Brown, 1991, 2000; and in this vol., see part 2, chapter 2.) Universals are made up of motive dispositions that combine in relatively stable and consistent ways. The same motive dispositions can also be elaborated and organized, at higher levels of cultural complexity, in ways that vary widely from culture to culture. For instance, all cultures have marriage, but some cultures are polygynous and some monogamous; some allow divorce, and some do not. All cultures have games, but not all cultures play whist or football. All cultures have language, but not all cultures are literate; not all literate cultures have produced highly developed forms of prose fiction; and not all cultures with highly developed forms of prose fiction have produced stream-of-consciousness narrative styles.

No culture can deviate from human universals (by definition), but many individual people can and do deviate from species-typical norms of behavior.

They murder their children, commit incest, fail to develop language, or otherwise behave in anomalous or dysfunctional ways. The behavior that is depicted in literary texts does not necessarily exemplify universal or species-typical behavioral patterns, but species-typical patterns form an indispensable frame of reference for the communication of meaning in literary representations. By appealing to this substratum of common human motives, authors activate a vein of common understanding in their readers. Consider maternal care and incest. Maternal care of infants is a "universal" feature of human nature, but all cultures make some provision for population control, and in cultures that do not have access to birth control and abortion, population control necessarily involves infanticide. (See Daly and Wilson, 1988; Low, 2000; Symons, 1979.) Literary authors can nonetheless depend on readers to feel the weight and value of maternal care. This is part of the common frame of reference, not just for any particular culture but for all cultures. Medea murders her own children, and Euripides can safely anticipate that the audience will react with instinctive shock and horror to the murder. So also, incest avoidance is a human universal. Different cultures define the details of incest in different ways, but certain kinds of incest are universally prohibited. No culture permits mother-son incest, and Sophocles can safely anticipate that his audience will instinctively sympathize with the revulsion of feeling that leads Oedipus to gouge out his own eyes. (See Daly and Wilson, 1990; Low, 2000; Sugiyama, 2001c.)

In the same way that each author has a unique fingerprint, he or she has also some unique configuration of identity—some individual variation of personality and experiential conditioning—and that identity defines itself in relation both to the cultural norms within which the author lives and also to the common elements of human nature. Individual identity is the basis for an author's point of view, and more often than not an author presents his or her own distinct point of view as a normative standard—as an ideal against which to judge other identities, other points of view. By appealing to "human nature," literary authors can ground their own values within what they take to be elemental realities. Sometimes, but not always, they contrast these elemental realities with the conventions of their own culture, suggesting that the conventions are shallow, perverse, artificial, unhealthy, or otherwise undesirable. (See Carroll, 1995; Jobling, 2001a, 2001b; Nesse, 1995; Nordlund, 2002; Sugiyama, in press; and in this vol., see part 2, chapter 3.)

Some distinctions of individual difference are obvious and available to untutored common sense—for instance, distinctions of age, sex, health, attractiveness, social affiliation, social status, vocational occupation, intelligence, and honesty. (The now pat triad of class, gender, and race—the standard topics of politicized literary criticism—is an arbitrary subset of these useful categories.) Such terms, available to common sense, are also necessary to a life history analysis of the human species. The common understanding operates as an intuitive or "folk" version of life history analysis. In addition to the distinctions from this range of analysis, all critics have access to the common vocabulary for assessing temperament and personality. Differences in personality are part of the adaptive environment among which individual humans make the choices that enable them to succeed in meeting the needs of their evolved motive dispositions. In traditional, belle-lettristic or impressionistic literary criticism, differences in the quality of critical perceptions depend in good part on the acuity any given critic displays in accessing this common vocabulary. Modern personality theory has now distilled, codified, and elaborated the common vocabulary of temperament and personality, and it is very much in a literary critic's interest to become familiar with this body of empirical research. At present, the best available theory is that of the five-factor system (extraversion, neuroticism, conscientiousness, agreeableness, and imaginative and intellectual "openness"). Since this system was drawn, in the first place, from the common lexicon, it is not surprising that its categories correlate well, as a first approximation, to the depiction of characters in fiction. In order to identify the relations of authors to their own characters, the use of this common vocabulary provides an invaluable tool for a shared and delimited analytic vocabulary. (See Bouchard, 1994; 1997; Buss, 1990, 1995; Costa and Widiger, 1994; Digman, 1990; Eysenck and Eysenck, 1985; McCrae, 1992; MacDonald, 1995b, 1998b; Pervin, 1990, 2003; Pervin and John, 1999; Segal and MacDonald, 1998; Wiggins, 1996.)

The fifth factor in the five-factor personality system—imaginative or intellectual openness to experience—is the factor most closely associated with domain-general intelligence, and it is itself roughly concordant with the cognitive behavioral system. MacDonald explains, "The Openness to Experience factor taps variation in intelligence and what one might term optimal Piagetian learning—intrinsically motivated curiosity and interest in intellectual and aesthetic experience combined with imagination and creativity in these areas" (1998b, p. 126). In virtually all literature, distinctions of wit or intelligence or imaginative vitality form a central distinguishing point of reference in the discrimination among characters and in the formation of a normative or dominant authorial point of view. Authors by nature have strong cognitive behavioral systems—they would be positioned at the far end of the right tail of the bell curve distribution measuring the fifth factor—and they tend strongly to value this same quality in their characters. They tend also to invite their audiences to share in their own normative approbation of this quality.

The primary purpose of literary criticism, as an objective pursuit of true knowledge about its subject, is to identify the specific configuration of meaning in any given text or set of texts. In order to make that identification, it is necessary for the critic to have three conceptual models or templates at his or her disposal: (a) a concept of human nature (like that in the diagram earlier); (b) a concept of the cultural ecology within which any given text has been constructed; and (c) a set of categories for analyzing individual differences. In order to make analytic use of these three templates, the critic must also assess the author's own understanding of human nature, identify the author's own stance toward the cultural context, and identify the distinctive characteristics of the author's individual identity

Life History Analysis and Cognitive Style in *Pride and Prejudice*

Before commenting on the relation of style to life history analysis in *Pride and Prejudice*, I shall take a moment to summarize the novel, as concisely as possible, for the benefit of any reader who has not read it, or who has not read it recently. The protagonist, Elizabeth Bennet, is twenty years old and the second of five daughters. Her father is a gentleman who married somewhat beneath his own social class and chose a wife for her physical charm. His wife's foolishness and vulgarity have alienated him, and he habitually engages in whimsical mockery of her. His estate is entailed to a cousin, a clergyman named Mr. Collins. When Mr. Bennet dies, Mr. Collins will inherit his estate, and Mr. Bennet's wife and five daughters will be left destitute. His wife is thus quite desperate to find rich husbands for her daughters. A wealthy and unmarried young man, Mr. Bingley, rents an estate in the Bennets' neighborhood, and his entourage includes two sisters and a friend, Mr. Darcy, who is also single and even more wealthy than Bingley. In short order, Bingley falls in love with Elizabeth Bennet's older sister, Jane, but Darcy discourages the match and persuades Bingley to leave the neighborhood. Darcy disapproves of the vulgarity of Elizabeth's mother and of her younger sisters, but he is himself nonetheless attracted to Elizabeth, whose wit and vivacity arouse his admiration. Mr. Collins, a monstrously foolish man, proposes to Elizabeth, and when she rejects him, he marries Elizabeth's best friend, Charlotte Lucas, who has little value on the marriage market and seeks only a comfortable establishment. Mr. Collins lives close to a wealthy, arrogant woman, Lady Catherine de Bourgh, who appointed him to his clerical living. Lady Catherine also happens to be Darcy's aunt, and when Elizabeth goes for an extended visit at Charlotte's new home, she again meets Darcy. He proposes to her, but does so in an insulting way, expressing his vivid sense of her social inferiority, and she angrily rejects him. In explaining her rejection, she accuses him of interfering in her sister's marriage prospects, and accuses him also of failing to meet his obligation to provide support for the son of his father's steward, Mr. Wickham, a man who grew up with Darcy. Wickham had recently been stationed with his regiment near Elizabeth's home, had become friendly with her, and had divulged his supposed mistreatment at Darcy's hands. In order to vindicate himself, Darcy writes a letter in which he explains that his own conduct to Wickham has been honorable and that Wickham is in fact a scoundrel and a prevaricator. His evidence is compelling, and Elizabeth realizes she has misjudged him. Her aunt and uncle invite her to accompany them on a vacation tour that leads them into the vicinity of Darcy's estate. They meet Darcy by accident, and his manners undergo a major change. He ceases being haughty and reserved and seeks to ingratiate himself with Elizabeth and her relatives. Elizabeth's views have also changed, and she is receptive to his address, but then she gets a letter from her sister Jane telling her that a younger sister, Lydia, has run off with Wickham, thus bringing disgrace on the whole family. Elizabeth returns home, and unbeknownst to her, Darcy finds Wickham and Lydia and bribes Wickham to marry Lydia. Elizabeth discovers this secret, and is duly grateful. When Bingley and Darcy return to Elizabeth's neighborhood, Bingley proposes to Jane and Darcy proposes, again, to Elizabeth. Both women accept the proposals, and the epilogue informs us that these two main couples live happily ever after.

Pride and Prejudice is universally recognized as a classic, and specifically as a classic distinguished by the economy of its narrative and the elegance of its style. That economy and elegance depend in large part on one central tension in the narrator's own point of view, a tension between two poles: at one pole, the tough-minded recognition of the fundamental realities of human life history, the primacy of resource acquisition and reproductive activity; and at the other pole, the determination to value individual qualities of mind and character. Austen herself grasps with a singular acuity the governing power of the somatic and reproductive foundation of human action, but virtually every character in the novel is assessed also on the basis of the quality of his or her mind. If you will refer again to the diagram of human nature, you can envision the novel as working itself out through a tension between the highest level of conscious human organization—the recognition of the primary need to acquire resources and to mate successfully—and the cognitive behavioral system. Everyone wants to marry well within the terms that are common knowledge among evolutionary sexual theorists—the women want wealth and status in their men, and the men want youth and beauty in their women. But the single most important criterion for registering personal quality in the novel is the degree to which both men and women rise above this basic standard and require also qualities of excellence in character and in mind.

The realization of character—and especially of conscientiousness—is best seen in action, in what the characters actually do. But the realization of mind is best revealed in their style—in what they say, and even more importantly, in how they say it. Austen's own style is "elegant" not in the sense of betraying effeminate delicacy or softness. It is elegant in the sense of being supple, sharp, quick, and crystal clear. It has less the quality of a brush held by a lady's gentle touch than of a finely tempered blade wielded by a hand that is strong, deft, and aggressive. The two chief characters, Elizabeth and Darcy, come to admire and love each other in good part because they share Austen's cognitive and stylistic powers. They select themselves out from the babble of folly, nonsense, and polite fatuities that make up the stylistic world of their associates, and they come to admire one another for qualities of wit and judgment that unfold themselves in sharp and serious dialogue on subjects of character, tone, and point of view. Darcy first offends Elizabeth, when they meet, by uttering some arrogant and defensive rationalizations for his own stiff behavior at a ball. (He is introverted and not very likable, but he is ultra-high on conscientiousness. Wickham, his chief rival for Elizabeth's romantic interest, is extraverted and charming but deceitful and utterly unreliable. As in many novels, one main plot line involves the long-term discrimination among superficially attractive qualities and the qualities that will wear well—a difference relevant to the basic distinction between short-term and long-term mating strategies.) Darcy first fundamentally changes Elizabeth's view of him in the letter he writes to her, after she rejects his proposal, explaining his conduct with respect to her sister's marriage prospects and his treatment of Wickham. Given the fact that he is an introvert and an intellectual, it is not surprising that he should present himself better in a letter than in a personal interview. The letter, which Austen transcribes in full, is the longest utterance he or anyone makes in the course of the novel, and if it does not display Austen's own humor—the subjects are somber, and Darcy is in no joking mood—it does display all of the precision, incisiveness, and acuity of her style. This style is itself a constant norm for the reader, and that same norm serves for all the main protagonistic characters as a measure of quality.

To take just one more of many possible examples for the signal importance of style as a measure of personal quality, Mr. Collins first introduces himself to the Bennet household in a letter that Mr. Bennet reads aloud to his family. The letter is an absolute marvel of fatuity and of pompous self-importance, and the way in which the individual family members respond to the letter reveals the quality of their own minds. Mary, the dull, plain younger sister who tries to build a niche for herself by diligent but uninspired study, thinks Mr. Collins's style rather good. Mrs. Bennet is as always simply indifferent to any quality of character or style and responds to all occasions solely on the basis of opportunistic interests. Elizabeth and her father alone register that the letter is a work of clownish absurdity. "'Can he be a sensible man, sir?'" "'No, my dear; I think not.'" (vol. 1, chapter 13) In that exchange, Austen reveals the foundation of the singular affinity that Elizabeth and her father feel for one another, and the reason that they have formed an inner circle of companionship separated from all the rest of the family. Elizabeth is fond of her older sister Jane, and Jane is not vulgar, but she is so excessively sweet-tempered, so almost pathologically high on the scale of likableness, that she is incapable of any negative judgment, and thus fails to see at least half of what passes in front of her. She is, for instance, merely puzzled by the nonsense in Mr. Collins's letter, but inclined to give him full credit for good intentions.

Elizabeth and her father form an inner circle of wit and judgment, and the central figure within that circle is Austen herself. She fashions the point of view as a field of intelligence, and within this field she creates a topography in which she locates all the characters and her audience. To get a sense for how this process works, consider the famous opening sentence of the novel: "It is a truth universally acknowledged, that a single man in possession of a good fortune, must be in want of a wife." There has been considerable difference of opinion over whether that sentence is meant to be taken ironically. The issue can be resolved by reference to the modifying effect of the sentence that follows the first sentence: "However little known the feelings or views of such a man may be on his first entering a neighborhood; this truth is so well fixed in the minds of the surrounding families, that he is considered as the rightful property of some one or other of their daughters." The first sentence is a good-humored affirmation of the rules of the game. Austen identifies the basic elements that are in play in social interactions (property and mating), and she acknowledges that the configuration of elements implied in her remarks constitutes a universal pattern of human behavior: men seek to acquire resources and to use them to acquire mates, and women seek mates who are in possession of resources. But the second sentence establishes a distance between the narrator and the common view she describes. She admits of anomalies, of individual differences. The "surrounding families" operate only on the basis of generalities, and they operate without regard to the inner lives of other people. They regard the man moving into the neighborhood not as a center of consciousness—a point of view—in his own right, but rather as their own property. This is a simple and elementary failure in "theory of mind"—a failure to recognize that other people have inner lives of their own. Failures of this nature inform much of Austen's satire, and indeed of all satire. It is one of the central principles of satire. People are preoccupied with their own needs, and they treat other people as props or furniture in the self-absorbed narratives they construct about themselves. (Mrs. Bennet and Darcy's aunt, Lady Catherine de Bourgh, are signal cases in point, and chief targets of the satire.)

As it happens, in this case, the common view holds good. Bingley is in fact in want of a wife. It is nonetheless the case that in the space of two sentences Austen has established a fundamental tension between her own perspective— a perspective that takes account both of point of view and of individual differences—and the common perspective of the neighborhood. That common perspective is also the perspective of the common world outside the novel. In the course of the novel, an inner core of protagonists, civilized, cultivated, and capable of making stylistic distinctions, will ultimately constitute a small ingroup that distinguishes itself from the common world of their own community. Elizabeth's aunt and uncle Gardiner belong to this inner group, and it is one of the triumphs for the ethos advanced by the novel that their cultivation and gentility of manner take precedence over their lower socioeconomic status (Mr. Gardiner is "in trade"). Austen's own point of view defines and dominates this inner group—she is its normative mind—and she tacitly invites receptive readers also to join this group. The criterion that permits a reader to join the group is the ability to read and judge the letters and conversational style of Darcy, Mr. Collins, Lady Catherine, and all the rest. Readers who pass this test of literacy succeed in segregating themselves from the common world that operates exclusively at the level of the lowest common denominators of life history analysis—the reduction of other people to general cases—and the identification of people exclusively in terms of "property."

Note that what has happened in the course of two sentences is that the author has established a set of relations among three points of view: her own, that of her characters, and that of her audience. This set of relations is not peripheral to the "meaning" of the story. By creating these relations, Austen creates an active field of communicative interaction. That is what hooks the reader, brings the reader in, rivets the reader's attention. All this happens before a single event has transpired, and before a single specific character has been introduced. To notice this is to realize that we cannot reduce the "meaning" of a story to the represented events. And even the very content of the two sentences admonishes us that if we reduce the events of the story to an exemplification of "human universals" or "species-typical behaviors," we shall have missed at least half the story. We shall in fact be on precisely the same level as the "surrounding families" personified for us, in the subsequent scene, by Mrs. Bennet. We shall be among the dullards and vulgarians who operate only on general rules and neglect to notice that every single character has a distinct center of consciousness.

Mrs. Bennet has access to a big chunk of the truth. Resources and mating do in fact form elementary building blocks in the human relations that provide the basis for stories. But in grasping this elemental reality, Mrs. Bennet neglects all other considerations of mind and character. She neglects the minds of other people, and she thus demonstrates the poverty of her own mind. The successful protagonists fully acknowledge the hard and sometimes harsh logic in the human reproductive economy, but they do so without neglecting the significance of the human mind and individual differences in identity.

Mate selection is the central behavioral system activated in this novel. That is a distinguishing, defining feature of the literary genre it exemplifies, the genre of "romantic comedy." (This genre probably provides at least half the literary biomass for the sum total of narratives in the world.) In its simplest designation, a romantic comedy is a love story that concludes in a happy marriage. Usually such stories are light in tone or enlivened with humor. But as it applies to Austen, the connotation of the words "romantic" and "comedy" could be a little misleading. There are many comical scenes, but the humor of the novel is often harsh, and the mating game is fierce and determined. Mr. Bingley's sister wants Darcy for herself and snipes incessantly, cattily, ineffectually at Elizabeth, denigrating her appearance, her temperament, her mind, and most of all her family and her social status. Miss Bingley also wants Darcy's younger sister, Georgiana, for her own brother—a liaison that would enhance her own social standing—and she thus conspires with Darcy to detach Bingley from Jane Bennet. She at first expresses the warmest friendship to Jane, activating Jane's own affectionate disposition, and then coldly cuts her. Lady Catherine wants Darcy to marry her own daughter, his cousin, but her daughter is sickly and peevish, and no one but her own mother and her governess pays her any regard at all. Austen's treatment of this girl betrays a certain streak of brutality. She sacrifices Miss de Bourgh on the altar of a ruthless principle of fitness, and the only sensation Elizabeth or Austen herself express toward this poor sick girl is that of vindictive contempt; there is no hint of pity. (To get an even better feel for this streak of brutality, one should read Austen's "juvenilia," the stories she wrote as a teenager. The stories consist of a rapid series of violent and grotesque events, many of them involving characters of certifiably psychopathic disposition.) Elizabeth's own chances of successful mating are seriously endangered when her sister Lydia runs off with Wickham, thus lowering the social standing of the whole family even further. There is a real possibility that by an inevitable progression Lydia would eventually be abandoned by Wickham and would "come on the town," living as a prostitute and in all likelihood dying early of disease and abuse. This doesn't happen because Darcy is determined in his choice of Elizabeth as a mate, and he exploits for his own purposes the opportunity Lydia's folly presents to him. By bribing Wickham to marry Lydia, Darcy does Elizabeth the greatest and most intimate service he could possibly do for her, and at the same time he decisively demonstrates the firmness of his commitment to her. He demonstrates that his preference for her outweighs even the disgrace of a marital association with a sluttish sister married to a reprobate of inferior birth.

The very nature of Wickham's disrepute signals the way in which resources and reproduction constitute the fundamental categories of human behavior in the novel—as they do in actual life. Wickham's evil-doing consists in two main forms of malfeasance: he leaves unpaid debts behind him, and he engages in illicit sexual liaisons with the daughters of the tradesmen and farmers in the neighborhoods he frequents. Before arriving in Elizabeth's neighborhood, he had even had the audacity to try running off with Darcy's sister. If he had succeeded, he would have damaged Darcy in his family pride and in his tenderest family feeling. He would have gained a fortune, advanced in status, and triumphed over a rival male. Darcy has good reason to resent Wickham, and this resentment renders his act of conciliation with Wickham all the more signal an instance of the self-sacrificing chivalry he displays in his commitment to Elizabeth.

Property and rank for men, and youth and beauty for women, count for much. They count almost more than anything, but within the normative perspective of the novel, they must at every point along the way be weighed in the balance of the total set of values that can be integrated within a well-proportioned economy of human life—the kind of economy that leads to the "rational" sort of happiness that Austen and Elizabeth both identify as their own central criterion of value. The total set of values that have to be given their due proportions to bring about rational happiness is not amorphous and unbounded. Sex and property, family or kin relations, parenting, social relations, and cognitive power—those are the central concerns of the book.

Next to sex and property, fidelity to kin presents itself as an urgent motivational force. Within the normative structure of values constituted by Austen's own point of view, even when family members are disgraceful and ridiculous, remaining loyal to them is a fundamental criterion of personal merit. Mr. Collins's baseness displays itself when he advises Mr. Bennet to abandon Lydia altogether after she runs off with Wickham, and Elizabeth displays her strength of character, in the epilogue, by effecting a rapprochement between Darcy and the alienated Lady Catherine, despite the insults Lady Catherine has heaped on Elizabeth herself.

The issue of parenting bulks large in the concerns of the book. The main background marriages—the marriages that serve as models or as warnings for the protagonists—are bad, either in their personal relations (as with Mr. and Mrs. Bennet) or in their parenting functions—as with both Darcy's and Elizabeth's parents. Elizabeth's mother is coarse, stupid, and frivolous, and her father is remote and detached. The situation of the family is bad, not just because of the entail but because he made a bad marriage, neglected to make the economies necessary to provide for his family after his death, neglected the discipline and education of his daughters, and failed to maintain the decorum of marital civility. (Jane and Elizabeth have educated themselves, but one chief attraction that Darcy holds for Elizabeth is that he is himself educated and holds out the promise for her of helping her to continue cultivating her own mind. Much is made of the magnificent library in his possession at his family estate.) Darcy's own parents, he says, were excellent people, but they neglected to form his temper, and they get the blame for the arrogance that first offends Elizabeth and that comes close to spoiling Darcy's ability to attract her to him, despite his wealth and rank. Mr. Collins is an oddity in part because he is a fool, a man of weak understanding, but the other half of the causal explanation is that he was raised by "an illiterate and miserly father" (vol. 1, chapter 15).

All the most intimate relations of sex, marriage, and family embed themselves within a larger social context. For this novel, one central plot question is whether Elizabeth will be accepted into the dominant social group. Her rivals hope she will not. Austen herself disparages their brittle snobbery (they laugh witlessly over the fact that she has an uncle in trade and another uncle who is a country attorney), but she also wishes for Elizabeth to gain access to the highest social level. She defines that level not only by wealth and status but by dignity and authority. One can be born into wealth and rank, but dignity and authority have to be earned by personal merit. Lady Catherine offers a self-parody of upper-class authority. Darcy is the real thing. When Elizabeth first sees Darcy's great estate, and hears his housekeeper praise his integrity and beneficence, she thinks to herself, "What praise is more valuable than the praise of an intelligent servant? As a brother, a landlord, a master, she considered how many people's happiness were in his guardianship!—How much of pleasure or pain it was in his power to bestow!—How much of good or evil must be done by him!" (vol. 3, chapter 1). Austen mocks false status—rank and wealth unsupported by education, wit, manners, and character—but she ultimately affirms the authority of legitimate social status as that is represented by the normative couple, Elizabeth and Darcy.

The chief social dynamic in the novel, the underlying social narrative, is that of a process in which dominant males marry down, selecting women of lower social rank but of superior personal quality. Conversely, women of high quality from a lower rank marry up into the higher gentry and thus integrate the standard of personal quality with the values of wealth and rank. Even Mr. Bennet, unhappily married though he is, has contributed to this process. He married a beautiful though silly woman from a social rank lower than his own. Two of his daughters are both beautiful and intelligent, and one (Elizabeth) is genuinely clever. And the two beautiful, intelligent girls both marry well, extremely well. Even Mrs. Bennet must be gratified with the results, though she understands so little of the process that produces those results.

And finally, again, in all the behavioral systems that have to be balanced in the economy of values in the novel, the cognitive system holds a place of predominating value. Mrs. Bennet contributes some heritable physical attractiveness, a matter not negligible in the total mix, but she contributes nothing of wit, and she is left almost wholly outside the scope of the inner social circle that constitutes the normative group at the end of the novel. "I wish I could say, for the sake of her family, that the accomplishment of her earnest desire in the establishment of so many of her children, produced so happy an effect as to make her a sensible, amiable, well-informed woman for the rest of her life; though perhaps it was lucky for her husband, who might not have relished domestic felicity in so unusual a form, that she was still occasionally nervous and invariably silly."

The Value of a Darwinian Literary Criticism

Previous criticism of Austen can be divided roughly into two bodies of work: (a) the traditional, common-language criticism that dominated academic literary study until the middle of the 1970s, and (b) the various forms of theory-driven criticism that emerged under the umbrella of postmodernism in the past three decades or so. The traditional criticism operates at the level of Austen's own lexicon. At its best, it makes alert observations about theme, tone, and formal organization, but its insights are impressionistic, opportunistic, and adventitious; it seeks no systematic reduction to simple principles that have large general validity. (See Bradley, 1929; C. L. Johnson, 1988; Lewes,

1859; Litz, 1965; Tanner, 1986; Van Ghent, 1953; Woolf, 1953.) At less than its best, traditional criticism consists only in otiose summary and formalistic elaboration punctuated by the occasional exercise in cranky emotional posturing. (See Butler, 1975; Duckworth, 1971; Halliday, 1960; Harding, 1940; Langland, 1984; Morgan, 1980; Mudrick, 1952; Phelan, 1989.) The positive rationale behind the revolution in theory-driven criticism is the recognition that all narratives have a surface-depth structure. Beneath the surface of local incident and occasional commentary in a narrative, there is a simpler, more basic structure of elemental motives and organizing principles. These motives and principles are the skeletal structure of the work. The business of interpretive criticism is to probe beneath the surface of common-language exposition and to find the skeletal structure. Theory-driven interpretation seeks to cut literary meaning at its joints.

The turn to theory-driven criticism answered to a manifest need, but the theoretical models that have been used, up to now, have been painfully inadequate. Deconstruction, Marxism, Freudianism, and Foucauldian political criticism have all presupposed ideas about human nature that conflict sharply with the Darwinian conception. The other main school, feminism, is less a single, coherent theory than a preoccupation about a specific subject matter—the condition of women—but the notions that cluster around this preoccupation often entail false ideas about human nature, and most feminist critics over the past thirty years have affiliated themselves with one or another of the dominant theoretical schools. All of the schools, as subsidiaries of postmodern theory, have fundamentally repudiated the idea of an innate, biologically constrained structure in the human motivational and cognitive system. Postmodern critics have sought the elemental forces of human experience in terms such as "semiosis," "textuality," "class struggle," "the Phallus," "bourgeois ideology," "desire," "discourse," "power," "gender," "dialogism," "heterosexism," "the Other," and "patriarchy," and they have contended that such terms reveal the underlying, governing forces in all literary production. In the degree to which they have succeeded in avoiding the passively reflexive character of traditional criticism, theory-driven criticism has offered distorted, skewed, and strained accounts of the elemental motives and governing principles in literary texts.

Literary criticism is both analytical and evaluative. Literary critics commit themselves to distinct concepts and to definite values. The values that animate postmodern theoretical criticism are emphatically radical, and the political critics incline either to disparage authors for their putative complicity with oppressive epistemes or, more frequently, to invest authors with their own characteristic attitudes of resentment, ideological indignation, and subversive animosity. Both the conceptual content and the political attitudes of the radical criticism are deeply alien to Austen. The conceptual content is alien to the elemental simplicity of her good sense, and the political attitudes are alien to the conservative temper of her wisdom. Many of the postmodern critics have nonetheless made some effort to assimilate Austen to an ethos of epistemological indeterminacy and political radicalism. They have sought to identify various "gaps" or "contradictions" between her overt meanings and this or that supposedly subversive implication in her style or tone. In Austen's case, particularly, these routine invocations of deconstructive formulas often appear half-hearted. The more sensitive postmodern critics evidently feel a certain queasy diffidence about pressing a case that can be made only by fabricating interpretive theses that run so clearly counter to Austen's own determinate meanings. Despite the obligatory invocation of deconstructive formulas, the bulk of commentary in the postmodern critiques blends insensibly into the thematic, tonal, and formal analyses of the traditional criticism. (See Ahearn, 1987; I. Armstrong, 1990; N. Armstrong, 1981, 1987; Auerbach, 1978; Belsey, 2002; Brownstein, 1988; Fraiman, 1989; Handler and Segal, 1990; Litvak, 1992; Newman, 1983; Newton, 1981; Poovey; 1981; Smith, 1993, 2000; Wylie, 2000.)

Darwinian literary criticism is grounded in the large facts of human evolution and human biology, facts much larger and more robust than the conceptions that characterize the various branches of postmodern theory. (See Boyd, 1998; Carroll, 1995; Dissanayake, 1995b; Storey, 1993, 1996.) Darwinian psychology provides a scientifically grounded and systematic account of human nature. This is the first time in our intellectual history that we have had such a theory, but the subject of this theory—human nature itself—is the very same nature that has always animated writers and readers. Most writers historically have not had access to the evolutionary explanation for how human nature came to be what it is, but they have nonetheless had a deep intuitive understanding of human motives and human feelings. What a Darwinian social science can now do for literary criticism is to give us conscious theoretical access to the elemental forces that have impelled all human beings throughout time and that have fundamentally informed the observations and reflections of all writers and all readers. Darwinian criticism can lift us above the superficial paraphrases of traditional criticism without forcing us into the often false reductions in the postmodern conceptions of human nature. It can help us to understand the source and subject of all literary representation, and it can help us to identify the sources of exceptional power in great literary works like *Pride and Prejudice*.

The Whole Story

More could be said, in detail, about *Pride and Prejudice*—much more. I hope I have said enough to give some indication of what I have in mind by insisting that to construct an even minimally adequate account of any literary representation, we have to set up a polar tension between the highest level of reduction in life history analysis—the level of the somatic and reproductive organization of life effort—and the most fine-grained analysis of formal organization: of theme, tone, and style. I hope to have convinced you that point of view is the central locus of literary meaning because it is the dimension within which people have mental experiences. The only people who can be involved in a literary social interaction are the author, the characters, and the audience, and those three sets of people *are* involved—all three sets—always. Delineating the dynamics of that specific set of social interactions—dynamics that vary from author to author and book to book—is a fundamental and indispensable procedure in literary criticism. Darwinian literary critics who ignore this dimension of analysis might be Darwinians, but they are not literary critics, and even as Darwinians, they are missing a major part of the story.

Many Darwinian psychologists and anthropologists have been missing a major part of the larger human story—that whole part of the story that concerns itself with the evolution of the cognitive behavioral system: the fifth personality factor, "g," domain-general intelligence. They have told us a good deal about life in a supposedly stable and homogeneous EEA, but they have neglected to tell us much about the evolution and adaptive functions of the distinctively human mind. A number of Darwinian anthropologists and psychologists are now correcting that signal omission, and Darwinian literary critics should rejoice that the development of the whole field is now producing a model of human nature that converges with their needs and interests as literary critics. The benefits can be reciprocal. Darwinian psychologists and Darwinian anthropologists take human nature as their field of study. Literature can provide important information on that topic, and Darwinian literary critics can help them to gain access to that information. Practitioners on both sides will need to make some allowances for differences of idiom and method. If they make these allowances, they will benefit not just in the gain of needful information but also in a closer acquaintance with the skills and cognitive habits that constitute the characteristic strengths in each discipline.

Part 3
Darwin and Darwinism

1
The Origin of Charles Darwin
A Review of Three Darwin Biographies

The following books are here under review:

John Bowlby. *Charles Darwin: A New Life* (1990).
Janet Browne. *Charles Darwin: Voyaging* (1995).
Adrian Desmond and James Moore. *Darwin* (1992).

For the past several years, I have been working to integrate literary study with Darwinian ideas about psychology and culture. Here I am going to talk about three big recent biographies of Darwin. I shall be considering aspects of biography that are not peculiar to Darwin's case—matters of method and point of view, temper and style—but I shall also be considering the question of how Darwin's own thinking can or should enter into the writing and reading of biographies at the present time. One of the three biographies affiliates itself with Darwinian theory, and two of them adopt, in contrast, the broadly Marxist conceptions that Paul Gross and Norman Levitt (1994) characterize as "the academic left." The Darwinian biography is written by the late John Bowlby, a distinguished psychologist who has corrected Freudian notions of child development through research into the evolved structure of human nature. The other two biographies are written by established scholars of Victorian science and intellectual history. One is co-authored by Adrian Desmond and James Moore, both highly regarded specialists in this period, and the other is written by Janet Browne, an editor of Darwin's correspondence.

My response to these books takes a polemical and partisan slant. Each of the biographies has been praised by qualified judges, but Bowlby's has been the least noticed and admired. I shall argue that the relative public success of these books betrays a deep deficiency in the judgments that are regulated by certain widespread conventional expectations, and I shall sketch out alternative criteria of judgment. Within these alternative criteria, Bowlby's biography is by far the most valuable of these books, and beyond this particular set of books, it should take an honored place within the canon of contemporary biographies. For me, it already takes a place within a very small set of contemporary scholarly books that seem to have classical stature and that serve as a touchstone for distinction and high merit. In explaining the value I place on the book, I shall appeal to critical criteria that can be applied not only to biographies but also to works of literature, criticism, and cultural history.

Bowlby's work as a psychologist culminated in *Attachment and Loss* (1960–1982), a magisterial three-volume study of traumatic separation between children and parents. This work has high prominence within its own clinical field, and it has far-reaching implications beyond this field—for psychoanalytic thought generally, and for all behavioral and social science. Bowlby assimilates Freud's insight into the formative influence of childhood experience, but he also constructs a model of human nature that replaces the Freudian model, and he presents his own research as a prototype for a unified behavioral science grounded in evolutionary biology. Situating human psychology within the broader study of animal ethology, he rejects Freud's belief that human nature consists in a few basic, unstructured drives such as hunger, thirst, and sex. For Freud, all other behavior is derived from these basic drives through a process of social learning, and in this respect, Freud's views are closely aligned with the views that have dominated social science for most of this century. In opposition to these views, and in concordance with the school of thought now gaining widespread recognition under the rubric of "evolutionary psychology," Bowlby maintains that human nature has evolved as a complex set of adaptive psychological structures. Thus, whereas Freud regards the child's attachment to its mother as the "secondary" effect of receiving food and warmth from her, Bowlby explains that attachment is itself a primary adaptive characteristic. Expanding from such findings to principles of the broadest import, he argues that "not a single feature of a species' morphology, physiology, or behaviour can be understood or even discussed intelligently except in relation to that species' environment of evolutionary adaptedness" (1982, p. 64).

Bowlby is not a professional historian or biographer. He is nonetheless a fine scholar, and he does a highly creditable job of situating Darwin in his historical setting. Still, he cannot compete with the other big biographies in the sheer wealth of contextual detail that constitutes their chief merit. His own chief merits are a sensitive appreciation for Darwin's personal and intellectual character, and a firm imaginative grasp of his scientific vision. I shall cite a couple of introductory passages in which Bowlby gives a summary impression of his subject. In the first passage, he is explaining how his full-scale biography developed out of his more narrowly focused concern with Darwin's chronic psychosomatic illness:

> I found myself captivated by Darwin as a maturing personality and gifted scientist, and also by the large extended family in which he grew to manhood, by his devoted wife and their numerous children, by his circle of scientific friends and colleagues, in short by the whole drama of his eventful, troubled and extraordinarily productive life. . . .

> [Darwin] is the most influential biologist to have lived. Not only did he change the course of biological science but he changed for ever how philosophers and theologians conceive of man's place in nature. An outstanding scientist who excelled first as an observer and later as a theorist and experimenter, he was also a singularly attractive character beloved by family and colleagues alike. (1990, pp. viii, 1)

Bowlby does not hesitate to offer expressions of personal response—of being "captivated" and of finding Darwin "singularly attractive"—but these expressions are supported by observations of fact. Darwin was demonstrably a gifted scientist; his work did in fact have a revolutionary impact; and he was indisputably beloved by his family and friends. Not all admiration and affection are naive or misplaced. Biographies are not likely to be written about men or women who have no outstanding merit. To register such merit, to realize it vividly and bring it home to the heart and imagination of the reader, is surely a primary duty of a biographer. But it is a duty that runs counter to deep-seated impulses of invidious egoism, and it runs counter also to powerful forces in the set of mind that currently prevails in the humanities—in literary history and criticism as in the history of science. In this respect, the conventional point of view has undergone a virtual reversal. Thirty years ago, a conventional work of biography or of literary criticism might easily have fallen into fatuous adulation or insincere admiration. At the present time, for a biographer to be both just and generous to Darwin, or to Matthew Arnold, George Eliot or Joseph Conrad, requires a truly exceptional largeness of spirit, both a liberality of feeling and an independence from conventional expectations.

The biography by Desmond and Moore has won widespread admiration among reputable scholars. For instance, Marjorie Greene regards the biography as "a magnificent piece of work" (1993, p. 666). George Levine considers it "arguably now the best biography of Darwin we have" (1994, p. 194). And Stephen Jay Gould declares roundly that it is "unquestionably the finest ever written about Darwin" (1992, p. 215). The prominence that has been given to this biography is an important, symptomatic fact in contemporary cultural history. The most striking feature in the reception of the book is that most reviewers, no matter how enthusiastic their delight, have felt it incumbent on them, as historians, to point out that the authors are thoroughly and systematically dishonest in their use of evidence. Desmond and Moore very frequently wrench quotations wholly out of context, and not seldom wander off into historical fiction and fantasy, presented as fact. The reviewers have regretted these infractions against scholarly integrity, but have apparently not felt that mere honesty was a primary criterion of worthiness in a biography. It has also been noted that Desmond and Moore adopt a tone that is often snide and disparaging, that their style is sensationalistic, and that their own moral and political stance is self-righteous. If reviewers note such things, why do they then still regard the book with such favor? The most important reason is that Desmond and Moore energetically endorse the Marxist thesis that Darwin's "key ideas" have "political roots" (1992, p. xx). They contend that the theory of natural selection is really only a "metaphoric extension" of the ideology arising from the socioeconomic conditions of Victorian Britain (p. 420). This contention would be fashionable when applied to any writer, but it must be received with particularly high favor when it is applied to Darwin. Within the Darwinian paradigm, all political structures are rooted in the biological nature of human beings. By treating the development of Darwin's ideas as an example of the Marxist creed, Desmond and Moore outflank Darwin, and by treating Darwin himself with ridicule they make it easier to hold his theory in contempt.

For the sake of a comparison with Bowlby, I'll give just one example of the manner they adopt toward their subject. One of Bowlby's central themes is the development of Darwin's sense of scientific method. In his autobiography, Darwin himself reports that while he was at Cambridge he read two books that together had a transformative influence on his conception of science and that did much to crystallize his sense of vocation. One book was a theoretical work on scientific method by John Herschel and the other a memoir of scientific exploration by Alexander von Humboldt. Darwin declares that these books "stirred up in me a burning zeal to add even the most humble contribution to the noble structure of Natural Science" (1958, p. 68). Bowlby cites the appropriate passage, analyzes Herschel's theory, and integrates it with his larger understanding of Darwin's method. If we are to construct an intelligible account of how an unformed young man ever became one of the world's great scientists, it is indispensable that we register the imaginative quality of such moments. And for this particular moment imaginative literature offers an instructive parallel. In *Middlemarch*, George Eliot describes the growth of a scientific passion in her young doctor Lydgate, and to evoke this passion she uses a rhetoric very similar to that which Darwin uses. "He was fired with the possibility that he might work out the proof of an anatomical conception and make a link in the chain of discovery. . . . He longed to demonstrate the more intimate relations of living structure, and help to define men's thought more accurately after the true order" (2000, chapter 15). Now consider the way Desmond and Moore treat a similar episode in Darwin's life. They start by posing the question of scientific method:

> What sorts of "evidence," "facts," and "laws of nature" were acceptable, and how were they established? Darwin swotted up the subject from a new, compact book by the doyen of science, Sir John Herschel. . . . It ignited Darwin. He glimpsed the limitless scope for scientific explanation and the rapid progress of every branch of knowledge. . . . The sky was the limit. Darwin closed his eyes and exuded a "burning zeal" for science. (p. 91)

There are many such moments of slap-dash caricature in the book, flippant mockery appealing to idle cynicism, but the cheap laughs are dearly bought at the price of distorting and trivializing Darwin's experience. The bouncy vulgarity of style in this passage is kept up for nearly 700 pages, and it is a style in which no meditative depth or dignity of mind could possibly be registered.

Janet Browne's biography is the first of two projected volumes. (This essay was written in 1998. The second volume of Browne's biography was published in 2002.) The first volume takes Darwin's life up to the mid-1850s, after his theory of natural selection was fully worked out but not yet published. At the end of this first volume, she summarizes the theory of natural selection and offers an interpretive statement that accords fully with the Marxist views of Desmond and Moore:

> Much of this was perhaps familiar to a nation immersed in competitive affairs. Darwin had transformed the generalised entrepreneurial ethos of English life into a biological theory which, in turn, derived much of its support from these all-pervasive cultural commitments. The theory of natural selection could only have emerged out of the competitive context of Victorian England. (1995, p. 545)

To present the theory in this way as nothing more than a superstructural reflex of a capitalist base neatly begs the question as to whether the theory is actually true. But if the theory is true, Darwin has gained insight into natural processes that are deeper than any specific form of economic organization.

For Desmond and Moore, the idea that social and political events shape all scientific ideas serves as a convenient substitute for more complex forms of causal analysis. They can simply give a running narrative of social and political events and point to the theory as the supposed result. Browne's case is rather different. Despite the statement in her conclusion, on the level of causal analysis she is by no means a thorough and committed Marxist. She has very few such programmatic statements as that which I just quoted, and she gives relatively scant attention to political movements and events. Her conclusion thus seems to come out of nowhere. It is not a statement of conviction but rather a substitute for convictions. Browne lacks any larger framework of explanation, and she must consequently make use of an explanation that she takes from the store of commonplace ideas that are currently available within the prevailing ideology.

Commenting on one of the characters in *Middlemarch*, George Eliot observes that "a kind Providence furnishes the limpest personality with a little gum or starch in the form of tradition" (2000, chap. 2). A similar comment could be applied to Browne. Although she gives no evidence of being doctrinally committed to Marxism, she adopts the commonplace sentiments that accompany the ideas in the prevailing doctrine. Like the Marxist thesis invoked in her conclusion, and more consistently invoked by Desmond and Moore, these sentiments fill a gap. They take the place of any independently articulated ideas and any individually realized values. They serve as a substitute for a distinct point of view. By characterizing this substitute, we can obtain a reasonably full portrait of the conventional sentiments that constitute the common public person at the present time.

Browne can serve exceptionally well for this kind of analysis. If she were a scholar of a lower order, the characterization might be confounded with adventitious elements of intellectual mediocrity. But she is an immensely capable scholar. She has immersed herself in all the multifarious social and professional networks of Victorian science. She understands very clearly the status of complex theories at precise moments of history, and she is able to locate all the individual actors within densely realized social and institutional structures. She has little feeling for the emotional life and the intimate personal relations of her characters. In comparison with Bowlby's rich and subtle evocations of personality and personal relations, her characters are largely blank. But if she lacks the novelist's sense of a private inner life, she has in compensation a novelistic sense of the more public forms of social interaction. Her own values and feelings are merely conventional, but in compensation she has an intuitive feel for the force of convention. She understands convention as virtually a living thing, a semi-autonomous thing in itself, a medium for the common intellectual life of the time.

Browne is a historian. When we ask what kind of gum or starch ideological convention provides for her, it is appropriate to start with her sense of history, and all the more appropriate since the ideological conventions she adopts are those of New Historicism. To my ear, the term New Historicism has an unintentionally ironic overtone, for it almost always implies a failure to participate with imaginative sympathy in the deeper forces at work in cultural history. New historicists seldom give us any feeling for the constructive energy that has been necessary to create the great civilizations. What they give us instead is a formulaic, two-dimensional pattern of history as a record of wanton oppression. This is history as complaint and condemnation, written from a perspective of a facile moral superiority. To get a sense of the kind of historical imagination at work here, I recommend that you compare Browne's treatment of Darwin's parents and grandparents with Bowlby's treatment of the same figures. Bowlby makes it possible for us to understand what went into the making of the Darwin and Wedgwood dynasties—the energy, initiative, and ability, the personal decency, and the public integrity. Browne, in contrast, treats the older generations as members of a sinister conspiracy of industrial intrigue and social exploitation. The same basic stance reappears, more centrally for Darwin himself, in her descriptions of the social and professional connections he used to further his scientific projects.

If New Historicism fails to register the creative forces in history, in what sense is it specifically historicist? One main feature of New Historicism is the deprecation or suppression of individual agency. For the New Historicist imagination, history is not the collective product of many individuals. It is rather a transcendent force that renders all individual identity nugatory. I'll give two examples. After listing in detail all the people who in one way or another provided support or information to Darwin, including aunts, nephews, and "unsuspecting household pets," Browne declares, "Darwin's work was entirely a social process in this sense" (pp. xii–xiii). Browne's insistence on the all-sufficiency of the social process probably reflects her own temperamental disposition to weigh public life more heavily than private, and this disposition merges with a common if regrettable failing among biographers and literary critics, a yearning to belittle their subjects. In this case, both the social disposition and the invidious egoism join hands with the conventional New Historicist impulse to deprecate the individual. Browne argues, "Because Darwin believed in the Victorian ethos of character—in the inbuilt advantages of mind—and unconsciously endorsed the cult of great men and public heroes that was so much a part of nineteenth-century life, he did not—could not—see that figures like himself were the product of a complex interweaving of personality and opportunity with the movements of the times" (p. xi). Now, Darwin himself would readily have acknowledged the importance of historical opportunities. Indeed, no one has done more to deepen our sense of contingency in the total process of life. Browne's critique is designed not to expose any actual lack of insight in Darwin but rather to diminish the singularity of his achievement while simultaneously crediting Browne herself with a critical acuity greater than that of her subject. Note the formulation "figures like himself." This phrase reduces Darwin to the member of a commonplace group, just one of a crowd. For most of us, most of the time, such formulations would be unexceptionable, but when dealing with figures of world-historical magnitude, such formulations are misleading. For writers like Browne, there are no great men, and to recognize greatness is to participate in a "cult" that extends throughout a whole century and that makes that whole century susceptible to supercilious condescension.

Browne succeeds in situating Darwin within his own time, the world of Victorian science. But because she participates in the conventional ideology of her own time, what she cannot do is to locate him within the far deeper time within which his own imagination moves. Bowlby offers less circumstantial detail about Darwin's time than either Browne or Desmond and Moore, but he nonetheless gives a more complete and adequate sense of the world in which Darwin lives. He can give this sense because there are two levels at which he makes much closer contact with Darwin's life and experience. One level is that of the individual human being. Bowlby is a trained psychologist, and he has an intuitive sensitivity to the complexities of personal identity. In his handling, Darwin and his family and friends come alive as people, with all their own quite particular affections and sorrows, their faults, their virtues, and their talents. Beginning with Erasmus Darwin, Charles' grandfather and a precursor to his theory of evolution, Bowlby constructs a narrative of family dynamics that crosses the generations and that includes affections and ambitions so intense they can result in crippling griefs and suicidal depressions. The other level is that of a human nature beyond all local differences of culture and period. Darwin himself is the chief scientific source for our modern vision of human nature, and Bowlby, unlike the other biographers, has had the good sense to learn from his subject. Discussing an early essay in which Darwin "outlines theories not dissimilar to those current today in sociobiology," Bowlby quotes a passage in which Darwin proposes "'looking at Man, as a naturalist would at any other Mammiferous animal'" (p. 388). From this angle of vision, Darwin concludes that humans have "'parental, conjugal and social instincts'" (p. 388). This is the conclusion Bowlby also reaches, and it is on the basis of this conclusion that he revises Freud's crudely oversimplified conception of human motivation.

Bowlby observes that Darwin's psychological research was long neglected and that this neglect was "a tragedy for the study of socio-emotional development which, lacking an evolutionary perspective, almost expired in the wastes of behaviourism and the jungle of psychoanalysis" (p. 403). Bowlby is among the first and the most important of the behavioral theorists to have revived Darwinian thinking, and by doing so he has helped to breathe new life into psychology. By turning his psychological insight to Darwin himself, he demonstrates the imaginative value of the lessons he has learned from Darwin.

Bowlby has assimilated Darwin's naturalistic vision, and he shares as well Darwin's sense of civilization. He feels strongly the elementary value of the common human affections, and he uses his intelligence not to derogate from the achievements of genius but to appreciate them and to make them his own. Such an accomplishment is rare. It is one of those products of the critical imagination that is in itself a contribution to literature.

2

Modern Darwinism and the Pseudo-Revolutions of Stephen Jay Gould

This critique of Gould was originally designed as the final segment of the introduction to my edition of Darwin's *On the Origin of Species* (2003). The critique was written shortly before the publication of Gould's last big book, *The Structure of Evolutionary Theory* (2002). In that book, he recapitulates the ideas and stratagems he had developed over the past three decades: anti-adaptationism, "pluralism," "punctuated equilibrium," and "spandrels." All these topics have already been adequately considered in this critique of his previous work. No good critical purpose would be served by appending a critique of his last book.

I discuss Gould's introduction to Kurtén's *Dance of the Tiger* in this vol., part 2, chapter 5.

Stephen Jay Gould is the most widely read contemporary popular commentator on evolution, and he is also the chief critic of contemporary Darwinism. He has done field work on land snails in the West Indies, has written a long series of popular essays and scholarly studies on natural history and the history of biology, and until his death in 2002 occupied something like the unofficial chair of evolutionary biology in the pages of the *New York Review of Books*. His chief claim to scientific eminence is to have proposed putative corrections and alternatives to mainstream Darwinism, especially to the idea that adaptation through natural selection is the main engine of evolutionary change. In reality, Gould has offered no truly original and genuinely significant contributions to evolutionary theory. Instead, he has created a vast rhetorical tissue of sophistical equivocations.

If Gould has formulated no significant revisions of Darwinian theory, why is it necessary to take account of his views? Maynard Smith poses this question and provides an answer:

> Gould occupies a rather curious position, particularly on his side of the Atlantic. Because of the excellence of his essays, he has come to be seen by non-biologists as the preeminent evolutionary theorist. In contrast, the evolutionary biologists with whom I have discussed his work tend to see him as a man whose ideas are so

confused as to be hardly worth bothering with, but as one who should not be publicly criticized because he is at least on our side against the creationists. All this would not matter, were it not that he is giving non-biologists a largely false picture of the state of evolutionary theory. (1995, p. 46)

By describing the failure of Gould's efforts to undermine the modern Darwinian synthesis, we can confirm the continuing strength of that synthesis. While examining the issues Gould has brought forward, we shall also be taking account of the current state of knowledge in evolutionary biology. We shall identify which ideas are firmly established and which still generate fruitful controversy. Gould makes frequent appeal to Darwin as an authority and example, and by assessing these appeals we shall be able to situate Darwin's own work in relation to current knowledge in evolutionary biology.

As an evolutionary theorist, Gould provides an illuminating contrast with Darwin in two ways. The sophistical procedures through which he constructs his critique of Darwinism contrast sharply with the integrity of argument that is so signal a feature of Darwin's own work, and the pseudo-revolutions generated by these sophistical procedures contrast sharply with the real revolution in thought and knowledge that was produced by Darwin.

Gould's claims for revolutionary revision depend on combining a few basic techniques of sophistical argument. In its simplest version, Gould's technique involves two steps. The first is to create a straw man by giving a falsely simplified description of the received view. The second is to propose what is actually the received view and to present this standard view as if it were a revolutionary correction. In his falsely simplified representation, the Modern Synthesis and its current acolytes consist of "ultra-Darwinians" and "panadaptationists" who are oblivious to all adaptively neutral phenomena and who fervently believe that all of evolution consists in the production of maximally efficient adaptations unconstrained by inheritance or contingent historical circumstance. In order to rescue evolutionary theory from these strangely narrow and obsessive "Darwinian fundamentalists," Gould propounds an array of concepts to which, he intimates, they are strangers. These broader concepts include the observations that adaptations are not ideally perfect but only relatively, competitively perfect, that inherited structures constrain adaptive change, that previously existing structures can be modified for some new adaptive purpose, that some structures are not themselves adaptive but are nonetheless sustained by natural selection because they happen to be connected, in inheritance, with structures that are adaptive, and that evolutionary change proceeds at a varying pace, depending both on the appearance of favorable variations and on alterations in the total set of ecological conditions. In reality, all of these concepts are standard features in the complex of ideas that constitutes the Modern Synthesis.

Gould's largest rhetorical strategy is to acknowledge adaptation through natural selection but to place all his emphasis against it. He seeks to create a pervasive rhetorical blur in which adaptation seems to be set in contrast or opposition to other elements of the total evolutionary process, and he often appeals to Darwin as a supposed precedent for this maneuver. Consider, for example, the following thumbnail sketch of modern Darwinian theory, from an essay first published in 1981:

> Darwin acknowledged the provisional nature of natural selection while affirming the fact of evolution. The fruitful theoretical debate that Darwin initiated has never ceased. From the 1940s through the 1960s, Darwin's own theory of natural selection did achieve a temporary hegemony that it never enjoyed in his lifetime. But renewed debate characterizes our decade, and, while no biologist questions the importance of natural selection, many now doubt its ubiquity. In particular, many evolutionists argue that substantial amounts of genetic change may not be subject to natural selection and may spread through populations at random. Others are challenging Darwin's linking of natural selection with gradual, imperceptible change through all intermediary degrees; they are arguing that most evolutionary events may occur far more rapidly than Darwin envisioned....
>
> Yet amidst all this turmoil no biologist has been led to doubt the fact that evolution occurred; we are debating *how* it happened. (1984, pp. 255–256)

In such passages, Gould is trying to turn back the clock on the history of evolutionary theory, and at the same time he is attempting to depict this retrograde movement as the resumption of a basically sound tradition that includes Darwin and that was only temporarily interrupted by the Modern Synthesis. In this Gouldian version of the history of Darwinism, Darwin himself treated the theory of natural selection as only "provisional"—a word presumably signifying "hypothetical," "tentative," or "temporary." His contemporaries and successors followed his lead in adopting this skeptical or diffident attitude toward natural selection, and except for the one deviant generation that produced the Modern Synthesis, all subsequent evolutionists have accepted "the fact of evolution" but have bracketed or suspended natural selection as the cause or "*how*" of evolution. This sound Darwinian tradition has consistently acknowledged a mélange of causal mechanisms. Some radical anti-adaptationists, among them presumably Gould himself, are even arguing that natural selection does not work through "gradual, imperceptible change through all intermediary degrees," and if it does not work in this way, it can work only through sudden macromutational leaps or the appearance of what are known as "hopeful monsters." (The idea of sudden macromutational leaps or "saltation" was prominent in the early decades of the twentieth century, but the proponents of the Modern Synthesis believed that it had been decisively falsified by the development of modern genetics.) Within the larger mélange of causal mechanisms recognized by the new, Gouldian generation, natural selection still has some indefinite "importance," but clearly, since we are now debating "*how*" evolution occurred, natural selection is no longer regarded as the central mechanism. It is once again "provisional," and that is all to the good.

As history, this Gouldian narrative is of course quite false, and as theory it is misleading in a number of ways. It is—to adapt Gould's disparaging term for all adaptive explanations—a "just-so story." As any reader of the *Origin* can readily attest, Darwin himself saw nothing "provisional" or marginal about natural selection. And as anyone reading current biological theory can attest, the Modern Synthesis is in fact the dominant, mainstream view among evolutionists. Since the time of the Modern Synthesis, almost all eminent evolutionists have accepted natural selection as the central mechanism of evolutionary change. The proponents of the modern theory have assimilated the findings of Kimura and others on the evolution of adaptively neutral nucleotides—nucleotides that are by definition outside the purview of natural selection—and none of them regards this theory as a challenge to the Darwinian theory that attributes all complex functional structure to the action of natural selection. Similarly, while most evolutionists have displayed some interest in the debate over the pace of evolutionary change, almost none of them believes that this debate challenges the centrality of natural selection. And finally, no reputable current evolutionary theorist, not even Gould, overtly and unequivocally proclaims a belief in macromutational leaps as a mechanism of evolutionary change.

The term that Gould uses to link himself with Darwin and set himself and Darwin together in ostensible opposition to the Modern Synthesis is "pluralism." By this word, Gould means a view of evolution that takes account of an array of causal mechanisms different from natural selection. Darwin himself consistently declared that adaptation through natural selection is the main but not the only mechanism of evolutionary change. In addition to natural selection, he acknowledged two other mechanisms: the inherited effects of direct environmental influence, and the inherited effects of habit or the use and disuse of organs (2003, chap. 5, pp. 178–185.) Use and disuse and the direct effect of the environment are concessions to ignorance—to what was not yet known about the mechanisms of inheritance. They are forms of what is commonly regarded as "Lamarckian" inheritance or the inheritance of acquired characteristics. Neither of these supplementary mechanisms is central to the argument of the *Origin*. In later editions, the supplementary mechanisms were given greater play as Darwin hedged against the criticisms of Fleeming Jenkin on the effects of blending inheritance and of Lord Kelvin on the extent of geological time, but natural selection remained unequivocally the core of Darwin's argument. Later discoveries have proved that the supplementary mechanisms do not work. They can and must be eliminated from the set of recognized causal mechanisms. Fortunately for the standing of Darwin's book as a scientific classic, dispensing with the supplementary mechanisms does no serious damage to the structure of his argument, and very little even to the details of his exposition. The overwhelming majority of his examples and causal analyses directly concern natural selection, not the supplementary mechanisms.

There are three sophistical twists in Gould's appeal to Darwin's "pluralism." (a) He takes Darwin's pluralism as a precedent for his own, blurring over the fact that the supplementary mechanisms Darwin acknowledged have been scientifically disconfirmed and were never, in any case, central to Darwin's argument. (b) He identifies as the constituents of his own "pluralism" ideas that are already part of the Modern Synthesis and that are either compatible with adaptation through natural selection or actually integral with it. And (c) he poses this putative "pluralism" as if it is an *alternative* to the "adaptationism" of the Modern Synthesis. The ideas that are already part of the Modern Synthesis and that are compatible with natural selection include correlated growth, adaptively neutral changes, and variable pace in evolutionary change. (Correlated growth is the idea that certain features not in themselves adaptive are linked genetically to features that are adaptive and that are thus targeted by selection. The non-adaptive features hitchhike on the adaptive features to which they are joined. Darwin cites as an example the shape of pelvises and kidneys in birds [2003, chapter 5, p. 186]. In modern genetics, correlated growth is associated with the term "pleiotropy," meaning genes that have multiple, diverse effects.) The chief idea that is actually integral with natural selection is that of inherited constraints on adaptive structure.

Gould's article "Darwinian Fundamentalism" (1997) offers a representative instance of his technique with respect to "pluralism." First, he cites a passage from the sixth and last edition of the *Origin* in which Darwin denies the charge that "I attribute the modification of species exclusively to natural selection" (p. 34). On the basis of this defensive disavowal, Gould declares that "Darwin himself strongly opposed the ultras of his own day" (p. 34). In contrast to the restrictive influence of supposed "ultra-Darwinians" such as Maynard Smith, Dawkins, and Dennett, Gould celebrates "the invigoration of modern evolutionary biology with exciting *nonselectionist and nonadaptationist* data from the three central disciplines of population genetics, developmental biology, and paleontology" (p. 34; my italics). Gould celebrates population genetics because it provides evidence of changes in adaptively neutral nucleotides; paleontology because it provides evidence for variations in the pace of evolutionary change; and developmental biology because it provides evidence for the idea of "developmental constraints," an idea Gould sets forth as clearly distinct from that of "natural selection" (pp. 35, 36). This supposedly non-adaptationist matrix of disciplines renders the 1990s "an especially unpropitious time for Darwinian fundamentalism—and seems only to reconfirm Darwin's own eminently sensible pluralism" (p. 34). In this specific article, Gould does not include pleiotropy or "correlated growth" within his canon of "nonselectionist or nonadaptationist" ideas. For the inclusion of this idea, we can cite "A Hearing for Vavilov" (1984) and "The Spandrels of San Marco and the Panglossian Paradigm: A Critique of the Adaptationist Programme" (Gould and Lewontin, 1979). In the former essay, Gould presents correlated growth as an instance of "the limits placed upon selection by structure and development" (p. 144), and in the latter essay, he presents the "production of nonadaptive structures by developmental correlation" as part of his catalogue of phenomena that supposedly stand outside the scope of "the adaptationist programme" (p. 581).

Gould's implied contrast between the various ideas he describes and the adaptationism and selectionism of the Modern Synthesis is transparently but breathtakingly bogus. In the case of variations in the pace of evolutionary change, the evolution of adaptively neutral nucleotides, and correlated growth, the contrast is bogus because none of these processes has any bearing on the evolution of complex functional structure, and that is the one central feature of evolution that adaptation by means of natural selection is designed to explain. Only natural selection produces complex functional structure, and in this sense it is the only answer to "*how*" evolution occurred. In the case of inherited constraints on functional structure, the supposed contrast is bogus because inherited constraint is an integral and indispensable *component* of natural selection.

Darwin's supposed "pluralism" consists of one major and two minor mechanisms for the creation of adaptive structure. In addition to these mechanisms, Darwin acknowledges the whole array of phenomena that Gould identifies as the key components of his own pluralism, and these components are also standard parts of modern evolutionary theory as it was constituted by the Modern Synthesis. In speaking of "Organs of little apparent importance," in chapter 6, "Difficulties on Theory," Darwin gives full consideration to the existence of nonfunctional structures:

> I fully admit that many structures are of no direct use to their possessors. . . . Correlation of growth has no doubt played a most important part, and a useful modification of one part will often have entailed on other parts diversified changes of no direct use. So again characters which formerly were useful, or which formerly had arisen from correlation of growth, or from other unknown causes, may reappear from the law of reversion, though now of no direct use. . . . But by far the most important consideration is that the chief part of the organisation of every being is simply due to inheritance; and consequently, though each being assuredly is well fitted for its place in nature, many structures now have no direct relation to the habits of life of each species. . . . We cannot believe that the same bones in the arm of the monkey, in the fore-leg of the horse, in the wing of the bat, and in the flipper of the seal, are of special use to these animals. (2003, chap. 6, pp. 219–220)

Darwin's argument for adaptation through natural selection explains both complex functional structure and also the limitations on maximal efficiency that flow necessarily from the constraints of inheritance. The constraint of inheritance is an overt and pervasive theme in the *Origin*, and indeed it is formulated as an explicit and emphatic thesis in both of Darwin's early sketches of his theory in 1842 and 1844 (Darwin and Wallace, 1958, pp. 78, 170). This theme is equally overt and pervasive in the work of virtually all prominent contemporary Darwinians. It is for example one of Richard Dawkins' constant themes, and Dawkins is one of the most prominent of the evolutionists whom Gould identifies as "ultra-Darwinians." Following in the line of Darwin's own logic, Dawkins observes that "evolution never starts from a clean drawing board. It has to start from what is already there" (1987, p. 92). One result is that many designs are not optimally efficient. As an instance of imperfect design, Dawkins' describes the wiring of the optic nerve in the vertebrate eye. One of the consequences of building step by step is that all previous steps constrain succeeding developments. In the case of the eye, Dawkins observes, one previous step, so far back in evolutionary time as to be lost to explanation, has resulted in a tiny but ubiquitous imperfection of design. "Each photocell is, in effect, wired in backwards," and this arrangement, of no apparent adaptive utility, produces an untidy and inefficient tangle of nerves (p. 93). The idea of inherited constraint, with all its attendant imperfections, is central to Darwin's own logic; it is one of his chief forms of proof for natural selection, and it is a constant feature in the entire subsequent history of Darwinian adaptationist thinking.

Dawkins' choice of the eye to illustrate imperfection in design is particularly felicitous in that, among adaptationists, the eye is the most prominently and frequently cited instance of an organ that displays complex functional structure. Paley takes the eye as a central exhibit in his argument for the existence of a divine designer, and Darwin, G. G. Simpson, and Dawkins all take it as a challenge to the proposition that any complex organ can be built up by infinitesimally small steps, beginning, in this case, with nothing more than a light-sensitive nerve. In "The Psychological Foundations of Culture" (1992)—an essay that has already achieved something like canonical status in modern evolutionary psychology—Tooby and Cosmides make the mechanics of vision a central illustration for the idea that complex functional structure is the key indicator of adaptation through natural selection. In *How the Mind Works* (1997b), an exposition that integrates evolutionary psychology with cognitive neuroscience, Steven Pinker analyzes the mechanics of sight at a length and with a precision of detail that would weary an ophthalmologist.

Dawkins' treatment of the eye follows the pattern set by Darwin. Complex functional structure can be produced only by adaptation through natural selection, but adaptations are only relatively "perfect." And indeed, by reconstructing the evolutionary history in the development of the eye, any evolutionist tacitly acknowledges that at earlier evolutionary periods the eyes of various ancestral organisms were less efficient, less complex and less capable of various kinds of visual resolution, than the organs of their descendants. Simpson brings this implication clearly into the open. He identifies various, currently existing levels of complexity and functional efficiency in the eyes of various organisms, and he situates these organs of sight on a scale, from simple to complex, that helps to us to understand the evolution of vision as a series of increments in structural complexity (1967, pp. 168–176). If the eyes of ancestral organisms were less efficient than those of at least some of their descendants, there could be no reason to assume that the eye of any organism is now truly "perfect" and could not, at some future point, become still more complex and efficient. No Darwinian would make so absurd an assumption. Nor would any Darwinian deny that it is equally possible that in cases in which eyes have ceased to be adaptive and have hence ceased to be targeted by natural selection—as in the case of animals living deep in caves—the eyes can degenerate over evolutionary time and become less efficient than those of ancestral organisms. "Panadaptationism" or "ultra-Darwinism" are thus chimeras of Gould's own imagining. Or, more precisely, they are figments of his rhetorical procedures. The purpose of the procedure is to attach a stigma to all adaptationist explanation, and the means to accomplish this purpose is to attribute to evolutionists a proclivity for gross fallacies that in reality and in the simple logic of the case—the logic of adaptationist reasoning—they virtually never display.

The two ideas for which Gould has generated the most publicity are "punctuated equilibrium" and "spandrels." The elements in these two ideas that are substantive and valid were integral parts of Darwinism before Gould formulated them, associated them spuriously with anti-adaptationist intimations, and popularized them with catchy phrases. Gould's own distinctive contribution to these two concepts, insofar as they have consisted of ideas that were substantive and that were not already part of the Darwinian synthesis, have proven to be either compatible with mainstream adaptationist thinking, relatively unimportant, or simply wrong.

Punctuated equilibrium has taken diverse forms over the years, but the different versions can be located on a scale between the strong and weak forms of the theory. The form that is specific and peculiar to Gould is the strong form; this form involves "saltation" or "big jumps" in the evolutionary process—speciation through macromutations. The idea of saltation appears in Gould's thumbnail sketch of modern Darwinian theory cited above, but it appears there only as an idea that Gould attributes to some unidentified speculators: "Others are challenging Darwin's linking of natural selection with gradual, imperceptible change through all intermediary degrees; they are arguing that most evolutionary events may occur far more rapidly than Darwin envisioned" (1984, p. 255). Despite the link between saltation and certain unidentified paleontologists who are questioning the pace of evolution, Gould does not quite overtly declare himself as one of this speculative band who are challenging Darwin's core theory. The idea of saltation as an idea that Gould himself embraces and does not merely attribute to unidentified others who look like him makes a more distinct appearance in an essay of 1980, "Is a New and General Theory of Evolution Emerging?" In this essay, Gould correctly characterizes the standard view of speciation as "a cumulative and sequential process powered by selection through large numbers of generations" (p. 122), and he clearly positions himself apart from this standard view. "I have no doubt that many species originate in this way; but it now appears that many, perhaps most, do not" (p. 122). He invokes new models of evolutionary change that involve "nonadaptive" processes, and he maintains that speciation represents a "discontinuity in our hierarchy of explanations" (pp. 122, 123). In these remarkable statements, Gould radically and openly subverts the core elements of Darwin's theory of descent with modification by means of natural selection. He explicitly affirms the proposition that species originate not through small, incremental changes that are adaptive in character but through processes that are nonadaptive and discontinuous.

The claims made in this essay of 1980 constituted a truly bold and startling move—too bold and too startling. Segregating himself so decisively from the central Darwinian tradition did not serve Gould's purposes. He wished only to be considered as at best an original theorist and at worst a gadfly, in no case as a mere crank on the fringe of legitimate evolutionary theory. He quickly backed off from saltation (the production of a new species within a single generation), and since this early, indiscreet foray into overt anti-Darwinism Gould's program has claimed (equivocally, but primarily) only to be "expanding" mainstream Darwinism, not replacing it. This program of expansion has had one main substantive element—an inflated claim for the significance of selection operating at the level of whole species rather than at the level of individual organisms. Gould has continued to suggest or hint at macromutation, but only by the rhetorical devices of blending it into selection at the level of species and by speaking of geologically "instantaneous" moments (that is, thousands of generations) as if these ideas somehow radically challenged Darwinian notions of "gradualism" (that is, the incremental change of species through micromutations introduced in a long series of generations).

Saltation is now almost universally regarded as biologically impossible. Species selection—natural selection operating at the level of species rather than that of individual organisms within species—is possible, but it is probably not a major factor in evolutionary change, and it is in any case not incompatible with the Darwinian theory of adaptation through natural selection. Mark Ridley (1983, pp. 136–140), Maynard Smith (1989, pp. 129, 140–141, 154), and E. O. Wilson (1992, pp. 89–92)—all eminent mainstream Darwinians—make it clear that (a) selection at the level of species is not nonadaptationist, and (b) there are no significant forms of species selection that do not work through the selection of individual organisms. Hence it does not, as Gould suggests, decouple microevolution from macroevolution.

In its weak form, punctuated equilibrium means only that the pace of evolution varies, that some species can remain in stasis for long periods, probably by means of stabilizing selection, while others evolve rapidly (perhaps under the stress of changing environmental conditions). This idea appears prominently in Darwin's own work (2003, chap. 10, pp. 289–292) and in that of G. G. Simpson, the most distinguished representative of the Modern Synthesis in the paleontological area (1967, pp. 20–22, 98). As Dawkins (1987, pp. 241–248) and several other writers have explained—trying to clear up some of the confusion generated by Gould—the idea of varying pace in evolutionary change is in no way opposed to Darwinian gradualism. Gradualism means change through a long sequence of micromutations. It is thus set in opposition to the idea of saltational change or the change from one species to another through macromutations. The *pace* of these changes is not at issue.

One distinctive aspect of the strong form of punctuated equilibrium is the idea that change can occur *only* during speciation events. This claim has been proven to be empirically incorrect. (See Mark Ridley, 1983, pp. 121–133.) In its weak form, punctuated equilibrium incorporates an idea that was put forward by Darwin (2003, chap. 4, pp. 157–161; chap. 6, p. 204) and given prominence by Ernst Mayr—the idea that speciation events can be facilitated by the isolation of small populations. The question of whether speciation can take place *only* through the isolation of small populations remains a live issue subject to empirical study. The best evidence seems to suggest that this is not in fact the case. (See Ridley, 1983, chap. 8.) E. O. Wilson summarizes the long debate over punctuated equilibrium and makes it clear that once the false claims and confusions have been cleared away, little of substance remains:

> [The argument for punctuated equilibrium] claims that not only does evolution periodically bound forward but it tends to flow to a virtual halt at other times. Species emerge quickly and fully formed after a rapid burst of evolution, then persist almost unchanged for millions of years. And, conversely, rapid evolution is driven mostly or entirely during species formation. The alternation between leaps and pauses creates a jerky pattern, a punctuated equilibrium, so extreme as to point to novel processes of evolution beyond the natural selection of genes and chromosomes. Macroevolution, the reasoning in its most radical form concludes, is in some fashion unique, not the same as microevolution. (1992, pp. 88–89)

Wilson explains that the theory "was at first promoted as a challenge to the neo-Darwinian theory of evolution" and that it was presented as "in effect, a new theory of evolution," but that claim, he observes "has been abandoned by most of its proponents. The fossil evidence for the widespread occurrence of jerky patterns proved weak, and most examples put forth at the outset were discredited" (p. 89). He notes that standard Darwinian theory already took account of the varying pace of evolution, so that those parts of the theory that were correct were not new, whereas those parts that were new were not correct. Macroevolution has not been decoupled, as Gould wished, from microevolution.

Gould's one other big idea is that of "spandrels" or nonadaptive structures. "The Spandrels of San Marco and the Panglossian Paradigm: A Critique of the Adaptationist Programme" is probably Gould's best-known essay—so well known that an entire book of essays in rhetorical analysis has been devoted to it (Selzer, 1993). In this essay, Gould, in company with Richard Lewontin, explains that spandrels are "the tapering triangular spaces formed by the intersection of two rounded arches at right angles" (1979, p. 581). Such spaces are "necessary architectural by-products of mounting a dome on rounded arches." The arches provide structural support for the dome, and the "tapering triangular spaces" (the spandrels) that are produced by this support structure are walled in. The resulting surfaces are often decorated, and in Saint Marks Church in Venice, they are covered with gold mosaic. The point of the metaphor is that not every feature of a complex structure is adaptive. Some features, like the areas of wall between the arches, are side effects or byproducts of some structural feature—in this case, the feature of intersecting arches. The spandrel walls are not created, Gould and Lewontin argue, to provide a surface for the application of gold mosaic. The areas of wall just happen to be there, but since they are there, some use is found for them.

In making spandrels into a biological metaphor, Gould blends two legitimate Darwinian concepts, but he spuriously represents this blended concept as an alternative or supplement to the idea of adaptation through natural selection. One of these legitimate Darwinian concepts is pleiotropy or multiple genic effects: what Darwin calls correlated growth. The other legitimate Darwinian concept is the idea that previously existing structures can be altered through natural selection to fulfill adaptive functions. Darwin offers as an example the swim bladder that in the course of evolution is transformed into a lung (2003, chap. 6, p. 214). The tetrapod body plan also caught Darwin's attention (pp. 219–220) and has remained a favorite example among evolutionists. The forelimbs evolve from fins to legs, and from legs sometimes to wings and sometimes to flippers. Another favorite example, discovered after Darwin's time, is that of the reptilian jaw bones that have been transformed into the mammalian ossicles—the bones of the inner ear. (See Young, 1992, pp. 185–186; Moore, 1993, pp. 176–177, 412–414.) For adaptations that use either previous adaptive structures or previous structures of no adaptive value, Gould and Vrba (1982) have invented the term "exaptation." This term is a variant of a term that was previously current—"preadaptation"—and the concept is itself a commonplace in standard Darwinian theory.

If we examine the metaphor of architectural spandrels more closely, we shall see—contrary to the implications in the argument presented by Gould and Lewontin—that "spandrels" are in fact an integral part of an adaptive design. If the spandrels were not walled in—if the architect chose to leave triangular holes in the walls below the dome—the architectural effect would be absurd, both eccentric in appearance and unpleasantly drafty. In the degree to which the architect operates within the range of architectural good sense and thus does not choose to create a perforated building, spandrel walls are a necessary part of the larger structure—a dome supported on arches. If a dome supported on arches is the adaptive target structure, in the degree to which the spandrels are a necessary part of that structure they are themselves an integral part of the adaptation. Spandrels are in this respect like the whiteness of bone. The bone could be any color, so far as color is concerned. But it could not be composed of any mineral. For the sake of hardness, a bone needs to be composed of calcium, and calcium, as it happens, is white. In that nontrivial sense, then, whiteness is an indispensable component of the whole adaptive design of bones. No whiteness, no calcium; no calcium, no hardness. Hardness is the target feature, but calcium, which happens to be white, is the means through which this feature is realized.

It would be unwise to make too much of the architectural metaphor. All metaphors contain adventitious and misleading associations, and they can be treacherous guides in the construction of scientific hypotheses. But for what it is worth, we can draw out an implication of the spandrels metaphor that is almost the opposite of that which Gould intends. Spandrels can be taken to illustrate the opportunistic process through which natural selection uses whatever structures are available to gain some advantage for an organism. Unless we choose to produce perforated buildings, spandrel walls inevitably accompany arches, and since they are there, they might as well be used, even if only for ornamentation. But is ornamentation adventitious or irrelevant to the functions of architecture? Both Dissanayake (1995b, p, 230) and Dennett (1995, pp. 273–274) go so far as to claim that ornamentation is itself the central target feature for selection. What purpose does a dome itself have other than to produce an aesthetic effect? In any case, ornamentation is integral with the total set of aesthetic and cultural functions a Byzantine-style church is designed to fulfill. The spandrel walls are there, as a byproduct of a structural feature, and they are then adapted to fulfill at least one of the functions appropriate to the church. They are, metaphorically, adaptive.

Despite the confusions and ambiguities introduced through the architectural metaphor, none of the implications in the idea of spandrels is in any way contrary to standard adaptationist thinking. What Gould and Lewontin have attempted to do, though, is to use the metaphor to suggest, without quite saying it, that major features of complex functional structures have been produced independently of adaptive processes. Put this baldly, the claim is simply and obviously false, but unless it is put this way, the claim has no actual content that is not already part and parcel of standard Darwinian thinking. Since the time of his youthful foray into saltation, Gould himself has usually been careful, whenever he implies or suggests this false idea, also to say that he recognizes that complex functional designs result from adaptation, or that adaptation through natural selection is an "important" feature of the evolutionary process. The false and obfuscatory implications in the more radical understanding of "spandrels" are nonetheless its *raison d'être*, its chief purpose and function. It subserves the larger Gouldian program of minimizing in whatever way he can the general significance of adaptation through natural selection.

In order to achieve their aim of minimizing the significance of adaptation through natural selection without clearly and decisively cutting themselves off from mainstream Darwinism, Gould and Lewontin are driven to the necessity of perpetual equivocation, and the equivocation is rendered all the more impenetrable by being commingled with a pseudo-concept produced by breaking a single, valid concept into two parts and representing these parts as antithetical. The single, valid concept is that of "selection," and the two parts are "selective force" and "constraints." We shall begin with the equivocation and then consider the pseudo-concept. Spuriously invoking Darwin as an antecedent for their own anti-adaptationism, Gould and Lewontin repudiate the idea that Darwin was himself "a radical selectionist at heart who invoked other mechanisms only in retreat, and only as a result of his age's own lamented ignorance about the mechanisms of heredity" (1979, p. 589). "This view," they declare, "is false." But then they also declare, in the very next sentence, that "Darwin regarded selection as the most important of evolutionary mechanisms. As do we." *As do we.* Strange, then, that the whole thrust of their essay should be toward the conclusion that "constraints restrict possible paths and modes of change so strongly that the constraints themselves become much the most interesting aspect of evolution" (p. 594). Or as they explain in the head note to the essay, "the constraints themselves become more interesting in delimiting pathways of change than the selective force that may mediate change when it occurs" (p. 581). Selection is the most important mechanism, but despite its importance, it is still not very interesting, somehow, not nearly so interesting as other things that are not so important.

The idea of a selective force operating independently of constraints—the idea of selection operating in a vacuum, independently of all actually existing conditions—is something like the idea of one hand clapping. When the idea of selection is placed in antithesis to the idea of constraints, it ceases altogether to be an intelligible idea. It becomes a pseudo-concept, a rhetorical term that is devoid of any conceptual content other than the confusion caused by the faulty way in which it is formulated. One might suppose that this feature of the concept—its lack of any content other than the confusion generated by the way it is formulated—would help to explain why it is so uninteresting, but it could hardly also explain why it is still "important." Gould and Lewontin have here drifted into a very strange region of "thought," a region much more familiar within the confines of postmodern literary theory than within those of evolutionary biology. Like Derrida or Foucault, Gould and Lewontin bring to bear sophisticated analytic and rhetorical skills, but these skills are oriented not to the production of clear and distinct ideas but to exactly the opposite, to the construction of pseudo-concepts that obstruct clear thinking.

There is one chief difference between the work of Gould/Lewontin and that of the postmodernists. Derrida, Foucault, and their many acolytes overtly declare irrationalism as their creed. It is the substance and burden of their theory, and in this sense their central theoretical claims are integral with their rhetorical methods. Gould and Lewontin use the techniques of sophistical equivocation in a virtuoso way, but they do not overtly and forthrightly declare that their purpose is to suspend the capacity for rational thought. There is, in that respect, something less complete and robust about their work. It is a sort of hybrid between sophistry and science.

Confusion is not itself the targeted feature under selection in "The Spandrels of San Marco." It is a means to an end, and that end is to achieve the appearance of revolutionary transformation without formulating ideas that are clear and distinct enough to be vulnerable to refutation. Since Gould and Lewontin are arguing only about degrees of difference ("so strongly") in subjective responses ("most interesting"), they cannot be held to have affirmed any specific proposition. Because they have produced no clear and distinct ideas, their claims cannot be falsified. They have nonetheless created a rhetorical facsimile of contrasting theoretical positions, and they can thus present themselves as having constructed a solid foundation for a revolutionary transformation of "the adaptationist programme" (1979, p. 581).

In his eagerness to minimize the significance of adaptation through natural selection, Gould is, in wish and emphasis, anti-Darwinian. But since, within the range of scientifically reputable evolutionary theory, there is no actual alternative to Darwinism—no alternative, that is, to adaptation through natural selection as an explanation for complex functional structure—Gould can never say fully what he wants to say. His plight recalls that of "Atticus" in Alexander Pope's "An Epistle from Mr. Pope to Dr. Arbuthnot." In Pope's depiction, Atticus (Addison) wished to satisfy envy and spite without making himself vulnerable through open attack. He thus developed a proto-Gouldian rhetorical technique that enabled him to "Damn with faint praise, assent with civil leer, / And without sneering, teach the rest to sneer; / Willing to wound, and yet afraid to strike, / Just hint a fault, and hesitate dislike" (1969, ll. 201–204).

In an article that offers a thorough and precise analysis of Gould's rhetorical strategies, John Alcock identifies a number of Gould's feints and dodges, and he observes that, while Gould frequently makes pretenses of affirming the centrality of adaptation, he also perpetually employs sophistical formulations intended to eliminate adaptation from the conceptual repertory of evolutionary biology. With respect to one such formulation, Alcock notes that "by 'adaptation'" Gould "means a trait that evolved without historical constraints, which means that almost no trait qualifies for the title. And I think that this is essentially what Stephen Jay Gould has in mind" (1998, p. 332).

Alcock persuasively argues that one animating motive in Gould's campaign against adaptation is his commitment to Marxist ideology. From a Marxist perspective, to affirm adaptive design is to acknowledge that the existing structure of social and political power is constrained in some way by the nature of things, and to acknowledge that much is to come too close, the Marxist feels, to justifying the existing social order. Marxist utopianism requires that human beings not be constrained by evolved motives; "human nature" is to consist in little more than a capacity for culture that entails infinite flexibility. It is certainly the case that from the very beginning Gould's ideological career has been punctuated repeatedly by attacks on human sociobiology and evolutionary psychology, and it seems more than probable that this social and political animus has helped to shape his formulations of general evolutionary theory, even when that theory directly concerns only insects, snails, pandas, flamingoes, horses, dinosaurs, and Cambrian phyla, not human beings. (On Gould's ideological motives, also see Gross, 2002.)

Gould's primary field of specialization is paleontology, and for a paleontologist the one most significant modern find—the one find that offers the greatest opportunity for drawing conclusions of broad general import in the field of evolutionary theory—are the fossils of the Burgess shale. Gould gives a historical and theoretical account of the Burgess fossils in his popular book *Wonderful Life: The Burgess Shale and the Nature of History* (1989). He uses the fossils to support his claim that evolution is wholly "contingent." By totalizing and hypostatizing this word—that is, by treating "contingency" as a distinct, substantive entity rather than a logical category—he creates the impression that evolution is altogether unpredictable and chaotic. The idea of contingency as *events resulting from unforeseen causal relations* bleeds over, in Gould's formulations, into the idea of contingency as *events happening in ways that are not subject to causal analysis because they happen without cause*. The idea of contingency as somehow distinct from adaptation is closely affiliated with the idea of constraints that are somehow more interesting than the selection that works on them. Insofar as it is not merely a form of obfuscation, this notion of contingency is a form of mysticism or irrationalism. We hear again the sound of one hand clapping.

Simon Conway Morris is a Cambridge paleontologist who performed an important part of the primary scientific work on the Burgess shale fossils. In *Wonderful Life*, Gould gives Conway Morris good press, but he does not thereby succeed in blunting the edge of the criticism that Conway Morris levels at him in his own subsequent book. In *The Crucible of Creation* (1998), Conway Morris opposes Gould's interpretation of the Burgess fossils on two main counts: the relative diversity of Burgess and modern phyla, and the significance of constraints. He argues that Gould is wrong in claiming that the Burgess animals displayed greater disparity of body form and a larger number of phyla than present animals. The appearance of greater disparity, he argues, is an artifact of classification (pp. 205–206, 218; also see Mark Ridley's (1990) review of *Wonderful Life*). Like Gould, Conway Morris emphasizes constraints, but he draws a radically different inference from them. One major feature of evolution, convergent evolution, powerfully supports the idea that viable forms are constrained in certain directions by the conditions of life on earth. Organisms that display convergent evolution have functionally similar adaptations that have evolved independently in distinct phylogenetic lineages. Signal instances include the eyes of insects, vertebrates, and cephalopods (squids), and the wings of birds, insects, and bats. By emphasizing the significance of the constraints evidenced by convergent evolution, Conway Morris undermines Gould's claims for unpredictability (pp. 139, 201–202).

David Hull, a leading figure in the history and philosophy of biology, takes Gould as an illustration of his thesis that "scientists are engaged in the ongoing process of jockeying for recognition in science" (1988, p. 202). Hull treats of science chiefly as an institutional and social process, and the "process" he describes consists largely in choosing strategies for the advancement of scientific careers. There are two basic strategies. Scientists can present themselves as adherents to the received view, contributing only refinements of technical detail, or they can present themselves as radical revolutionaries. "The choice is between a safe strategy with a minor payoff versus a very dangerous strategy that promises great rewards" (p. 203). In biology, for instance, scientists can choose to "exaggerate their differences with the received view to emphasize how original their contributions are," or they can "exaggerate the similarities between their views and those of contemporary Darwinians in order to throw the mantle of the great Darwin round their own shoulders" (p. 202). Gould has found a way to combine these two strategies. He presents himself as a radical opponent of the received view but—apart from his youthful fling with overt saltation— also as a Darwinist more truly Darwinian than the "Darwinian fundamentalists." He has found a way to seek great rewards with little risk, but the method he has chosen for thus maximizing his strategic advantages is to abandon any effort to produce substantive contributions to scientific knowledge and instead to generate verbal problematics.

There is a cost to the strategy Gould has adopted, even in the purely careerist terms described by Hull. As Alcock observes, "Gould's debating tactics may make his essays persuasive to a general audience, but rhetoric alone cannot overcome the research record established by persons willing to put their ideas about the adaptive design of traits on the table for honest testing" (1998, p. 335). In an exchange with Gould over evolutionary psychology, Steven

Pinker makes a similar appeal to positive research findings and cites an illustrative range of psychological topics:

> The adaptationist approach has, for over a century, driven the most rigorous, elegant, and empirically rich branch of psychology, perception. Today it is spawning new insights and intensive modeling and data-gathering on every other aspect of the mind, including reasoning, mental imagery, memory, language, beauty, sexual desire, autism, emotions such as fear and disgust, violence, the numerical abilities of children and animals, and the shaping of personality." (1997a, p. 56)

Alcock and Pinker both believe in the ultimate integrity of the scientific process. On the basis of this belief, Alcock declares, "I am confident that, in the long run, Gould's polemical essays will be just an odd footnote in the history of evolutionary thought, a history that has been shaped in a wonderfully productive manner by the adaptationist perspective" (p. 335). Gould's situation is something like that in the story of the man, hungry for fame, who made a particularly ingenious bargain with the devil—ingenious, that is, on the devil's side. In return for his soul, the man would be famous in his own day, but only on the condition that after his death all trace of his works would be eradicated from the memory of men.

Several eminent evolutionists have reflected on the quality of sophistry that pervades Gould's theoretical writing. Daniel Dennett, Richard Dawkins, Simon Conway Morris, and E. O. Wilson have all described the way in which Gould exaggerates the revolutionary significance of his ideas. In a chapter of *Darwin's Dangerous Idea: Evolution and the Meanings of Life* (1995), Dennett gives a penetrating and comprehensive critique of Gould's theoretical career and describes it, correctly, as a series of factitious revolutions. One of the chapter sections is tellingly titled "The Boy Who Cried Wolf." Summarizing his chapter, Dennett concludes, "*Gould's self-styled revolutions, against adaptationism, gradualism, and extrapolationism, and for 'radical contingency,' all evaporate, their good points already firmly incorporated into the modern synthesis, and their mistaken points dismissed. Darwin's dangerous idea emerges strengthened, its dominion over every corner of biology more secure than ever*" (p. 312). Rather more bluntly, Dawkins complains that "Gould seems to be saying things that are more radical than they really are. He pretends" (1995, p. 84). Dawkins is openly hostile toward Gould, and he gives his reasons. "I'm extremely hostile towards any sort of obscurantism, pretension. If I think somebody's a fake, if somebody isn't genuinely concerned about what actually is true but is instead doing something for some other motive, if somebody is trying to appear like an intellectual, or trying to appear more profound than he is, or more mysterious than he is, I'm very hostile to that" (p. 85). As we have seen, Conway Morris provides a sober specialist critique of Gould's conclusions about the fossils of the Burgess shale, but he also fashions an evocative

and humorous image of Gould's whole career as an ostensible post-adapta-
tionist founder of new evolutionary theories:

> Again and again Gould has been seen to charge into battle, sometimes hardly
> visible in the struggling mass. Strangely immune to seemingly lethal lunges he fi-
> nally re-emerges. Eventually the dust and confusion die down. Gould announces
> to the awestruck onlookers that our present understanding of evolutionary pro-
> cesses is dangerously deficient and the theory is perhaps in its death throes. We
> look beyond the exponent of doom, and there standing in the sunlight is the ed-
> ifice of evolutionary theory, little changed. (1998, p. 10)

In a similar vein, commenting specifically on the debate over punctuated equilibrium, E. O. Wilson suggests that Gould's claims for revolutionary novelty
were more a matter of rhetorical posturing than of substantive conceptual
proposals. "Neo-Darwinian theory was not challenged in substance, only se-
mantically—a renaming, so to speak, as opposed to a reinventing of the wheel"
(1992, p. 89). The term "punctuated equilibrium" has survived, but it "is now
used mostly as a descriptive term for a pattern of alternating rapid and slow
evolution, especially when the rapid phase is accompanied by species formation. Its fate illustrates the principle that in science failed ideas live on as ghosts
in the glossaries of the survivors."

Early in his career as the boy who cried wolf, Gould responded to the complaint that he is generating confusion by creating pseudo-issues. Backing off
from the strong, saltational version of punctuated equilibrium, he acknowledged that punctuated equilibrium "may not be directed at the heart of natural selection," but he still claimed that "it remains an important critique of
the Darwinian tradition" (1982, p. 383). His supporting inference for the importance of his idea is that "he world is not inhabited exclusively by fools, and
when a subject arouses intense interest and debate, as this one has, something
other than semantics is usually at stake" (p. 383). Evolutionary biologists do
not tend to be fools, but they do tend to be ingenuously straightforward, and
they are often poorly equipped to deal with provocative challenges wrapped in
obfuscatory equivocation. Gould's pluralism, his punctuationism, and his
spandrels can be likened to the eggs of a cuckoo in the nest of evolutionary biology. The eggs look enough like legitimate eggs to cause consternation in the
minds of the parent birds, but targeted birds eventually evolve defenses against
the cuckoo's parasitism. They count eggs or assess size, and oust the illegitimate intruders. The affair costs them some little effort, but it hardly seems fair
for the cuckoo then to proclaim that the effort taken to oust his illegitimate
offspring constitutes evidence of his own legitimacy.

Among Darwin's contemporaries, the one figure who most resembles
Gould in his use of sophistical equivocation is the paleontologist Richard
Owen (1804–1892), who wished, on the one hand, to affirm that animal forms
are determined by "archetypes" that are not related to one another by lineage

and, on the other, to represent himself as having originated proto-Darwinian evolutionary ideas. Darwin responds to Owen's equivocations in the historical sketch appended to the third edition of the *Origin*, and he comes closer there to a snort of satirical contempt than he ever comes in responding to any other writer, even to Lamarck. "It is consolatory to me that others find Professor Owen's controversial writings as difficult to understand and to reconcile with each other, as I do" (2003, p. 84). Darwin himself operates in good faith, and his overriding assumption is that others do also, even when he fundamentally disagrees with them. In his *Autobiography*, he remarks, "I have almost always been treated honestly by my reviewers, passing over those without scientific knowledge as not worthy of notice" (1958, p. 125). Coming from a man who had received so many violently hostile reviews, this remark reflects a presumption of good faith so ingenuous in its benignity as to fall little short of the sublime. But Owen is so flagrantly and unmistakably not operating in good faith that even Darwin's simplicity of good will is finally roused to an awareness of Owen's deviousness and duplicity. One can only speculate how Darwin would have responded to Gould. He might well have wondered whether Gould is, as Maynard Smith characterizes him, merely confused, or, as Dawkins characterizes him, downright dishonest. To my own eye, it seems evident that Gould is not himself confused, though it is his purpose that his readers should be.

References

Abrams, M. H. (1953). *The Mirror and the Lamp: Romantic Theory and the Critical Tradition.* Oxford: Oxford University Press.

Abrams, M. H. (1986). Poetry, theories of. In A. Preminger et al. (eds.), *Princeton Encyclopedia of Poetic Terms* (pp. 203–214). Princeton, NJ: Princeton University Press.

Abrams, M. H. (1995), What is a humanistic criticism? In D. Eddins (ed.), *The Emperor Redressed: Critiquing Critical Theory* (pp. 13–44). Tuscaloosa: University of Alabama Press.

Abrams, M. H. (1997). The transformation of English studies: 1930–1995. *Daedalus,* 126, 105–132.

Acocella, J. (2000). *Willa Cather and the Politics of Criticism.* Lincoln: University of Nebraska Press.

Ahearn, E. J. (1987). *Marx and Modern Fiction.* New Haven, CT: Yale University Press.

Alcock, J. (1998). Unpunctuated equilibrium in the *Natural History* essays of Stephen Jay Gould. *Evolution and Human Behavior,* 19, 321–336.

Alcock, J. (2001). *The Triumph of Sociobiology.* Oxford: Oxford University Press.

Alexander, R. D. (1979). *Darwinism and Human Affairs.* Seattle: University of Washington Press.

Alexander, R. D. (1987). *The Biology of Moral Systems.* Hawthorne, NY: Aldine de Gruyter.

Alexander, R. D. (1990). Epigenetic rules and Darwinian algorithms: The adaptive study of learning and development. *Ethology and Sociobiology* 11, 241–303.

Anderson, J. D. (1996). *The Reality of Illusion: An Ecological Approach to Cognitive Film Theory.* Carbondale: Southern Illinois University Press.

Anderson, L. R. (1988). *Bennett, Wells, and Conrad: Narrative in Transition.* New York: St. Martin's Press.

Argyros, A. J. (1991). *A Blessed Rage for Order: Deconstruction, Evolution, and Chaos.* Ann Arbor: University of Michigan Press.

Aristotle (1982). *Aristotle's "Poetics"* (J. Hutton, trans.) New York: W.W. Norton.

Armstrong, I. (1990). Introduction. In J. Austen, *Pride and Prejudice* (J. Kingsley, ed.) (pp. vii–xxx). New York: Oxford University Press.

Armstrong, N. (1981). Inside Greimas's square: Literary characters and cultural constraints. In W. Steiner (ed.), *The Sign in Music and Literature* (pp. 52–66). Austin: University of Texas Press.

Armstrong, N. (1987). *Desire and Domestic Fiction: A Political History of the Novel.* New York: Oxford University Press.

Arnhart, L. (1998). *Darwinian Natural Right: The Biological Ethics of Human Nature.* Albany: State University of New York Press.

Arnold, M. (1962a). Democracy. In R. H. Super (ed.), *The Complete Prose Works of Matthew Arnold* (vol. 2, pp. 3–211). Ann Arbor: University of Michigan Press. (Original work published 1861)

Arnold, M. (1962b). The function of criticism at the present time. In R. H. Super (ed.), *The Complete Prose Works of Matthew Arnold* (vol. 3, pp. 258–285). Ann Arbor: University of Michigan Press. (Original work published 1864)

Arnold, M. (1965). *Culture and Anarchy.* In R. H. Super (ed.), *The Complete Prose Works of Matthew Arnold* (vol. 5, pp. 85–256). Ann Arbor: University of Michigan Press. (Original work published 1869)

Arnold, M. (1974). Literature and science. In R. H. Super (ed.), *The Complete Prose Works of Matthew Arnold* (vol. 10, pp. 53–73). Ann Arbor: University of Michigan Press. (Original work published 1882)

Arnold, M. (1979). Preface to the first edition of *Poems.* In R. H. Super (ed.), *The Complete Prose Works of Matthew Arnold* (vol. 1, pp. 1–15). Ann Arbor: University of Michigan Press. (Original work published 1853)

Ashton, M. C., Paunonen, S. V., Helmes, E., and Jackson, D. N. (1998). Kin altruism, reciprocal altruism, and the big five personality factors. *Evolution and Human Behavior,* 19, 243–255.

Asimov. I., and Silverberg, R. (1992). *The Ugly Little Boy.* New York: Doubleday.

Atran, S. (1990). *Cognitive Foundations of Natural History: Towards an Anthropology of Science.* Cambridge: Cambridge University Press.

Auel, J. (1981). *The Clan of the Cave Bear.* New York: Bantam Books.

Auel, J. (1983). *The Valley of Horses.* New York: Bantam Books.

Auerbach, N. (1978). *Communities of Women: An Idea in Fiction.* Cambridge, MA: Harvard University Press.

Austen, J. (1993). *Pride and Prejudice: An Authoritative Text, Backgrounds, Reviews, and Essays in Criticism* (D. J. Gray, ed., 2nd ed.). New York: W.W. Norton. (Original work published 1813)

Austen, J. (1998). *Sense and Sensibility* (J. Kinsley, ed.). Oxford: Oxford University Press. (Original work published 1811)

Babb, H. S. (1954). *The Novels of William Golding.* Columbus: Ohio State University Press.

Bailey, J. M. (1997). Are genetically based individual differences compatible with species-wide adaptations? In N. L. Segal, G. E. Weisfeld, and C. C. Weisfeld (eds.), *Uniting Psychology and Biology: Integrative Perspectives on Human Development* (pp. 81–100). Washington, DC: American Psychological Association.

Bailey, J. M. (1998). Can behavior genetics contribute to evolutionary behavioral science? In C. C. Crawford and D. L. Krebs (eds.), *Handbook of Evolutionary Psychology: Ideas, Issues, Applications* (pp. 211–233). Mahway, NJ: Lawrence Erlbaum Associates.

Baker, B. (1982). *O Pioneers!* The problem of structure. *Great Plains Quarterly,* 2, 218–223.

Barash, D. P. (1997). In search of behavioral individuality. *Human Nature,* 8, 153–169.

Barash, D. P., and Barash, N. (2002, October 18). Biology as a lens: Evolution and literary criticism. *Chronicle of Higher Education,* 49, B7–B9.

Barkow, J.H. (1989). *Darwin, Sex, and Status: Biological Approaches to Mind and Culture.* Toronto: University of Toronto Press.

Barkow, J. H. (1990). Beyond the DP/DSS controversy. *Ethology and Sociobiology,* 11, 341–351.

Baron-Cohen, S. (1996). *Mindblindness: An Essay on Autism and Theory of Mind.* Cambridge, MA: MIT Press.

Baron-Cohen, S., Tager-Flusberg, H., and Cohen, D. J. (eds.). (2000). *Understanding Other Minds: Perspectives from Developmental Cognitive Neuroscience* (2nd ed.). Oxford: Oxford University Press.

Barrett, L., Dunbar, R., and Lycett, J. (2002). *Human Evolutionary Psychology.* Princeton, NJ: Princeton University Press.

Barrish, P. (1991). Accumulating variation: Darwin's *On the Origin of Species* and contemporary literary and cultural theory. *Victorian Studies,* 34, 431–453.

Barrow, J. D. (1995). *The Artful Universe.* Oxford: Clarendon Press.

Barthes, R. (1972). To write: An intransitive verb? In R. Macksey and E. Donato (eds.), *The Structuralist Controversy: The Languages of Criticism and the Sciences of Man.* Baltimore, MD: Johns Hopkins University Press.

Bate, J. (1991). *Romantic Ecology: Wordsworth and the Environmental Tradition.* New York: Routledge.

Bauer, H. P. (1992). Spiritual maternity and self-fulfillment in Arnold Bennett's *Anna of the Five Towns.* In M. Pearlman (ed.), *The Anna Book: Searching for Anna in Literary History.* Westport, CT: Greenwood.

Bedaux, J. B., and Cooke, B. (eds.). (1999). *Sociobiology and the Arts.* Amsterdam: Editions Rodopi.

Beer, G. (1983). *Darwin's Plots: Evolutionary Narrative in Darwin, George Eliot, and Nineteenth-Century Fiction.* London: Routledge.

Beja, M. (1979). *Film and Literature: An Introduction.* New York: Longman.

Belsey, C. (2002). Making space: Perspective vision and the Lacanian real. *Textual Practice,* 16, 31–55.

Bender, B. (1996). *The Descent of Love: Darwin and the Theory of Sexual Selection in American Fiction, 1871–1926.* Philadelphia: University of Pennsylvania Press.

Bennett, A. (1997). *Anna of the Five Towns* (P. Preston, ed.). London: J. M. Dent. (Original work published 1902)

Betzig, L. (1986). *Despotism and Differential Reproduction: A Darwinian View of History.* Hawthorne, NY: Aldine de Gruyter.

Betzig, L. (1991). History. In M. Maxwell (ed.), *The Sociobiological Imagination.* Albany: State University of New York.

Betzig, L. (1998). Not whether to count babies, but which. In C. C. Crawford and D. L. Krebs (eds.), *Handbook of Evolutionary Psychology: Ideas, Issues, Applications* (pp. 265–273). Mahway, NJ: Lawrence Erlbaum Associates.

Betzig, L. (ed.). (1997). *Human Nature: A Critical Reader.* New York: Oxford University Press.

Bickerton, D. (1990). *Language and Species.* Chicago: University of Chicago Press.

Bierce, A. (1946). *The Devil's Dictionary.* In C. Fadiman (ed.), *The Collected Writings of Ambrose Bierce* (pp. 187–392). Secaucus, NJ: Citadel.

Biles, J. I. (1970). *Talk: Conversations with William Golding.* New York: Harcourt Brace Jovanovich.

Blake, W. (1965). Annotations to the works of Sir Joshua Reynolds (E. Malone, ed.), in D. V. Erdman & H. Bloom (Eds.), *The Poetry and Prose of William Blake.* Garden City, NY: Doubleday.

Bluestone, G. (1957). *Novel into Film.* Berkeley: University of California Press.

Booth, W. (1996). Distance and point of view: An essay in classification. In M. J. Hoffman and P. D. Murphy (eds.), *Essentials of the Theory of Fiction* (pp. 116–133). Durham, NC: Duke University Press.

Bouchard, T. J., Jr. (1994, June 17). Genes, environment, and personality. *Science,* 264, 1700–1701.

Bouchard, T. J., Jr. (1997). The genetics of personality. In K. Blum and E. P. Noble (eds.), *Handbook of Psychiatric Genetics* (pp. 267–290). Boca Raton, FL: CRC Press.

Bowlby, J. (1973). *Attachment and Loss:* vol. 2. *Separation: Anxiety and Anger.* New York: Basic Books.

Bowlby, J. (1980). *Attachment and Loss:* vol. 3. *Loss.* New York: Basic Books.

Bowlby, J. (1982). *Attachment and loss:* vol. 1. *Attachment* (2nd edition). New York: Basic Books.

Bowlby, J. (1990). *Charles Darwin: A New Life.* New York: W.W. Norton.

Bowler, P. J. (1989). *Evolution: The History of an Idea.* Berkeley: University of California Press.

Boyd, B. (1998). "Jane, meet Charles": Literature, evolution, and human nature. *Philosophy and Literature,* 22, 1–30.

Boyd, B. (1999). Literature and discovery. *Philosophy and Literature,* 23, 313–333.

Boyd, B. (2001). The origin of stories: *Horton Hears a Who. Philosophy and Literature,* 25, 197–214.

Boyd, B. (in press). Evolutionary theories of art. In J. Gottschall and D. S. Wilson, (eds.), *Literature and the Human Animal.* Evanston, IL: Northwestern University Press.

Boyd, B. (in press). Kind and unkindness: Aaron in *Titus Andronicus.* In B. Boyd (ed.), *Words that Count: Essays on Early Modern Authorship in Honor of MacDonald P. Jackson.* Newark, NJ: University of Delaware Press.

Boyd, B. (in press). Laughter and literature: A play theory of humor. *Philosophy and Literature.*

Boyum, J. (1989). *Double Exposure: Fiction into Film.* New York: Mentor.

Bradley, A. C. (1929). Jane Austen. In *A Miscellany* (pp. 32–72). London: Macmillan and Company.

Bridgeman, B. (2003). *Psychology and Evolution: The Origins of Mind.* Thousand Oaks, CA: Sage.

Brontë, C. (1990). *Villette* (M. Smith and H. Rosengarten, eds.). Oxford: Oxford University Press. (Original work published 1853)

Brontë, E. (2003). *Wuthering Heights: The 1847 Text, Backgrounds, and Criticism* (R. J. Dunn, ed., 4th edition). New York: W.W. Norton. (Original work published 1847)

Brooks, C. (1947). *The Well Wrought Urn: Studies in the Structure of Poetry.* New York: Harcourt, Brace, World.

Brooks, C., and Warren, R. P. (1949). *Modern Rhetoric.* New York: Harcourt.

Brooks, C., and Warren, R. P. (1976). *Understanding Poetry* (4th edition). New York: Holt, Rinehart, and Winston.

Brown, D. E. (1991). *Human Universals.* Philadelphia, PA: Temple University Press.

Brown, D. E. (2000). *Human Universals and Their Implications.* In N. Roughley (ed.), *Being Humans: Anthropological Universality and Particularity in Transdisciplinary Perspectives* (pp. 156–174). New York: Walter de Gruyter.

Browne, J. (1995). *Charles Darwin: Voyaging.* New York: Alfred A. Knopf.

Browning, R. (1981). An essay on Percy Bysshe Shelley. *The Complete Works of Robert Browning, with Variant Readings and Annotations* (R. A. King, J. W. Herring, P. Honan, A. N. Kincaid, and A. C. Dooley, eds., vol. 5), (pp. 135–151). Athens: Ohio University Press.

Brownstein, R. M. (1988). Jane Austen: Irony and authority. *Women's Studies,* 15, 57–70.

Buell, L. (1995). *The Environmental Imagination: Thoreau, Nature Writing, and the Formation of American Culture.* Cambridge, MA: Harvard University Press.

Buss, D. M. (1990). Toward a biologically informed psychology of personality. *Journal of Personality,* 58, 1–16.

Buss, D. M. (1994). *The Evolution of Desire: Strategies of Human Mating.* New York: Basic Books.

Buss, D. M. (1995). Evolutionary psychology: A new paradigm for psychological science. *Psychological Inquiry,* 6, 1–30.

Buss, D. M. (1999). *Evolutionary Psychology: The New Science of the Mind.* Boston: Allyn & Bacon.

Buss, D. (2000). *The Dangerous Passion: Why Jealousy Is as Necessary as Love and Sex.* New York: Free Press.

Butler, M. (1975). *Jane Austen and the War of Ideas.* Oxford: Clarendon Press.

Cain, W. (1984). *The Crisis in Criticism: Theory, Literature, and Reform in English Studies.* Baltimore: Johns Hopkins University Press.

Campbell, D. T. (1988). *Methodology and Epistemology for Social Science: Selected Papers* (E. S. Overman, ed.). Chicago: University of Chicago Press.

Campbell, S. (1996). The land and language of desire: Where deep ecology and post-structuralism meet. In C. Glotfelty and H. Fromm (eds.), *The Ecocriticism Reader: Landmarks in Literary Ecology* (pp. 124–136). Athens: University of Georgia Press.

Cardwell, S. (2000). Present(ing) tense: Temporality and tense in comparative theories of literature-film adaptation. *Scope.* Retrieved June 2, 2001, from www.nottinghma.ac.uk/film/journal/articles/presenting-tense.htm

Carey, S., and Spelke, E. (1994). Domain-specific knowledge and conceptual change. In L. A. Hirschfeld and S. A. Gelman (eds.), *Mapping the Mind: Domain Specificity in Cognition and Culture* (pp. 169–200). Cambridge: Cambridge University Press.

Carlisle, J. (1979). The face in the mirror: *Villette* and the conventions of autobiography. *ELH,* 46, 262–289.

Carroll, J. (1982). *The Cultural Theory of Matthew Arnold.* Berkeley: University of California Press.

Carroll, J. (1994). Arnold, Matthew. In M. Groden and M. Kreiswirth (eds.), *The Johns Hopkins Guide to Literary Theory and Criticism* (pp. 45–48). Baltimore, MD: Johns Hopkins University Press.

Carroll, J. (1995). *Evolution and Literary Theory.* Columbia: University of Missouri Press.

Carroll, J. (1998). Arnold, Matthew. In M. Kelly (ed.), *Encyclopedia of Aesthetics,* vol. 1 (pp. 114–118). New York: Oxford University Press.

Carroll, J. (2003a). Adaptationist literary study: An emerging research program. *Style,* 36, 596–617.

Carroll, J. (2003b). Introduction. In C. Darwin, *On the Origin of Species by Means of Natural Selection* (J. Carroll, ed.), (pp. 9–75). Peterborough, Ontario: Broadview.

Carroll, J. (in press). Evolutionary psychology and literature. In D. Buss (ed.), *The Evolutionary Psychology Handbook.* Hoboken, NJ: John Wiley & Sons.

Carroll, N. (1988). *Mystifying Movies: Fads and Fallacies in Contemporary Film Theory.* New York: Columbia University Press.

Carruthers, P., and Smith, P. K. (eds.). (1996). *Theories of Theories of Mind.* Cambridge: Cambridge University Press.

Cather, W. (1995). *O Pioneers!* (D. Grumbach, ed.). Boston: Houghton Mifflin. (Original work published 1913)

Chagnon, N. A. (1979). *Yanomamö: The Fierce People* (3rd edition). New York: Holt, Rinehart, and Winston.

Chagnon, N. A, and Irons, W. (eds.). (1979). *Evolutionary Biology and Human Social Behavior: An Anthropological Perspective.* North Scituate, MA: Duxbury Press.

Charles, P. D. (1965). Love and death in Willa Cather's *O Pioneers! CLA Journal,* 9, 140–150.

Chiappe, D. L. (2000). Metaphor, modularity, and the evolution of conceptual integration. *Metaphor and Symbol,* 15, 137–158.

Chiappe, D. L. and MacDonald, K. B. (2003). *The Evolution of Domain-general Mechanisms in Intelligence and Learning.* Manuscript submitted for publication.

Clark, R. (ed.) (1994). *Sense and Sensibility and Pride and Prejudice—Jane Austen.* New York: St. Martin's.

Coleridge, S. T. (1984). *Biographia Literaria* (J. Engell and W. J. Bate, eds., vols. 1–2 in one vol.), in K. Coburn and B. Winer (eds.), *The Collected Works of Samuel Taylor Coleridge* (vol. 7). Princeton, NJ: Princeton University Press.

Conrad, J. (1990). *The Secret Agent* (M. Seymour-Smith, ed.). London: Penguin. (Original work published 1907)

Conrad, J. (1995). *Heart of Darkness* (R. Hampson, ed.). London: Penguin. (Original work published 1902)

Constable, J. (1997). Verse forms: a pilot study in the epidemiology of representations. *Human Nature*, 8, 171–203.

Conway Morris, S. (1998). *The Crucible of Creation: The Burgess Shale and the Rise of Animals.* Oxford: Oxford University Press.

Cooke, B. (1995). Microplots: The case of *Swan Lake. Human Nature*, 6, 183–196.

Cooke, B. (1999a). Edward O. Wilson on art. In B. Cooke and F. Turner (eds.), *Biopoetics: Evolutionary Explorations in the Arts* (pp. 97–118). Lexington, KY: ICUS.

Cooke, B. (1999b). On the evolution of interest: Cases in serpent art. In D. H. Rosen and M. Luebbert (eds.), *Evolution of the Psyche* (pp. 150–168). Westport, CT: Praeger.

Cooke, B. (1999c). The promise of a biothematics. In J. B. Bedaux and B. Cooke (eds.), *Sociobiology and the Arts* (pp. 43–62). Amsterdam: Editions Rodopi.

Cooke, B. (1999d). Sexual property in Pushkin's "The Snowstorm": A Darwinist perspective. In B. Cooke and F. Turner (eds.), *Biopoetics: Evolutionary Explorations in the Arts* (pp. 175–204). Lexington, KY: ICUS.

Cooke, B. (2002). *Human Nature in Utopia: Zamyatin's We.* Evanston, IL: Northwestern University Press.

Cooke, B. (ed.). (2001). *Interdisciplinary Literary Studies* [Special issue on Darwinian literary study], 2 (2).

Cooke, B., and Turner, F. (eds.). (1999). *Biopoetics: Evolutionary Explorations in the Arts.* Lexington, KY: ICUS.

Cooper, F. T. (1984). Review of *O Pioneers!.* In J. J. Murphy (ed.), *Critical Essays on Willa Cather* (pp. 112–113; reprinted from *Bookman*, 37, August 1913, pp. 666–667). Boston: G.K. Hall.

Cosmides, L. Tooby, J. (1992). Cognitive adaptations for social exchange. In J. H. Barkow, L. Cosmides, and J. Tooby (eds.), *The Adapted Mind: Evolutionary Psychology and the Generation of Culture.* New York: Oxford University Press.

Cosmides, L., and Tooby, J. (1994). Origins of domain specificity: the evolution of functional organization. In L. A. Hirschfeld and S. A. Gelman (eds.), *Mapping the Mind: Domain Specificity in Cognition and Culture* (pp. 85–116). Cambridge: Cambridge University Press.

Costa, P. T., and Widiger, T. A. (eds.). (1994). *Personality Disorders and the Five-factor Model of Personality.* Washington, DC: American Psychological Association.

Crawford, C. (1998). Environments and adaptations: Then and now. In C. Crawford and D. L. Krebs, *Handbook of Evolutionary Psychology: Ideas, Issues, Applications* (pp. 275–302). Mahway, NJ: Lawrence Erlbaum Associates.

Crawford, C., and Krebs, D. L. (eds.). (1998). *Handbook of Evolutionary Psychology: Ideas, Issues, Applications.* Mahway, NJ: Lawrence Erlbaum Associates.

Crews, F. (2001). *Postmodern Pooh.* New York: Northpoint Press.

Cronk, L., Chagnon, N., and Irons, W. (2000). *Adaptation and Human Behavior: An Anthropological Perspective.* New York: Aldine de Gruyter.

Cureton, R. (1997a). Linguistics, stylistics, and poetics. *Language and Literature*, 22, 1–43.

Cureton, R. (1997b). Toward a temporal theory of language. *Journal of English Linguistics*, 25, 287–303.

Daiches, D. (1951). *Willa Cather: A Critical Introduction.* Ithaca, NY: Cornell University Press.

Daly, M., and Wilson, M. (1983). *Sex, Evolution, and Behavior* (2nd edition). Belmont, CA: Wadsworth.

Daly, M., and Wilson, M. (1988). *Homicide.* Hawthorne, NY: Aldine de Gruyter.

Daly, M., and Wilson, M. (1990). Is parent-offspring conflict sex-linked? Freudian and Darwinian models. *Journal of Personality*, 58, 163–189.

Damasio, A. (1994). *Descartes' Error: Emotion, Reason, and the Human Brain.* New York: G.P. Putnam.

Darwin, C. (1845). *Journal of Researches into the Geology and Natural History of the Various Countries Visited by H.M.S. Beagle, Under the Command of Captain Fitzroy from 1832 to 1836* (2nd edition). London: Murray.

Darwin, C. (1958). *The Autobiography of Charles Darwin, 1809–1882. With Original Omissions Restored* (N. Barlow, ed.). London: Collins. (Original work published 1892)

Darwin, C. (1959). *The Life and Letters of Charles Darwin, Including an Autobiographical Chapter* (F. Darwin, ed., vols. 1–2). New York: Basic Books. (Original work published 1887)

Darwin, C. (1981). *The Descent of Man, and Selection in Relation to Sex* (J. T. Bonner and R. M. May, eds., 2 vols. in 1). Princeton, NJ: Princeton University Press. (Original work published 1871)

Darwin, C. (1998). *The Expression of the Emotions in Man and Animals* (P. Ekman, ed.) (3rd edition). New York: Oxford University Press. (Original work published 1872)

Darwin, C. (2003). *On the Origin of Species by Means of Natural Selection* (J. Carroll, ed.). Peterborough, Ontario: Broadview. (Original work published 1859)

Darwin, C., and Wallace, A. R. (1958). *Evolution by Natural Selection* (G. de Beer, ed.). Cambridge: Cambridge University Press. (Contains Darwin's 1842 sketch and 1844 manuscript, and the 1858 Linnaean Society papers by Darwin and Wallace)

Dawkins, R. (1982). *The Extended Phenotype: The Gene as the Unit of Selection.* San Francisco: Freeman.

Dawkins, R. (1987). *The Blind Watchmaker.* New York: W.W. Norton.

Dawkins, R. (1989). *The Selfish Gene* (new edition). Oxford: Oxford University Press.

Dawkins, R. (1995). A survival machine. In J. Brockman (ed.), *The Third Culture: Beyond the Scientific Revolution.* New York: Simon and Schuster.

Degler, C. (1991). *In Search of Human Nature: The Decline and Revival of Darwinism in American Social Thought.* Oxford: Oxford University Press.

DeLaura, D. J. (1973). Matthew Arnold. In D. J. DeLaura (ed.), *Victorian Prose: A Guide to Research* (pp. 249–320). New York: Modern Language Association.

Dennett, D. C. (1995). *Darwin's Dangerous Idea: Evolution and the Meanings of Life.* New York: Simon and Schuster.

Derrida, J. (1976). *Of Grammatology* (G. C. Spivak, trans.). Baltimore: Johns Hopkins University Press.

Derrida, J. (1981). The law of genre. In W. J. T. Mitchell (ed.), *On Narrative.* Chicago: University of Chicago Press.

Desmond, A. and Moore, J. (1992). *Darwin.* New York: Warner.

Devall, B., and Sessions, G. (1985). *Deep Ecology: Living as if Nature Mattered.* Salt Lake City: Gibbs M. Smith.

De Waal, F. (1996). *Good Natured: The Origins of Right and Wrong in Humans and Other Animals.* Cambridge, MA: Harvard University Press.

Diamond, J. (1992). *The Third Chimpanzee: The Evolution and Future of the Human Animal.* New York: HarperCollins.

Dickens, C. (1956). *Bleak House* (M. D. Zabel, ed.). Boston: Houghton Mifflin. (Original work published 1853)

Digman, J. M. (1990). Personality structure: Emergence of the five-factor model. *Annual Review of Psychology,* 41, 417–440.

Dissanayake, E. (1988). *What Is Art For?* Seattle: University of Washington Press.

Dissanayake, E. (1995a). Chimera, spandrel, or adaptation: Conceptualizing art in human evolution. *Human Nature,* 6, 99–117.

Dissanayake, E. (1995b). *Homo Aestheticus: Where Art Comes From and Why.* Seattle: University of Washington Press. (Original work published 1992)

Dissanayake, E. (2000). *Art and Intimacy: How the Arts Began.* Seattle: University of Washington Press.

Dissanayake, E. (2001). Aesthetic incunabula. *Philosophy and Literature,* 25, 335–346.

Dissanayake, E. (in press). Art in global context: An evolutionary/functionalist perspective for the twenty-first century. *International Journal of Anthropology.*

Drabble, M. (1974). *Arnold Bennett.* New York: Alfred A. Knopf.

Dryden, J. (1970). Of dramatic poesy: An essay. In J. Kinsley and G. Parfitt (eds.), *Selected Criticism* (pp. 16–76). Oxford: Oxford University Press.

Duckworth, A. (1971). *The Improvement of the Estate: A Study in Jane Austen's Novels.* Baltimore, MD: Johns Hopkins University Press.

Dunbar, R., Nettle, D., and Stiller, J. (2003). *Drama as the Mirror of the Mind: Exploring the Psychological Underpinnings of Shakespeare's Plays.* Manuscript in preparation.

Duncan, I. (1991). Darwin and the savages. *Yale Journal of Criticism,* 4, 13–45.

Dupré, J. (1998, May 29). Unification not proved. *Science,* 280, 1395.

Easterlin, N. (1993). Play, mutation, and reality acceptance: Toward a theory of literary experience. In N. Easterlin and B. Riebling (eds.), *After Poststructuralism: Interdisciplinary and Literary Theory* (pp. 105–125). Evanston, IL: Northwestern University Press.

Easterlin, N. (1999a). Do cognitive predispositions predict or determine literary value judgments? Narrativity, plot, and aesthetics. In B. Cooke and F. Turner (eds.), *Biopoetics: Evolutionary Explorations in the Arts* (pp. 241–262). Lexington, KY: ICUS.

Easterlin, N. (1999b). Making knowledge: Bioepistemology and the foundations of literary theory. *Mosaic*, 32, 131–147.

Easterlin, N. (2000). Psychoanalysis and the "discipline of love." *Philosophy and Literature*, 24, 261–279.

Easterlin, N. (2001a). Hans Christian Andersen's fish out of water. *Philosophy and Literature*, 25, 251–277.

Easterlin, N. (2001b). Voyages in the verbal universe: The role of speculation in Darwinian literary criticism. *Interdisciplinary Literary Studies*, 2, 59–73.

Easterlin, N. (2002). Romanticism's gray matter. *Philosophy and Literature*, 443–455.

Easterlin, N., and Riebling, B. (eds.). (1993). *After Poststructuralism: Interdisciplinarity and Literary Theory*. Evanston, IL: Northwestern University Press.

Eaves, L. J., Eysenck, H. J., and Martin, N. G. (1989). *Genes, Culture, and Personality: An Empirical Approach*. London: Harcourt.

Eibl-Eibesfeldt, I. (1989). *Human Ethology*. Hawthorne, NY: Aldine de Gruyter.

Ekman, P. (1994). Antecedent events and emotion metaphors. In P. Ekman and R. J. Davidson (eds.), *The Nature of Emotion: Fundamental Questions* (pp. 146–149). New York: Oxford University Press.

Ekman, P. (2003). *Emotions Revealed: Recognizing Faces and Feelings to Improve Communication and Emotional Life*. New York: Henry Holt.

Ekman, P., and Davidson, R. J. (eds.). (1994). *The Nature of Emotion: Fundamental Questions*. New York: Oxford University Press.

Eliot, G. (2000). *Middlemarch: An Authoritative Text, Backgrounds, Reviews, and Criticism* (B. G. Hornback, ed., 2nd edition). New York: W.W. Norton. (Original work published 1871– 1872)

Ellis, J. M. (1997). *Literature Lost: Social Agendas and the Corruption of the Humanities*. New Haven, CT: Yale University Press.

Evans, D. A. (1998). Evolution and literature. *South Dakota Review*, 36 (4), 33–45.

Everett, B. (1986). Golding's pity. In John Carey (ed.), *William Golding: The Man and His Books: A Tribute on His 75th Birthday* (pp. 110–125). London: Faber & Faber.

Eysenck, H. J. (1967). *The Biological Basis of Personality*. Springfield, IL: Charles C. Thomas.

Eysenck, H. J. (1979). *The Structure and Measurement of Intelligence*. Berlin: Springer-Verlag.

Eysenck, H. J. (1980). The biosocial nature of man. *Journal of Social and Biological Structures*, 3, 125–134.

Eysenck, H. J. (1995). *Genius: The Natural History of Creativity*. Cambridge: Cambridge University Press.

Eysenck, H. J., and Eysenck, M. W. (1985). *Personality and Individual Differences: A Natural Science Approach*. New York: Plenum.

Eysenck, H. J., and Wilson, G. D. (1978). Conclusion: Ideology and the study of social attitudes. In H. J. Eysenck and G. D. Wilson (eds.). *The Psychological Basis of Ideology*. Baltimore, MD: University Park Press.

Fish, S. (1989). *Doing What Comes Naturally: Change, Rhetoric, and the Practice of Theory in Literary and Legal Studies*. Durham, NC: Duke University Press.

Foley, R. A. (1996). The adaptive legacy of human evolution: A search for the environment of evolutionary adaptedness. *Evolutionary Anthropology*, 4, 194–203.

Foucault, M. (1972). *The Archaeology of Knowledge and the Discourse on Language* (A. M. Sheridan Smith, trans.). New York: Pantheon.

Foucault, M. (1973). *The Order of Things: An Archaeology of the Human Sciences*. New York: Vintage.

Foucault, M. (1977). *Language, Counter-memory, Practice: Selected Essays and Interviews* (D. F. Bouchard and S. Simon, trans., D. F. Bouchard, ed.). Ithaca, NY: Cornell University Press.

Fox, R. (1989). *The Search for Society: Quest for a Biosocial Science and Morality*. New Brunswick, NJ: Rutgers University Press.

Fox, R. (1995). Sexual conflict in the epics. *Human Nature*, 6, 135–144.

Fox, W. (1989). "The deep ecology-ecofeminism debate and its parallels. *Environmental Ethics*, 11, 5–25.

Fraiman, S. (1989). The humiliation of Elizabeth Bennet. In P. Yaeger and B. Kowaleski-Wallace (eds.), *Refiguring the Father: New Feminist Readings of Patriarchy* (pp. 168–187). Carbondale: Southern Illinois University Press.

Frank, R. (1988). *Passions within Reason: The Strategic Role of the Emotions*. New York: W.W. Norton.

Freeman, D. (1992). Paradigms in collision. *Academic Questions*, 5, 23–33.

Freeman, D. (1999). *The Fateful Hoaxing of Margaret Mead: A Historical Analysis of Her Samoan Research*. Boulder, CO: Westview.

Freud, S. (1959). Creative writers and daydreaming. In J. Strachey (ed. and trans.), *The Standard Edition of the Complete Psychological Works of Sigmund Freud*. (vol. 9, pp. 142–153). London: Hogarth. (Original work published 1907)

Friedman, L. S. (1993). *William Golding*. New York: Frederick Ungar.

Fromm, H. (1996). From transcendence to obsolescence: A route map. In C. Glotfelty and H. Fromm (eds.), *The Ecocriticism Reader: Landmarks in Literary Ecology* (pp. 30–39). Athens: University of Georgia Press.

Fromm, H. (1998). Ecology and ecstasy on Interstate 80. *Hudson Review*, 51, 65–78.

Fromm, H. (2001). A crucifix for Dracula: Wendell Berry meets Edward O. Wilson. *Hudson Review*, 53, 657–664.

Fromm, H. (2003a). The new Darwinism in the humanities: From Plato to Pinker. *Hudson Review*, 56, 89–99.

Fromm, H. (2003b). The new Darwinism in the humanities, part two: Back to nature again. *Hudson Review*, 56, 315–327.

Frye, N. (1957). *Anatomy of Criticism: Four Essays*. Princeton, NJ: Princeton University Press.

Frye, N. (1971). *The Critical Path: An Essay on the Social Context of Literary Criticism*. Bloomington: Indiana University Press.

The function of Matthew Arnold at the present time [special section]. (1983). *Critical Inquiry*, 9, 415–516.

Gaulin, S. J. C., and McBurney, D. H. (2001). *Psychology: An Evolutionary Approach*. Upper Saddle River, NJ: Prentice Hall.

Gazzaniga, M. S. (1997). What are brains for? In R. L. Solso (ed.), *Mind and Brain Sciences in the Twenty-First Century* (pp. 157–171). Cambridge, MA: MIT Press.

Geary, D. C. (1998). *Male, Female: The Evolution of Human Sex Differences*. Washington, DC: American Psychological Association.

Geary, D. C., and K. J. Huffman. (2002). Brain and cognitive evolution: Forms of modularity and functions of mind. *Psychological Bulletin*, 128, 667–698.

Ghiselin, M. (1969). *The Triumph of the Darwinian Method*. Chicago: University of Chicago Press.

Giddings, R., Selby, K., and Wensley, C. (1990). *Screening the Novel: The Theory and Practice of Literary Dramatization*. New York: St. Martin's.

Gilbert, S. M., and Gubar, S. (1979). *The Madwoman in the Attic: The Woman Writer and the Nineteenth-Century Literary Imagination*. New Haven, CT: Yale University Press.

Glotfelty, C., and Fromm, H. (eds.). (1996). *The Ecocriticism Reader: Landmarks in Literary Ecology*. Athens: University of Georgia Press.

Goldberg, S. (1993). *Why Men Rule: A Theory of Male Dominance*. Chicago: Open Court.

Golding, W. (1955). *The Inheritors*. San Diego: Harcourt.

Gose, E. B. (1963). Psychic evolution: Darwinism and initiation in *Tess*. *Nineteenth-Century Fiction*, 18, 261–272.

Gottschall, J. (2001). Homer's human animal: Ritual combat in the *Iliad*. *Philosophy and Literature*, 25, 278–294.

Gottschall, J. (in press). An evolutionary perspective on Homer's invisible daughters. *Interdisciplinary Literary Studies*.

Gottschall, J. (in press). The heroine with a thousand faces. In J. Gottschall and D. S. Wilson (eds.), *Literature and the Human Animal*. Evanston, IL: Northwestern University Press.

Gottschall, J. (in press). Patterns of characterization in folk tales across geographic regions and levels of cultural complexity: Literature as a neglected source of quantitative data. *Human Nature*.

Gottschall, J. (in press). The tree of knowledge and Darwinian literary study. *Philosophy and Literature*.

Gottschall, J., Allison, E., De Rosa, J., and Klockeman, K. (in press). Can literary study be scientific? Results of an empirical search for the virgin/whore dichotomy. *Interdisciplinary Literary Studies*.

Gould, S. J. (1980). Is a new and general theory of evolution emerging? *Paleobiology*, 6, 119–130.

Gould, S. J. (1982, April 23). Darwinism and the expansion of evolutionary theory. *Science*, 216, 380–387.

Gould, S. J. (1984). *Hen's Teeth and Horse's Toes*. New York: W.W. Norton.

Gould, S. J. (1989). *Wonderful Life: The Burgess Shale and the Nature of History.* New York: W.W. Norton.

Gould, S. J. (1992, January 16). The paradox of genius. *Nature,* 355, 215–16.

Gould, S. J. (1995). Introduction. In B. Kurtén, *Dance of the Tiger: A Novel of the Ice Age* (pp. xii–xix). Berkeley: University of California Press.

Gould, S. J. (1997, June 12). Darwinian fundamentalism. *The New York Review of Books* 44 (10), 34–37.

Gould, S. J. (2002). *The Structure of Evolutionary Theory.* Cambridge, MA: Harvard University Press.

Gould, S. J., and Lewontin, R. J. (1979). The spandrels of San Marco and the panglossian paradigm: A critique of the adaptationist programme. *Proceedings of the Royal Society of London* (Series B), 205, 581–598.

Gould, S. J., and Vrba, E. S. (1982). Exaptation—a missing term in the science of form. *Paleobiology,* 8, 4–15.

Graff, G. (1987). *Professing Literature: An Institutional History.* Chicago: University of Chicago Press.

Grene, M. (1993). Recent biographies of Darwin: The complexity of context. *Perspectives on Science,* 1, 659–675.

Griffiths, P. E. (1997). *What Emotions Really Are: The Problem of Psychological Categories.* Chicago: University of Chicago Press.

Gross, P. R. (2002). The apotheosis of Stephen Jay Gould. *The New Criterion,* 21 (2), 77–80.

Gross, P. R., and Levitt, N. (1994). *Higher Superstition: The Academic Left and Its Quarrels with Science.* Baltimore: Johns Hopkins University Press.

Gross, P. R., Levitt, N., and Lewis, M. W. (eds.). (1997). *The Flight from Science and Reason.* Baltimore, MD: Johns Hopkins University Press.

Haack, S. (1998). The ants and us. *Academic Questions,* 11(3), 64–68.

Hall, J. (1959). *Arnold Bennett: Primitivism and Taste.* Seattle: University of Washington Press.

Halliday, E. M. (1960). Narrative perspective in *Pride and Prejudice. Nineteenth-Century Fiction,* 15, 65–71.

Hamilton, W. D. (1996). Evolution of social behavior. In *Narrow Roads of Gene Land: The Collected Papers of W. D. Hamilton* (vol. 1). Oxford: W.H. Freeman.

Hamilton, W. D. (2001). Evolution of sex. In *Narrow Roads of Gene Land: The Collected Papers of W. D. Hamilton* (vol. 2). Oxford: Oxford University Press.

Handler, R., and Segal, D. (1990). *Jane Austen and the Fiction of Culture: An Essay on the Narration of Social Realities.* Tucson: University of Arizona Press.

Harding, D. W. (1940). "Regulated hatred": An aspect in the work of Jane Austen. *Scrutiny,* 8, 346–347, 351–354, 362.

Hardy, T. (1991). *Tess of the d'Urbervilles: An Authoritative Text, Backgrounds and Sources, Criticism* (S. Elledge, ed., 3rd edition). New York: W.W. Norton. (Original work published 1891)

Hart, F. Elizabeth. (2001). The epistemology of cognitive literary studies. *Philosophy and Literature,* 25, 314–334.

Hassan, I. (1986). Pluralism in postmodern perspective. *Critical Inquiry,* 12, 503–520.

Heilman, R. B. (1991). Innovations in gothic: Charlotte Brontë. In *The Workings of Fiction: Essays by Robert Berchtold Heilman* (pp. 41–54). Columbia: University of Missouri Press.

Hernadi, P. (1976). Literary theory: A compass for critics. *Critical Inquiry,* 3, 369–386

Herrnstein, R. J., and Murray, C. (1994). *The Bell Curve: Intelligence and Class Structure in American Life.* New York: The Free Press.

Hirsch, E. D. (1967). *Validity in Interpretation.* New Haven, CT: Yale University Press.

Hirsch, E. D. (1976). *The Aims of Interpretation.* Chicago: University of Chicago Press.

Hrdy, S. B. (1999). *Mother Nature: A History of Mothers, Infants, and Natural Selection.* New York: Pantheon.

Hughes, T. (1986). Baboons and Neanderthals: A rereading of *The Inheritors.* In J. Carey (ed.), *William Golding: The Man and His Books: A Tribute on His 75th Birthday* (pp. 161–168). London: Faber & Faber.

Hull, D. L. (1988). *Science as a Process: An Evolutionary Account of the Social and Conceptual Development of Science.* Chicago: University of Chicago Press.

Human Nature: An Interdisciplinary Biosocial Perspective. (1995). 6 (2) [special issue on Darwinian literary study].

Huxley, A. (1932). *Brave New World.* New York: HarperPerennial.

Irons, W. (1979). Cultural and biological success. In N. A. Chagnon and W. Irons (eds.), *Evolutionary Biology and Human Social Behavior: An Anthropological Perspective* (pp. 257–272). North Scituate, MA: Duxbury Press.

Irons, W. (1990). Let's make our perspective broader rather than narrower: A comment on Turke's "Which humans behave adaptively, and what does it matter?" *Ethology and Sociobiology*, 11, 361–374.

Irons, W. (1998). Adaptively relevant environments versus the environment of evolutionary adaptedness. *Evolutionary Anthropology*, 6, 194–204.

Jameson, F. (1991). *Postmodernism, or, the Cultural Logic of Late Capitalism*. Durham, NC: Duke University Press.

Jensen, A. R. (1998). *The g Factor: The Science of Mental Ability*. Westport, CT: Praeger.

Jobling, I. (2001a). Personal justice and homicide in Scott's *Ivanhoe*: An evolutionary psychological perspective. *Interdisciplinary Literary Studies*, 2, 29–43.

Jobling, I. (2001b). The psychological foundations of the hero-ogre story: A cross-cultural study. *Human Nature*, 12, 247–272.

Jobling, I. (2002). Byron as cad. *Philosophy and Literature*, 26, 296–311.

Johnson, B. (1977). "The perfection of species" and Hardy's *Tess*. In U. C. Knoepflmacher and G. B. Tennyson (eds.), *Nature and the Victorian Imagination*. Berkeley: University of California Press.

Johnson, C. L. (1988). *Jane Austen: Women, Politics, and the Novel*. Chicago: University of Chicago Press.

Johnson, M. 1987). *The Body in the Mind: The Bodily Basis of Meaning, Imagination, and Reason*. Chicago: University of Chicago Press.

Johnson, S. (1969). *The Rambler* (W. J. Bate and A. B. Strauss, eds.), in H. W. Liebert et al. (eds.), *The Yale Edition of the Works of Samuel Johnson* (vol. 3). New Haven, CT: Yale University Press.

Johnson, S. (1990). *Rasselas and Other Tales* (G. J. Kolb, ed.), in H. W. Liebert et al. (eds.), *The Yale Edition of the Works of Samuel Johnson* (vol. 16). New Haven, CT: Yale University Press.

Jones, S. (1998, April 23). In the genetic toyshop. *New York Review of Books*, 45 (7), 14–16.

Jung, C. (1966). On the relation of analytical psychology to poetry (R. F. C. Hull, trans.). In Sir H. Read, M. Fordham, G. Adler, and W. McGuire (eds.), *The Collected Works of C. G. Jung* (vol. 15, pp. 65–83). Princeton, NJ: Princeton University Press. (Original work published 1922)

Kellert, S. R. (1993). The biological basis for human values of nature. In S. R. Kellert and E. O. Wilson (eds.), *The Biophilia Hypothesis*. Washington, D.C.: Island Press.

Kermode, F. (1962). William Golding. In *Puzzles and Epiphanies: Essays and Reviews, 1958–1961* (pp. 198–213). New York: Chilmark Press.

Kinkead-Weekes, M., and Gregor, I. (1984). *William Golding: A Critical Study* (rev. edition). London: Faber & Faber.

Koch, W. A. (1993). *The Roots of Literature*. Bochum, Germany: Universitätsverlag Dr. Robert Brockmeyer.

Koertge, N. (ed.). (1998). *A House Built on Sand: Exposing Postmodern Myths about Science*. New York: Oxford University Press.

Kolodny, A. (1975). *The Lay of the Land: Metaphor as Experience and History in American Life and Letters*. Chapel Hill: University of North Carolina Press.

Kroeber, K. (1994). *Ecological Literary Criticism: Romantic Imagining and the Biology of Mind*. New York: Columbia University Press.

Kuhn, T. (1991). The road since structure. In A. Fine, M. Forbes, and L. Wessels (eds.), *PSA 1990: Proceedings of the 1990 Biennial Meeting of the Philosophy of Science Association*. 2 vols. East Lansing, MI: Philosophy of Science Association.

Kurtén, B. (1995). *Dance of the Tiger: A Novel of the Ice Age*. Berkeley: University of California Press. (Original work published 1978)

Lakoff, G. (1987). *Women, Fire, and Dangerous Things: What Categories Reveal about the Mind*. Chicago: University of Chicago Press.

Lakoff, G., and Johnson, M. (1980). *Metaphors We Live By*. Chicago: University of Chicago Press.

Lakoff, G., and Johnson, M. (1999). *Philosophy in the Flesh: The Embodied Mind and Its Challenge to Western Thought*. New York: Basic Books.

Langland, E. (1984). *Society in the Novel*. Chapel Hill: University of North Carolina Press.

Leaska, M. A. (1996). The concept of point of view. In M. J. Hoffman and P. D. Murphy (eds.), *Essentials of the Theory of Fiction* (pp. 158–171). Durham, NC: Duke University Press.

LeDoux, J. (1996). *The Emotional Brain: The Mysterious Underpinnings of Emotional Life.* New York: Simon and Schuster.

Lee, H. (1989). *Willa Cather: Double Lives.* New York: Pantheon.

Leopold, A. (1987). *A Sand County Almanac and Sketches Here and There.* New York: Oxford University Press. (Original work published 1949)

Levin, R. The new interdisciplinarity in literary criticism. In N. Easterlin and B. Riebling (eds.), *After Poststructuralism: Interdisciplinarity and Literary Theory* (pp. 13–43). Evanston, IL: Northwestern University Press.

Levine, G. (1988). *Darwin and the Novelists: Patterns of Science in Victorian Fiction.* Chicago: University of Chicago Press.

Levine, G. (1994). Darwin revised, and carefully edited. *Configuration*, 2, 191–202.

Lewes, G. H. (1859). The novels of Jane Austen. *Blackwood's Magazine*, 86, 99–113.

Lewis, M., and Haviland, J. M. (eds.). (2000). *Handbook of Emotions* (2nd edition). New York: Guilford Press.

Litvak, J. (1992). "Delicacy and disgust, mourning and melancholia, privilege and perversity." *Pride and Prejudice. Qui Parle*, 6, 35–51.

Litz, A. W. (1965). *Jane Austen: A Study of Her Artistic Development.* New York: Oxford University Press.

Lorenz, K. (1978). *Behind the Mirror: A Search for a Natural History of Human Knowledge* (R. Taylor, trans.). New York: Harcourt Brace Jovanovich.

Love, G. A. (1999a). Ecocriticism and science: Toward consilience? *New Literary History*, 30, 561–576.

Love, G. A. (1999b). Science, anti-science, and ecocriticism. *Interdisciplinary Studies in Literature and the Environment*, 6, 65–81.

Love, G. A. (2003). *Practical Ecocriticism: Literature, Biology, and the Environment.* Charlottesville: University of Virginia Press.

Low, B. S. (1998). The evolution of human life histories. In C. Crawford and D. L. Krebs (eds.), *Handbook of Evolutionary Psychology: Ideas, Issues, Applications* (pp. 131–161). Mahway, NJ: Lawrence Erlbaum Associates.

Low, B. S. (2000). *Why Sex Matters: A Darwinian Look at Human Behavior.* Princeton, NJ: Princeton University Press.

Lucas, J. (1974). *Arnold Bennett: A Study of His Fiction.* London: Methuen.

McCrae, R. R.. (1992). The five-factor model: Issues and applications [special issue]. *Journal of Personality*, 60 (2).

MacDonald, K. B. (1990). A perspective on Darwinian psychology: The importance of domain-general mechanisms, plasticity, and individual differences. *Ethology and Sociobiology*, 12, 449–480.

MacDonald, K. B. (1995a). The establishment and maintenance of socially imposed monogamy in Western Europe. *Politics and the Life Sciences*, 14, 3–46.

MacDonald, K. B. (1995b). Evolution, the five-factor model, and levels of personality. *Journal of Personality*, 63, 525–567.

MacDonald, K. B. (1997). Life history theory and human reproductive behavior: environmental/contextual influences and heritable variation. *Human Behavior*, 8, 327–359.

MacDonald, K. B. (1998a). Evolution and development. In A. Campbell and S. Muncer (eds.), *The Social Child* (pp. 21–49). Hove, East Sussex, England: Psychology Press.

MacDonald, K. B. (1998b). Evolution, culture, and the five-factor model, *Journal of Cross-Cultural Psychology*, 29, 119–149.

McGuire, M, and Troisi, A. (1998). *Darwinian Psychiatry.* New York: Oxford University Press.

Machann, C. (1993a). *The Essential Matthew Arnold: An Annotated Bibliography of Major Modern Studies.* New York: Macmillan.

Machann, C. (1993b). A report on "Matthew Arnold and Victorian Culture: An International Conference," April 15–17, 1993. (1993b). *Nineteenth-Century Prose* 20 (2), 15–22.

Manes, C. (1996). Nature and silence. In C. Glotfelty and H. Fromm (eds.), *The Ecocriticism Reader: Landmarks in Literary Ecology* (pp. 15–29). Athens: University of Georgia Press.

Martin, W. (1986). *Recent Theories of Narrative.* Ithaca, NY: Cornell University Press.

Martineau, H. (1990). Review of *Villette* by Currer Bell. In B. T. Gates (ed.), *Critical Essays on Charlotte Brontë* (pp. 253–256, reprinted from [London] *Daily News*, February 3, 1853, p. 2). Boston: G.K. Hall.

Marx, L. (1964). *The Machine in the Garden: Technology and the Pastoral Ideal in America.* New York: Oxford University Press.

Maxwell, M. (ed.). (1991). *The Sociobiological Imagination*. Albany: State University of New York Press.

Maynard, J. (1984). *Charlotte Brontë and Sexuality*. Cambridge: Cambridge University Press.

Maynard Smith, J. (1989). *Did Darwin Get It Right? Essays on Games, Sex, and Evolution*. New York: W.H. Freeman.

Maynard Smith, J. (1995, November 30). Genes, memes, and minds. *New York Review of Books*, 42 (19), 46–48.

Maynard Smith, J. (ed.) (1982). *Evolution Now: A Century after Darwin*. San Francisco: W.H. Freeman.

Mayr, E. (1982). *The Growth of Biological Thought: Diversity, Evolution, and Inheritance*. Cambridge, MA: Harvard University Press.

Mealey, L. (1995). The sociobiology of sociopathy: an integrated evolutionary model. *Behavioral and Brain Sciences*, 18, 523–541

Meeker, J. W. (1997). *The Comedy of Survival: Literary Ecology and a Play Ethic* (3rd edition). Tucson: University of Arizona Press.

Meisel, P. (1972). *Thomas Hardy: The Return of the Repressed, a Study of the Major Fiction*. New Haven, CT: Yale University Press.

Mellars, P. (1996). *The Neanderthal Legacy: An Archeological Perspective from Western Europe*. Princeton, NJ: Princeton University Press.

Miller, G. (1998a). How mate choice shaped human nature: A review of sexual selection and human evolution. In C. Crawford and D. Krebs (eds.), *Handbook of Evolutionary Psychology*. Mahwah, NJ: Lawrence Erlbaum Associates.

Miller, G. (1998b, October 16). Looking to be entertained: Three strange things that evolution did to our minds. *Times Literary Supplement*, 4985, 14–15.

Miller, G. (2000). *The Mating Mind: How Sexual Choice Shaped the Evolution of Human Nature*. New York: Doubleday.

Miller, J. H. (1986). Optic and semiotic in *Middlemarch*. In H. Bloom (ed.), *George Eliot* (pp. 99–110). New York: Chelsea House, 1986.

Millett, K. (1970). *Sexual Politics*. Garden City, NY: Doubleday.

Milton, J. (1968). *The Poems of John Milton* (J, Carey and A. Fowler, eds.). London: Longman. (Original work published 1667–1674)

Mithen, S. (1996). *The Prehistory of the Mind: The Cognitive Origins of Art, Religion, and Science*. London: Thames and Hudson.

Mithen, S. (2001). The evolution of imagination: An archaeological perspective. *SubStance*, 30, 28–54.

Moore, J. A. (1993). *Science as a Way of Knowing: The Foundations of Modern Biology*. Cambridge, MA: Harvard University Press.

Morgan, S. (1980). *In the Meantime: Character and Perception in Jane Austen's Fiction*. Chicago: University of Chicago Press.

Morton, P. R. (1984). *The Vital Science: Biology and the Literary Imagination, 1860–1900*. Boston: Allen and Unwin.

Moseley, A. (1985). Mythic reality: Structure and theme in Cather's *O Pioneers!* In B. H. Meldrum (ed.), *Under the Sun: Myth and Realism in Western American Literature*. Troy, NY: Whitston.

Mudrick, M. (1952). *Jane Austen: Irony as Defense and Discovery*. Princeton, NJ: Princeton University Press.

Murdock, G. P. (1945). The common denominator of cultures. In R. Linton (ed.), *The Science of Man in the World Crisis* (pp. 123–142). New York: Columbia University Press.

Murphy, J. J. (1984). A comprehensive view of Cather's *O Pioneers!* In J. J. Murphy (ed.), *Critical Essays on Willa Cather*. Boston: G.K. Hall.

Nash, R. (1982). *Wilderness and the American Mind* (3rd edition). New Haven, CT: Yale University Press.

Nesse, M. (1995). Guinevere's choice. *Human Nature*, 6, 145–163.

Nettle, D. (in press). What happens in Shakespeare: Evolutionary perspectives on dramatic form. In J. Gottschall and D. S. Wilson (eds.), *Literature and the Human Animal*. Evanston, IL: Northwestern University Press.

Newman, K. (1983). Can this marriage be saved: Jane Austen makes sense of an ending. *Journal of English Literary History*, 50, 693–708.

Newton, J. L. (1981). *Women, Power, and Subversion: Social Strategies in British Fiction, 1774–1860*. Athens: University of Georgia Press.

Nordlund, M. (2002). Consilient literary interpretation. *Philosophy and Literature*, 26, 312–333.

O'Brien, S. (1978). The unity of Willa Cather's "two–part pastoral": Passion in *O Pioneers! Studies in American Fiction*, 6, 157–171.

O'Brien, S. (1987). *Willa Cather: The Emerging Voice*. New York: Oxford University Press.

Palmer, J. A., and Palmer, L. K. (2002). *Evolutionary Psychology: The Ultimate Origins of Human Behavior*. Boston: Allyn & Bacon.

Panksepp, J. (1998). *Affective Neuroscience: The Foundations of Human and Animal Emotions*. New York: Oxford University Press.

Parsons, K. (ed.). (2003). *The Science Wars: Debating Scientific Knowledge and Technology*. Amherst, NY: Prometheus Books.

Pater, W. (1910). *Greek Studies*. London: Macmillan.

Pater, W. (1980). *The Renaissance: Studies in Art and Poetry* (D. L. Hill, ed.) Berkeley: University of California Press.

Pervin, L. A. (1990). A brief history of modern personality theory. In L. A. Pervin (ed.), *Handbook of Personality: Theory and Research* (pp. 3–18). New York: Guilford Press.

Pervin, L. A. (2003). *The Science of Personality* (2nd edition). New York: Oxford University Press.

Pervin, L A., and John, O. P. (eds.) (1999). *Handbook of Personality: Theory and Research* (2nd edition). New York: Guilford Press.

Phelan, J. (1989). *Reading People, Reading Plots: Characters, Progression, and the Interpretation of Narrative*. Chicago: University of Chicago Press.

Philosophy and Literature. (2001). 24 (2) [special issue on Darwinian literary study]

Pinker, S. (1994). *The Language Instinct: How the Mind Creates Language*. New York: William Morrow.

Pinker, S. (1995). Language is a human instinct." In Brockman, J. (ed.), *The Third Culture: Scientists on the Edge* (pp. 223–238). New York: Simon and Schuster.

Pinker, S. (1997a, October 9). Evolutionary psychology: An exchange. *The New York Review of Books*, 44 (15), 55–58.

Pinker, S. (1997b). *How the Mind Works*. New York: W. W. Norton.

Pinker, S. (2002). *The Blank Slate: The Modern Denial of Human Nature*. New York: Viking.

Pitts, M. E. (1990). The holographic paradigm: A new model for the study of literature and science. *Modern Language Studies*, 20 (4), 80–89.

Plato (1937). *The Republic*. In *The Dialogues of Plato* (B. Jowett, trans., vols. 1–2), (pp. 591–879). New York: Random House.

Poovey, M. (1984). *The Proper Lady and the Woman Writer: Ideology as Style in the Works of Mary Wollstonecraft, Mary Shelley, and Jane Austen*. Chicago: University of Chicago Press.

Pope, A. (1969). An epistle from Mr. Pope to Dr. Arbuthnot. In A. Williams (ed.), *Poetry and Prose of Alexander Pope* (pp. 196–211). Boston: Houghton Mifflin. (Work originally published in 1735)

Popper, K. (1979). *Objective Knowledge: An Evolutionary Approach* (rev. ed). Oxford: Oxford University Press.

Porter, K. A. (1940). Notes on a criticism of Thomas Hardy. *Southern Review*, 6, 150–161.

Potts, R. (1998). Variability selection in hominid evolution. *Evolutionary Anthropology*, 7, 81–96.

Rabkin, E. S., and Simon, C. P. (2001). Age, sex, and evolution in the science fiction marketplace. *Interdisciplinary Literary Studies*, 2, 45–58.

Remarque, E. M. (1975). *All Quiet on the Western Front* (A. W. Wheen, trans.). New York: Fawcett. (Original work published 1929)

Review of *Anna of the Five Towns* [anonymous]. (1981). In J. Hepburn (ed.), *Arnold Bennett: The Critical Heritage* (p. 164, reprinted from *Spectator*, September 20, 1902, p. 407). London: Routledge and Kegan Paul.

Richards, M. P. Pettitt, P. B., Trinkaus, E., Smith, F. H., Paunović, M., and Karavanić, I. (2000). Neanderthal diet at Vindija and Neanderthal predation: The evidence from stable isotopes. *PNAS*, 97, 7663–7666.

Richerson, P. J., and Boyd, R. (2000). Climate, culture, and the evolution of cognition. In C. Heyes and L. Huber (eds.), *The Evolution of Cognition* (pp. 329–346). Cambridge, MA: MIT Press.

Ridley, M[ark]. (1983). *The Problems of Evolution*. Oxford: Oxford University Press.

Ridley, M[ark]. (1990, June 28). Dreadful beasts. *London Review of Books*, 12, 11–12.

Ridley, M[att]. (1997). *The Origins of Virtue: Human Instincts and the Evolution of Cooperation*. New York: Penguin.

Ridley, M[att]. (1999). *Genome: Autobiography of a Species in 23 Chapters*. New York: HarperCollins.

Robinson, R. (1980). Hardy and Darwin. In N. Page (ed.), *Thomas Hardy: The Writer and His Background*. New York: St. Martin's Press.

Roele, M., and Wind, J. (1999). Sociobiology and the arts: An introduction. In J. B. Bedaux and B. Cooke (eds.), *Sociobiology and the Arts*. Amsterdam: Editions Rodopi.

Rorty, R. (1998). Against unity. *The Wilson Quarterly*, 22 (1), 28–38.

Rosny, J. H. (1985). *Roman Préhistoriques* (J-B. Baronian, ed.). Paris: Robert Lafont.

Rossano, M. J. (2003). *Evolutionary Psychology: The Science of Human Behavior and Evolution*. Hoboken, NJ: John Wiley & Sons.

Rushton, J. P. (1995). *Race, Evolution, and Behavior: A Life History Perspective*. New Brunswick, NJ: Transaction.

Sanders, S. R. (1996). Speaking a word for nature. In C. Glotfelty and H. Fromm (eds.), *The Ecocriticism Reader: Landmarks in Literary Ecology*. Athens: University of Georgia Press.

Schiller, F. (1965). *On the Aesthetic Education of Man in a Series of Letters* (R. Snell, trans.). New York: Frederick Ungar. (Original work published 1795)

Schiller, F. (1966). *Naive and Sentimental Poetry* and *On the Sublime: Two Essays* (J. A. Elias, trans.). New York: Frederick Ungar. (Original work published 1795–1796)

Searle, J. (1993). Rationality and realism, what is at stake? *Daedalus*, 122 (4), 55–83

Segal, N. L. (1997). Twin research perspective on human development. In Segal, N. L., Weisfeld, G. E., and Weisfeld, C. C. (eds.), *Uniting Psychology and Biology: Integrative Perspectives on Human Development* (pp. 145–173). Washington, DC: American Psychological Association.

Segal, N. L. (1999). *Entwined Lives: Twins and What They Tell Us about Human Behavior*. New York: Dutton.

Segal, N. L., and MacDonald, K. B. (1998). Behavioral genetics and evolutionary psychology: Unified perspective on personality research. *Human Biology*, 70, 159–184.

Segerstråle, Ullica. (2000). *Defenders of the Truth: The Battle for Science in the Sociobiology Debate and Beyond*. Oxford: Oxford University Press.

Seligman, D. (1992). *A Question of Intelligence: The IQ Debate in America*. New York: Carol.

Selzer, J. (ed.). (1993). *Understanding Scientific Prose*. Madison: University of Wisconsin Press.

Shakespeare, W. (1963). *Hamlet: An Authoritative Text, Intellectual Backgrounds, Extracts from the Sources, Essays in Criticism* (C. Hoy, ed.). New York: W.W. Norton. (Original work published 1603)

Shattuck, R. (1998). Does it all fit together: Evolution, the arts, and consilience. *Academic Questions*, 11 (3), 56–61.

Shelley, P. B. (1969). A defence of poetry. In J. Shawcroft (ed.), *Shelley's Literary and Philosophical Criticism* (pp. 120–159). Folcroft, PA: Folcroft. (Original work published 1840)

Shreeve, J. (1995). *The Neanderthal Enigma: Solving the Mystery of Modern Human Origins*. New York: Avon Books.

Silver, B. R. (1983). The reflecting reader in *Villette*. In E. Abel, M. Hirsch, and E. Langland (Eds.), *The Voyage In: Fictions of Female Development*. Hanover, NY: University Press of New England.

Silverberg, R., Greenberg, M. H., and Waugh, C. G. (eds.). (1987). *Neanderthals*. New York: Signet.

Simpson, G. G. (1967). *The Meaning of Evolution: A Study of the History of Life and of Its Significance for Man* (2nd edition). New Haven, CT: Yale University Press.

Smith, J. M. (1993). "I am a gentleman's daughter": A Marxist-feminist reading of *Pride and Prejudice*. In M. M. Folsom (ed.), *Approaches to Teaching Austen's Pride and Prejudice* (pp. 67–73). New York: Modern Language Association.

Smith, J. M. (2000). The oppositional reader and *Pride and Prejudice*. In L. C. Lambdin and R. T. Lambdin (eds.), *A Companion to Jane Austen Studies* (pp. 27–40). Westport, CT: Greenwood Press.

Sober, E., and Wilson, D. S. (1999). *Unto Others: The Evolution and Psychology of Unselfish Behavior*. Cambridge, MA: Harvard University Press.

Sokal, A. D. (1996). Transgressing the boundaries: Toward a transformative hermeneutics of quantum gravity. *Social Text*, 14, 217–252.

Sokal, A., and Bricmont, J. (1998). *Fashionable Nonsense: Postmodern Intellectuals' Abuse of Science*. New York: Picador.

Spencer, H. (1862). *First Principles*. London: Williams & Norgate.

Sperber, D. (1994). The modularity of thought and the epidemiology of representations. In L. A. Hirschfeld and S. A. Gelman (eds.), *Mapping the Mind: Domain Specificity in Cognition and Culture* (pp. 39–67). Cambridge: Cambridge University Press.

Spolsky, E. (1993). *Gaps in Nature: Literary Interpretation and the Modular Mind*. Albany: State University of New York Press.

Stelmack, R. M. (1990). Biological bases of extraversion: Psychophysiological evidence. *Journal of Personality*, 58, 293–312.

Stephen, L. (1949). *History of English Thought in the Eighteenth Century* (3rd edition, vols. 1–2). New York: Peter Smith. (Original work published 1902)

Stephen, L. (1990). Charlotte Brontë. In B. T. Gates (ed.), *Critical Essays on Charlotte Brontë* (pp. 17–33, reprinted from *Cornhill Magazine*, 36, November, 1877, pp. 723–739). Boston: G.K. Hall.

Stevenson, L. (1932). *Darwin Among the Poets*. Chicago: University of Chicago Press.

Stone, D. E. (1983). The art of Arnold Bennett: Transmutation and empathy in *Anna of the Five Towns* and *Riceyman Steps*. In R. Kiely (ed.), *Modernism Reconsidered*. Cambridge, MA: Harvard University Press.

Storey, R. (1993). "I am I because my little dog knows me": Prolegomenon to a theory of mimesis. In N. Easterlin and B. Riebling (eds.), *After Poststructuralism: Interdisciplinarity and Literary Theory* (pp. 45–70). Evanston, IL: Northwestern University Press.

Storey, R. (1996). *Mimesis and the Human Animal: On the Biogenetic Foundations of Literary Representation*. Evanston, IL: Northwestern University Press.

Storey, R. (2001). A critique of recent theories of laughter and humor, with special reference to the comedy of *Seinfeld*. *Interdisciplinary Literary Studies*, 2, 75–92.

Stouck, D. (1992). Historical essay. In S. J. Rosowski and C. W. Mignon (eds.), *O Pioneers!* Lincoln: University of Nebraska Press.

Stringer, C. and Gamble, C. (1993). *In Search of the Neanderthals: Solving the Puzzle of Human Origins*. New York: Thames & Hudson.

Sugiyama, M. S. (1996). On the origins of narrative: Storyteller bias as a fitness enhancing strategy. *Human Nature*, 7, 403–425.

Sugiyama, M. S. (2001a). Food, foragers, and folklore: The role of narrative in human subsistence. *Evolution and Human Behavior*, 22, 221–240.

Sugiyama, M. S. (2001b). Narrative theory and function: Why evolution matters. *Philosophy and Literature*, 25, 233–250.

Sugiyama, M. S. (2001c). New science, old myth: An evolutionary critique of the Oedipal paradigm. *Mosaic*, 34, 121–136.

Sugiyama, M. S. (In press). Cultural relativism in the bush: Toward a theory of narrative universals. *Human Nature*.

Symons, D. (1979). *The Evolution of Human Sexuality*. New York: Oxford University Press.

Symons, D. (1989). A critique of Darwinian anthropology. *Ethology and Sociobiology*, 10, 131–144.

Symons, D. (1992). On the use and misuse of Darwinism in the study of human behavior. In J. H. Barkow, L. Cosmides, and J. Tooby (eds.), *The Adapted Mind: Evolutionary Psychology and the Generation of Culture* (pp. 137–162). New York: Oxford University Press.

Taine, H. (1879). *History of English literature* (H. van Laun, trans.). (2 vols. in 1). New York: Henry Holt. (Original work published 1863–64)

Tanner, T. (1968). Colour and movement in Hardy's *Tess of the d'Urbervilles*. *Critical Quarterly*, 10, 219–239.

Tanner, T. (1979). Introduction. In *Villette* (M. Lilly, ed.). Harmondsworth, England: Penguin.

Tanner, T. (1986). *Jane Austen*. Cambridge, MA: Harvard University Press.

Tattersall, I. (1999). *The Last Neanderthal: The Rise, Success, and Mysterious Extinction of Our Closest Human Relatives* (rev. edition). New York: Westview Press.

Thiessen, D. and Umezawa, Y. (1998). The sociobiology of everyday life: A new look at a very old novel. *Human Nature*, 9, 293–320.

Tiger, V. (1976). *William Golding: The Dark Fields of Discovery*. London: Marion Boyars.

Tiger, L. and Fox, R. (1971). *The Imperial Animal*. New York: Holt, Rinehart, and Winston.

Todorov, T. (1998, April 27). The surrender to nature. *The New Republic*, 219, 29–33.

Tooby, J., and Cosmides, L. (1990). On the universality of human nature and the uniqueness of the individual: the role of genetics and adaptation. *Journal of Personality*, 58, 17–67.

Tooby, J., and Cosmides, L. (1992). The psychological foundations of culture. In J. H. Barkow, L. Cosmides, and J. Tooby (eds.), *The Adapted Mind: Evolutionary Psychology and the Generation of Culture* (pp. 19–136). New York: Oxford University Press.

Tooby, J., and Cosmides, L. (2001). Does beauty build adapted minds? Toward an evolutionary theory of aesthetics, fiction, and the arts. *SubStance* 30, 6–27.

Trivers, R. L. (1972). Parental investment and sexual selection. In B. G. Campbell (ed.), *Sexual Selection and the Descent of Man 1871–1971* (pp. 136–179). Chicago: Aldine de Gruyter.

Trivers, R. L. (1985). *Social Evolution*. Menlo Park, NJ: Benjamin/Cummings.

Turke, P. W. (1990). Which humans behave adaptively, and why does it matter? *Ethology and Sociobiology*, 11, 305–339.

Turner, F. (1992). *Natural Classicism: Essays on Literature and Science*. Charlottesville: University of Virginia Press. (Original work published 1985)

Turner, M. (1991). *Reading Minds: The Study of English in the Age of Cognitive Science*. Princeton, NJ: Princeton University Press.

Turner, M. (1996). *The Literary Mind*. New York: Oxford University Press.

Ulin, D. (1992). A clerisy of worms in Darwin's inverted world. *Victorian Studies*, 35, 295–308.

Van Ghent, D. (1953). *The English Novel: Form and Function*. New York: Holt, Rinehart, and Winston.

Wagenknecht, E. (1994). *Willa Cather*. New York: Continuum.

Watt, I. (1957). *The Rise of the Novel: Studies in Defoe, Richardson, and Fielding*. Berkeley: University of California Press.

Wellek, R. and Warren, A. (1977). *Theory of Literature* (new rev. edition). New York: Harcourt, Brace, and World.

Wells, H. G. (1971a). The grisly folk. In *The Complete Short Stories of H. G. Wells*. New York: St. Martin's. (Original work published 1921)

Wells, H. G. (1971b). A story of the Stone Age. In *The Complete Short Stories of H. G. Wells*. New York: St. Martin's. (Original work published 1897)

Wells, H. G. (1978). *The Complete Science Fiction Treasury of H. G. Wells*. New York: Wings.

Whelehan, I. (1999). Adaptations: The contemporary dilemmas. In D. Cartmell and I. Whelehan (eds.), *Adaptations: From Text to Screen, Screen to Text*. London: Routledge.

Whissel, C. (1996). Mate selection in popular women's fiction. *Human Nature*, 7, 427–447.

Wiggins, J. S. (ed.). (1996). *The Five-factor Model of Personality: Theoretical Perspectives*. New York: Guilford Press.

Williams, G. C. (1966). *Adaptation and Natural Selection: A Critique of Some Current Evolutionary Thought*. Princeton, NJ: Princeton University Press.

Wilson, D. S. (1994). Adaptive genetic variation and human evolutionary psychology. *Ethology and Sociobiology*, 15, 219–235.

Wilson, D. S. (1999). Tasty slice—but where is the rest of the pie? *Evolution and Human Behavior*, 20, 279–287.

Wilson, D. S. (2002). *Darwin's Cathedral: Evolution, Religion, and the Nature of Society*. Chicago: University of Chicago Press.

Wilson, D. S. (in press). Evolutionary social constructivism. In J. Gottschall and D. S. Wilson (eds.), *Literature and the Human Animal*. Evanston, IL: Northwestern University Press.

Wilson, D. S., Near, D. C., and Miller, R. R.. (1998). Individual differences in Machiavellianism as a mix of cooperative and exploitative strategies. *Evolution and Human Behavior*, 19, 203–211.

Wilson, E. (1931). *Axel's Castle: A Study in the Imaginative Literature of 1870–1930*. New York: W.W. Norton.

Wilson, E. O. (1975). *Sociobiology: The New Synthesis*. Cambridge, MA: Harvard University Press.

Wilson, E. O. (1978). *On Human Nature*. Cambridge, MA: Harvard University Press.

Wilson, E. O. (1984). *Biophilia*. Cambridge, MA: Harvard University Press.

Wilson, E. O. (1992). *The Diversity of Life*. Cambridge, MA: Harvard University Press.

Wilson, E. O. (1993). Biophilia and the conservation ethic. In S. R. Kellert and E. O. Wilson (eds.), *The Biophilia Hypothesis*. Washington, DC: Island Press.

Wilson, E. O. (1994). *Naturalist*. Washington, DC: Island Press.

Wilson, E. O. (1996). *In Search of Nature*. Washington, DC: Island Press.

Wilson, E. O. (1998). *Consilience: The Unity of Knowledge*. New York: Alfred A. Knopf.

Wilson, J. Q. (1993). *The Moral Sense*. New York: Macmillan.

Woolf, V. (1953). Jane Austen. In *The Common Reader: First Series* (pp. 137–149). New York: Harcourt, Brace, and World. (Original work published 1925)

Woolf, V. (1960). The novels of Thomas Hardy. In *The Second Common Reader* (pp. 222–233). New York: Harcourt, Brace, and World. (Original work published 1932)

Wordsworth, W. (1965). Preface to the second edition of *Lyrical Ballads*. In J. Stillinger (ed.), *Selected Poems and Prefaces*. Boston: Houghton Mifflin. (Original work published 1800)

Wylie, J. (2000). Dancing in chains: Feminist satire in pride and prejudice. *Persuasions: Journal of the Jane Austen Society of North America*, 22, 62–69.

Yeazell, R. B. (1991). *Fictions of Modesty: Women and Courtship in the English Novel.* Chicago: University of Chicago Press.

Young, D. (1992). *The Discovery of Evolution.* Cambridge: Cambridge University Press.

Zola, É. (1964). *The Experimental Novel and Other Essays* (B. M Sherman, trans.). New York: Haskell. (Original work published 1894)

Index

Abbey, Edward, 90

Abrams, M. H., 44, 147, 148, 163–64

Adaptations: display complex functional structure, xx, 110, 232, 238–39; Gould deprecates, xxiv, 227–45 *passim*; closed and open, 23; produce human universals, 117; are a result of a mechanical process, 122; and the EEA, 190–91; for the cognitive behavioral system, 198; are constrained by inheritance, 228. *See also* Art, adaptive functions of; Evolutionary theory (Darwin's); Literature, adaptive function of; Natural selection

Adaptationist literary study. *See* Darwinian literary study

Adaptationist program: definition of, vii; Pinker on, 63; Gould and Lewontin oppose, 237–40. *See also* Adapted mind, the; Adaptations; Evolutionary psychology; Evolutionary theory (Darwin's); Natural selection; Sociobiology

Adapted mind, the, vii, xii, 57. *See also* Adaptations; Adaptationist program; Cognitive modules; Darwinian social sciences; Evolutionary psychology; Sociobiology

Addison, Joseph, 240

Alcock, John, xxv, 240–41, 242

Alexander, Richard, 10–11, 43, 79, 108, 155

Althusser, Louis, 151

Andersen, Hans Christian, 190

Anderson, Joseph, 86, 92

Anderson, L. R., 140

Anthropology. *See* Darwinian social sciences

Archetypes: in Frye's theory, 21, 120, 121; in Koch's theory, 56; in E. O. Wilson's theory, 80–83; Jungian, 110; in Darwinian literary criticism, 130; in *Anna of the Five Towns*, 141; in *Tess of the d'Urbervilles*, 143; in *Clan of the Cave Bear*, 175; in Richard Owen's theory, 244–45

Argyros, Alexander, xii, xiii, xxiii, 49, 52–55, 60

Aristotle, 118, 119, 120, 122, 123

Arnhart, Larry, xxv

Arnold, Matthew: cultural theory of, xii, xxiii, 3–14 *passim*, 147; normative affirmations of, 32; on the function of literature, 33; on human universals, 119–20; on poetry and religion, 148; as subject of biography, 221

Art: adaptive functions of, vii-viii, xix-xxii, 69, 80, 159–60, 198; evaluation of, 5, 6; New Critical view of, 77; E. O. Wilson on, 79–83; evolutionary theories of, 80; and the Human Revolution, 104, 192; Paleolithic, 170; compared with science, 139, 171–72; integrity in, 171–72, 173. *See also* Literature

Association for the Study of Literature and Environment (ASLE), 147

Association of Literary Scholars and Critics (ALSC), 31

Audience. *See* Literature, as social exchange

Auel, Jean, xxiv, 164–65, 170–71, 173–77, 179

Austen, Jane: Boyd on, xvii; settings in, 96–97; critics on, 134–35, 145, 213–15; conservatism of, 135, 214; determinate meaning in, 135–36; Charlotte Brontë dislikes, 137; sexual identity of, 139; tone in, 169; style of, 207; brutality in, 211; central criterion of value in, 212; mentioned, xxv, 94, 159

works: *Mansfield Park*, xvii; *Pride and Prejudice*, xxiv, 38, 97, 114–15, 132, 133–34, 142, 144, 189, 190, 206–15; *Sense and Sensibility*, 96–97; juvenilia, 211

Austin, J. L., 49

Authors: as source of meaning, 18, 39, 81, 131, 133–34, 150, 188, 200–202, 202–3; as organisms, 19, 36, 157, 164; quality of mind in, 76, 164–85 *passim*; individuality of, 130–31, 150, 157, 187, 204, 206; and point of view, 131–32; and normative heterosexuality, 132–45 *passim*; in social exchange, 134; sexual identity of, 138–39; motives of, 154; and emotions, 158; understand human nature, 159, 204, 215; Abrams' concept of, 163–64; are people, 163, 202; poststructuralist conception of, 163–64; empathy in, 165; integrity of, 166; understand individual differences, 203; are intelligent, 205. *See also* Literature, as social exchange; Point of view

Autism, 66, 243. *See also* Theory of mind

Bakhtin, Mikhail, 85

Barash, David, xvii

Barash, Nanelle, xvii

Barkow, Jerome, 126

Bauer, H. P., 140

Beer, Gillian, 45, 144